CW00816214

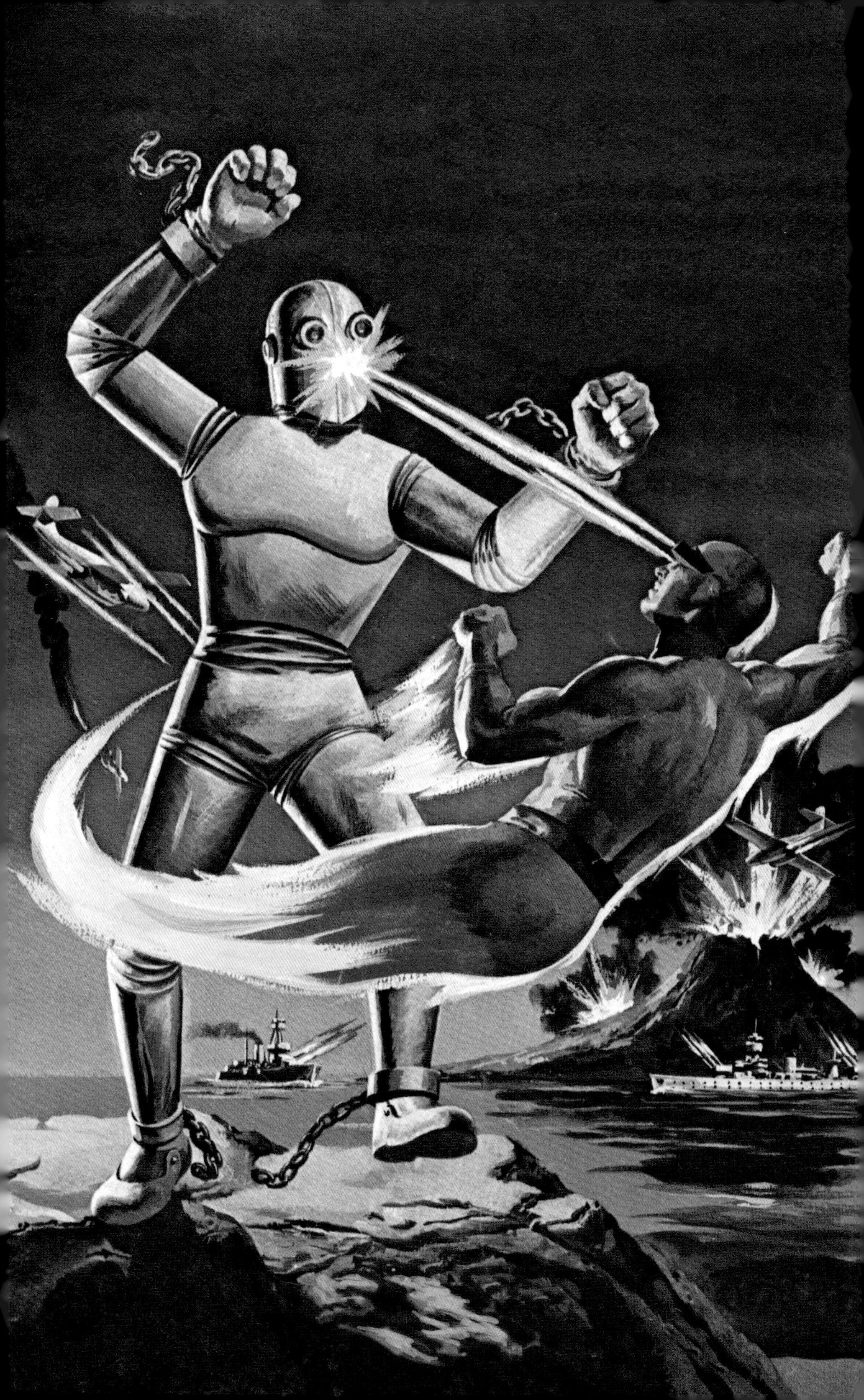

# DOCTOR SOLAR™

## MAN OF THE ATOM

### Volume Three

**WRITTEN BY**

Paul S. Newman

**ILLUSTRATED BY**

Frank Bolle
and others

DARK HORSE BOOKS™

**PUBLISHER**
Mike Richardson

**COLLECTION DESIGNER**
Joshua Elliott

**COLLECTION EDITOR**
Michael Carriglitto

**ART DIRECTOR**
Lia Ribacchi

**DIGITAL RETOUCH**
Chris Horn

Published by
Dark Horse Books
A division of Dark Horse Comics, Inc.

Dark Horse Comics, Inc.
10956 SE Main Street
Milwaukie, Oregon 97222

**www.darkhorse.com**

To find a comic shop in your area, call the
Comic Shop Locator Service: (888) 266-4226

First Edition: September 2005
ISBN: 1-59307-374-7

1 3 5 7 9 10 8 6 4 2

Printed in China

This volume collects issues fifteen through twenty-two of *Doctor Solar, Man of the Atom*, originally published from 1965 to 1968
by Gold Key, a division of K. K. Publications, Inc.

# TABLE OF CONTENTS

FOREWORD BY MIKE BARON

6

IN KEEPING WITH THE COMICS PUBLICATION STYLE OF ITS TIME, THE CREATIVE TEAM ON DOCTOR SOLAR, MAN OF THE ATOM WAS
NOT CREDITED FOR ITS WORK. WHILE WE STROVE FOR COMPLETE ACCURACY IN THIS VOLUME, WE REGRET THAT THE NATURE OF
THIS MATERIAL ALLOWS THE POSSIBILITY FOR INCORRECT OR INCOMPLETE ATTRIBUTIONS

# FOREWORD
## by Mike Baron

A child surveying the comics racks of the early sixties gazed upon a nuclear wasteland punctuated here and there with rare pockets of life. *Fantastic Four* appeared in 1961, followed a year later by *Spider-Man*, but it would be years before their long march achieved victory. Carl Barks' work was a bright spot, but for the adventure or superhero lover, it was slim pickings. In the first volume of this series Mark Evanier outlined how Western Publishing begat *Magnus Robot Fighter, Space Family Robinson,* and *Doctor Solar*, the Big Three of the Western adventure line. Of these, Dr. Solar, written by Paul Newman and Matt Murphy and drawn by Bob Fujitani and Frank Bolle evoked the most psychic and societal resonance.

It was the Age of the Atom, only seventeen years after Hiroshima. It was the height of the cold war, with the Soviet Union and United States engaged in a nuclear arms race. Like many Midwestern families, we had a bomb shelter in our basement stocked with canned food and bottled water. People in South Dakota took the nuclear threat seriously. After all—South and North Dakota were home to half the nation's Hardened missile sites, silos which have since been sold as surplus, turned into storage units, or in some cases, homes.

*Doctor Solar* captures the agonizing ambiguity of the times. On the one hand, the atom was our friend, providing a new, seemingly inexhaustible and clean source of energy. Doctor Solar, who might have been played by Fred MacMurray, captures the wholesome optimism of post-war America. On the other hand, the atom was the potential destroyer of life as we knew it. Solar's bizarre enemies and fear of the unknown represent the dark side. We would be incinerated by twin suns. We would freeze to death in a new ice age. Giants would stalk the earth, destroying everything in their path. Despite bold promises from *Life* and *Popular Science,* we had seen what the atom could do. The twin detonations of Hiroshima and Nagasaki blazed brighter than any possible peaceful application.

Doctor Solar the man represented the atom's bright future. *Doctor Solar* the comic represented our disturbing uncertainty toward this elemental, transformative force. It's interesting to note that in the comic, Atom Valley is only one of countless atomic power plants that exist throughout the country and the world, providing clean energy. Had *Solar*'s creators been able to look into the future they would have been astounded by today's energy grid. No nuclear power plants have gone online in the United States since 1996. There are currently 103 nuclear power plants online in the United States, producing 754 billion kilowatt-hours, 20% of our national supply. The rest is supplied by coal-burning generators.

The most serious nuclear accident to occur in the United States was a partial meltdown at Pennsylvania's Three Mile Island in 1979. There were no fatalities. Indeed, there are no known lasting health effects from the incident. The same cannot be said for the Chernobyl disaster which occurred in the Ukraine in 1986. A chain reaction went out of control, blowing the lid off the reactor, killing thirty people, and eventually killing thousands more affected by the radiation and turning an area of thousands of square miles into a nuclear wasteland. The Russians were notoriously sloppy about their safety procedures. In an effort to pull abreast with the United States they took short cuts on everything and regarded manpower as their most expendable resource. Americans in the sixties were astounded by the speed of Soviet nuclear subs until they learned that Soviet subs lacked radiation shielding because it weighed too much. Virtually every sailor who served aboard a Soviet nuclear sub in the sixties died of radiation poisoning.

*Doctor Solar* stepped into this atmosphere of gee-whiz paranoia. Writer Newman had a fine sense of the bizarre but his understanding of science was rudimentary. Solar's origin, exposing himself to extreme radiation, wouldn't wash today. Mr. Newman would have to construct a more elaborate and plausible origin were he to re-create *Doctor Solar* today. But the same can be said for the *Fantastic Four* or *Spider-Man*.

Newman gets off the occasional unintentional zinger: "He was raving ... but in a *positive* manner, Doctor!" And, "Our main objective is to protect humanity now by lighting the dark side of earth ... keeping the world under constant 24-hour sunlight ... "

Good plan.

By today's standards Frank Bolle's art seems crude and sketchy. But consider the man's challenge—to delineate fantastic amorphous plasma creatures. Primo today would be rendered with muscles in places most people don't even have places and fitted with elaborate weapons. Bolle excelled in rendering faces. Many artists have a standard face they slap on man, woman, child, and dog. Bolle appears to have based his characters on real people rendered in a style that has all but disappeared, that of the sixties-era ad illustrator. Some of these faces could only exist in the sixties. One marvels at the different facial types—heads that are ovals, triangles, or pyramids. One gets the sense Bolle drew these people from life, from those around him.

Another influence shaped the *Doctor Solar* series. In 1963, *Dr. No*, the first James Bond film, premiered. Men of a certain age will never forget having their lives turned upside down. Nuro, Doctor Solar's mysterious nemesis who had been present from the beginning, began to acquire the trappings of a James Bond villain: an elaborate underground lair, an East European henchman (Uzbek), and a robot assistant named Orun. Not even Atom Valley was immune to Bond's siren song. Check out the cutaway drawing of the Atom Valley bunker in "The War of the Suns."

For the first dozen issues, Nuro appears only from behind, a fat bald man not unlike the Kingpin. Finally, in "Solar vs. Solar" from 1967, Bolle gives the game away with a profile on page three—Nuro is one scary dude! Almost comically porcine, he has the brows and snout of a Tuscany wild boar. The only thing missing are the tusks. The late Oskar Homolka could have played him to perfection.

*Doctor Solar* was more than entertainment; it was a Rorschach check of our collective unconscious. One thing remains as true today as it was when these comics appeared: our ambiguity toward nuclear power.

—**Mike Baron**

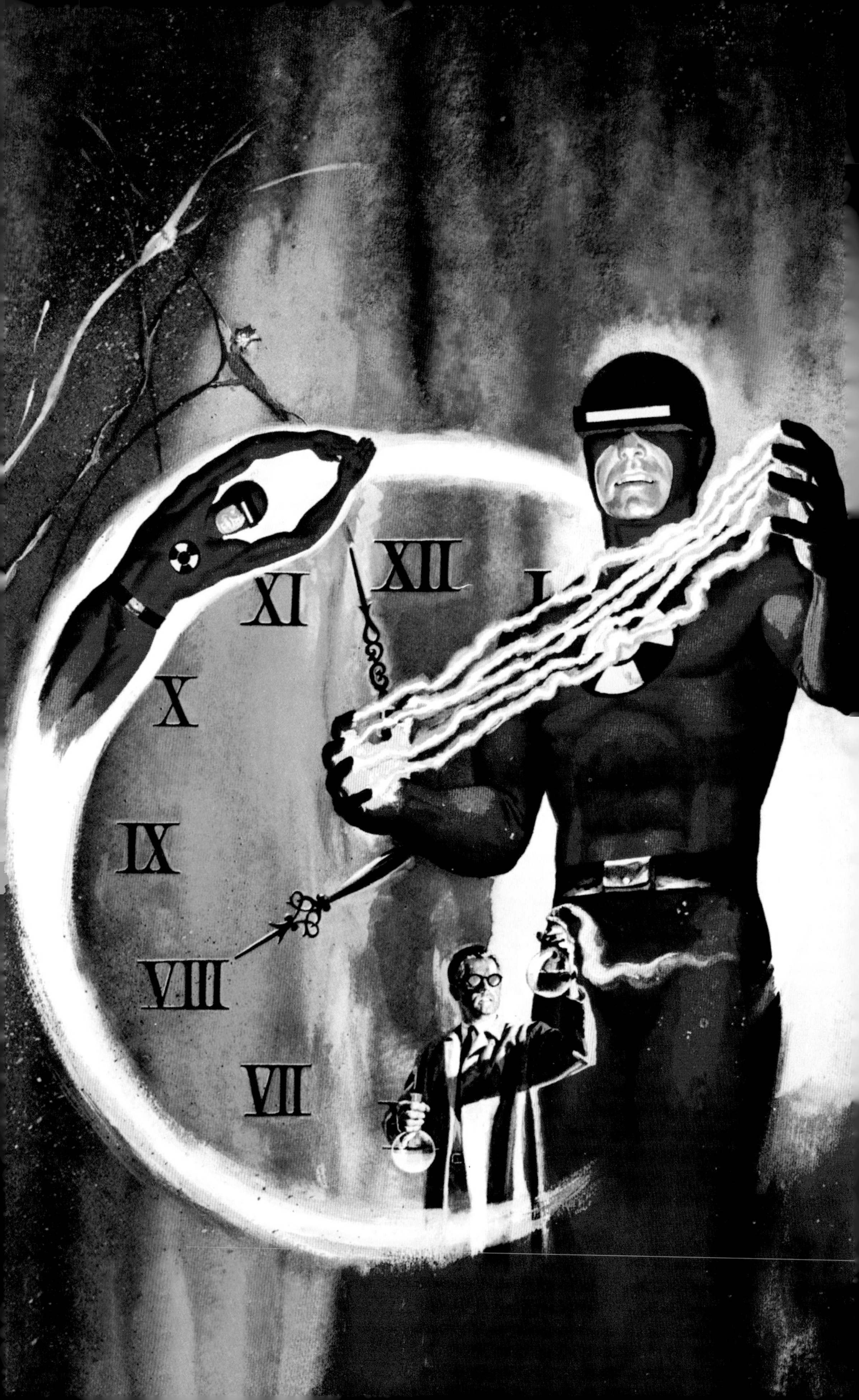

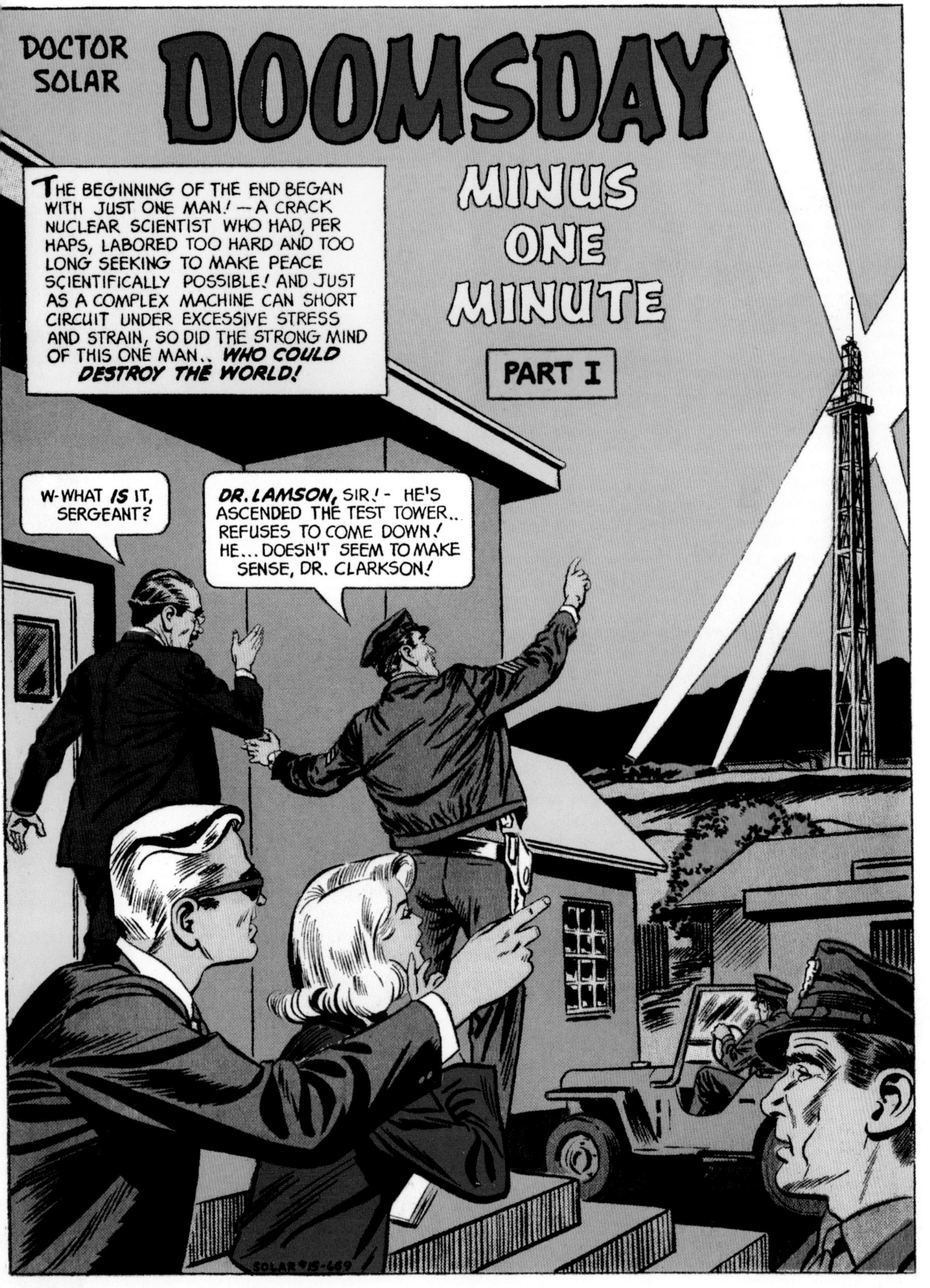
DOCTOR SOLAR
DOOMSDAY
MINUS ONE MINUTE
PART I
THE BEGINNING OF THE END BEGAN WITH JUST ONE MAN! — A CRACK NUCLEAR SCIENTIST WHO HAD, PER HAPS, LABORED TOO HARD AND TOO LONG SEEKING TO MAKE PEACE SCIENTIFICALLY POSSIBLE! AND JUST AS A COMPLEX MACHINE CAN SHORT CIRCUIT UNDER EXCESSIVE STRESS AND STRAIN, SO DID THE STRONG MIND OF THIS ONE MAN.. WHO COULD DESTROY THE WORLD!
W-WHAT IS IT, SERGEANT?
DR. LAMSON, SIR! - HE'S ASCENDED THE TEST TOWER.. REFUSES TO COME DOWN! HE... DOESN'T SEEM TO MAKE SENSE, DR. CLARKSON!
SOLAR #15-669

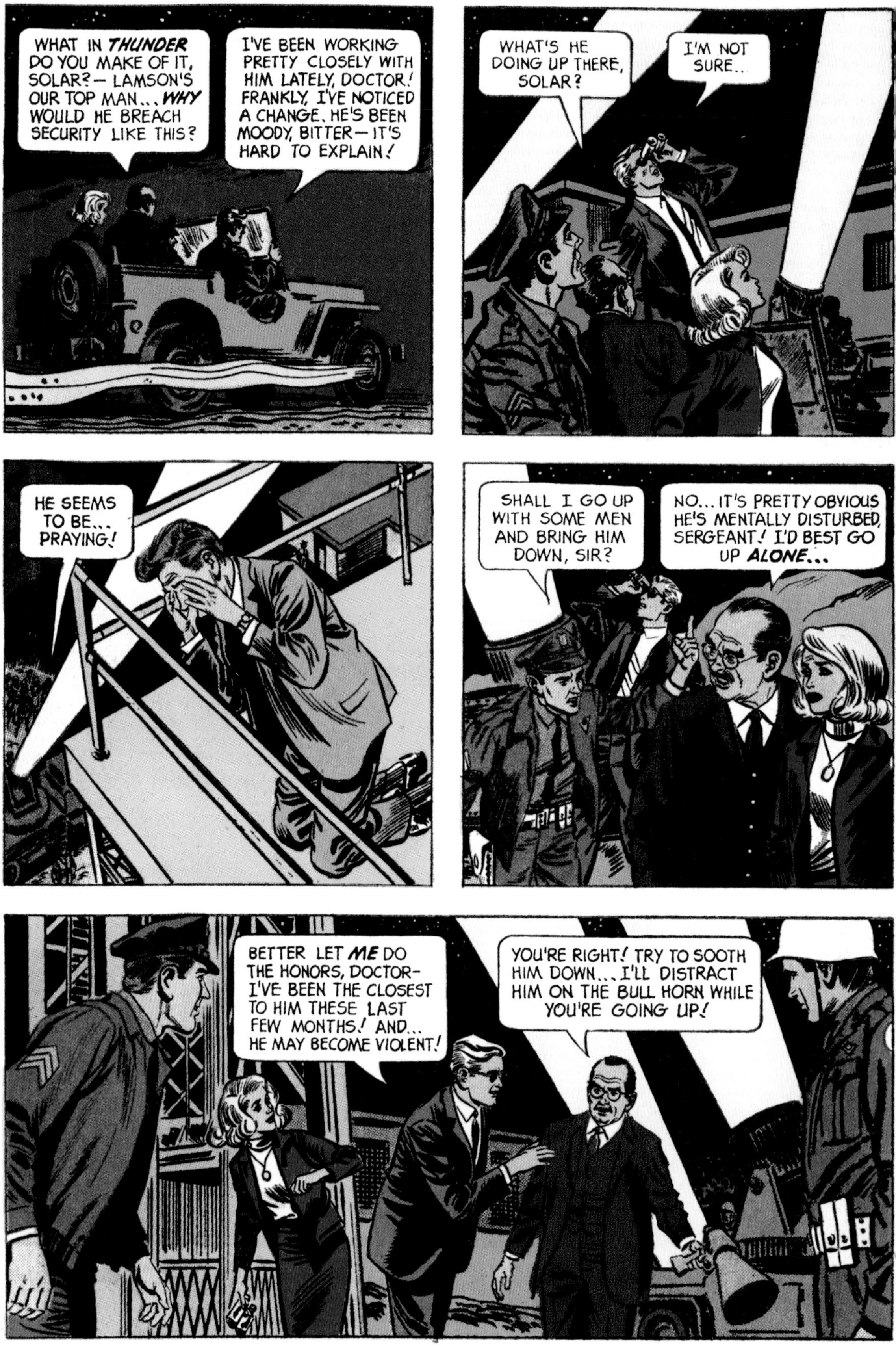
WHAT IN THUNDER DO YOU MAKE OF IT, SOLAR? — LAMSON'S OUR TOP MAN... WHY WOULD HE BREACH SECURITY LIKE THIS?
I'VE BEEN WORKING PRETTY CLOSELY WITH HIM LATELY, DOCTOR! FRANKLY, I'VE NOTICED A CHANGE. HE'S BEEN MOODY, BITTER— IT'S HARD TO EXPLAIN!
WHAT'S HE DOING UP THERE, SOLAR?
I'M NOT SURE...
HE SEEMS TO BE... PRAYING!
SHALL I GO UP WITH SOME MEN AND BRING HIM DOWN, SIR?
NO... IT'S PRETTY OBVIOUS HE'S MENTALLY DISTURBED, SERGEANT! I'D BEST GO UP ALONE...
BETTER LET ME DO THE HONORS, DOCTOR— I'VE BEEN THE CLOSEST TO HIM THESE LAST FEW MONTHS! AND... HE MAY BECOME VIOLENT!
YOU'RE RIGHT! TRY TO SOOTH HIM DOWN... I'LL DISTRACT HIM ON THE BULL HORN WHILE YOU'RE GOING UP!

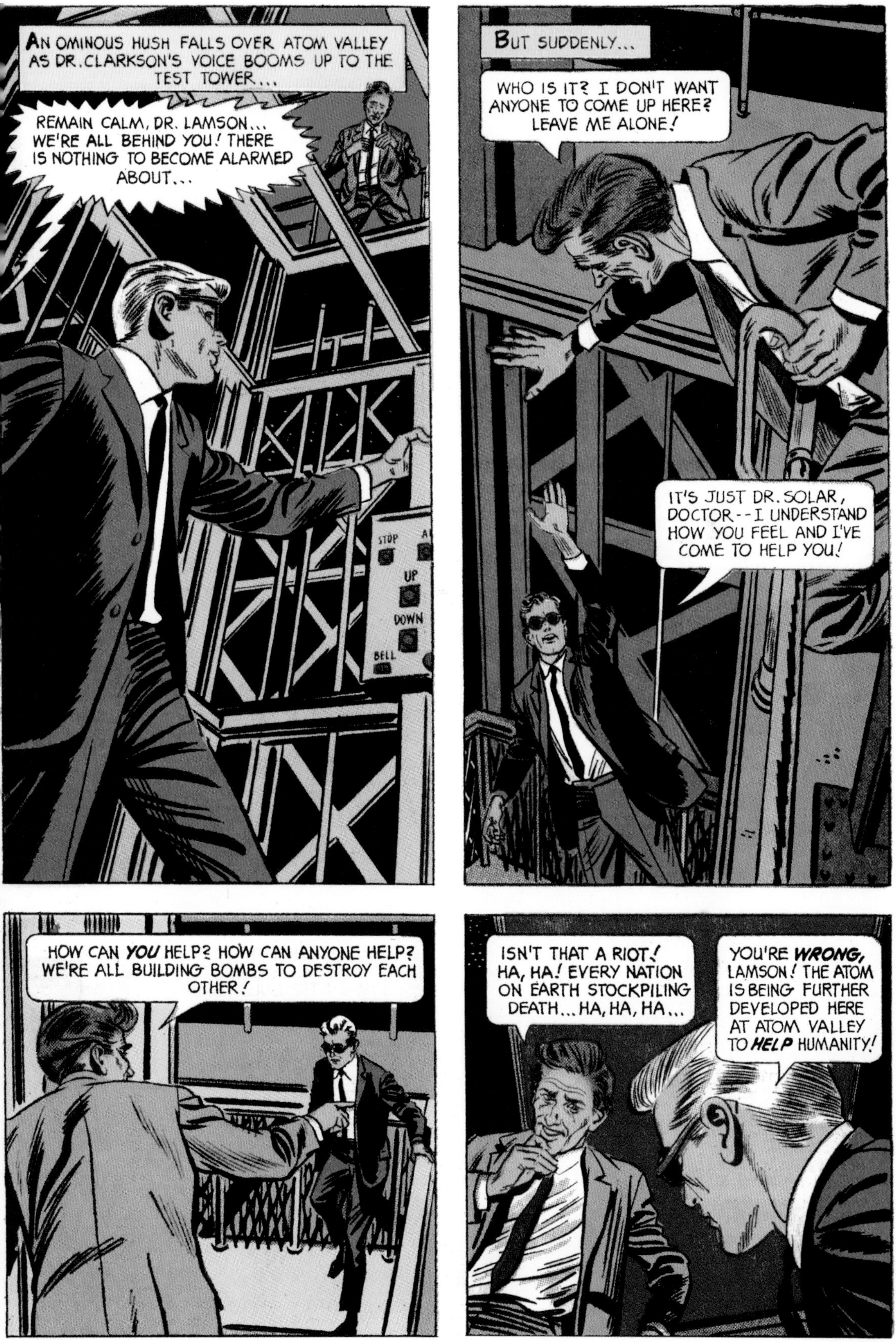
AN OMINOUS HUSH FALLS OVER ATOM VALLEY AS DR. CLARKSON'S VOICE BOOMS UP TO THE TEST TOWER...
REMAIN CALM, DR. LAMSON... WE'RE ALL BEHIND YOU! THERE IS NOTHING TO BECOME ALARMED ABOUT...
STOP
UP
DOWN
BELL
BUT SUDDENLY...
WHO IS IT? I DON'T WANT ANYONE TO COME UP HERE? LEAVE ME ALONE!
IT'S JUST DR. SOLAR, DOCTOR--I UNDERSTAND HOW YOU FEEL AND I'VE COME TO HELP YOU!
HOW CAN YOU HELP? HOW CAN ANYONE HELP? WE'RE ALL BUILDING BOMBS TO DESTROY EACH OTHER!
ISN'T THAT A RIOT! HA, HA! EVERY NATION ON EARTH STOCKPILING DEATH... HA, HA, HA...
YOU'RE WRONG, LAMSON! THE ATOM IS BEING FURTHER DEVELOPED HERE AT ATOM VALLEY TO HELP HUMANITY!

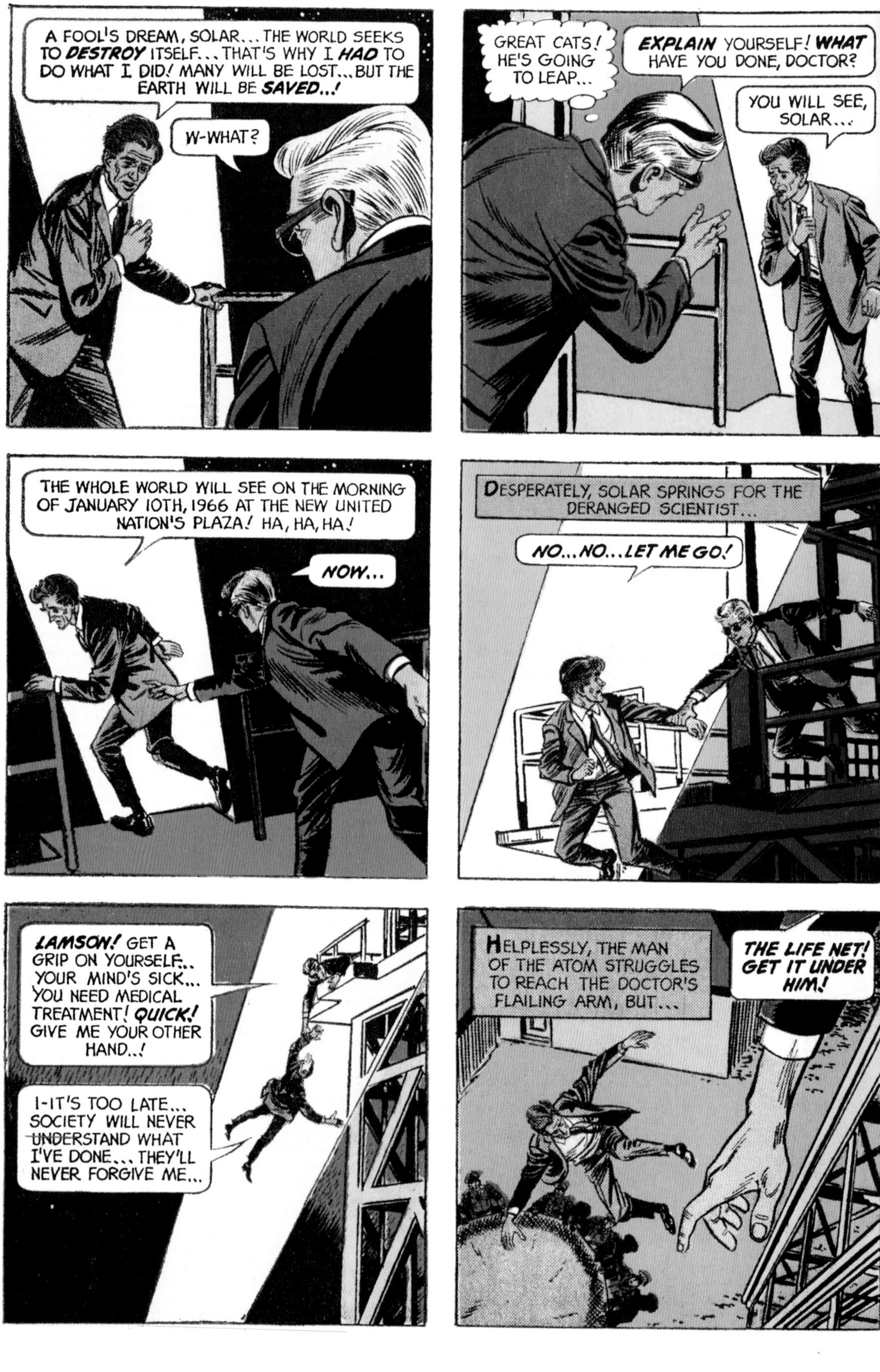
A FOOL'S DREAM, SOLAR... THE WORLD SEEKS TO DESTROY ITSELF... THAT'S WHY I HAD TO DO WHAT I DID! MANY WILL BE LOST... BUT THE EARTH WILL BE SAVED..!
W-WHAT?
GREAT CATS! HE'S GOING TO LEAP...
EXPLAIN YOURSELF! WHAT HAVE YOU DONE, DOCTOR?
YOU WILL SEE, SOLAR...
THE WHOLE WORLD WILL SEE ON THE MORNING OF JANUARY 10TH, 1966 AT THE NEW UNITED NATION'S PLAZA! HA, HA, HA!
NOW...
DESPERATELY, SOLAR SPRINGS FOR THE DERANGED SCIENTIST...
NO... NO... LET ME GO!
LAMSON! GET A GRIP ON YOURSELF... YOUR MIND'S SICK... YOU NEED MEDICAL TREATMENT! QUICK! GIVE ME YOUR OTHER HAND..!
I-IT'S TOO LATE... SOCIETY WILL NEVER UNDERSTAND WHAT I'VE DONE... THEY'LL NEVER FORGIVE ME...
HELPLESSLY, THE MAN OF THE ATOM STRUGGLES TO REACH THE DOCTOR'S FLAILING ARM, BUT...
THE LIFE NET! GET IT UNDER HIM!

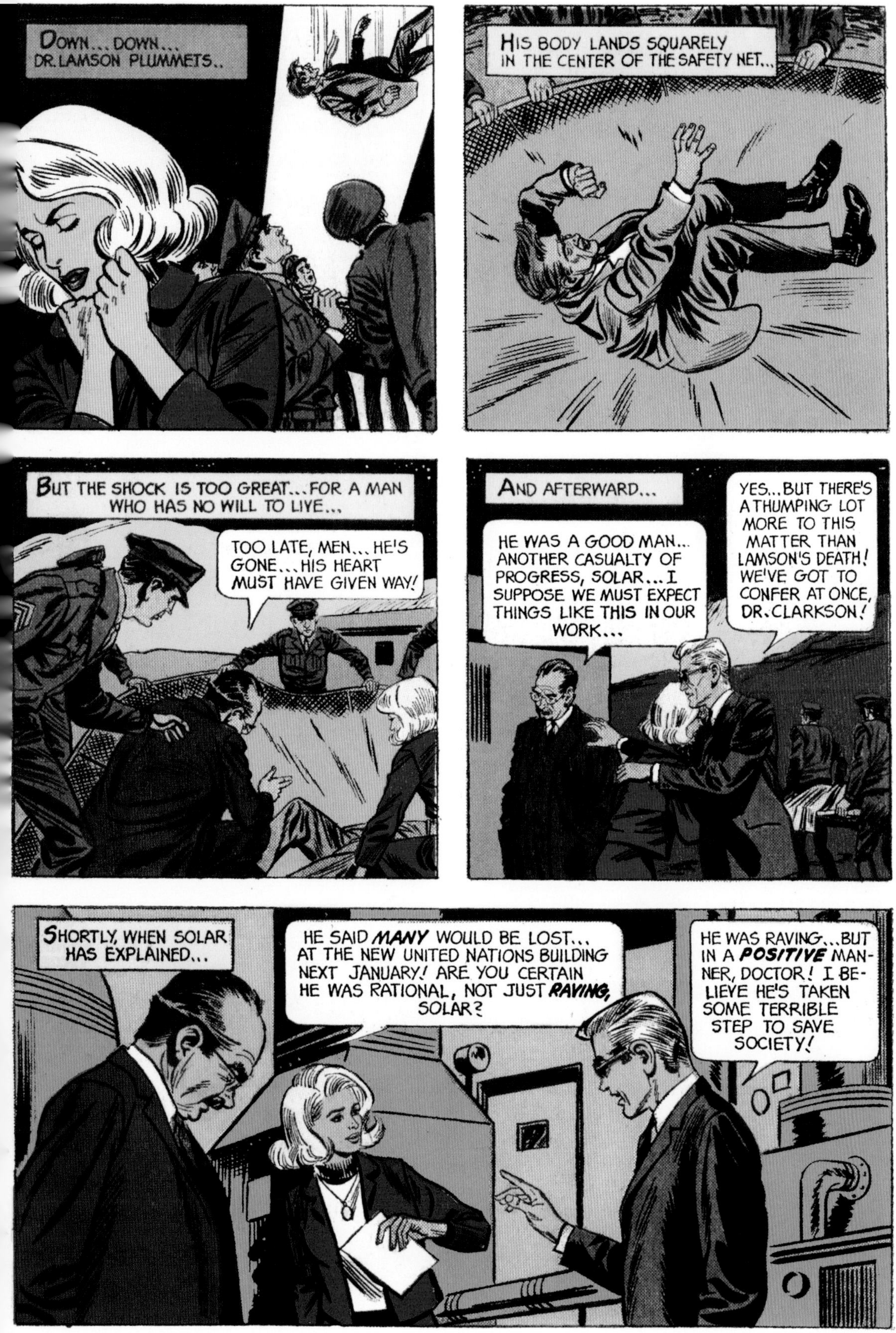
DOWN... DOWN... DR. LAMSON PLUMMETS..
HIS BODY LANDS SQUARELY IN THE CENTER OF THE SAFETY NET...
BUT THE SHOCK IS TOO GREAT... FOR A MAN WHO HAS NO WILL TO LIVE...
TOO LATE, MEN... HE'S GONE... HIS HEART MUST HAVE GIVEN WAY!
AND AFTERWARD...
HE WAS A GOOD MAN... ANOTHER CASUALTY OF PROGRESS, SOLAR... I SUPPOSE WE MUST EXPECT THINGS LIKE THIS IN OUR WORK...
YES... BUT THERE'S A THUMPING LOT MORE TO THIS MATTER THAN LAMSON'S DEATH! WE'VE GOT TO CONFER AT ONCE, DR. CLARKSON!
SHORTLY, WHEN SOLAR HAS EXPLAINED...
HE SAID MANY WOULD BE LOST... AT THE NEW UNITED NATIONS BUILDING NEXT JANUARY! ARE YOU CERTAIN HE WAS RATIONAL, NOT JUST RAVING, SOLAR?
HE WAS RAVING... BUT IN A POSITIVE MANNER, DOCTOR! I BELIEVE HE'S TAKEN SOME TERRIBLE STEP TO SAVE SOCIETY!

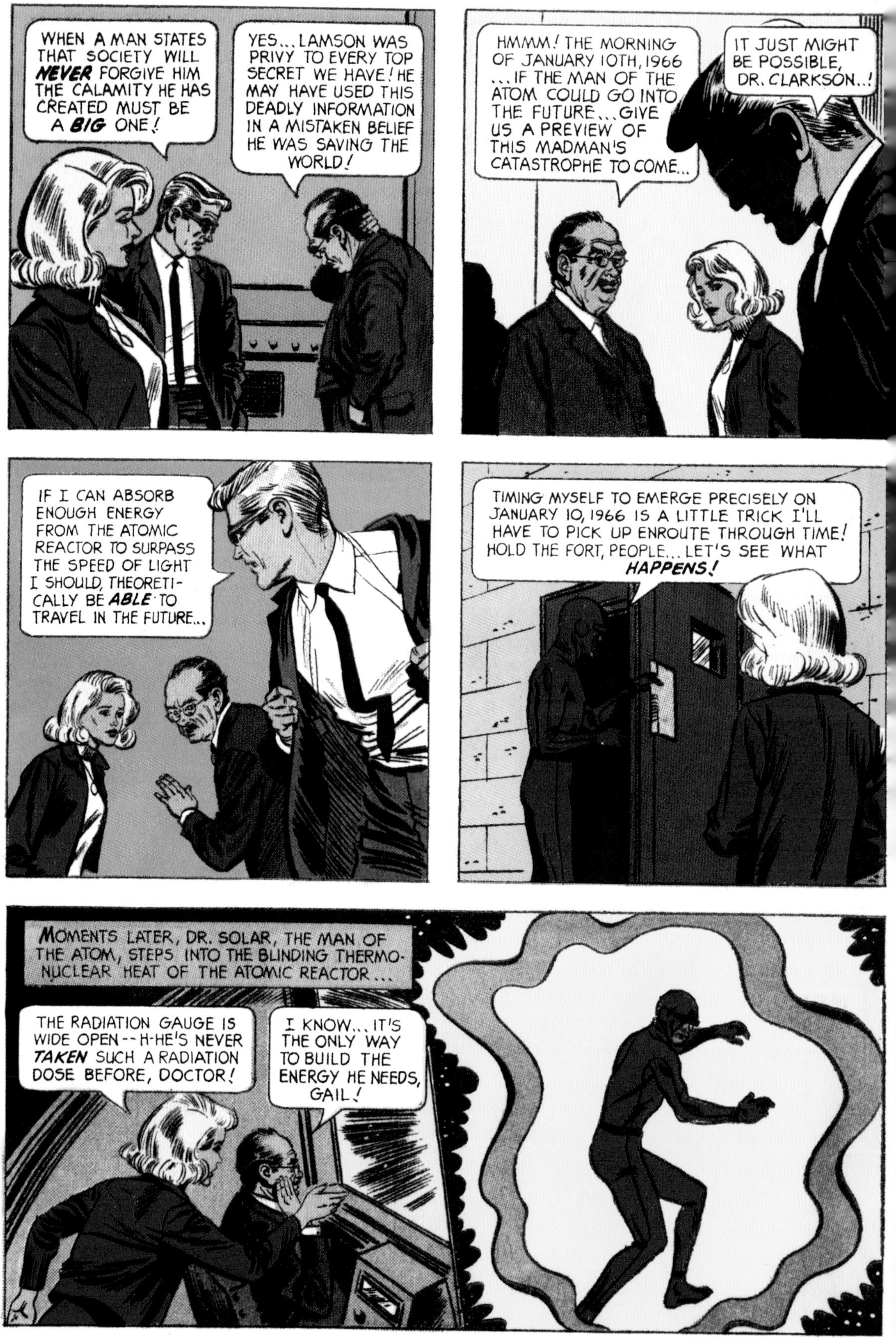

WHEN A MAN STATES THAT SOCIETY WILL NEVER FORGIVE HIM THE CALAMITY HE HAS CREATED MUST BE A BIG ONE!
YES... LAMSON WAS PRIVY TO EVERY TOP SECRET WE HAVE! HE MAY HAVE USED THIS DEADLY INFORMATION IN A MISTAKEN BELIEF HE WAS SAVING THE WORLD!
HMMM! THE MORNING OF JANUARY 10TH, 1966 ... IF THE MAN OF THE ATOM COULD GO INTO THE FUTURE... GIVE US A PREVIEW OF THIS MADMAN'S CATASTROPHE TO COME...
IT JUST MIGHT BE POSSIBLE, DR. CLARKSON...!
IF I CAN ABSORB ENOUGH ENERGY FROM THE ATOMIC REACTOR TO SURPASS THE SPEED OF LIGHT I SHOULD, THEORETICALLY BE ABLE TO TRAVEL IN THE FUTURE...
TIMING MYSELF TO EMERGE PRECISELY ON JANUARY 10, 1966 IS A LITTLE TRICK I'LL HAVE TO PICK UP ENROUTE THROUGH TIME! HOLD THE FORT, PEOPLE... LET'S SEE WHAT HAPPENS!
MOMENTS LATER, DR. SOLAR, THE MAN OF THE ATOM, STEPS INTO THE BLINDING THERMO-NUCLEAR HEAT OF THE ATOMIC REACTOR...
THE RADIATION GAUGE IS WIDE OPEN -- H-HE'S NEVER TAKEN SUCH A RADIATION DOSE BEFORE, DOCTOR!
I KNOW... IT'S THE ONLY WAY TO BUILD THE ENERGY HE NEEDS, GAIL!

INSIDE THE REACTOR, SOLAR'S BODY PULSATES AND THROBS AS NEUTRONS AND GAMMA RAYS BOMBARD IT IN EVER INCREASING FURY...
C-CAN I TAKE SUCH ENERGY..? WHAT WILL HAPPEN IF I OVER-SHOOT MY TARGET...GET LOST IN TIME...TRAPPED IN THE FUTURE...
1,000...2,000...3,000 ROENTGENS OF RADIA-TION CONTORT THE MAN OF THE ATOM'S FEATURES...
ROENTGENS
FINALLY, AS THE DOSAGE IS COMPLETE...
S-SOMETHING'S HAPPENING TO ME... THE ROOM SEEMS TO BE DRIFTING AWAY... I'M PACKED WITH SUPER ENERGY ...GOT TO START CRACKING THE SPEED-OF-LIGHT BARRIER...
QUICKLY, SOLAR CATAPULTS HIS BODY OUT OF ATOM VALLEY...
FASTER...FASTER... GOT TO PACK EVERY OUNCE OF ENERGY INTO SPEED...
THEN, AS THE MAN OF THE ATOM CIRCLES ATOM VALLEY IN AN INCREASING CYCLE OF SPEED...
I-IT'S WORKING... THAT NEW BUILDING WON'T BE FINISHED UNTIL THE 1ST OF JANUARY... I'VE PASSED THE SPEED OF LIGHT... I'M MOVING INTO THE FUTURE!

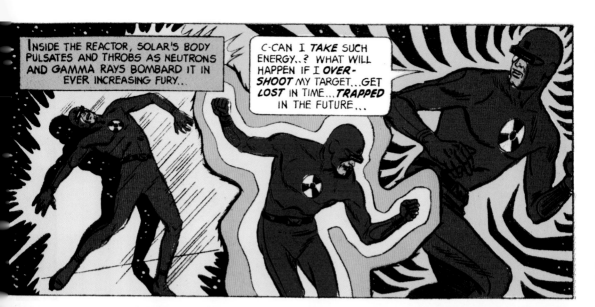

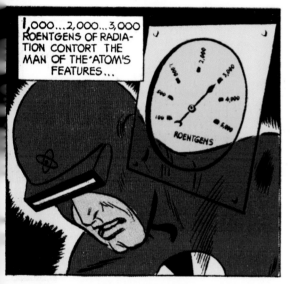

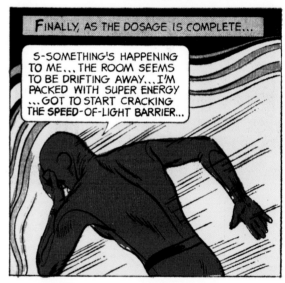

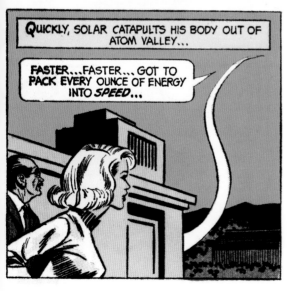

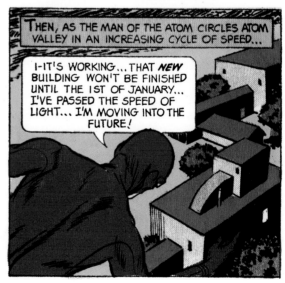

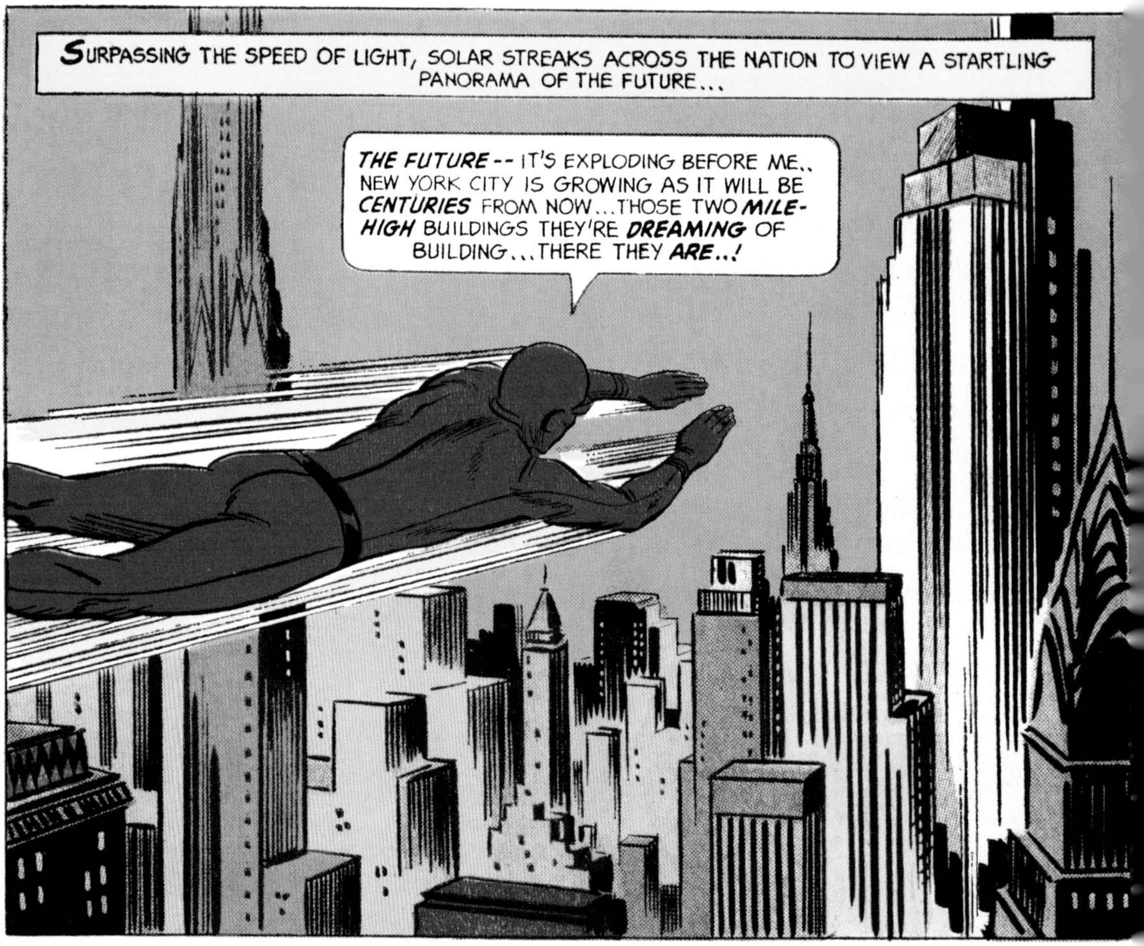
SURPASSING THE SPEED OF LIGHT, SOLAR STREAKS ACROSS THE NATION TO VIEW A STARTLING PANORAMA OF THE FUTURE...
THE FUTURE -- IT'S EXPLODING BEFORE ME.. NEW YORK CITY IS GROWING AS IT WILL BE CENTURIES FROM NOW...THOSE TWO MILE-HIGH BUILDINGS THEY'RE DREAMING OF BUILDING...THERE THEY ARE..!

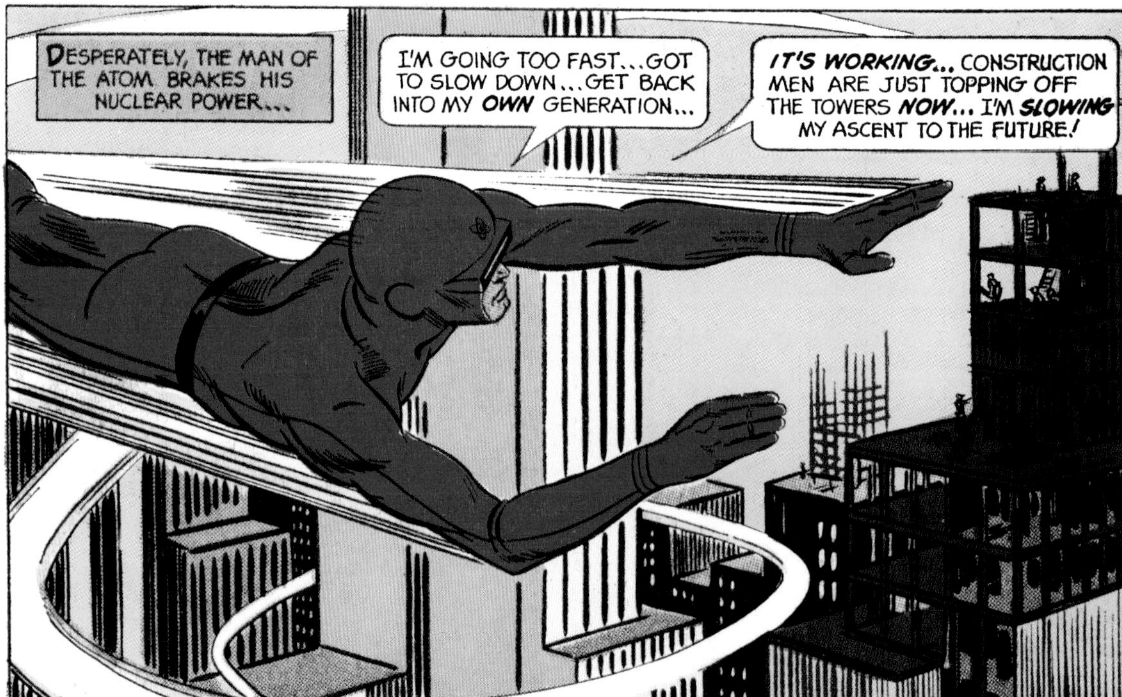
DESPERATELY, THE MAN OF THE ATOM BRAKES HIS NUCLEAR POWER...
I'M GOING TOO FAST...GOT TO SLOW DOWN...GET BACK INTO MY OWN GENERATION...
IT'S WORKING... CONSTRUCTION MEN ARE JUST TOPPING OFF THE TOWERS NOW... I'M SLOWING MY ASCENT TO THE FUTURE!

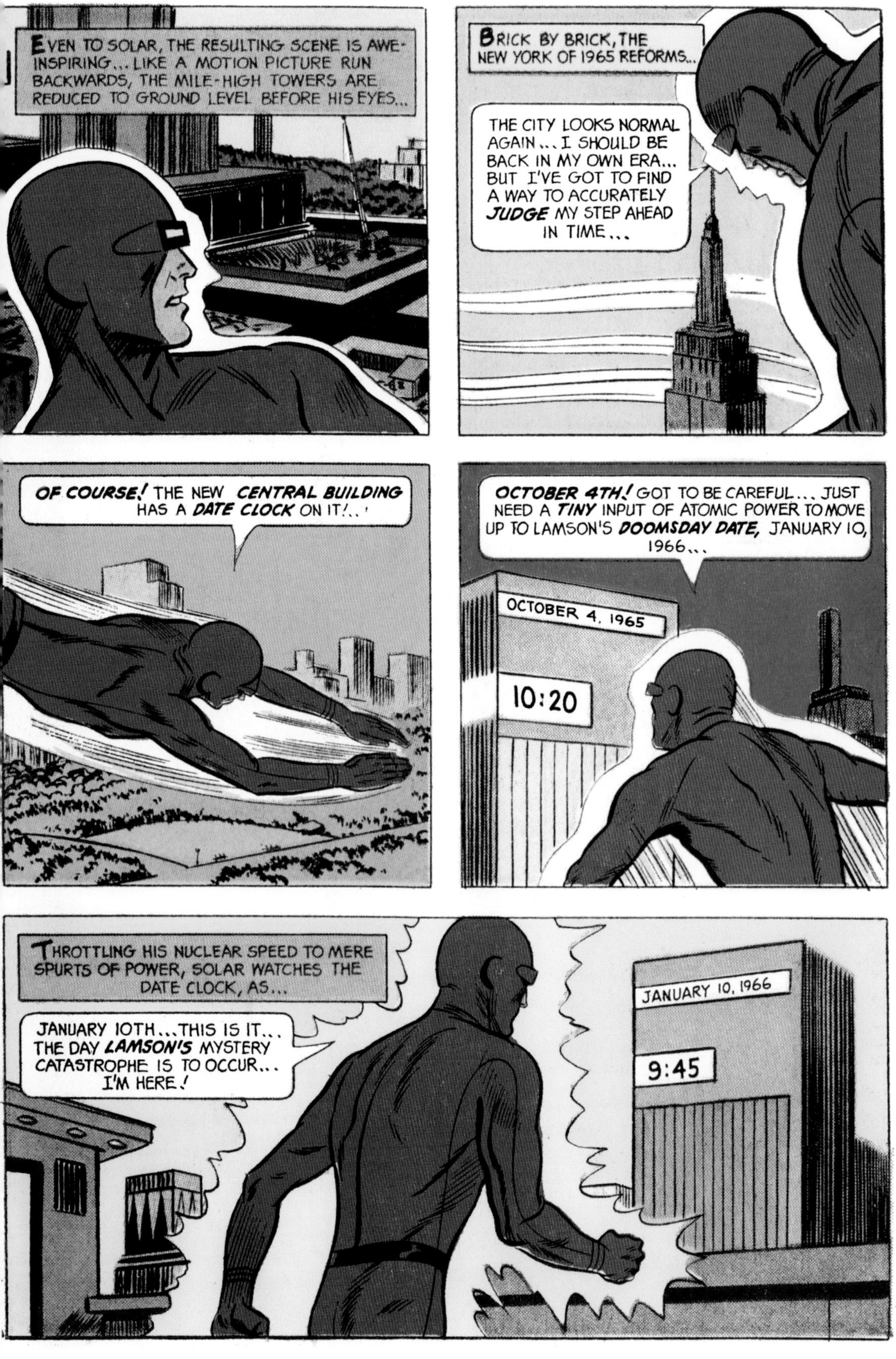
EVEN TO SOLAR, THE RESULTING SCENE IS AWE-INSPIRING... LIKE A MOTION PICTURE RUN BACKWARDS, THE MILE-HIGH TOWERS ARE REDUCED TO GROUND LEVEL BEFORE HIS EYES...
BRICK BY BRICK, THE NEW YORK OF 1965 REFORMS...
THE CITY LOOKS NORMAL AGAIN... I SHOULD BE BACK IN MY OWN ERA... BUT I'VE GOT TO FIND A WAY TO ACCURATELY JUDGE MY STEP AHEAD IN TIME...
OF COURSE! THE NEW CENTRAL BUILDING HAS A DATE CLOCK ON IT!..
OCTOBER 4TH! GOT TO BE CAREFUL... JUST NEED A TINY INPUT OF ATOMIC POWER TO MOVE UP TO LAMSON'S DOOMSDAY DATE, JANUARY 10, 1966...
OCTOBER 4, 1965
10:20
THROTTLING HIS NUCLEAR SPEED TO MERE SPURTS OF POWER, SOLAR WATCHES THE DATE CLOCK, AS...
JANUARY 10TH... THIS IS IT... THE DAY LAMSON'S MYSTERY CATASTROPHE IS TO OCCUR... I'M HERE!
JANUARY 10, 1966
9:45

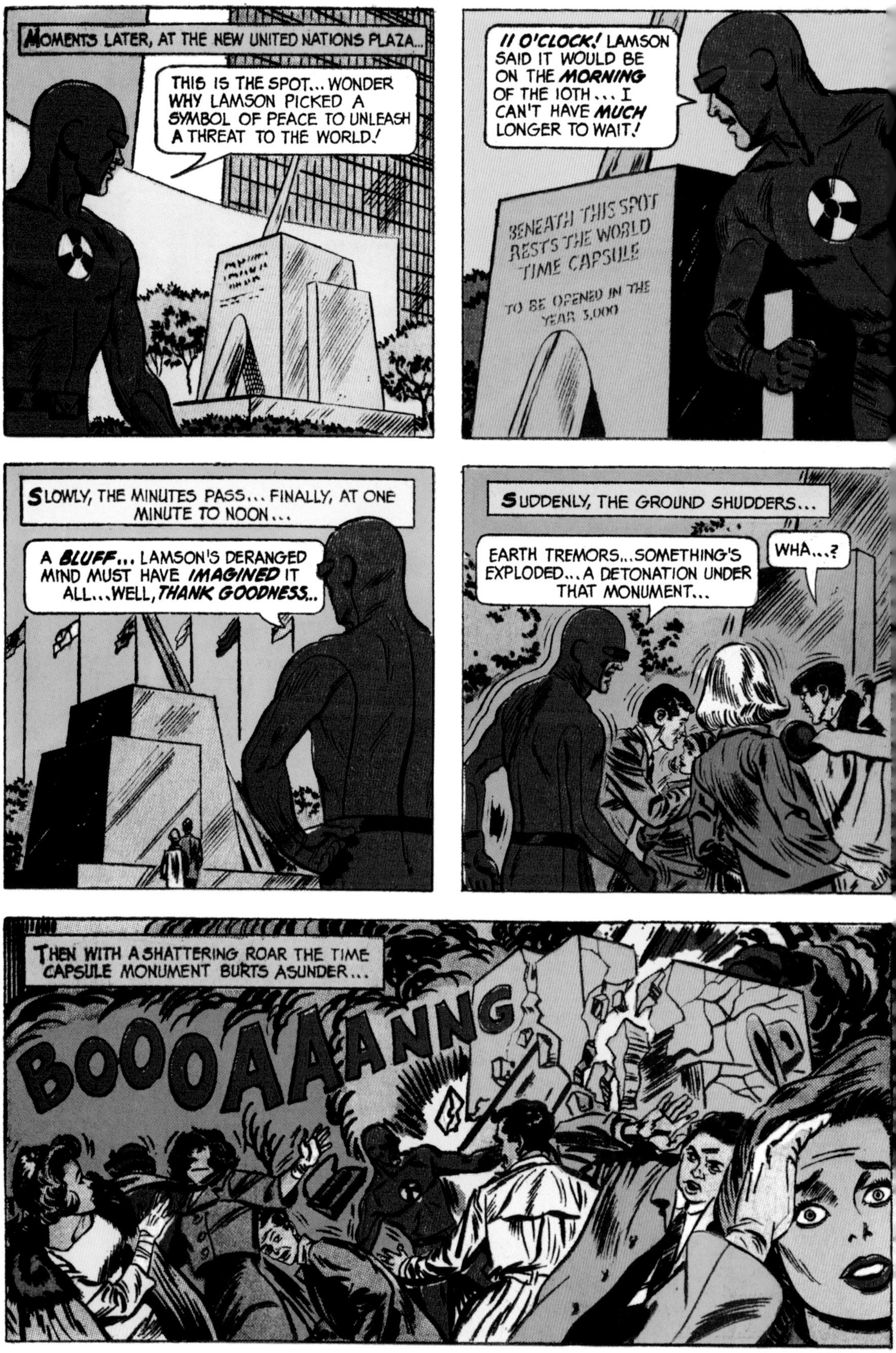
MOMENTS LATER, AT THE NEW UNITED NATIONS PLAZA...
THIS IS THE SPOT... WONDER WHY LAMSON PICKED A SYMBOL OF PEACE TO UNLEASH A THREAT TO THE WORLD!
11 O'CLOCK! LAMSON SAID IT WOULD BE ON THE MORNING OF THE 10TH... I CAN'T HAVE MUCH LONGER TO WAIT!
BENEATH THIS SPOT RESTS THE WORLD TIME CAPSULE
TO BE OPENED IN THE YEAR 3,000
SLOWLY, THE MINUTES PASS... FINALLY, AT ONE MINUTE TO NOON...
A BLUFF... LAMSON'S DERANGED MIND MUST HAVE IMAGINED IT ALL...WELL, THANK GOODNESS...
SUDDENLY, THE GROUND SHUDDERS...
EARTH TREMORS...SOMETHING'S EXPLODED...A DETONATION UNDER THAT MONUMENT...
WHA...?
THEN WITH A SHATTERING ROAR THE TIME CAPSULE MONUMENT BURTS ASUNDER...
BOOOAAANNG

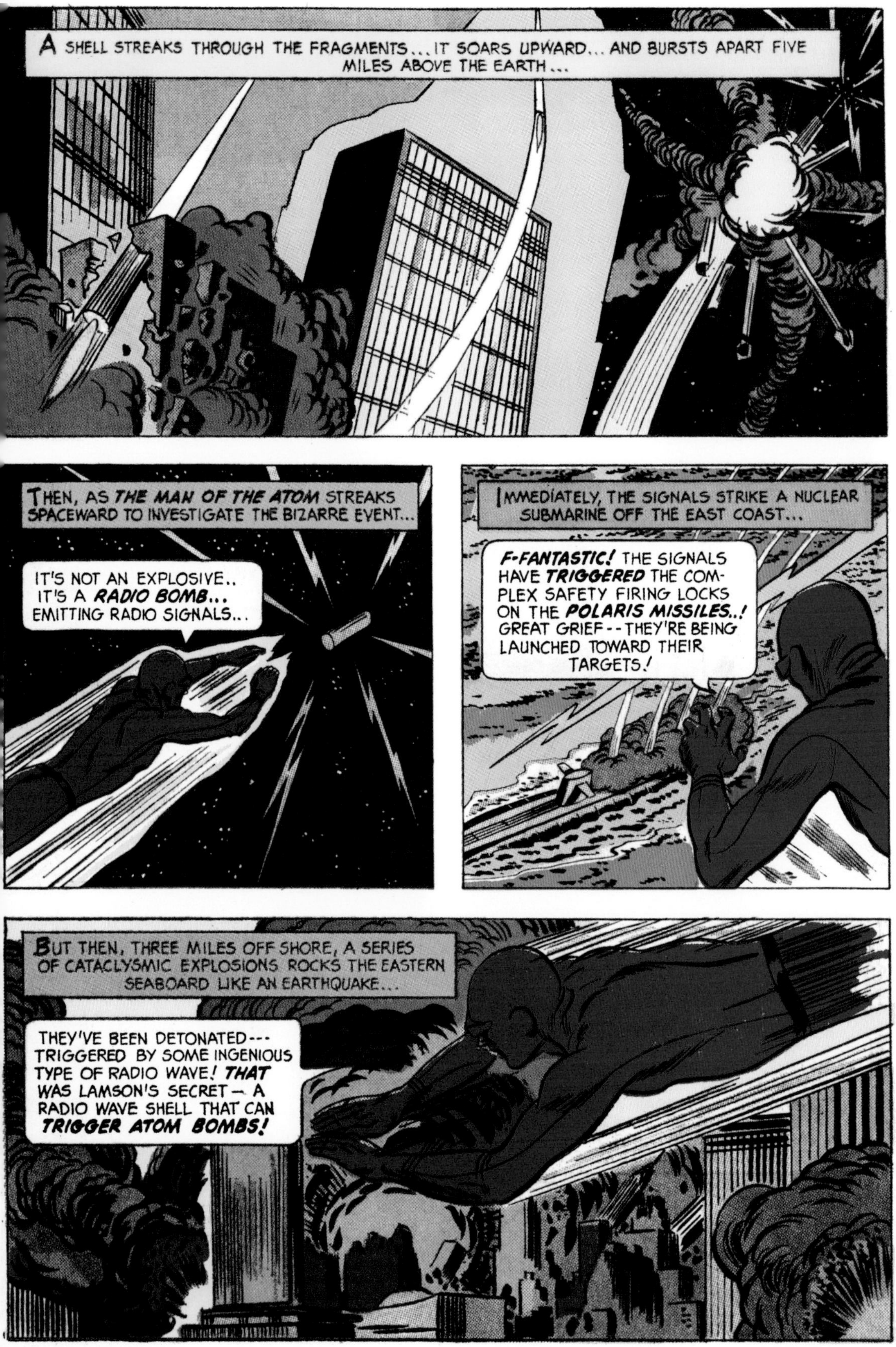
A SHELL STREAKS THROUGH THE FRAGMENTS... IT SOARS UPWARD... AND BURSTS APART FIVE MILES ABOVE THE EARTH...
THEN, AS THE MAN OF THE ATOM STREAKS SPACEWARD TO INVESTIGATE THE BIZARRE EVENT...
IT'S NOT AN EXPLOSIVE.. IT'S A RADIO BOMB... EMITTING RADIO SIGNALS...
IMMEDIATELY, THE SIGNALS STRIKE A NUCLEAR SUBMARINE OFF THE EAST COAST...
F-FANTASTIC! THE SIGNALS HAVE TRIGGERED THE COMPLEX SAFETY FIRING LOCKS ON THE POLARIS MISSILES..! GREAT GRIEF--THEY'RE BEING LAUNCHED TOWARD THEIR TARGETS!
BUT THEN, THREE MILES OFF SHORE, A SERIES OF CATACLYSMIC EXPLOSIONS ROCKS THE EASTERN SEABOARD LIKE AN EARTHQUAKE...
THEY'VE BEEN DETONATED--- TRIGGERED BY SOME INGENIOUS TYPE OF RADIO WAVE! THAT WAS LAMSON'S SECRET— A RADIO WAVE SHELL THAT CAN TRIGGER ATOM BOMBS!

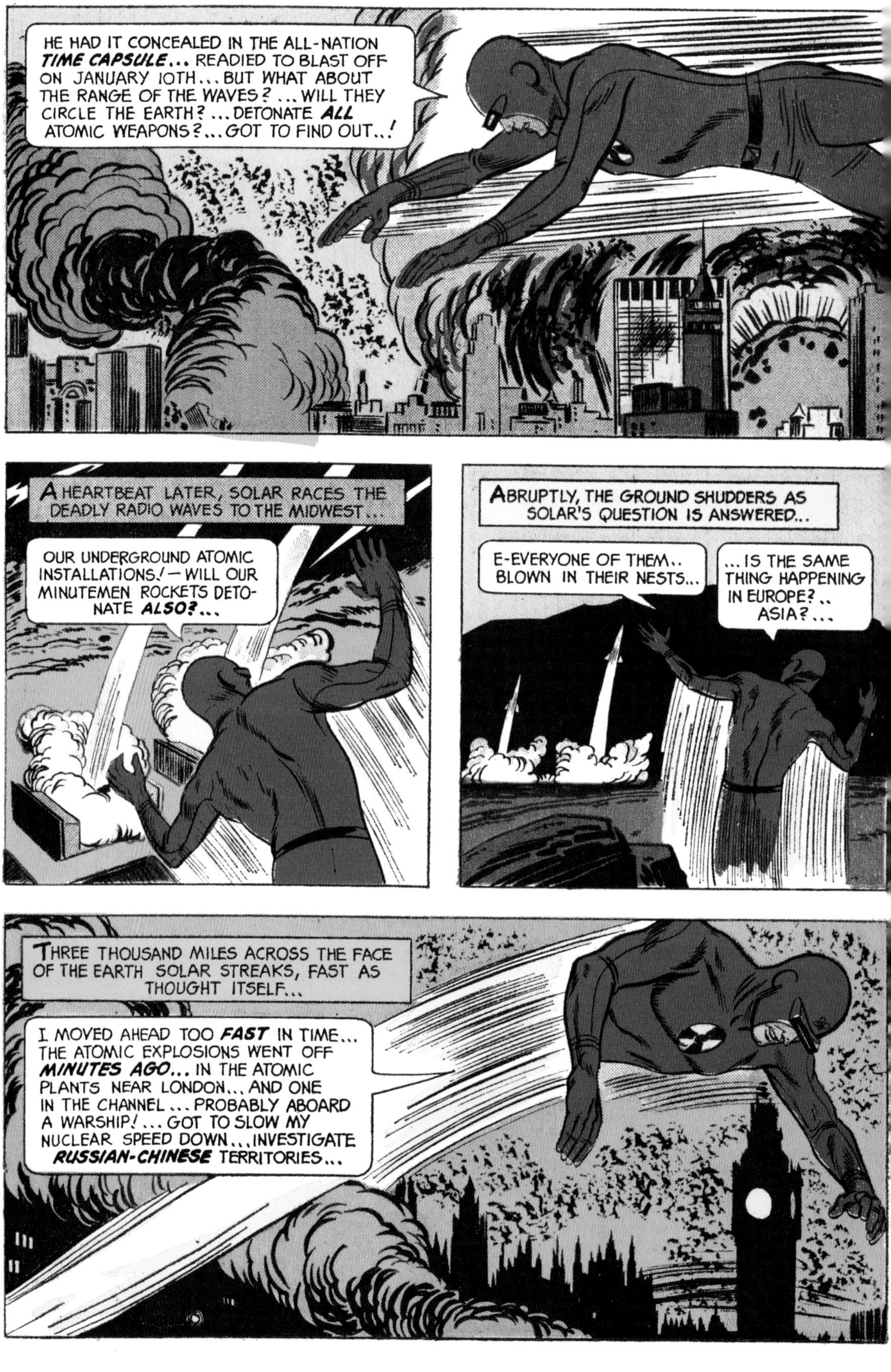
HE HAD IT CONCEALED IN THE ALL-NATION TIME CAPSULE... READIED TO BLAST OFF ON JANUARY 10TH... BUT WHAT ABOUT THE RANGE OF THE WAVES? ...WILL THEY CIRCLE THE EARTH? ...DETONATE ALL ATOMIC WEAPONS?...GOT TO FIND OUT..!
A HEARTBEAT LATER, SOLAR RACES THE DEADLY RADIO WAVES TO THE MIDWEST...
OUR UNDERGROUND ATOMIC INSTALLATIONS!—WILL OUR MINUTEMEN ROCKETS DETONATE ALSO?...
ABRUPTLY, THE GROUND SHUDDERS AS SOLAR'S QUESTION IS ANSWERED...
E-EVERYONE OF THEM.. BLOWN IN THEIR NESTS...
...IS THE SAME THING HAPPENING IN EUROPE?.. ASIA?...
THREE THOUSAND MILES ACROSS THE FACE OF THE EARTH SOLAR STREAKS, FAST AS THOUGHT ITSELF...
I MOVED AHEAD TOO FAST IN TIME... THE ATOMIC EXPLOSIONS WENT OFF MINUTES AGO... IN THE ATOMIC PLANTS NEAR LONDON... AND ONE IN THE CHANNEL ... PROBABLY ABOARD A WARSHIP! ... GOT TO SLOW MY NUCLEAR SPEED DOWN... INVESTIGATE RUSSIAN-CHINESE TERRITORIES...

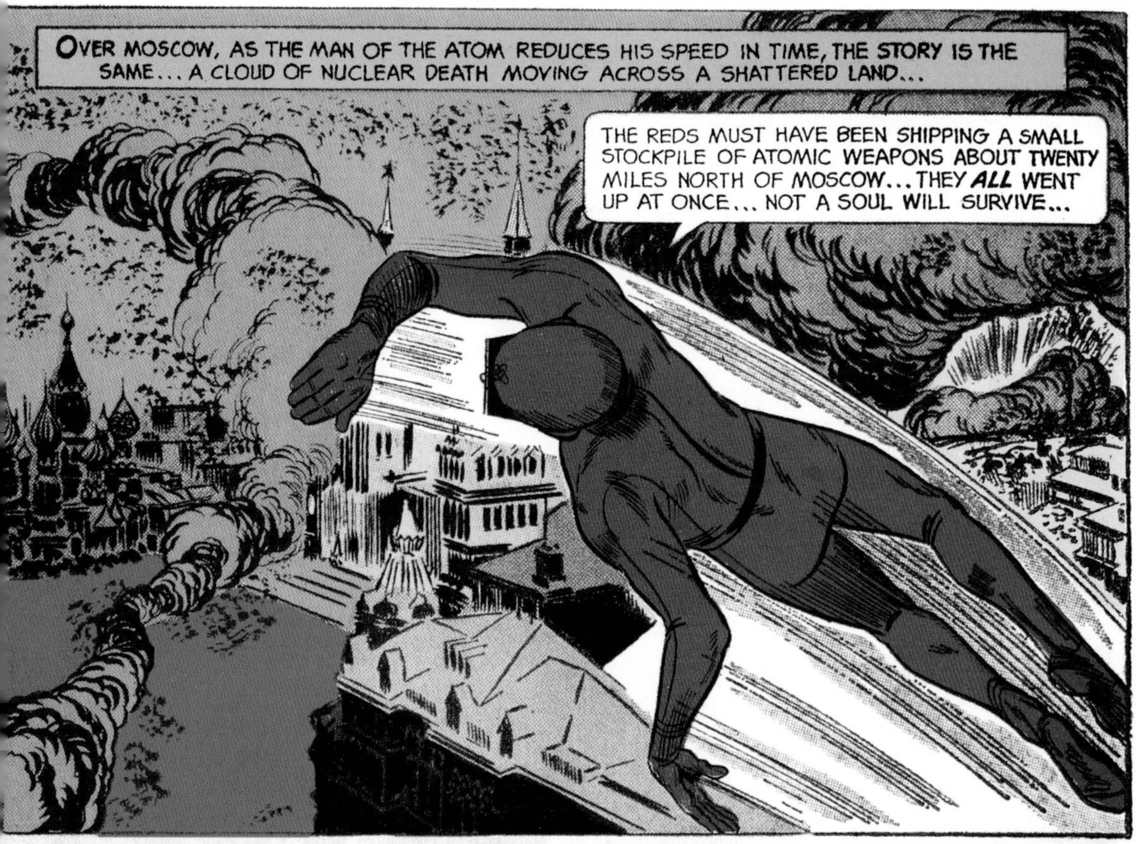
OVER MOSCOW, AS THE MAN OF THE ATOM REDUCES HIS SPEED IN TIME, THE STORY IS THE SAME... A CLOUD OF NUCLEAR DEATH MOVING ACROSS A SHATTERED LAND...
THE REDS MUST HAVE BEEN SHIPPING A SMALL STOCKPILE OF ATOMIC WEAPONS ABOUT TWENTY MILES NORTH OF MOSCOW... THEY *ALL* WENT UP AT ONCE... NOT A SOUL WILL SURVIVE...

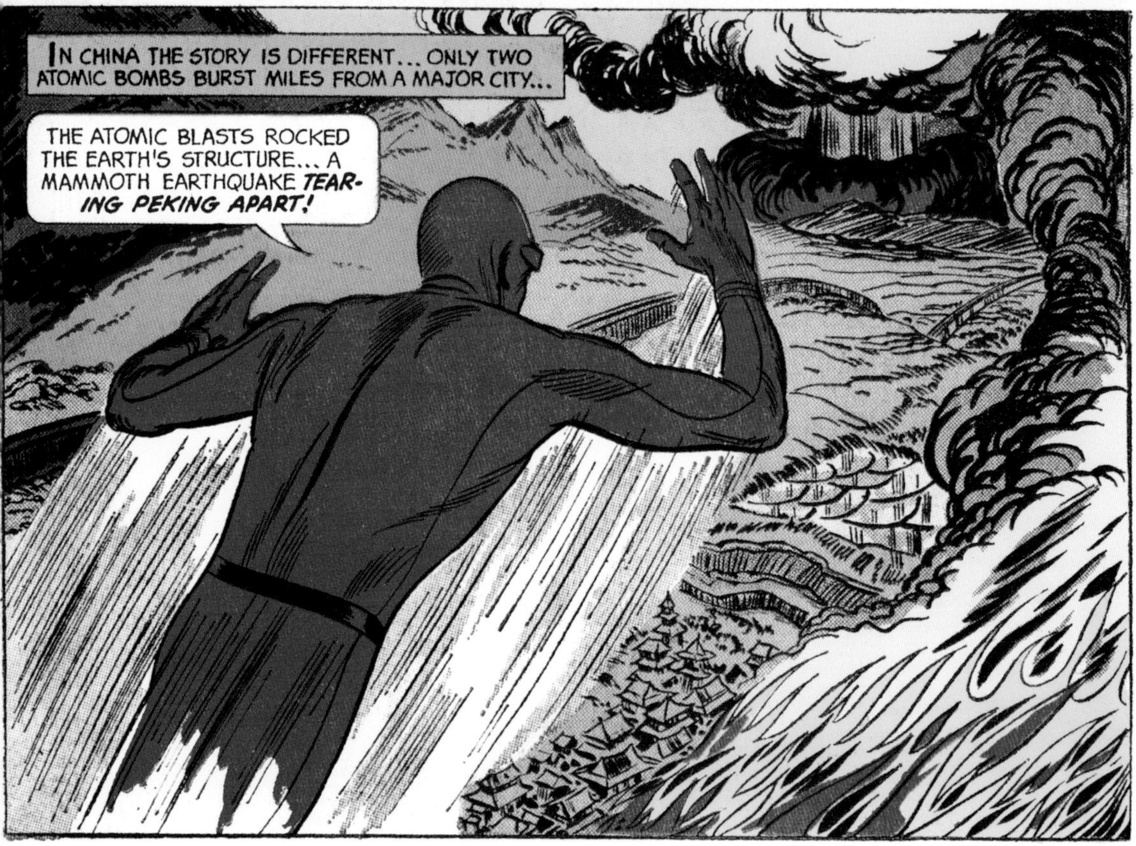
IN CHINA THE STORY IS DIFFERENT... ONLY TWO ATOMIC BOMBS BURST MILES FROM A MAJOR CITY...
THE ATOMIC BLASTS ROCKED THE EARTH'S STRUCTURE... A MAMMOTH EARTHQUAKE ***TEAR-ING PEKING APART!***

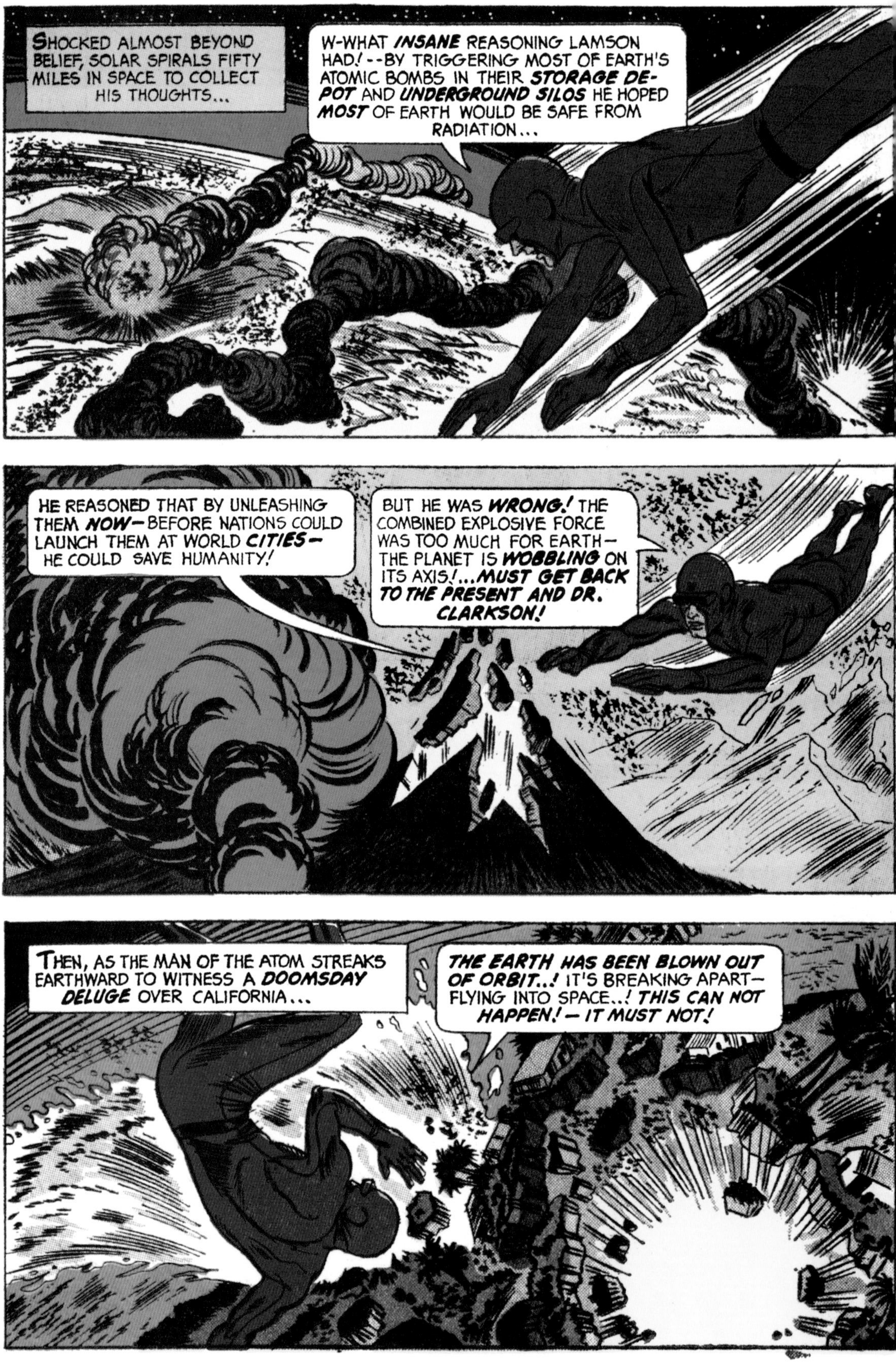
SHOCKED ALMOST BEYOND BELIEF, SOLAR SPIRALS FIFTY MILES IN SPACE TO COLLECT HIS THOUGHTS...
W-WHAT *INSANE* REASONING LAMSON HAD! --BY TRIGGERING MOST OF EARTH'S ATOMIC BOMBS IN THEIR *STORAGE DEPOT* AND *UNDERGROUND SILOS* HE HOPED *MOST* OF EARTH WOULD BE SAFE FROM RADIATION...
HE REASONED THAT BY UNLEASHING THEM *NOW*-- BEFORE NATIONS COULD LAUNCH THEM AT WORLD *CITIES*-- HE COULD SAVE HUMANITY!
BUT HE WAS *WRONG!* THE COMBINED EXPLOSIVE FORCE WAS TOO MUCH FOR EARTH-- THE PLANET IS *WOBBLING* ON ITS AXIS! ...*MUST GET BACK TO THE PRESENT AND DR. CLARKSON!*
THEN, AS THE MAN OF THE ATOM STREAKS EARTHWARD TO WITNESS A *DOOMSDAY DELUGE* OVER CALIFORNIA...
*THE EARTH HAS BEEN BLOWN OUT OF ORBIT..!* IT'S BREAKING APART-- FLYING INTO SPACE..! *THIS CAN NOT HAPPEN! -- IT MUST NOT!*

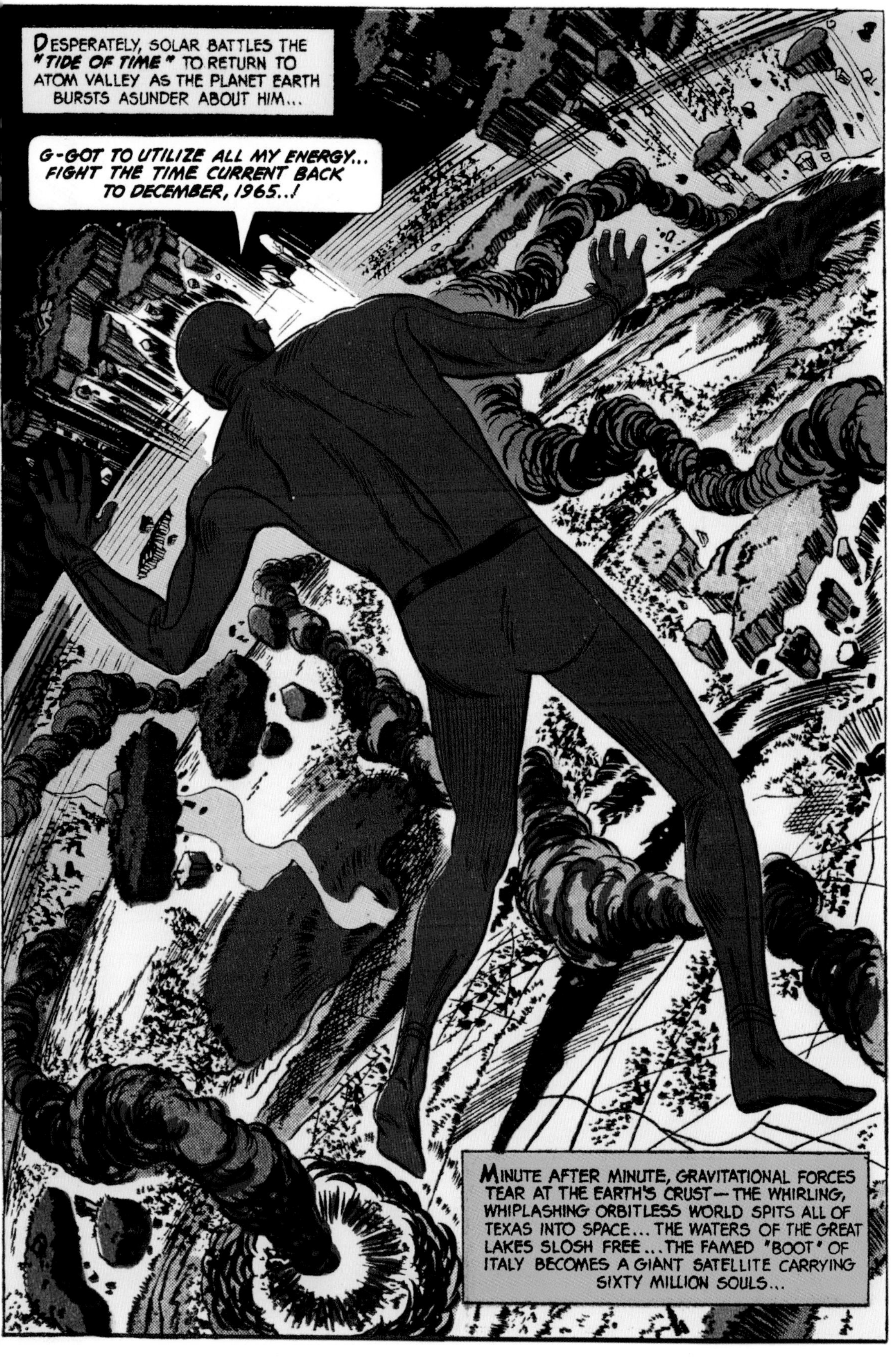
DESPERATELY, SOLAR BATTLES THE "TIDE OF TIME" TO RETURN TO ATOM VALLEY AS THE PLANET EARTH BURSTS ASUNDER ABOUT HIM...
G-GOT TO UTILIZE ALL MY ENERGY... FIGHT THE TIME CURRENT BACK TO DECEMBER, 1965...!
MINUTE AFTER MINUTE, GRAVITATIONAL FORCES TEAR AT THE EARTH'S CRUST—THE WHIRLING, WHIPLASHING ORBITLESS WORLD SPITS ALL OF TEXAS INTO SPACE... THE WATERS OF THE GREAT LAKES SLOSH FREE... THE FAMED "BOOT" OF ITALY BECOMES A GIANT SATELLITE CARRYING SIXTY MILLION SOULS...

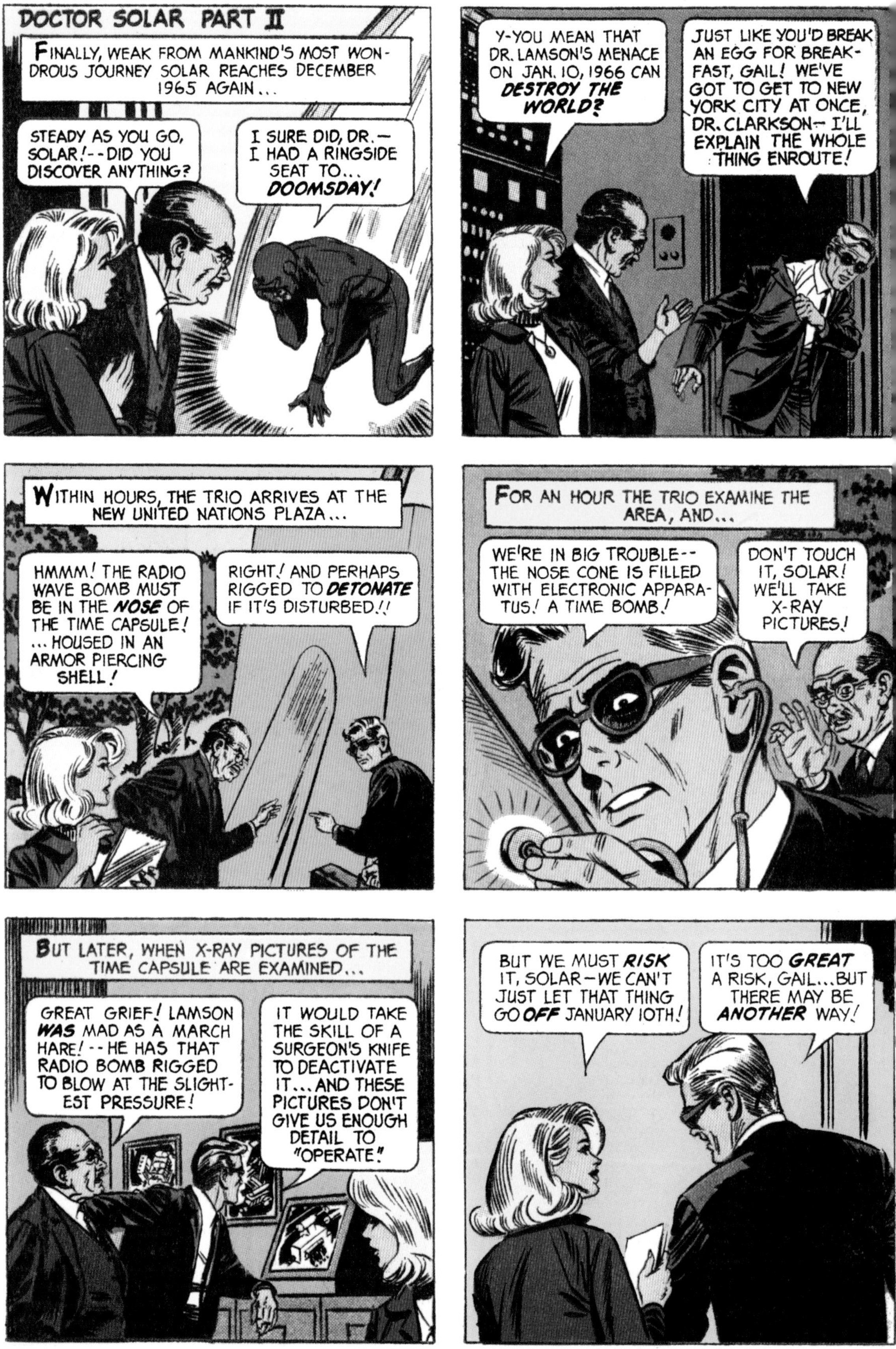
DOCTOR SOLAR PART II
FINALLY, WEAK FROM MANKIND'S MOST WONDROUS JOURNEY SOLAR REACHES DECEMBER 1965 AGAIN...
STEADY AS YOU GO, SOLAR!--DID YOU DISCOVER ANYTHING?
I SURE DID, DR.— I HAD A RINGSIDE SEAT TO... DOOMSDAY!
Y-YOU MEAN THAT DR. LAMSON'S MENACE ON JAN. 10, 1966 CAN DESTROY THE WORLD?
JUST LIKE YOU'D BREAK AN EGG FOR BREAKFAST, GAIL! WE'VE GOT TO GET TO NEW YORK CITY AT ONCE, DR. CLARKSON— I'LL EXPLAIN THE WHOLE THING ENROUTE!
WITHIN HOURS, THE TRIO ARRIVES AT THE NEW UNITED NATIONS PLAZA...
HMMM! THE RADIO WAVE BOMB MUST BE IN THE NOSE OF THE TIME CAPSULE! ...HOUSED IN AN ARMOR PIERCING SHELL!
RIGHT! AND PERHAPS RIGGED TO DETONATE IF IT'S DISTURBED!!
FOR AN HOUR THE TRIO EXAMINE THE AREA, AND...
WE'RE IN BIG TROUBLE-- THE NOSE CONE IS FILLED WITH ELECTRONIC APPARATUS! A TIME BOMB!
DON'T TOUCH IT, SOLAR! WE'LL TAKE X-RAY PICTURES!
BUT LATER, WHEN X-RAY PICTURES OF THE TIME CAPSULE ARE EXAMINED...
GREAT GRIEF! LAMSON WAS MAD AS A MARCH HARE! --HE HAS THAT RADIO BOMB RIGGED TO BLOW AT THE SLIGHTEST PRESSURE!
IT WOULD TAKE THE SKILL OF A SURGEON'S KNIFE TO DEACTIVATE IT...AND THESE PICTURES DON'T GIVE US ENOUGH DETAIL TO "OPERATE."
BUT WE MUST RISK IT, SOLAR—WE CAN'T JUST LET THAT THING GO OFF JANUARY 10TH!
IT'S TOO GREAT A RISK, GAIL...BUT THERE MAY BE ANOTHER WAY!

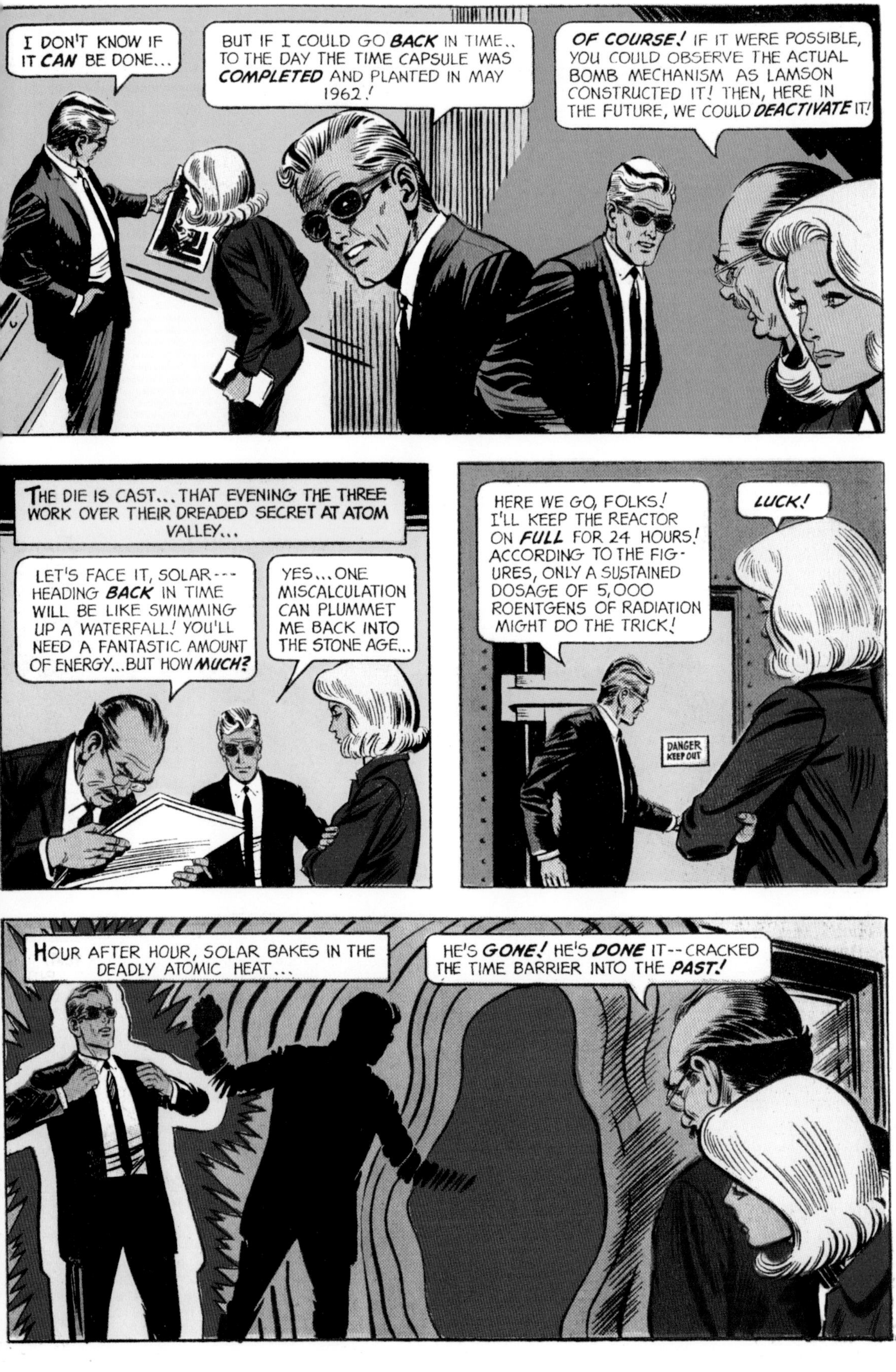

I DON'T KNOW IF IT CAN BE DONE...
BUT IF I COULD GO BACK IN TIME.. TO THE DAY THE TIME CAPSULE WAS COMPLETED AND PLANTED IN MAY 1962!
OF COURSE! IF IT WERE POSSIBLE, YOU COULD OBSERVE THE ACTUAL BOMB MECHANISM AS LAMSON CONSTRUCTED IT! THEN, HERE IN THE FUTURE, WE COULD DEACTIVATE IT!
THE DIE IS CAST... THAT EVENING THE THREE WORK OVER THEIR DREADED SECRET AT ATOM VALLEY...
LET'S FACE IT, SOLAR--- HEADING BACK IN TIME WILL BE LIKE SWIMMING UP A WATERFALL! YOU'LL NEED A FANTASTIC AMOUNT OF ENERGY...BUT HOW MUCH?
YES... ONE MISCALCULATION CAN PLUMMET ME BACK INTO THE STONE AGE...
HERE WE GO, FOLKS! I'LL KEEP THE REACTOR ON FULL FOR 24 HOURS! ACCORDING TO THE FIG-URES, ONLY A SUSTAINED DOSAGE OF 5,000 ROENTGENS OF RADIATION MIGHT DO THE TRICK!
LUCK!
DANGER KEEP OUT
HOUR AFTER HOUR, SOLAR BAKES IN THE DEADLY ATOMIC HEAT...
HE'S GONE! HE'S DONE IT--CRACKED THE TIME BARRIER INTO THE PAST!

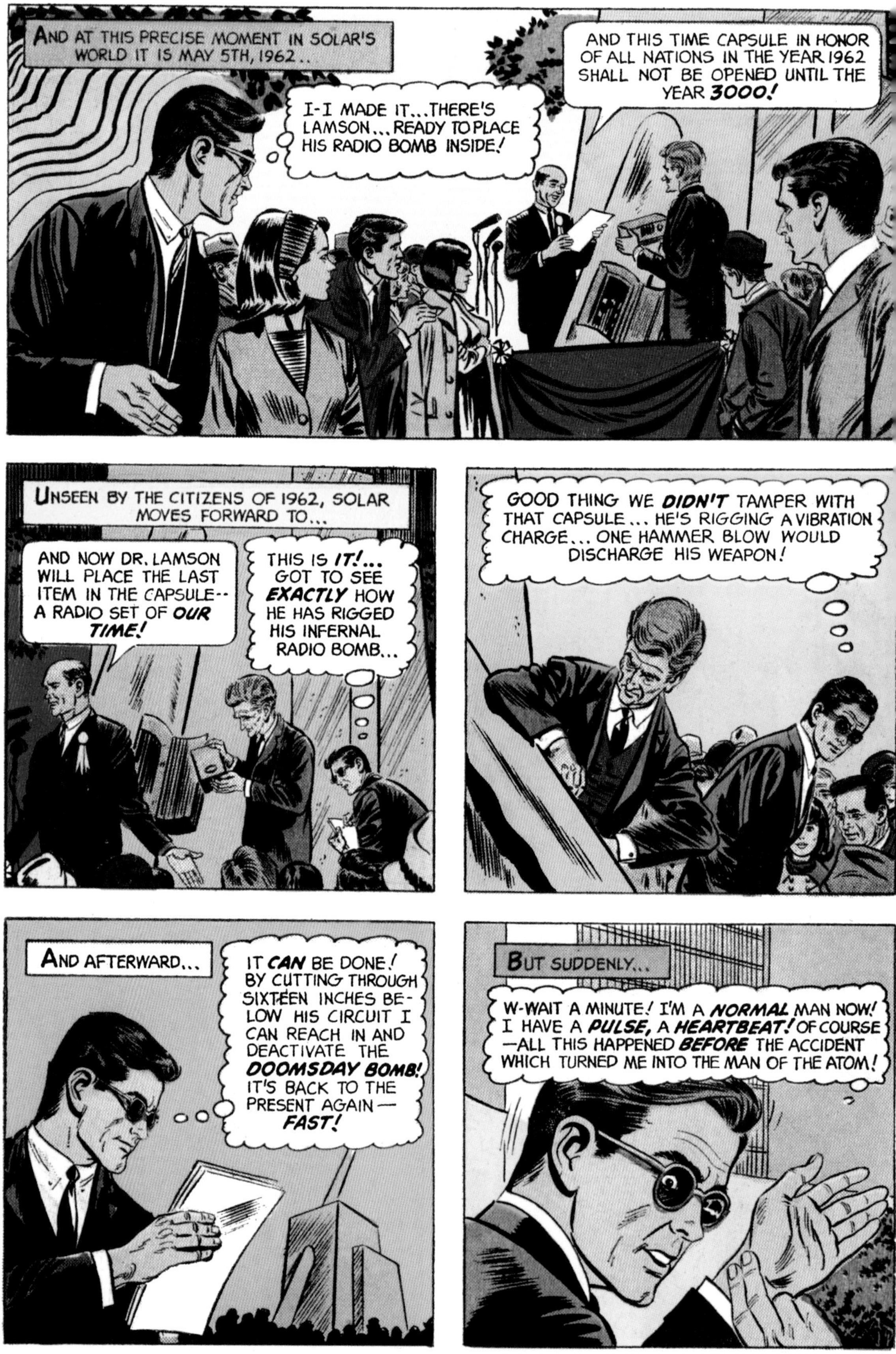

AND AT THIS PRECISE MOMENT IN SOLAR'S WORLD IT IS MAY 5TH, 1962..
I-I MADE IT...THERE'S LAMSON... READY TO PLACE HIS RADIO BOMB INSIDE!
AND THIS TIME CAPSULE IN HONOR OF ALL NATIONS IN THE YEAR 1962 SHALL NOT BE OPENED UNTIL THE YEAR 3000!
UNSEEN BY THE CITIZENS OF 1962, SOLAR MOVES FORWARD TO...
AND NOW DR. LAMSON WILL PLACE THE LAST ITEM IN THE CAPSULE-- A RADIO SET OF OUR TIME!
THIS IS IT!... GOT TO SEE EXACTLY HOW HE HAS RIGGED HIS INFERNAL RADIO BOMB...
GOOD THING WE DIDN'T TAMPER WITH THAT CAPSULE... HE'S RIGGING A VIBRATION CHARGE... ONE HAMMER BLOW WOULD DISCHARGE HIS WEAPON!
AND AFTERWARD...
IT CAN BE DONE! BY CUTTING THROUGH SIXTEEN INCHES BE-LOW HIS CIRCUIT I CAN REACH IN AND DEACTIVATE THE DOOMSDAY BOMB! IT'S BACK TO THE PRESENT AGAIN— FAST!
BUT SUDDENLY...
W-WAIT A MINUTE! I'M A NORMAL MAN NOW! I HAVE A PULSE, A HEARTBEAT! OF COURSE —ALL THIS HAPPENED BEFORE THE ACCIDENT WHICH TURNED ME INTO THE MAN OF THE ATOM!

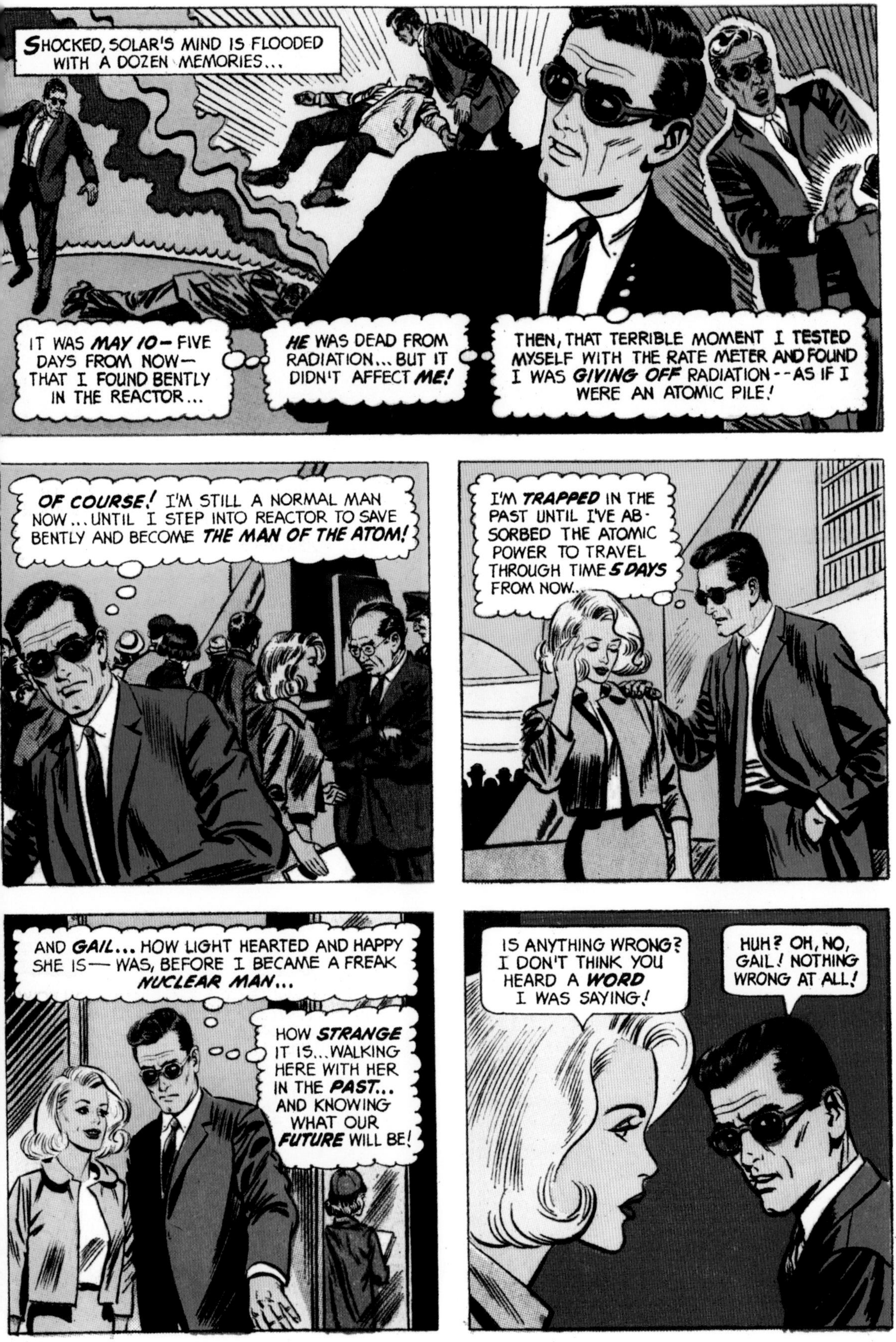
SHOCKED, SOLAR'S MIND IS FLOODED WITH A DOZEN MEMORIES...
IT WAS MAY 10 — FIVE DAYS FROM NOW— THAT I FOUND BENTLY IN THE REACTOR...
HE WAS DEAD FROM RADIATION... BUT IT DIDN'T AFFECT ME!
THEN, THAT TERRIBLE MOMENT I TESTED MYSELF WITH THE RATE METER AND FOUND I WAS GIVING OFF RADIATION--AS IF I WERE AN ATOMIC PILE!
OF COURSE! I'M STILL A NORMAL MAN NOW... UNTIL I STEP INTO REACTOR TO SAVE BENTLY AND BECOME THE MAN OF THE ATOM!
I'M TRAPPED IN THE PAST UNTIL I'VE AB-SORBED THE ATOMIC POWER TO TRAVEL THROUGH TIME 5 DAYS FROM NOW...
AND GAIL... HOW LIGHT HEARTED AND HAPPY SHE IS— WAS, BEFORE I BECAME A FREAK NUCLEAR MAN...
HOW STRANGE IT IS... WALKING HERE WITH HER IN THE PAST... AND KNOWING WHAT OUR FUTURE WILL BE!
IS ANYTHING WRONG? I DON'T THINK YOU HEARD A WORD I WAS SAYING!
HUH? OH, NO, GAIL! NOTHING WRONG AT ALL!

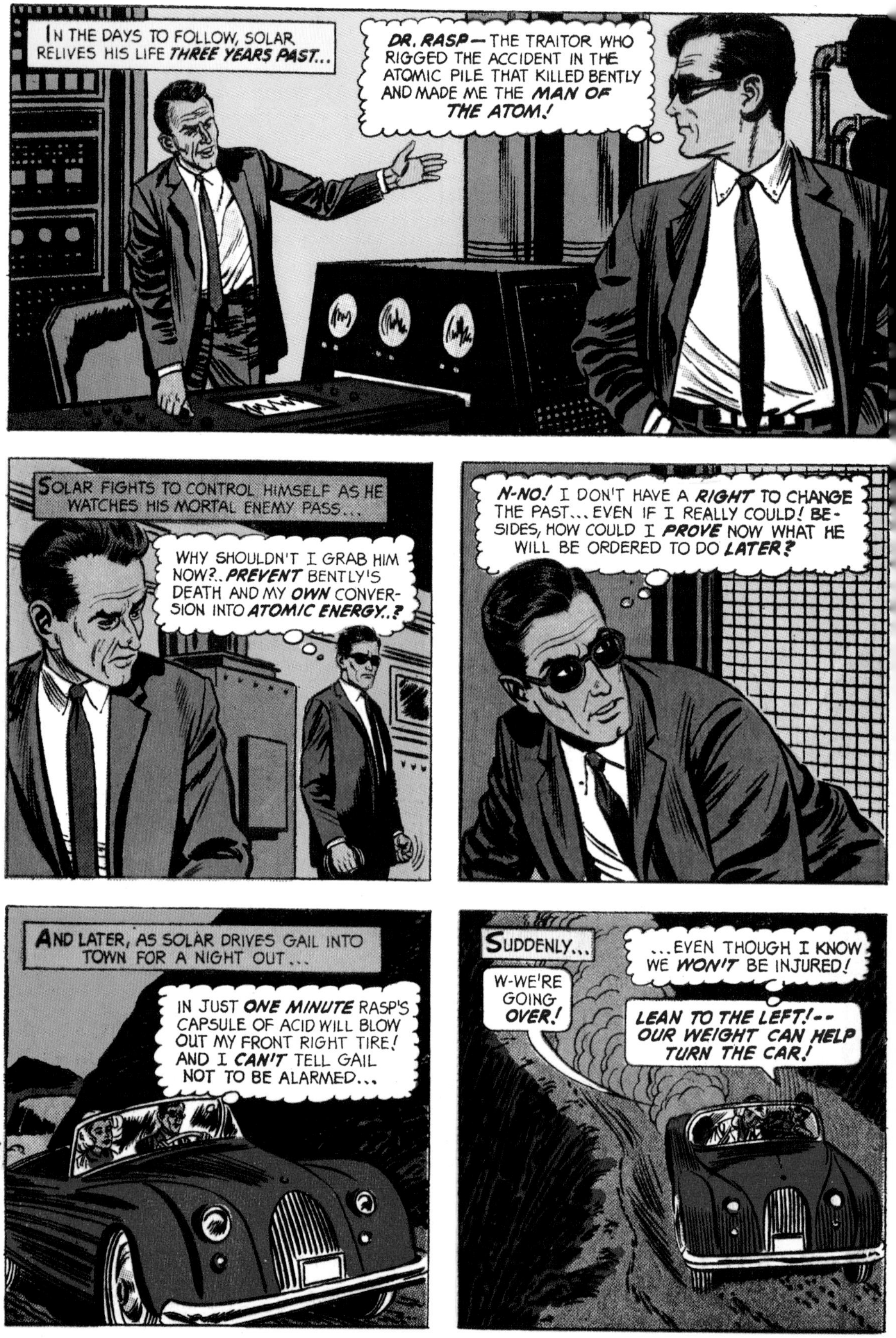
IN THE DAYS TO FOLLOW, SOLAR RELIVES HIS LIFE THREE YEARS PAST...
DR. RASP— THE TRAITOR WHO RIGGED THE ACCIDENT IN THE ATOMIC PILE THAT KILLED BENTLY AND MADE ME THE MAN OF THE ATOM!
SOLAR FIGHTS TO CONTROL HIMSELF AS HE WATCHES HIS MORTAL ENEMY PASS...
WHY SHOULDN'T I GRAB HIM NOW?.. PREVENT BENTLY'S DEATH AND MY OWN CONVERSION INTO ATOMIC ENERGY..?
N-NO! I DON'T HAVE A RIGHT TO CHANGE THE PAST... EVEN IF I REALLY COULD! BESIDES, HOW COULD I PROVE NOW WHAT HE WILL BE ORDERED TO DO LATER?
AND LATER, AS SOLAR DRIVES GAIL INTO TOWN FOR A NIGHT OUT...
IN JUST ONE MINUTE RASP'S CAPSULE OF ACID WILL BLOW OUT MY FRONT RIGHT TIRE! AND I CAN'T TELL GAIL NOT TO BE ALARMED...
SUDDENLY...
W-WE'RE GOING OVER!
...EVEN THOUGH I KNOW WE WON'T BE INJURED!
LEAN TO THE LEFT!-- OUR WEIGHT CAN HELP TURN THE CAR!

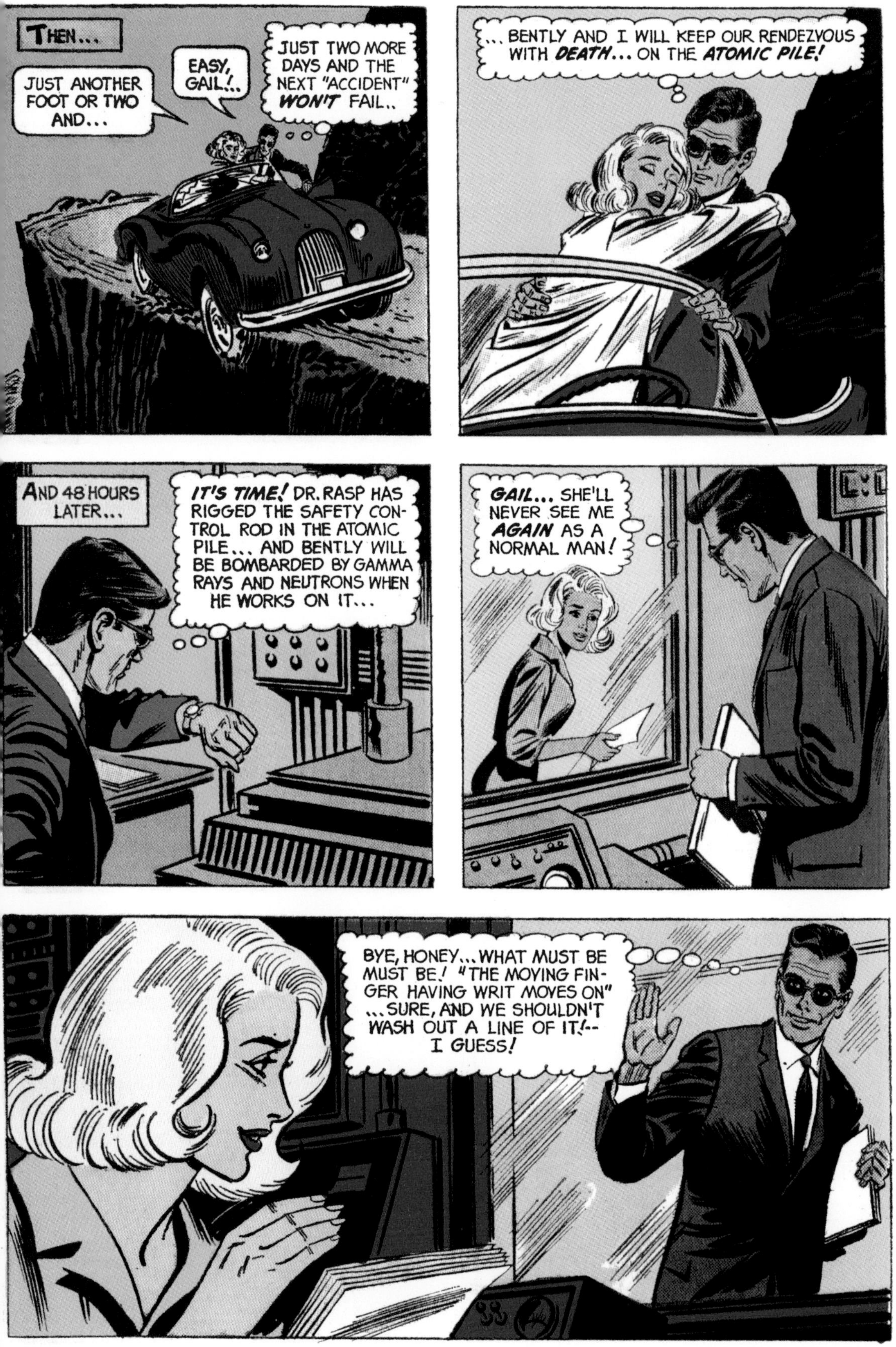
THEN...
JUST ANOTHER FOOT OR TWO AND...
EASY, GAIL!..
JUST TWO MORE DAYS AND THE NEXT "ACCIDENT" WON'T FAIL..
... BENTLY AND I WILL KEEP OUR RENDEZVOUS WITH DEATH... ON THE ATOMIC PILE!
AND 48 HOURS LATER...
IT'S TIME! DR. RASP HAS RIGGED THE SAFETY CONTROL ROD IN THE ATOMIC PILE... AND BENTLY WILL BE BOMBARDED BY GAMMA RAYS AND NEUTRONS WHEN HE WORKS ON IT...
GAIL... SHE'LL NEVER SEE ME AGAIN AS A NORMAL MAN!
BYE, HONEY... WHAT MUST BE MUST BE! "THE MOVING FINGER HAVING WRIT MOVES ON" ...SURE, AND WE SHOULDN'T WASH OUT A LINE OF IT!-- I GUESS!

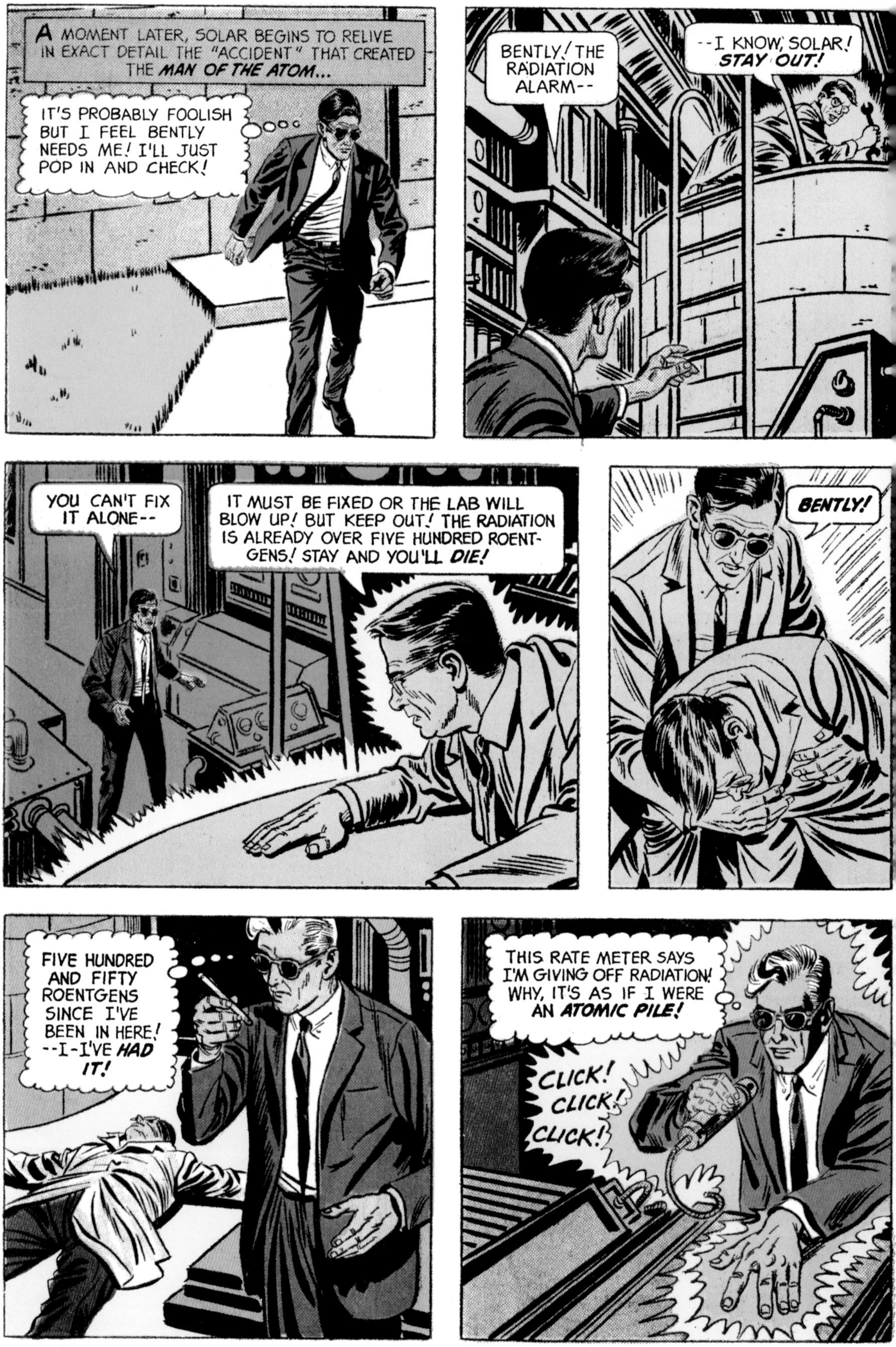
A MOMENT LATER, SOLAR BEGINS TO RELIVE IN EXACT DETAIL THE "ACCIDENT" THAT CREATED THE MAN OF THE ATOM...
IT'S PROBABLY FOOLISH BUT I FEEL BENTLY NEEDS ME! I'LL JUST POP IN AND CHECK!
BENTLY! THE RADIATION ALARM--
--I KNOW, SOLAR! STAY OUT!
YOU CAN'T FIX IT ALONE--
IT MUST BE FIXED OR THE LAB WILL BLOW UP! BUT KEEP OUT! THE RADIATION IS ALREADY OVER FIVE HUNDRED ROENTGENS! STAY AND YOU'LL DIE!
BENTLY!
FIVE HUNDRED AND FIFTY ROENTGENS SINCE I'VE BEEN IN HERE! --I-I'VE HAD IT!
THIS RATE METER SAYS I'M GIVING OFF RADIATION! WHY, IT'S AS IF I WERE AN ATOMIC PILE!
CLICK! CLICK! CLICK!

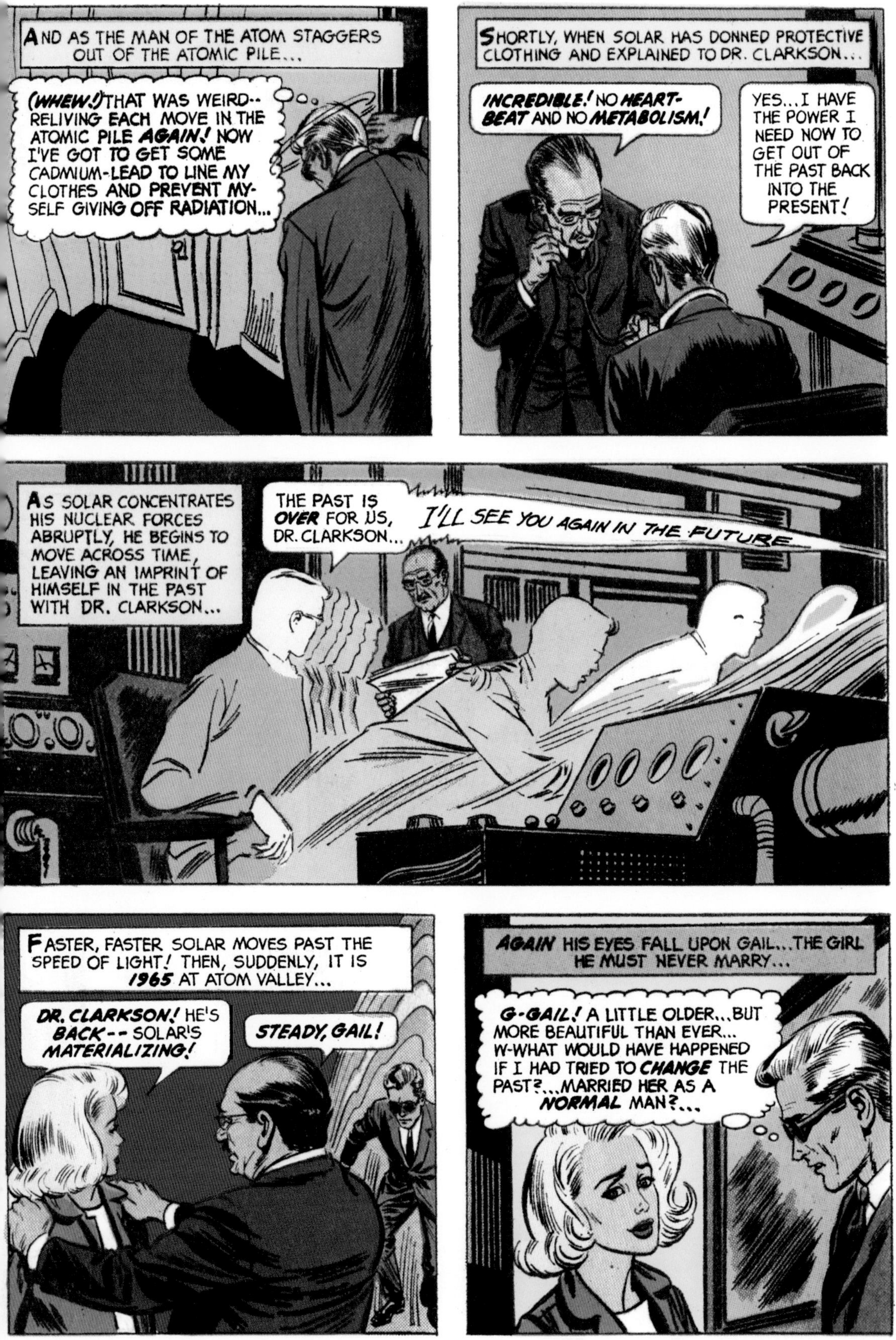
AND AS THE MAN OF THE ATOM STAGGERS OUT OF THE ATOMIC PILE...
(WHEW!) THAT WAS WEIRD-- RELIVING EACH MOVE IN THE ATOMIC PILE AGAIN! NOW I'VE GOT TO GET SOME CADMIUM-LEAD TO LINE MY CLOTHES AND PREVENT MY-SELF GIVING OFF RADIATION...
SHORTLY, WHEN SOLAR HAS DONNED PROTECTIVE CLOTHING AND EXPLAINED TO DR. CLARKSON...
INCREDIBLE! NO HEART-BEAT AND NO METABOLISM!
YES... I HAVE THE POWER I NEED NOW TO GET OUT OF THE PAST BACK INTO THE PRESENT!
AS SOLAR CONCENTRATES HIS NUCLEAR FORCES ABRUPTLY, HE BEGINS TO MOVE ACROSS TIME, LEAVING AN IMPRINT OF HIMSELF IN THE PAST WITH DR. CLARKSON...
THE PAST IS OVER FOR US, DR. CLARKSON...
I'LL SEE YOU AGAIN IN THE FUTURE
FASTER, FASTER SOLAR MOVES PAST THE SPEED OF LIGHT! THEN, SUDDENLY, IT IS 1965 AT ATOM VALLEY...
DR. CLARKSON! HE'S BACK-- SOLAR'S MATERIALIZING!
STEADY, GAIL!
AGAIN HIS EYES FALL UPON GAIL... THE GIRL HE MUST NEVER MARRY...
G-GAIL! A LITTLE OLDER... BUT MORE BEAUTIFUL THAN EVER... W-WHAT WOULD HAVE HAPPENED IF I HAD TRIED TO CHANGE THE PAST?... MARRIED HER AS A NORMAL MAN?...

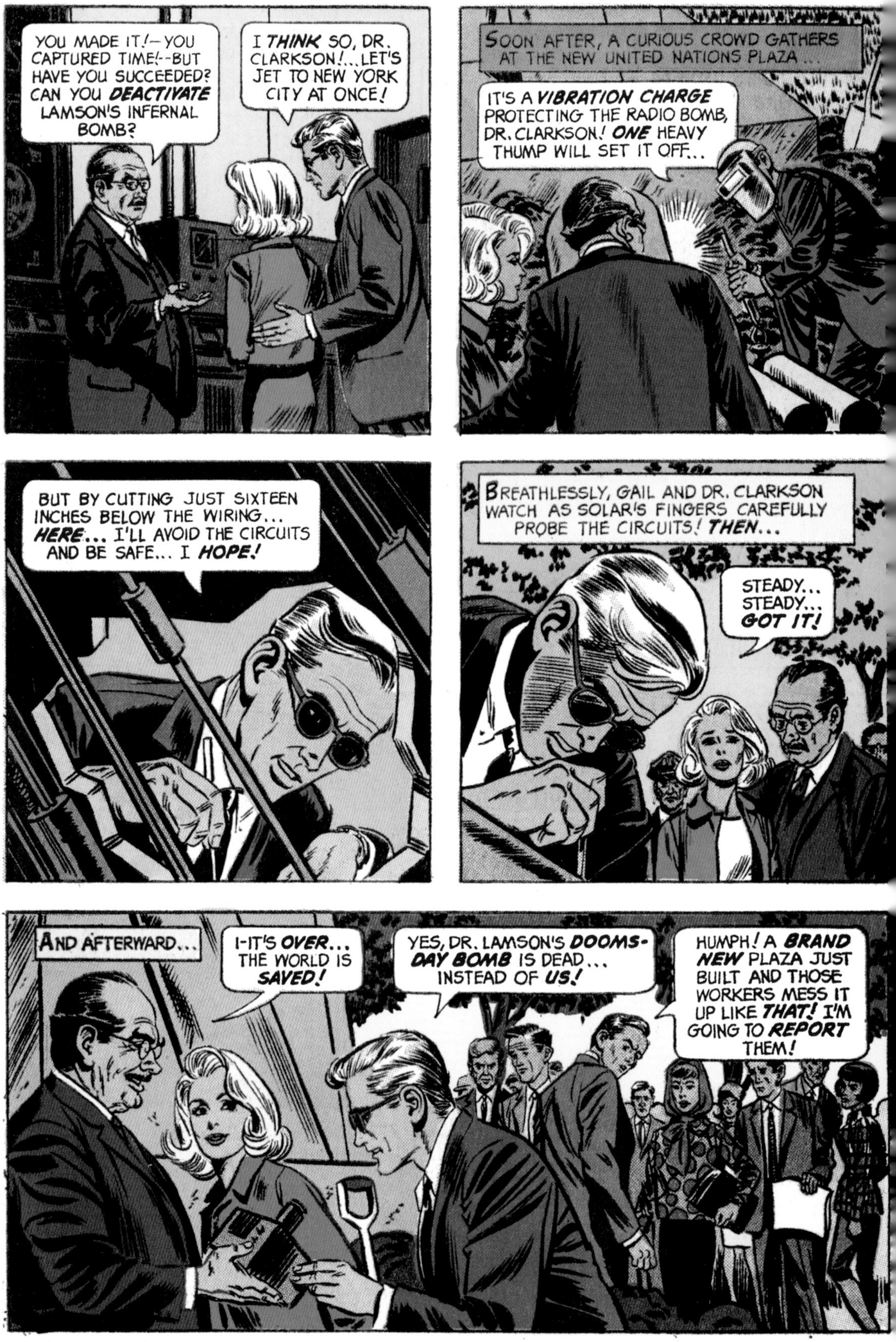
YOU MADE IT!—YOU CAPTURED TIME!--BUT HAVE YOU SUCCEEDED? CAN YOU DEACTIVATE LAMSON'S INFERNAL BOMB?
I THINK SO, DR. CLARKSON!...LET'S JET TO NEW YORK CITY AT ONCE!
SOON AFTER, A CURIOUS CROWD GATHERS AT THE NEW UNITED NATIONS PLAZA...
IT'S A VIBRATION CHARGE PROTECTING THE RADIO BOMB, DR. CLARKSON! ONE HEAVY THUMP WILL SET IT OFF...
BUT BY CUTTING JUST SIXTEEN INCHES BELOW THE WIRING... HERE... I'LL AVOID THE CIRCUITS AND BE SAFE... I HOPE!
BREATHLESSLY, GAIL AND DR. CLARKSON WATCH AS SOLAR'S FINGERS CAREFULLY PROBE THE CIRCUITS! THEN...
STEADY... STEADY... GOT IT!
AND AFTERWARD...
I-IT'S OVER... THE WORLD IS SAVED!
YES, DR. LAMSON'S DOOMS-DAY BOMB IS DEAD... INSTEAD OF US!
HUMPH! A BRAND NEW PLAZA JUST BUILT AND THOSE WORKERS MESS IT UP LIKE THAT! I'M GOING TO REPORT THEM!

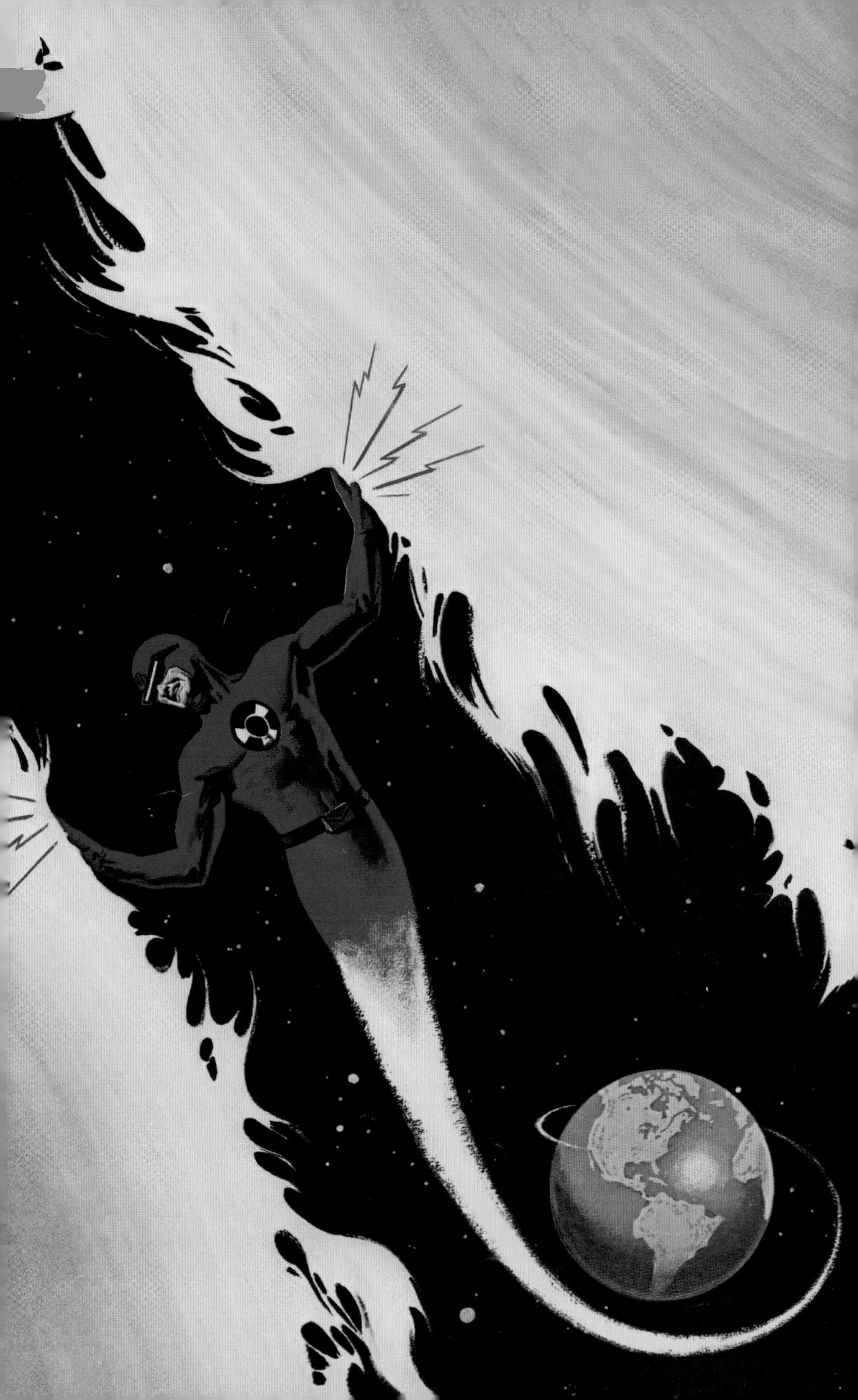

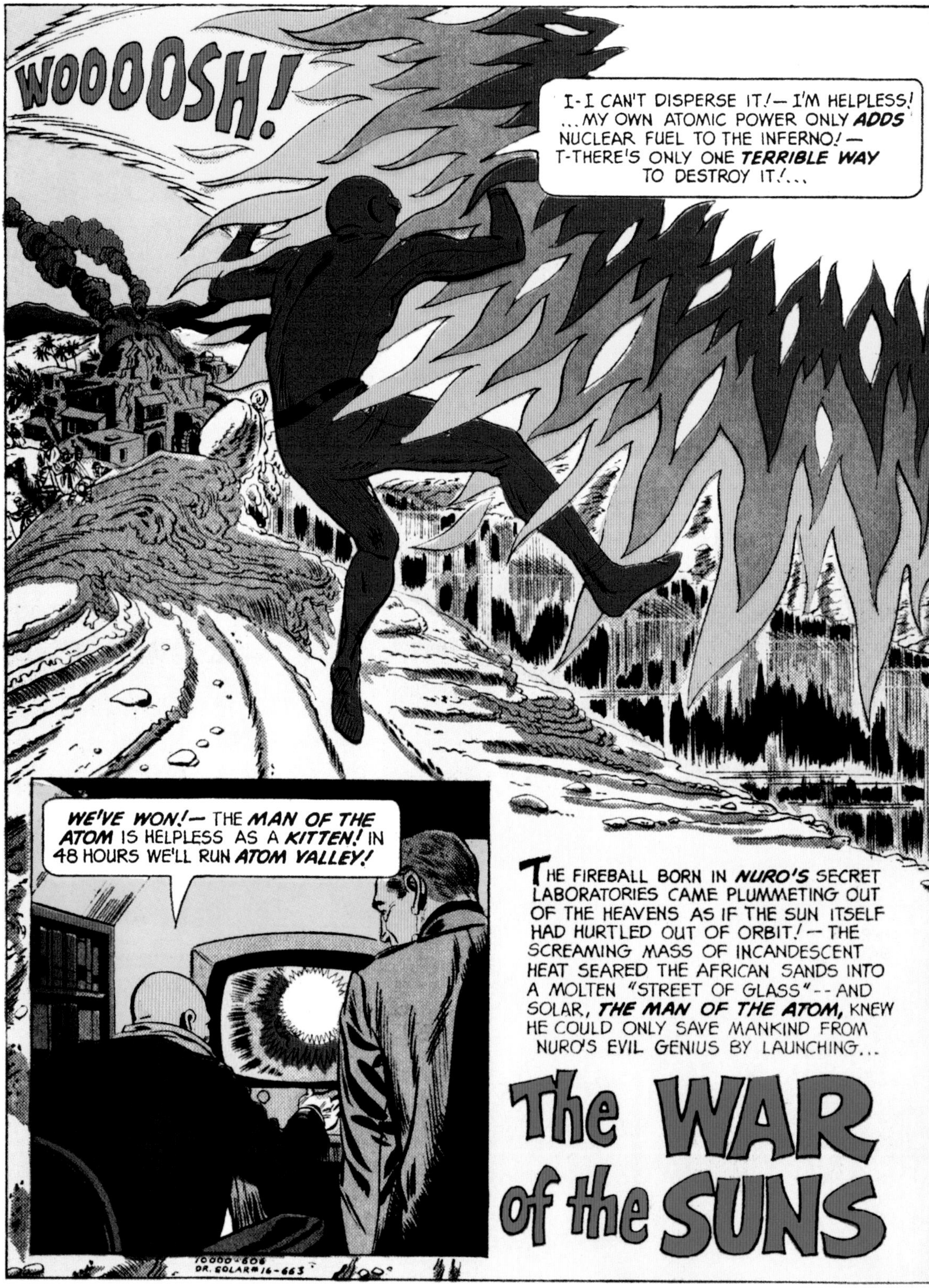
WOOOOSH!
I-I CAN'T DISPERSE IT!—I'M HELPLESS! ...MY OWN ATOMIC POWER ONLY ADDS NUCLEAR FUEL TO THE INFERNO!—T-THERE'S ONLY ONE TERRIBLE WAY TO DESTROY IT!...
WE'VE WON!—THE MAN OF THE ATOM IS HELPLESS AS A KITTEN! IN 48 HOURS WE'LL RUN ATOM VALLEY!
THE FIREBALL BORN IN NURO'S SECRET LABORATORIES CAME PLUMMETING OUT OF THE HEAVENS AS IF THE SUN ITSELF HAD HURTLED OUT OF ORBIT!—THE SCREAMING MASS OF INCANDESCENT HEAT SEARED THE AFRICAN SANDS INTO A MOLTEN "STREET OF GLASS"--AND SOLAR, THE MAN OF THE ATOM, KNEW HE COULD ONLY SAVE MANKIND FROM NURO'S EVIL GENIUS BY LAUNCHING...
The WAR of the SUNS
10000-606
DR. SOLAR #16-663

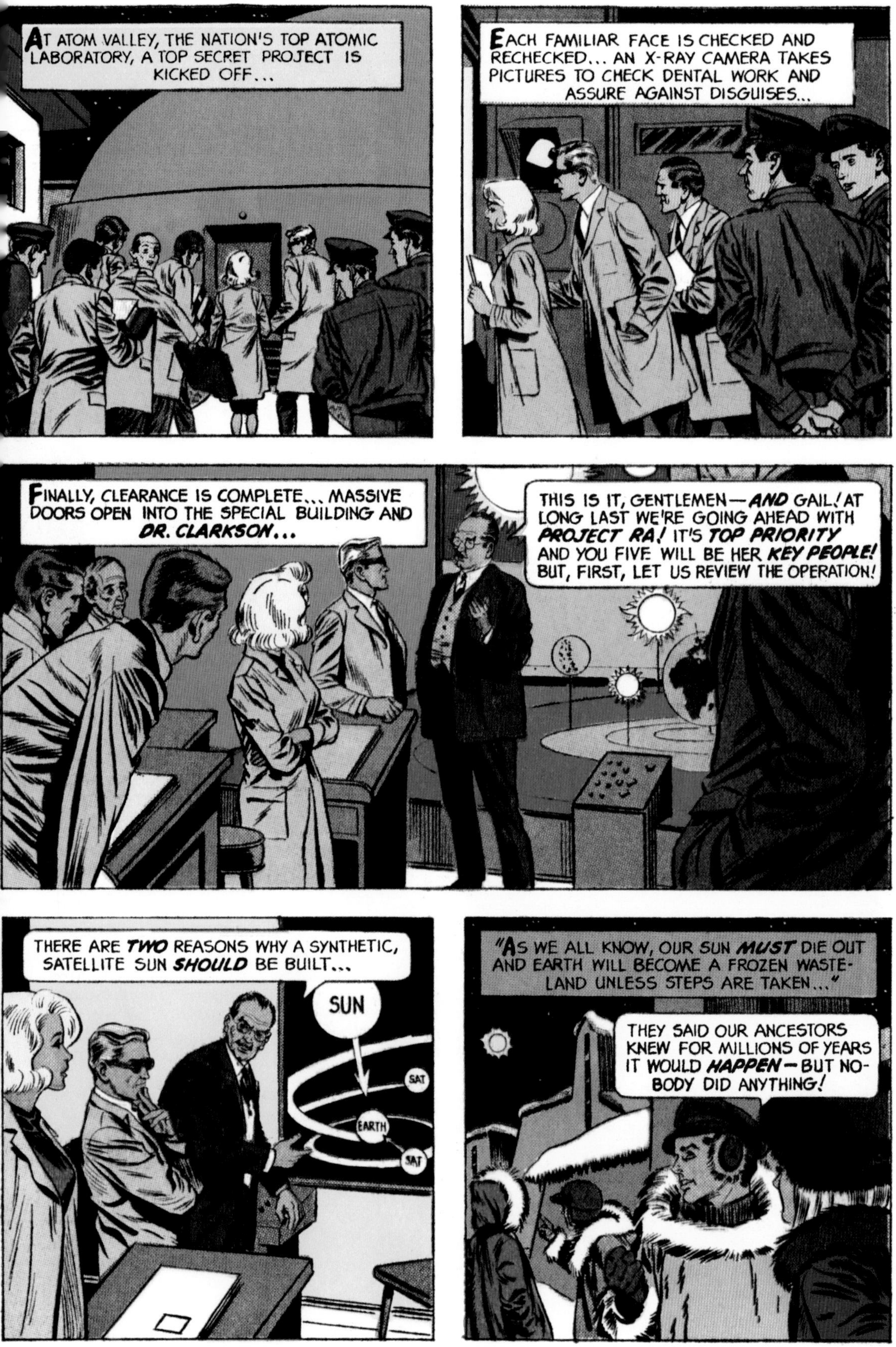
AT ATOM VALLEY, THE NATION'S TOP ATOMIC LABORATORY, A TOP SECRET PROJECT IS KICKED OFF...
EACH FAMILIAR FACE IS CHECKED AND RECHECKED... AN X-RAY CAMERA TAKES PICTURES TO CHECK DENTAL WORK AND ASSURE AGAINST DISGUISES...
FINALLY, CLEARANCE IS COMPLETE... MASSIVE DOORS OPEN INTO THE SPECIAL BUILDING AND DR. CLARKSON...
THIS IS IT, GENTLEMEN—AND GAIL! AT LONG LAST WE'RE GOING AHEAD WITH PROJECT RA! IT'S TOP PRIORITY AND YOU FIVE WILL BE HER KEY PEOPLE! BUT, FIRST, LET US REVIEW THE OPERATION!
THERE ARE TWO REASONS WHY A SYNTHETIC, SATELLITE SUN SHOULD BE BUILT...
SUN
SAT
EARTH
SAT
"AS WE ALL KNOW, OUR SUN MUST DIE OUT AND EARTH WILL BECOME A FROZEN WASTE-LAND UNLESS STEPS ARE TAKEN..."
THEY SAID OUR ANCESTORS KNEW FOR MILLIONS OF YEARS IT WOULD HAPPEN—BUT NO-BODY DID ANYTHING!

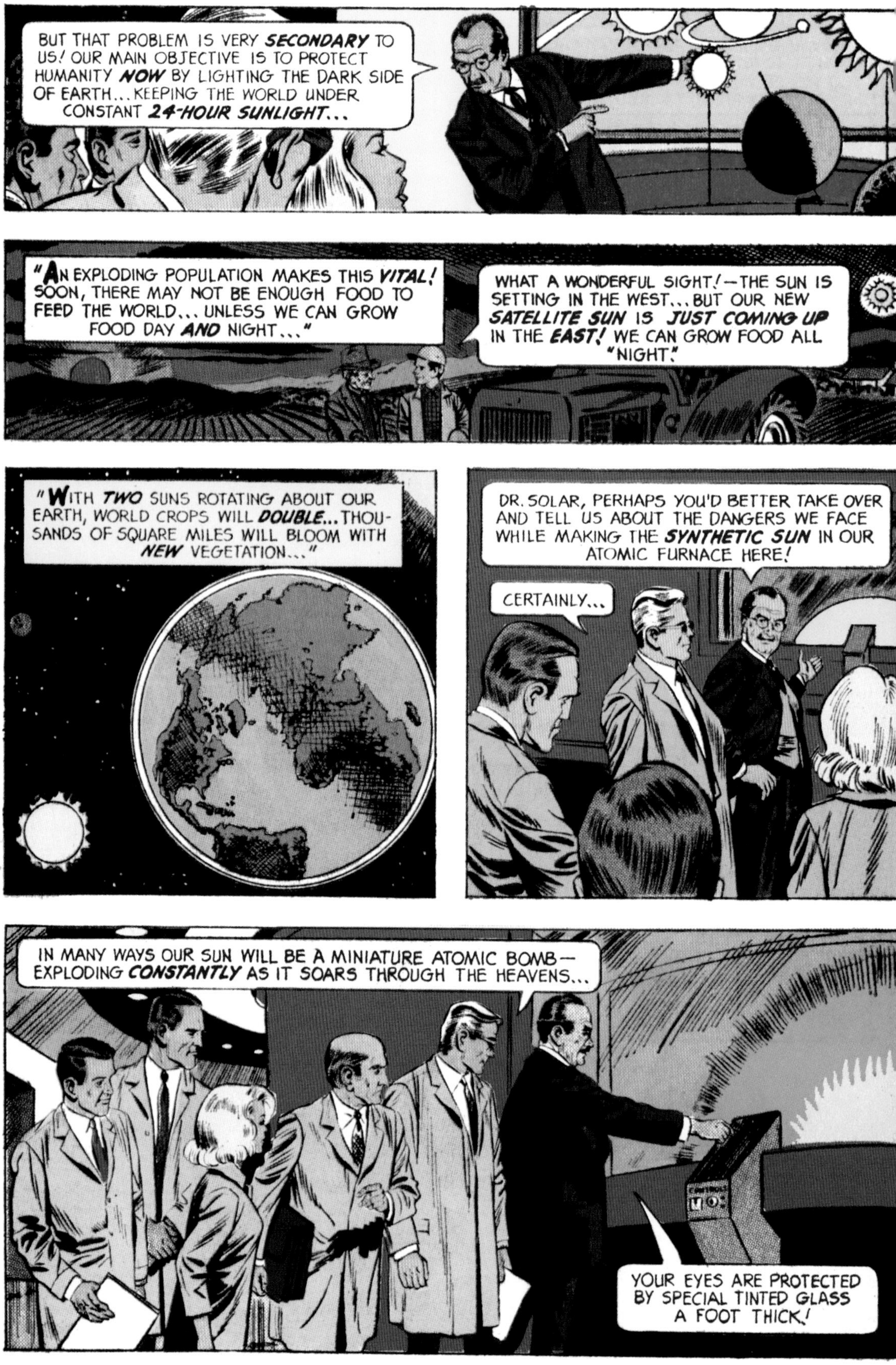
BUT THAT PROBLEM IS VERY SECONDARY TO US! OUR MAIN OBJECTIVE IS TO PROTECT HUMANITY NOW BY LIGHTING THE DARK SIDE OF EARTH... KEEPING THE WORLD UNDER CONSTANT 24-HOUR SUNLIGHT...
"AN EXPLODING POPULATION MAKES THIS VITAL! SOON, THERE MAY NOT BE ENOUGH FOOD TO FEED THE WORLD... UNLESS WE CAN GROW FOOD DAY AND NIGHT..."
WHAT A WONDERFUL SIGHT! —THE SUN IS SETTING IN THE WEST... BUT OUR NEW SATELLITE SUN IS JUST COMING UP IN THE EAST! WE CAN GROW FOOD ALL "NIGHT."
"WITH TWO SUNS ROTATING ABOUT OUR EARTH, WORLD CROPS WILL DOUBLE... THOUSANDS OF SQUARE MILES WILL BLOOM WITH NEW VEGETATION..."
DR. SOLAR, PERHAPS YOU'D BETTER TAKE OVER AND TELL US ABOUT THE DANGERS WE FACE WHILE MAKING THE SYNTHETIC SUN IN OUR ATOMIC FURNACE HERE!
CERTAINLY...
IN MANY WAYS OUR SUN WILL BE A MINIATURE ATOMIC BOMB— EXPLODING CONSTANTLY AS IT SOARS THROUGH THE HEAVENS...
YOUR EYES ARE PROTECTED BY SPECIAL TINTED GLASS A FOOT THICK!

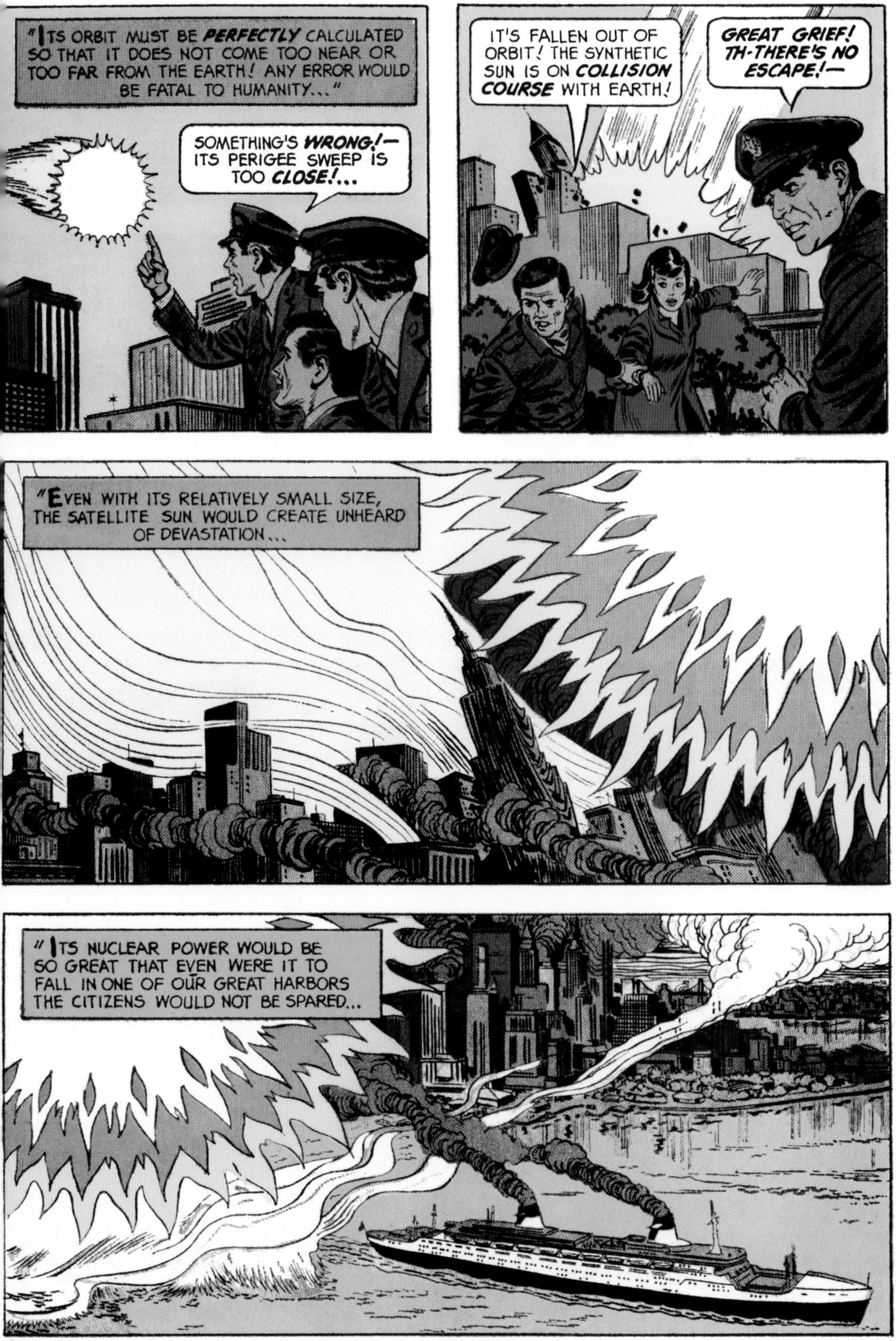
"ITS ORBIT MUST BE PERFECTLY CALCULATED SO THAT IT DOES NOT COME TOO NEAR OR TOO FAR FROM THE EARTH! ANY ERROR WOULD BE FATAL TO HUMANITY..."
SOMETHING'S WRONG!— ITS PERIGEE SWEEP IS TOO CLOSE!...
IT'S FALLEN OUT OF ORBIT! THE SYNTHETIC SUN IS ON COLLISION COURSE WITH EARTH!
GREAT GRIEF! TH-THERE'S NO ESCAPE!—
"EVEN WITH ITS RELATIVELY SMALL SIZE, THE SATELLITE SUN WOULD CREATE UNHEARD OF DEVASTATION...
"ITS NUCLEAR POWER WOULD BE SO GREAT THAT EVEN WERE IT TO FALL IN ONE OF OUR GREAT HARBORS THE CITIZENS WOULD NOT BE SPARED...

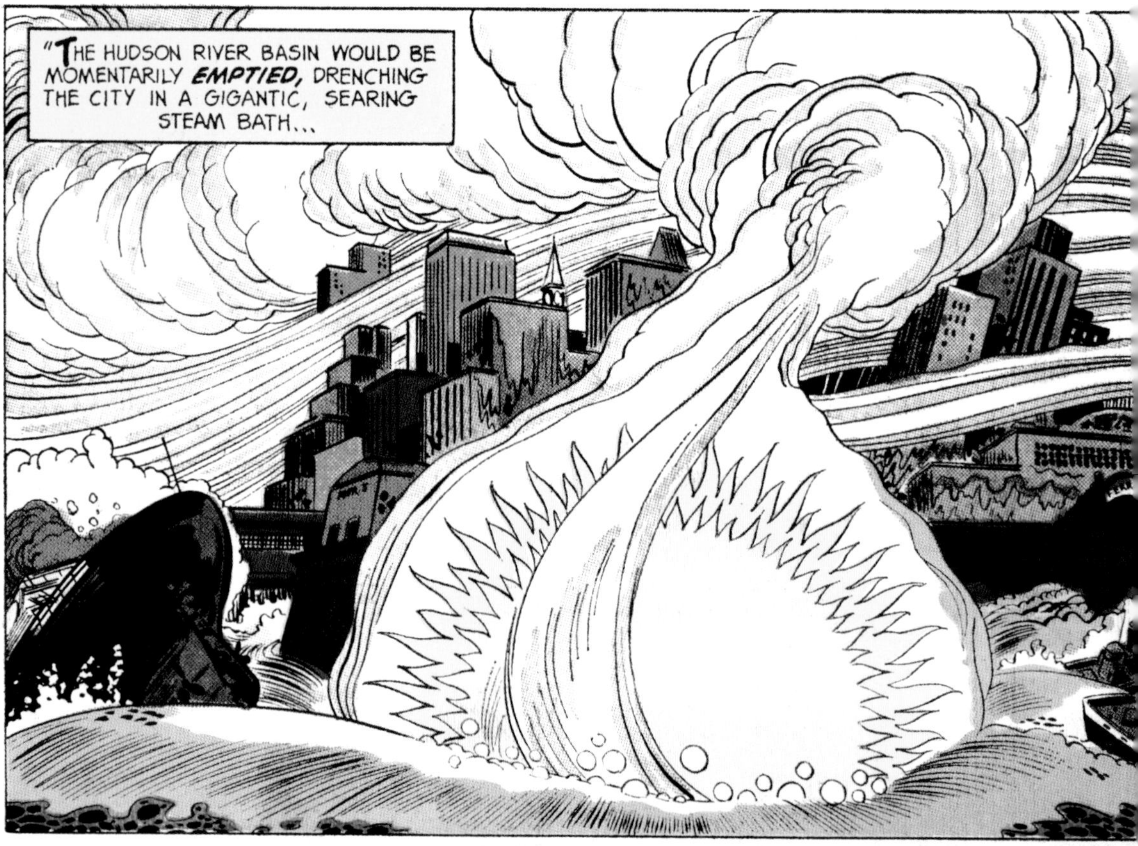
"THE HUDSON RIVER BASIN WOULD BE MOMENTARILY *EMPTIED*, DRENCHING THE CITY IN A GIGANTIC, SEARING STEAM BATH...

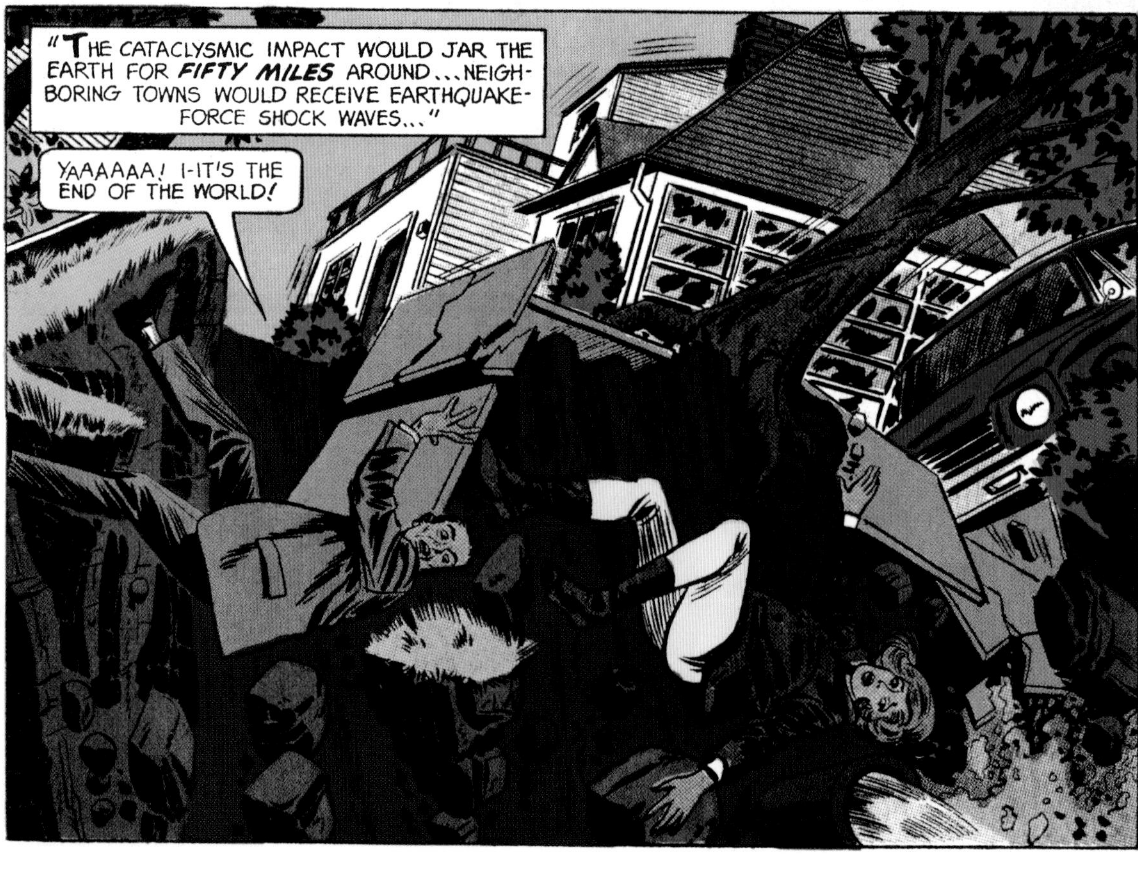
"THE CATACLYSMIC IMPACT WOULD JAR THE EARTH FOR *FIFTY MILES* AROUND... NEIGHBORING TOWNS WOULD RECEIVE EARTHQUAKE-FORCE SHOCK WAVES..."
YAAAAAA! I-IT'S THE END OF THE WORLD!

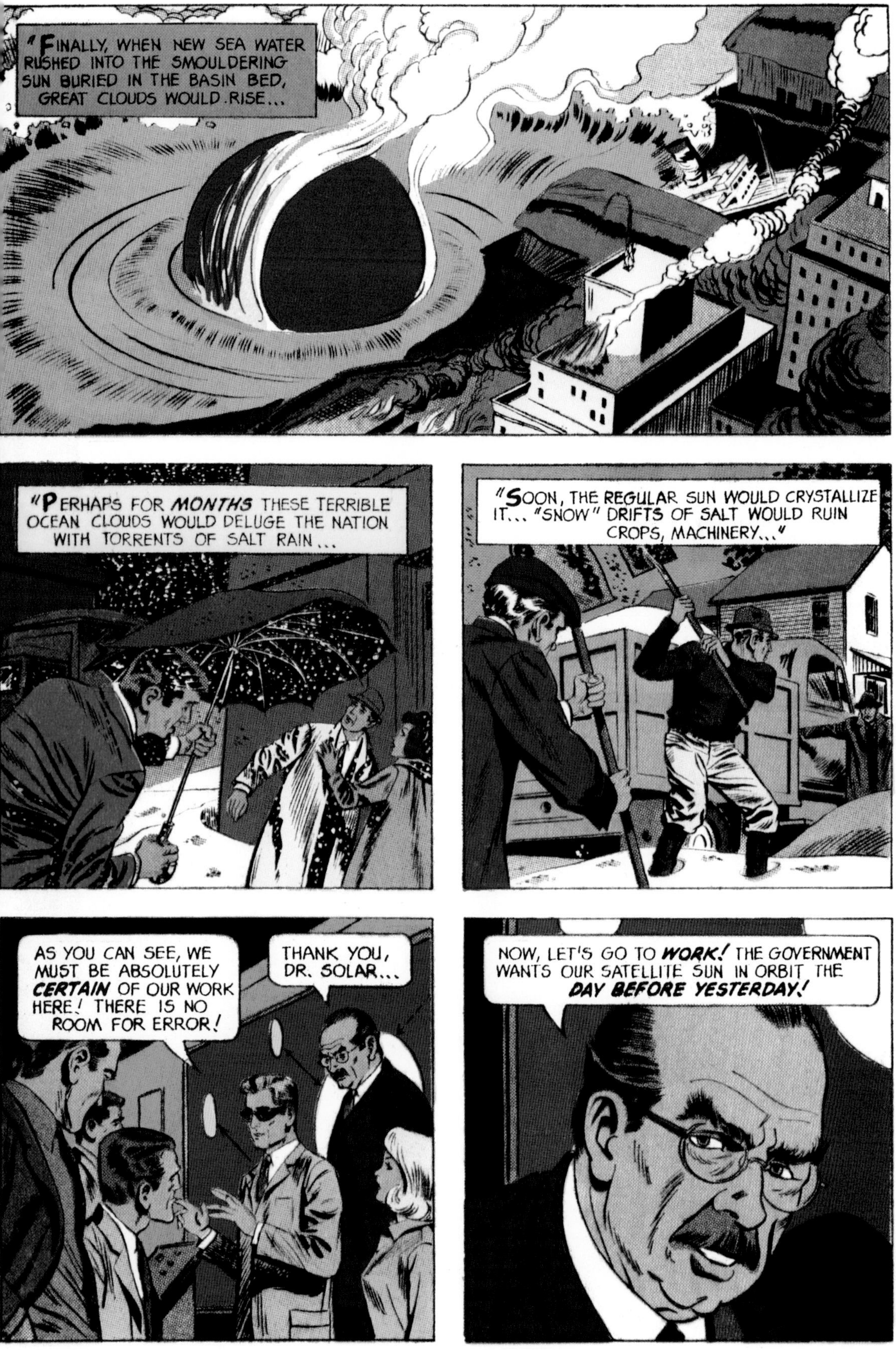
"FINALLY, WHEN NEW SEA WATER RUSHED INTO THE SMOULDERING SUN BURIED IN THE BASIN BED, GREAT CLOUDS WOULD RISE...
"PERHAPS FOR MONTHS THESE TERRIBLE OCEAN CLOUDS WOULD DELUGE THE NATION WITH TORRENTS OF SALT RAIN...
"SOON, THE REGULAR SUN WOULD CRYSTALLIZE IT... "SNOW" DRIFTS OF SALT WOULD RUIN CROPS, MACHINERY..."
AS YOU CAN SEE, WE MUST BE ABSOLUTELY CERTAIN OF OUR WORK HERE! THERE IS NO ROOM FOR ERROR!
THANK YOU, DR. SOLAR...
NOW, LET'S GO TO WORK! THE GOVERNMENT WANTS OUR SATELLITE SUN IN ORBIT THE DAY BEFORE YESTERDAY!

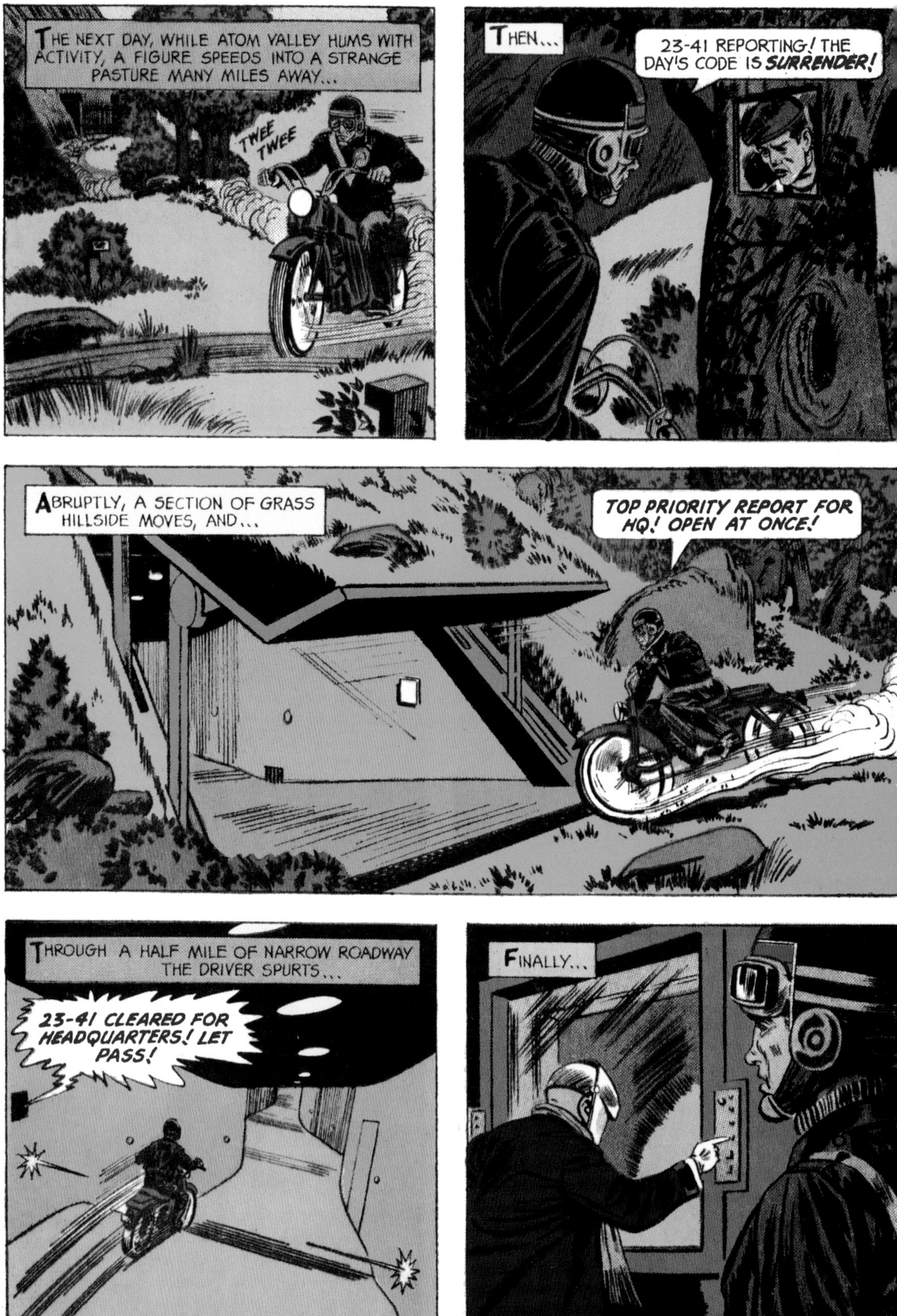
THE NEXT DAY, WHILE ATOM VALLEY HUMS WITH ACTIVITY, A FIGURE SPEEDS INTO A STRANGE PASTURE MANY MILES AWAY...
TWEE TWEE
THEN...
23-41 REPORTING! THE DAY'S CODE IS SURRENDER!
ABRUPTLY, A SECTION OF GRASS HILLSIDE MOVES, AND...
TOP PRIORITY REPORT FOR HQ! OPEN AT ONCE!
THROUGH A HALF MILE OF NARROW ROADWAY THE DRIVER SPURTS...
23-41 CLEARED FOR HEADQUARTERS! LET PASS!
FINALLY...

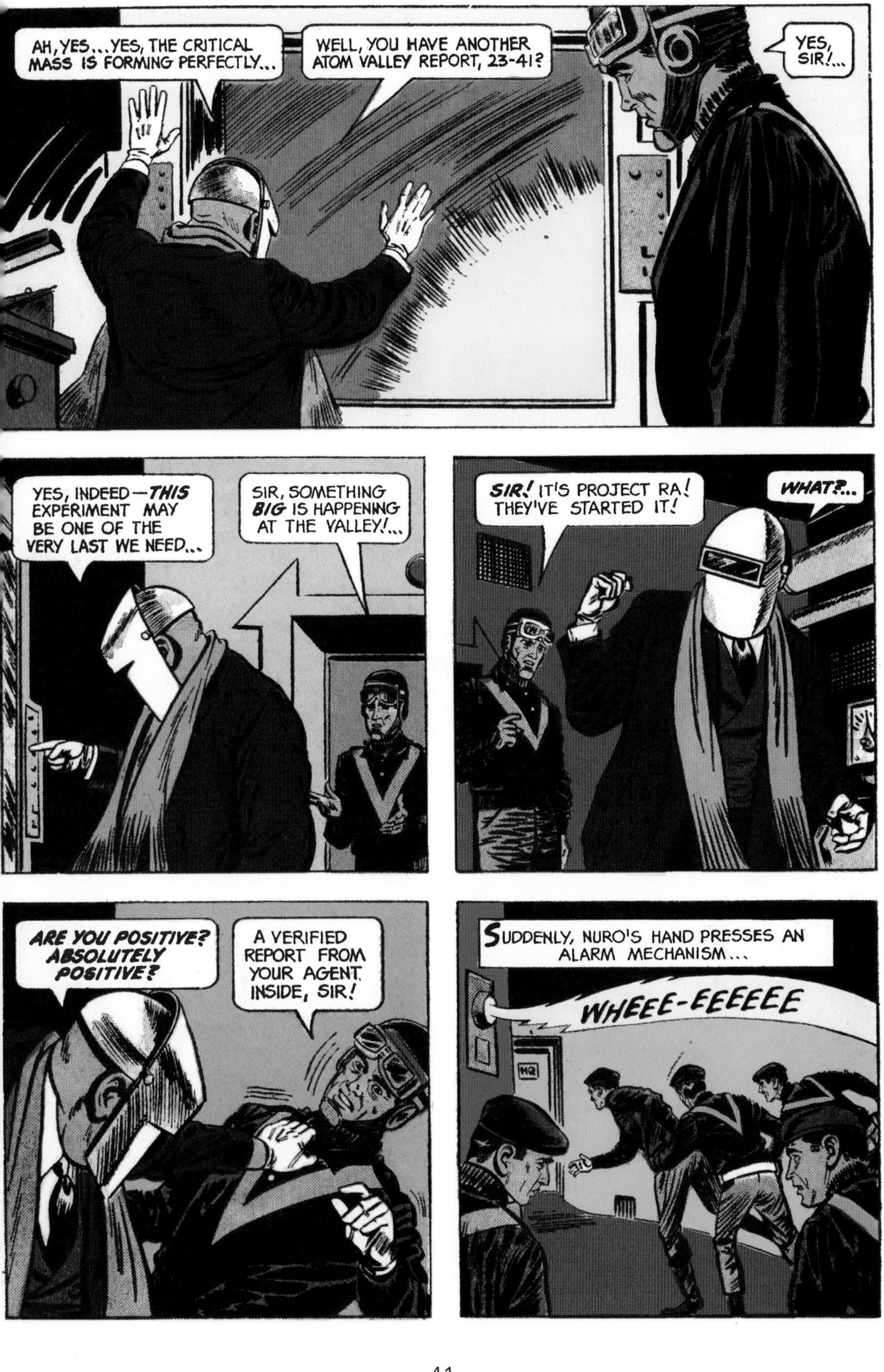
AH, YES... YES, THE CRITICAL MASS IS FORMING PERFECTLY...
WELL, YOU HAVE ANOTHER ATOM VALLEY REPORT, 23-41?
YES, SIR!...
YES, INDEED—THIS EXPERIMENT MAY BE ONE OF THE VERY LAST WE NEED...
SIR, SOMETHING BIG IS HAPPENING AT THE VALLEY!...
SIR! IT'S PROJECT RA! THEY'VE STARTED IT!
WHAT?...
ARE YOU POSITIVE? ABSOLUTELY POSITIVE?
A VERIFIED REPORT FROM YOUR AGENT INSIDE, SIR!
SUDDENLY, NURO'S HAND PRESSES AN ALARM MECHANISM...
WHEEE-EEEEEE
HQ

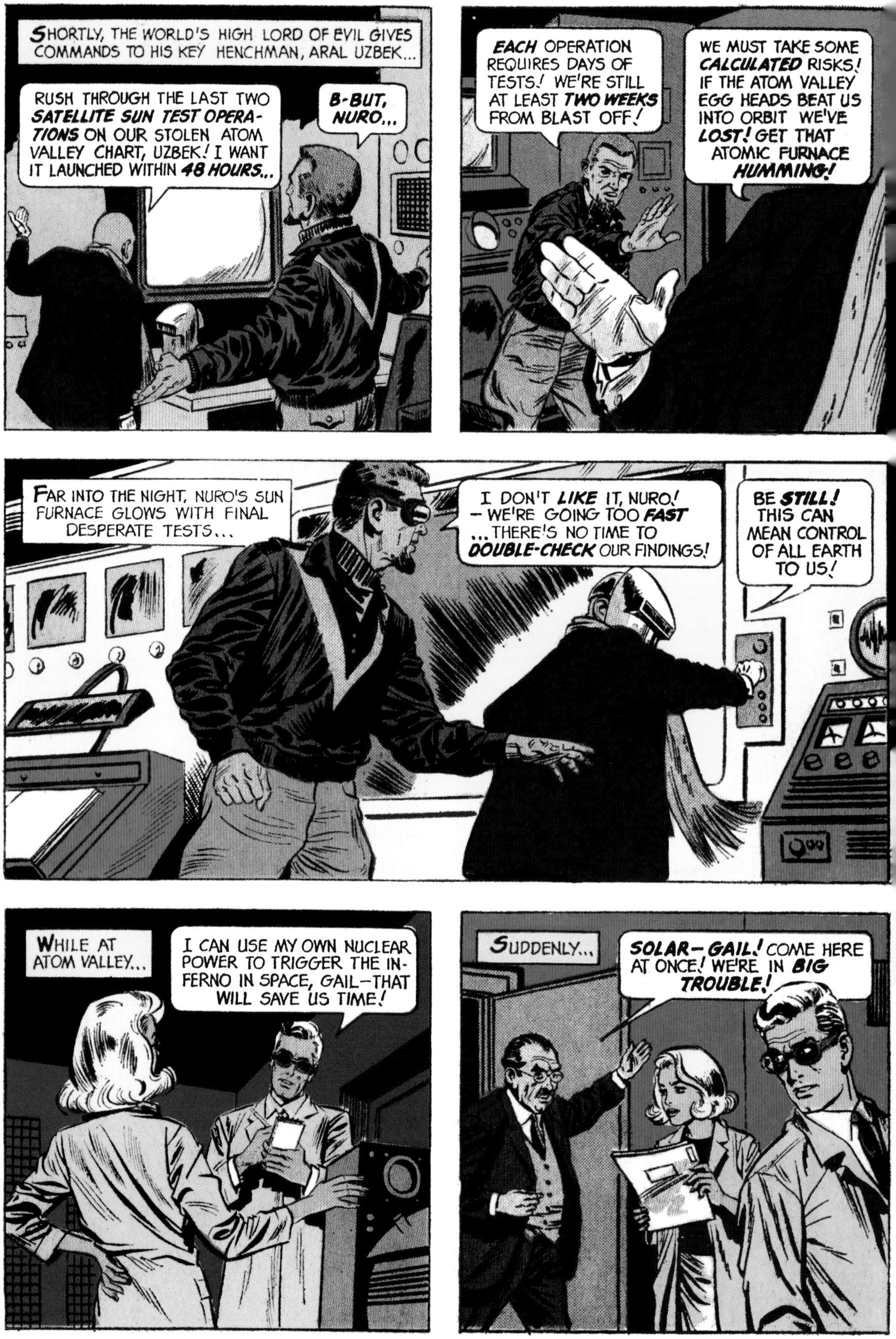
SHORTLY, THE WORLD'S HIGH LORD OF EVIL GIVES COMMANDS TO HIS KEY HENCHMAN, ARAL UZBEK...
RUSH THROUGH THE LAST TWO SATELLITE SUN TEST OPERATIONS ON OUR STOLEN ATOM VALLEY CHART, UZBEK! I WANT IT LAUNCHED WITHIN 48 HOURS...
B-BUT, NURO...
EACH OPERATION REQUIRES DAYS OF TESTS! WE'RE STILL AT LEAST TWO WEEKS FROM BLAST OFF!
WE MUST TAKE SOME CALCULATED RISKS! IF THE ATOM VALLEY EGG HEADS BEAT US INTO ORBIT WE'VE LOST! GET THAT ATOMIC FURNACE HUMMING!
FAR INTO THE NIGHT, NURO'S SUN FURNACE GLOWS WITH FINAL DESPERATE TESTS...
I DON'T LIKE IT, NURO! - WE'RE GOING TOO FAST ...THERE'S NO TIME TO DOUBLE-CHECK OUR FINDINGS!
BE STILL! THIS CAN MEAN CONTROL OF ALL EARTH TO US!
WHILE AT ATOM VALLEY...
I CAN USE MY OWN NUCLEAR POWER TO TRIGGER THE INFERNO IN SPACE, GAIL—THAT WILL SAVE US TIME!
SUDDENLY...
SOLAR—GAIL! COME HERE AT ONCE! WE'RE IN BIG TROUBLE!

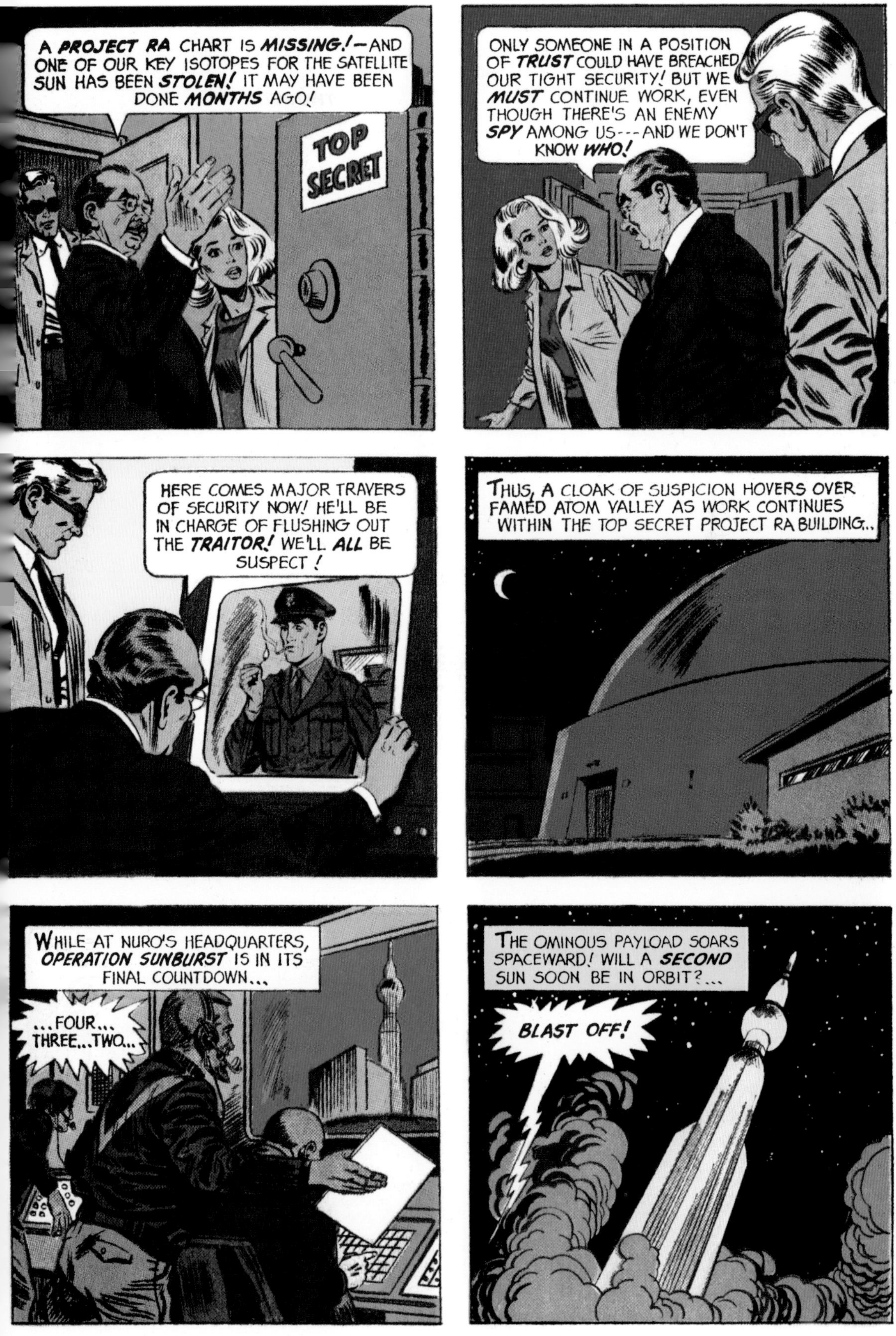
A PROJECT RA CHART IS MISSING!—AND ONE OF OUR KEY ISOTOPES FOR THE SATELLITE SUN HAS BEEN STOLEN! IT MAY HAVE BEEN DONE MONTHS AGO!
TOP SECRET
ONLY SOMEONE IN A POSITION OF TRUST COULD HAVE BREACHED OUR TIGHT SECURITY! BUT WE MUST CONTINUE WORK, EVEN THOUGH THERE'S AN ENEMY SPY AMONG US---AND WE DON'T KNOW WHO!
HERE COMES MAJOR TRAVERS OF SECURITY NOW! HE'LL BE IN CHARGE OF FLUSHING OUT THE TRAITOR! WE'LL ALL BE SUSPECT!
THUS, A CLOAK OF SUSPICION HOVERS OVER FAMED ATOM VALLEY AS WORK CONTINUES WITHIN THE TOP SECRET PROJECT RA BUILDING..
WHILE AT NURO'S HEADQUARTERS, OPERATION SUNBURST IS IN ITS FINAL COUNTDOWN...
...FOUR... THREE...TWO...
THE OMINOUS PAYLOAD SOARS SPACEWARD! WILL A SECOND SUN SOON BE IN ORBIT?...
BLAST OFF!

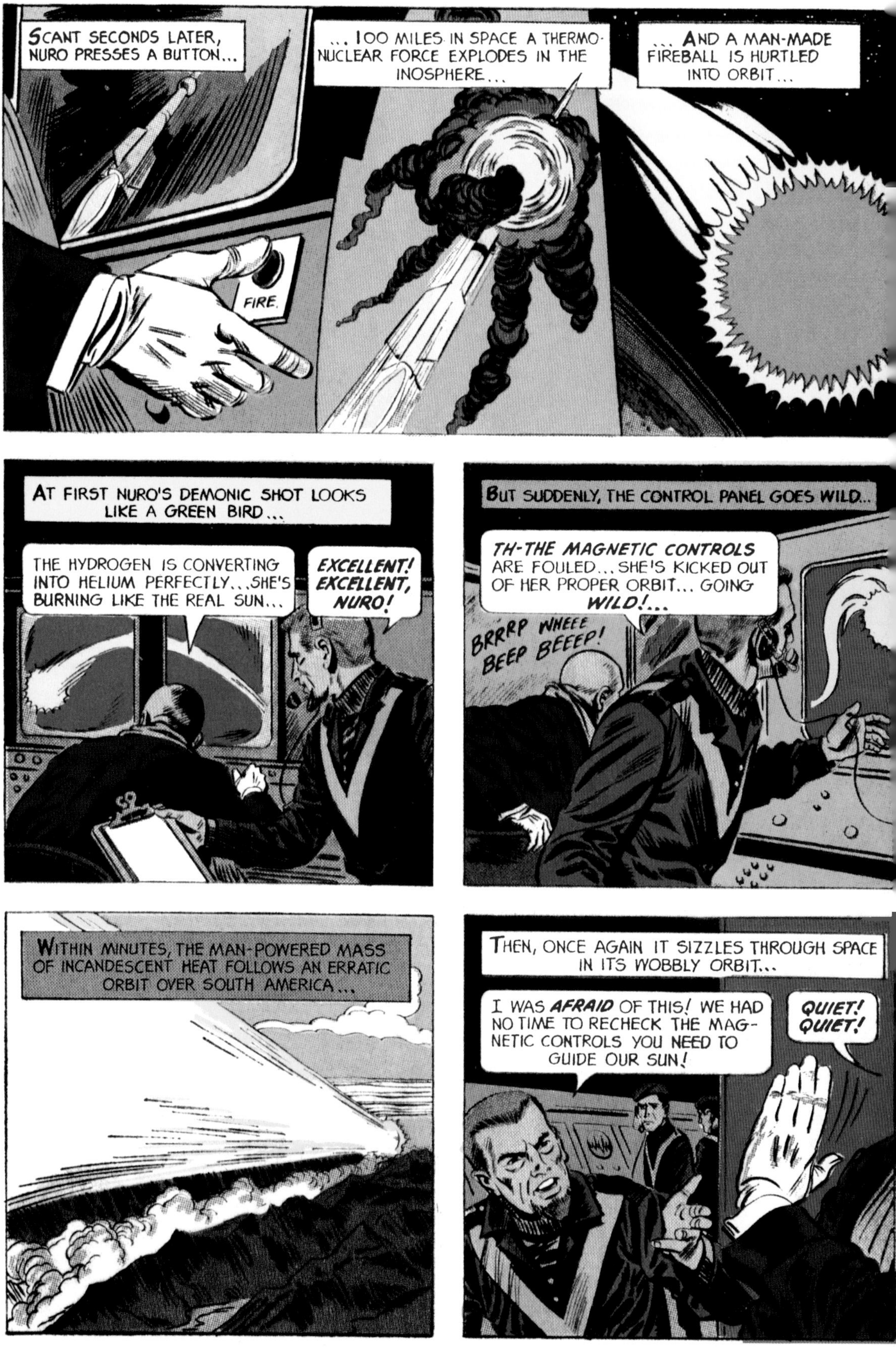
SCANT SECONDS LATER, NURO PRESSES A BUTTON...
FIRE
...100 MILES IN SPACE A THERMO-NUCLEAR FORCE EXPLODES IN THE INOSPHERE...
...AND A MAN-MADE FIREBALL IS HURTLED INTO ORBIT...
AT FIRST NURO'S DEMONIC SHOT LOOKS LIKE A GREEN BIRD...
THE HYDROGEN IS CONVERTING INTO HELIUM PERFECTLY...SHE'S BURNING LIKE THE REAL SUN...
EXCELLENT! EXCELLENT, NURO!
BUT SUDDENLY, THE CONTROL PANEL GOES WILD...
TH-THE MAGNETIC CONTROLS ARE FOULED...SHE'S KICKED OUT OF HER PROPER ORBIT... GOING WILD!...
BRRRP WHEEE BEEP BEEEP!
WITHIN MINUTES, THE MAN-POWERED MASS OF INCANDESCENT HEAT FOLLOWS AN ERRATIC ORBIT OVER SOUTH AMERICA...
THEN, ONCE AGAIN IT SIZZLES THROUGH SPACE IN ITS WOBBLY ORBIT...
I WAS AFRAID OF THIS! WE HAD NO TIME TO RECHECK THE MAGNETIC CONTROLS YOU NEED TO GUIDE OUR SUN!
QUIET! QUIET!

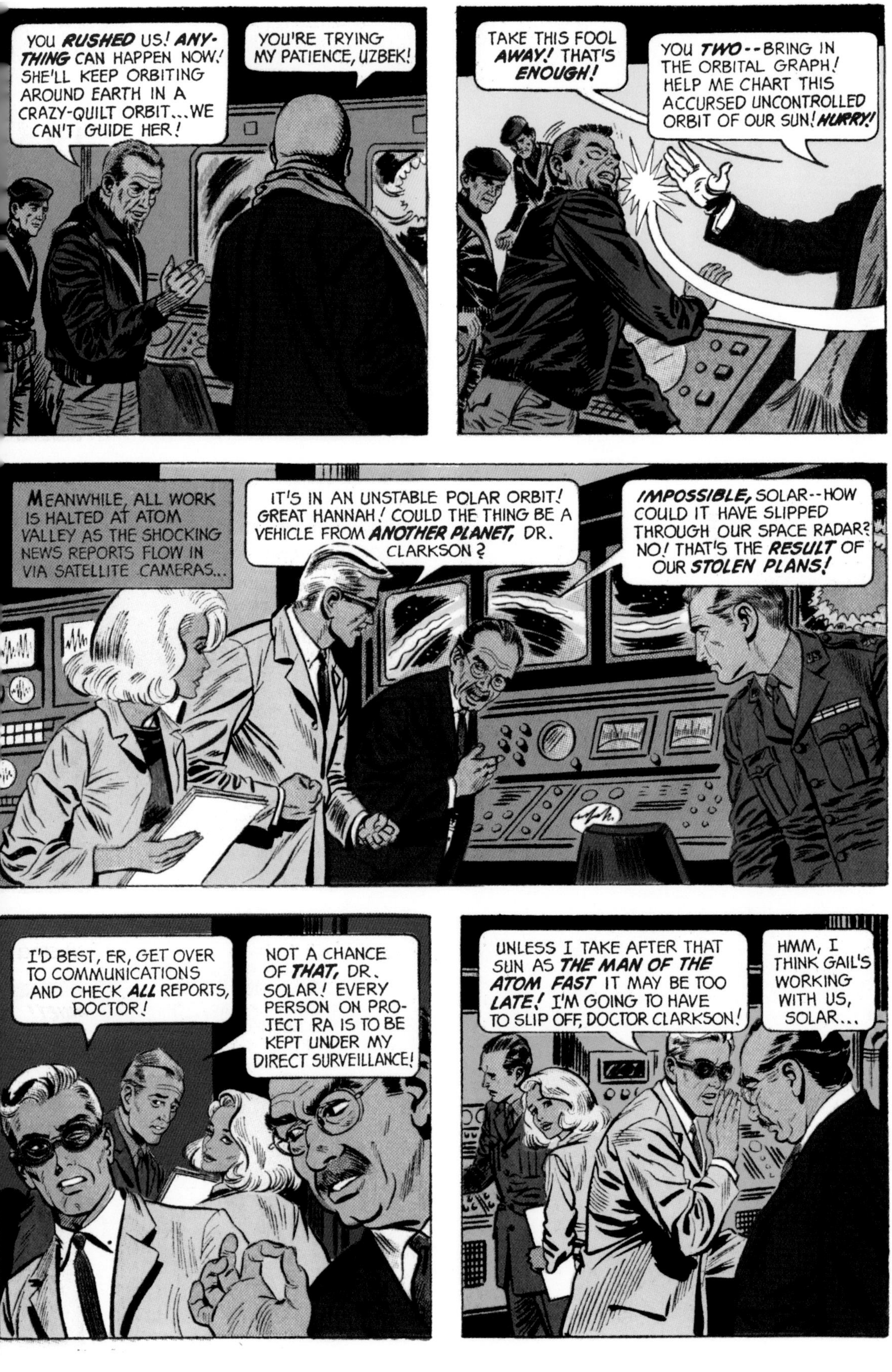
YOU RUSHED US! ANYTHING CAN HAPPEN NOW! SHE'LL KEEP ORBITING AROUND EARTH IN A CRAZY-QUILT ORBIT...WE CAN'T GUIDE HER!
YOU'RE TRYING MY PATIENCE, UZBEK!
TAKE THIS FOOL AWAY! THAT'S ENOUGH!
YOU TWO--BRING IN THE ORBITAL GRAPH! HELP ME CHART THIS ACCURSED UNCONTROLLED ORBIT OF OUR SUN! HURRY!
MEANWHILE, ALL WORK IS HALTED AT ATOM VALLEY AS THE SHOCKING NEWS REPORTS FLOW IN VIA SATELLITE CAMERAS...
IT'S IN AN UNSTABLE POLAR ORBIT! GREAT HANNAH! COULD THE THING BE A VEHICLE FROM ANOTHER PLANET, DR. CLARKSON?
IMPOSSIBLE, SOLAR--HOW COULD IT HAVE SLIPPED THROUGH OUR SPACE RADAR? NO! THAT'S THE RESULT OF OUR STOLEN PLANS!
I'D BEST, ER, GET OVER TO COMMUNICATIONS AND CHECK ALL REPORTS, DOCTOR!
NOT A CHANCE OF THAT, DR. SOLAR! EVERY PERSON ON PROJECT RA IS TO BE KEPT UNDER MY DIRECT SURVEILLANCE!
UNLESS I TAKE AFTER THAT SUN AS THE MAN OF THE ATOM FAST IT MAY BE TOO LATE! I'M GOING TO HAVE TO SLIP OFF, DOCTOR CLARKSON!
HMM, I THINK GAIL'S WORKING WITH US, SOLAR...

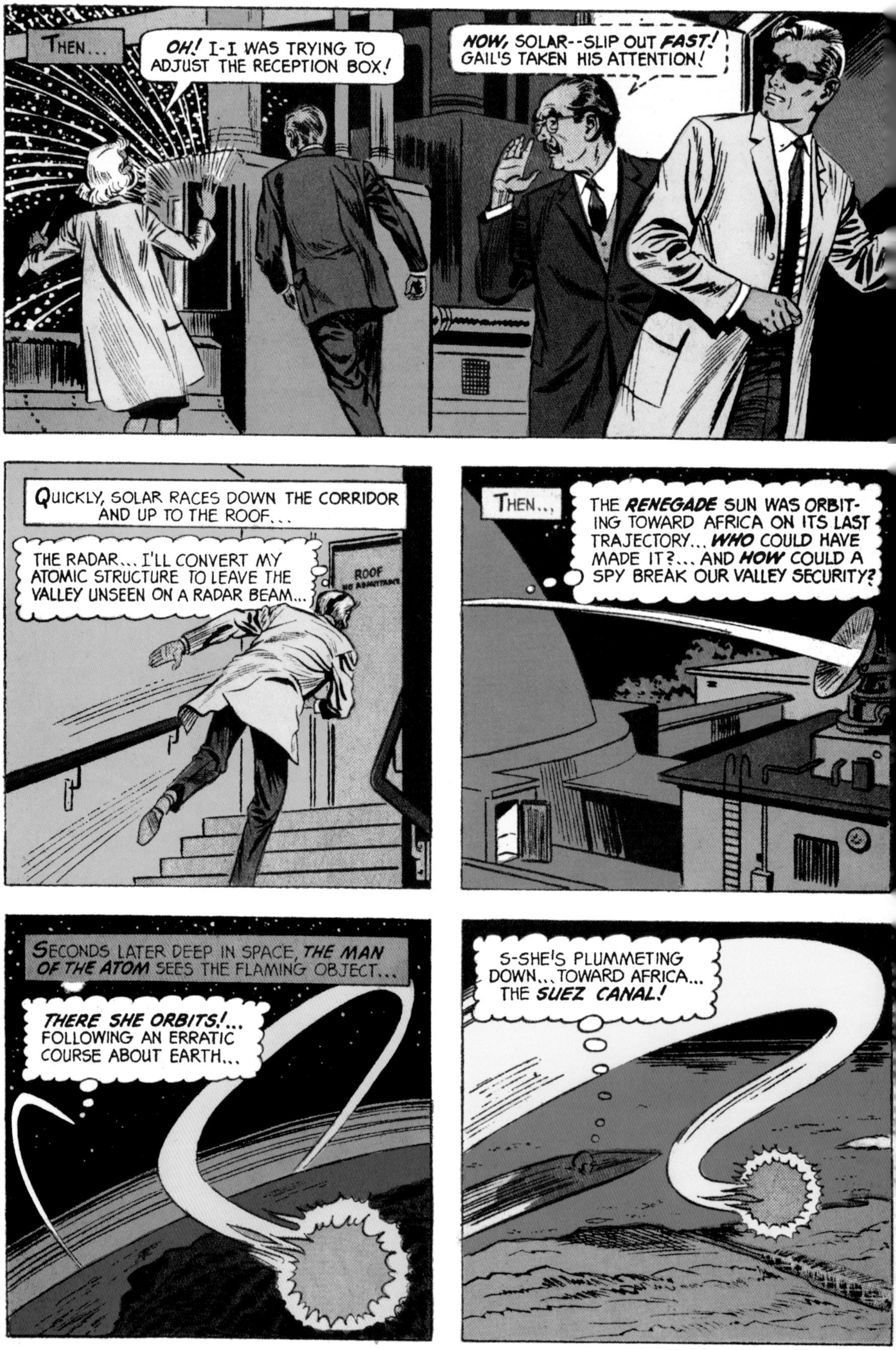
THEN...
OH! I-I WAS TRYING TO ADJUST THE RECEPTION BOX!
NOW, SOLAR--SLIP OUT FAST! GAIL'S TAKEN HIS ATTENTION!
QUICKLY, SOLAR RACES DOWN THE CORRIDOR AND UP TO THE ROOF...
THE RADAR... I'LL CONVERT MY ATOMIC STRUCTURE TO LEAVE THE VALLEY UNSEEN ON A RADAR BEAM...
ROOF
THEN...
THE RENEGADE SUN WAS ORBITING TOWARD AFRICA ON ITS LAST TRAJECTORY... WHO COULD HAVE MADE IT?... AND HOW COULD A SPY BREAK OUR VALLEY SECURITY?
SECONDS LATER DEEP IN SPACE, THE MAN OF THE ATOM SEES THE FLAMING OBJECT...
THERE SHE ORBITS!... FOLLOWING AN ERRATIC COURSE ABOUT EARTH...
S-SHE'S PLUMMETING DOWN... TOWARD AFRICA... THE SUEZ CANAL!

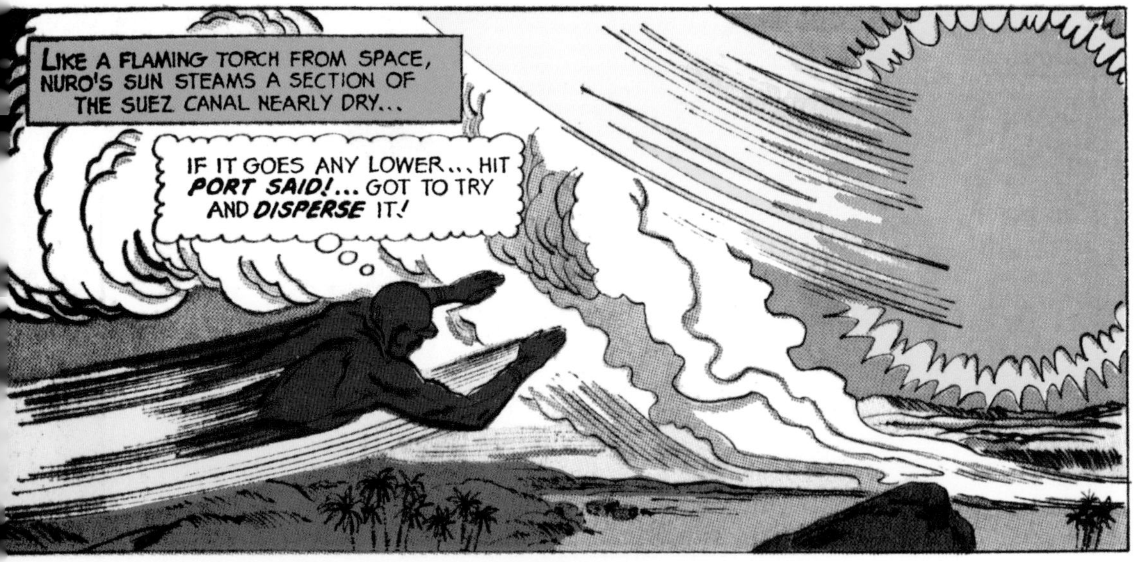
LIKE A FLAMING TORCH FROM SPACE, NURO'S SUN STEAMS A SECTION OF THE SUEZ CANAL NEARLY DRY...
IF IT GOES ANY LOWER... HIT PORT SAID!... GOT TO TRY AND DISPERSE IT!

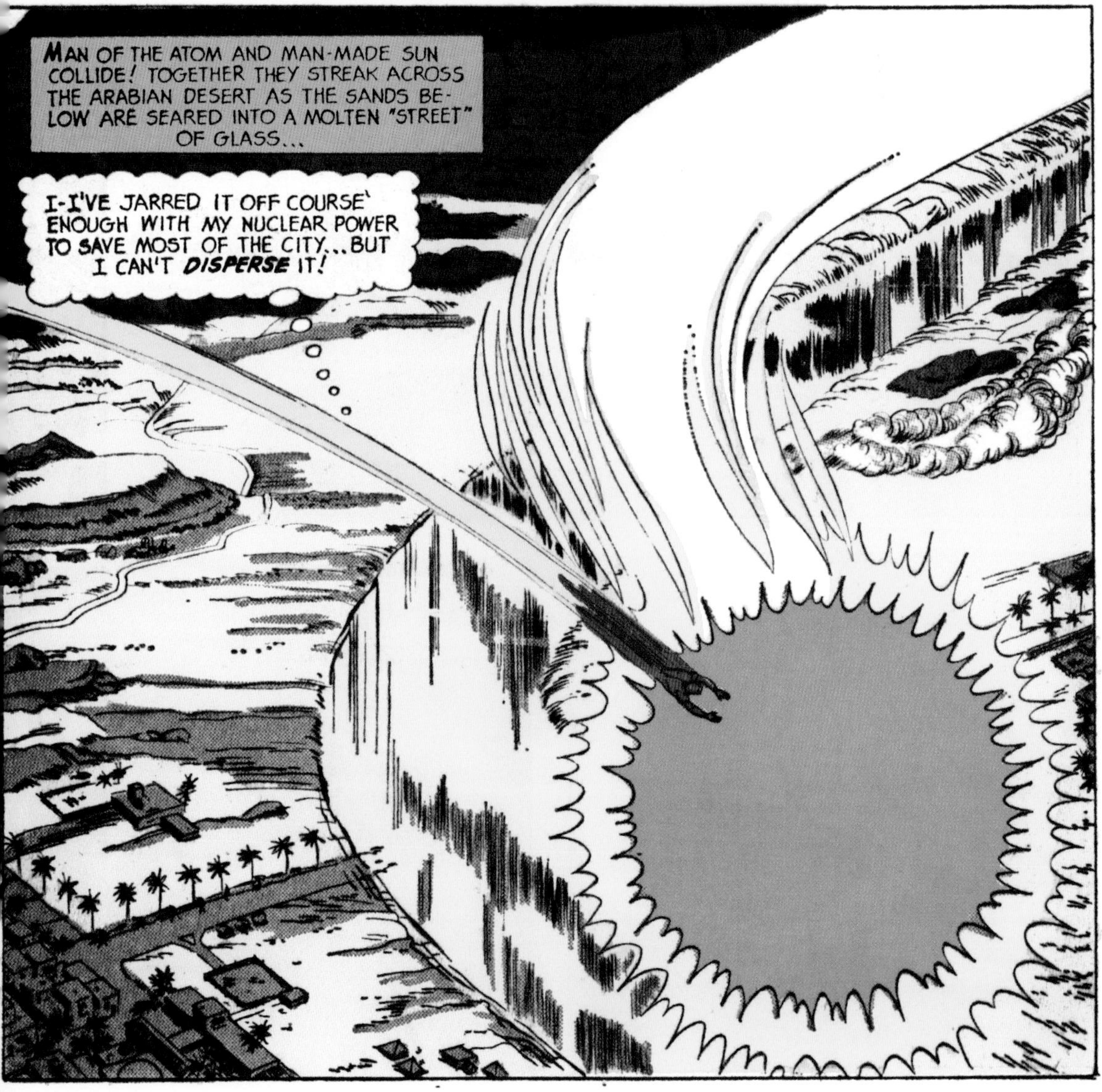
MAN OF THE ATOM AND MAN-MADE SUN COLLIDE! TOGETHER THEY STREAK ACROSS THE ARABIAN DESERT AS THE SANDS BE-LOW ARE SEARED INTO A MOLTEN "STREET" OF GLASS...
I-I'VE JARRED IT OFF COURSE ENOUGH WITH MY NUCLEAR POWER TO SAVE MOST OF THE CITY...BUT I CAN'T DISPERSE IT!

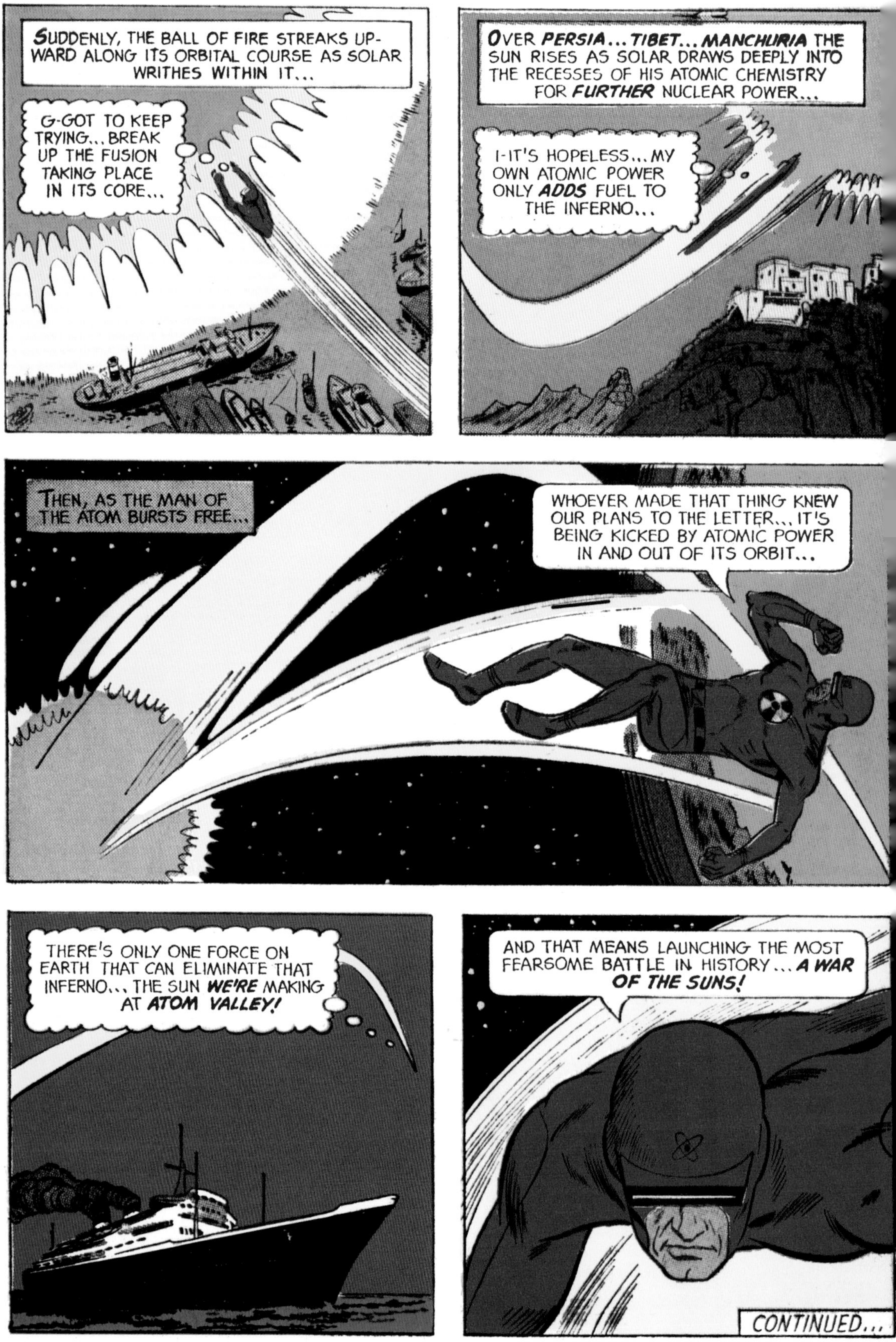
SUDDENLY, THE BALL OF FIRE STREAKS UPWARD ALONG ITS ORBITAL COURSE AS SOLAR WRITHES WITHIN IT...
G-GOT TO KEEP TRYING... BREAK UP THE FUSION TAKING PLACE IN ITS CORE...
OVER PERSIA... TIBET... MANCHURIA THE SUN RISES AS SOLAR DRAWS DEEPLY INTO THE RECESSES OF HIS ATOMIC CHEMISTRY FOR FURTHER NUCLEAR POWER...
I-IT'S HOPELESS... MY OWN ATOMIC POWER ONLY ADDS FUEL TO THE INFERNO...
THEN, AS THE MAN OF THE ATOM BURSTS FREE...
WHOEVER MADE THAT THING KNEW OUR PLANS TO THE LETTER... IT'S BEING KICKED BY ATOMIC POWER IN AND OUT OF ITS ORBIT...
THERE'S ONLY ONE FORCE ON EARTH THAT CAN ELIMINATE THAT INFERNO... THE SUN WE'RE MAKING AT ATOM VALLEY!
AND THAT MEANS LAUNCHING THE MOST FEARSOME BATTLE IN HISTORY... A WAR OF THE SUNS!
CONTINUED...

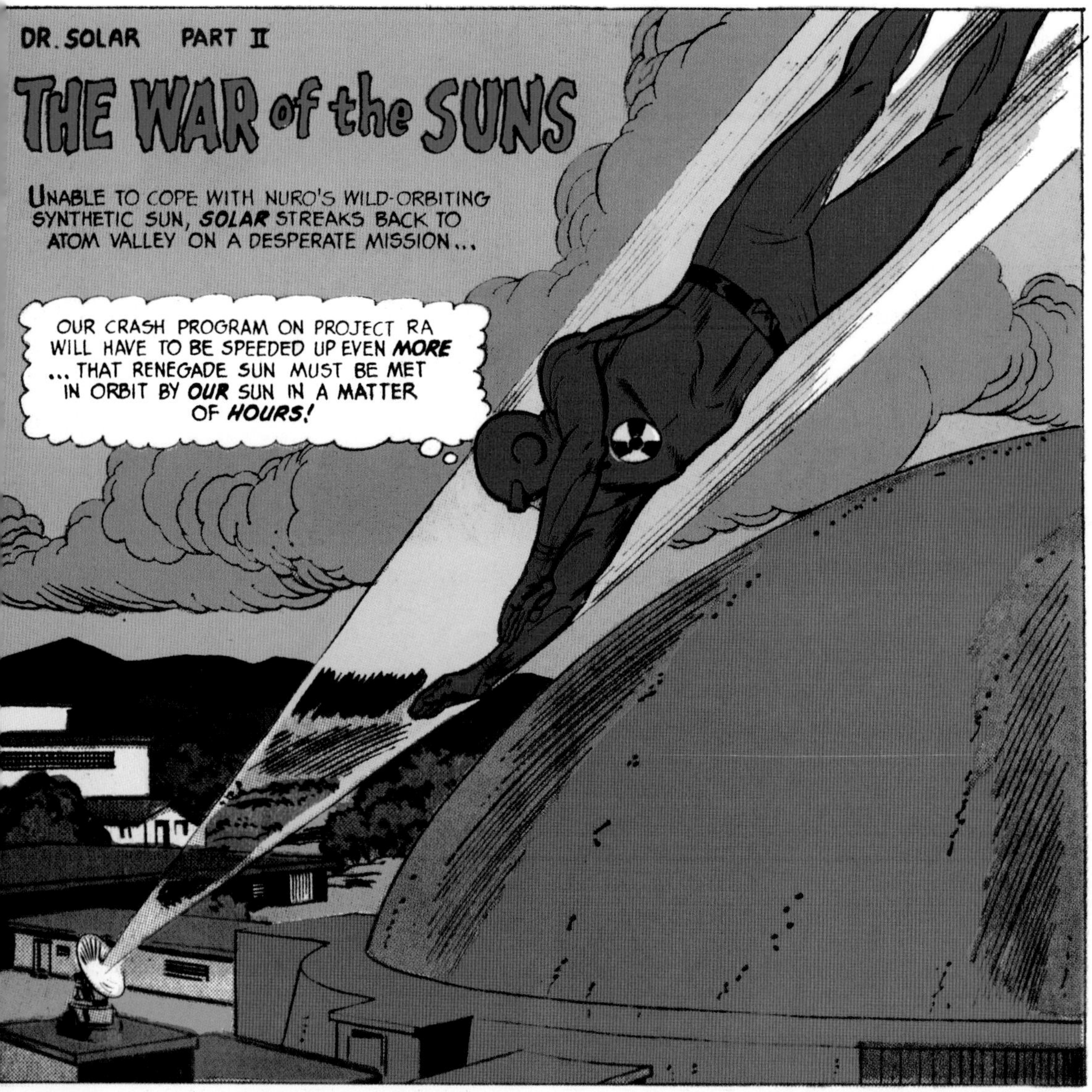
DR. SOLAR PART II
THE WAR of the SUNS
UNABLE TO COPE WITH NURO'S WILD-ORBITING SYNTHETIC SUN, SOLAR STREAKS BACK TO ATOM VALLEY ON A DESPERATE MISSION...
OUR CRASH PROGRAM ON PROJECT RA WILL HAVE TO BE SPEEDED UP EVEN MORE ... THAT RENEGADE SUN MUST BE MET IN ORBIT BY OUR SUN IN A MATTER OF HOURS!

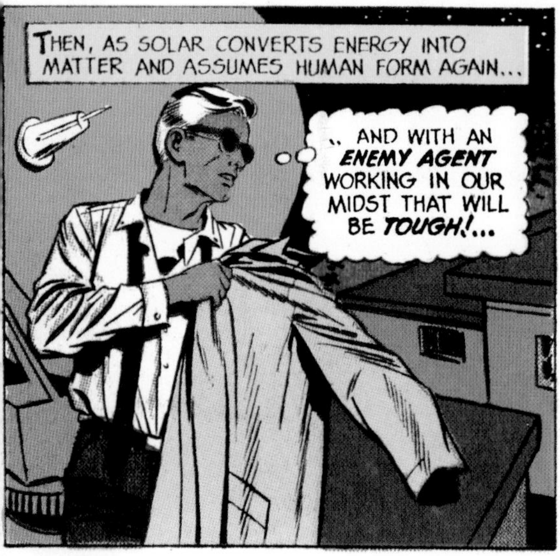
THEN, AS SOLAR CONVERTS ENERGY INTO MATTER AND ASSUMES HUMAN FORM AGAIN...
.. AND WITH AN ENEMY AGENT WORKING IN OUR MIDST THAT WILL BE TOUGH!...

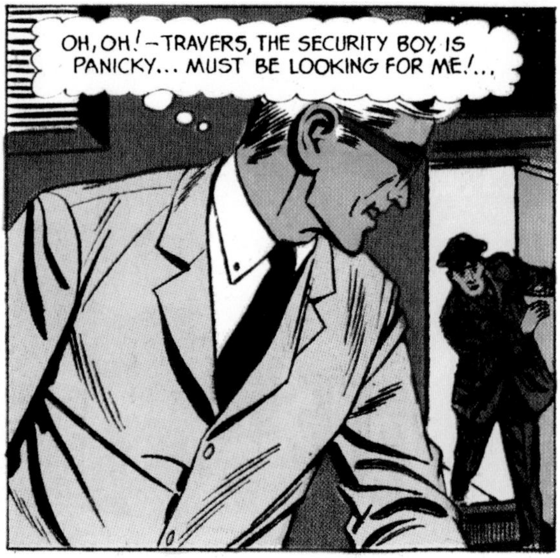
OH, OH!—TRAVERS, THE SECURITY BOY, IS PANICKY... MUST BE LOOKING FOR ME!...

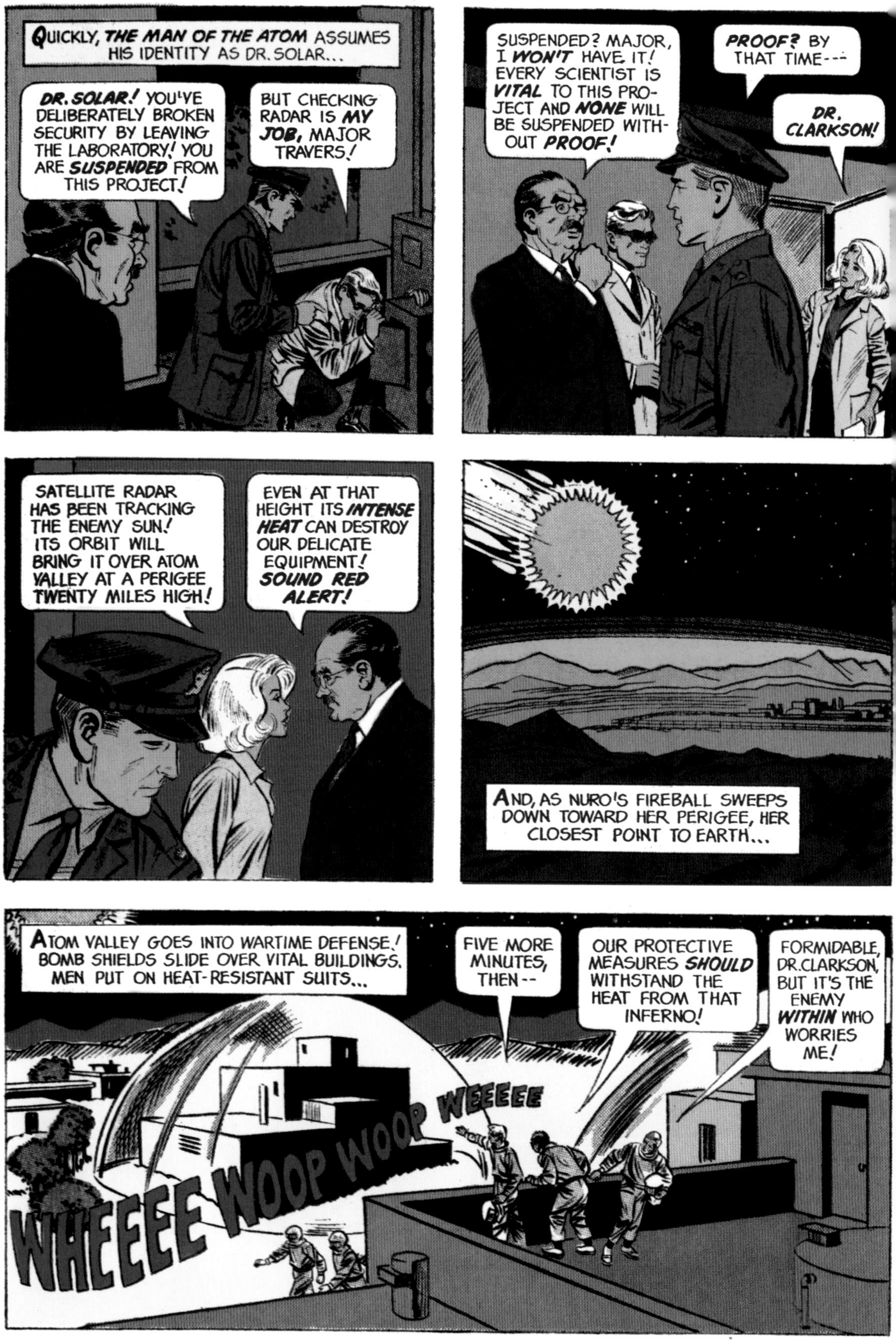
QUICKLY, THE MAN OF THE ATOM ASSUMES HIS IDENTITY AS DR. SOLAR...
DR. SOLAR! YOU'VE DELIBERATELY BROKEN SECURITY BY LEAVING THE LABORATORY! YOU ARE SUSPENDED FROM THIS PROJECT!
BUT CHECKING RADAR IS MY JOB, MAJOR TRAVERS!
SUSPENDED? MAJOR, I WON'T HAVE IT! EVERY SCIENTIST IS VITAL TO THIS PROJECT AND NONE WILL BE SUSPENDED WITHOUT PROOF!
PROOF? BY THAT TIME---
DR. CLARKSON!
SATELLITE RADAR HAS BEEN TRACKING THE ENEMY SUN! ITS ORBIT WILL BRING IT OVER ATOM VALLEY AT A PERIGEE TWENTY MILES HIGH!
EVEN AT THAT HEIGHT ITS INTENSE HEAT CAN DESTROY OUR DELICATE EQUIPMENT! SOUND RED ALERT!
AND, AS NURO'S FIREBALL SWEEPS DOWN TOWARD HER PERIGEE, HER CLOSEST POINT TO EARTH...
ATOM VALLEY GOES INTO WARTIME DEFENSE! BOMB SHIELDS SLIDE OVER VITAL BUILDINGS. MEN PUT ON HEAT-RESISTANT SUITS...
FIVE MORE MINUTES, THEN--
OUR PROTECTIVE MEASURES SHOULD WITHSTAND THE HEAT FROM THAT INFERNO!
FORMIDABLE, DR. CLARKSON, BUT IT'S THE ENEMY WITHIN WHO WORRIES ME!
WHEEEE WOOP WOOP WOOP WEEEEE

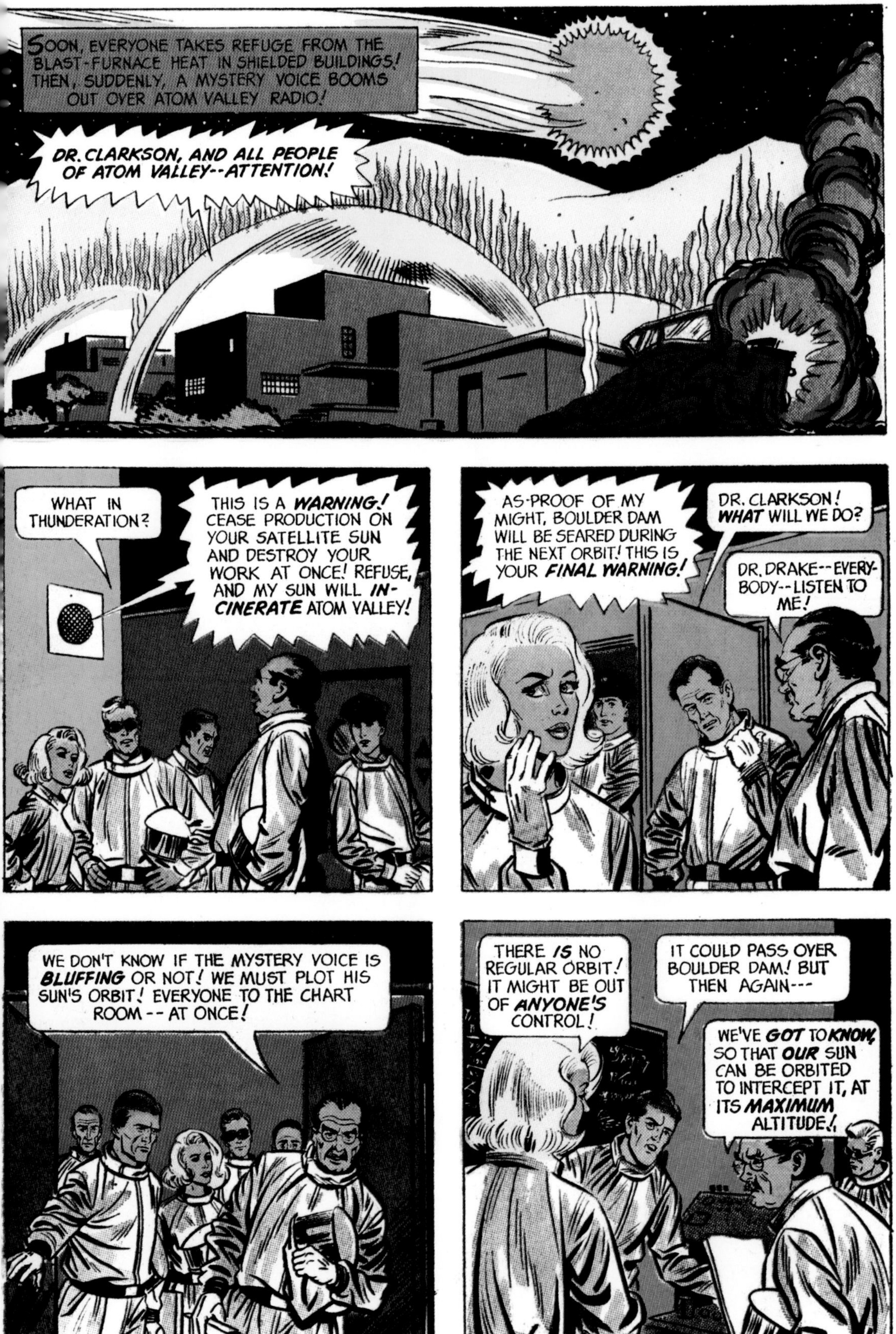
SOON, EVERYONE TAKES REFUGE FROM THE BLAST-FURNACE HEAT IN SHIELDED BUILDINGS! THEN, SUDDENLY, A MYSTERY VOICE BOOMS OUT OVER ATOM VALLEY RADIO!
DR. CLARKSON, AND ALL PEOPLE OF ATOM VALLEY--ATTENTION!
WHAT IN THUNDERATION?
THIS IS A WARNING! CEASE PRODUCTION ON YOUR SATELLITE SUN AND DESTROY YOUR WORK AT ONCE! REFUSE, AND MY SUN WILL INCINERATE ATOM VALLEY!
AS PROOF OF MY MIGHT, BOULDER DAM WILL BE SEARED DURING THE NEXT ORBIT! THIS IS YOUR FINAL WARNING!
DR. CLARKSON! WHAT WILL WE DO?
DR. DRAKE--EVERYBODY--LISTEN TO ME!
WE DON'T KNOW IF THE MYSTERY VOICE IS BLUFFING OR NOT! WE MUST PLOT HIS SUN'S ORBIT! EVERYONE TO THE CHART ROOM -- AT ONCE!
THERE IS NO REGULAR ORBIT! IT MIGHT BE OUT OF ANYONE'S CONTROL!
IT COULD PASS OVER BOULDER DAM! BUT THEN AGAIN---
WE'VE GOT TO KNOW, SO THAT OUR SUN CAN BE ORBITED TO INTERCEPT IT, AT ITS MAXIMUM ALTITUDE!

GAIL, YOU AND DR. KINDER KEEP FEEDING RADAR DATA INTO THE COMPUTERS TILL YOU *CAN* PREDICT ITS TRAJECTORY! MEANWHILE, WE GO ON WITH PROJECT RA!

THE TRIGGERING MECHANISM IS ALMOST READY, DR. CLARKSON! JUST GIVE ME A LITTLE MORE TIME--

TIME IS THE *ONE* THING WE *DON'T* HAVE, DRAKE-- *IF* OUR ENEMY'S THREAT IS NO BLUFF!

THERE'S ONE HOPE LEFT, MAJOR TRAVERS! SECRET, SUBTERRANEAN FACILITIES NO ONE KNOWS ABOUT! WE CAN *APPEAR* TO GIVE IN--

YES, AND COMPLETE THE PROJECT UNDERGROUND! BUT WE *MUST* PREVENT OUR SPY FROM GETTING WORD TO HIS MASTER!

NEXT MORNING, THE WORLD WAITS AS BOULDER DAM IS EVACUATED...THEN...

*LOOK!* LOOK THERE! THAT'S NOT THE *REAL* SUN! IT'S NOT DUE TO RISE FOR ANOTHER *HOUR!*

*GREAT SCOTT!* THEN THE DAM--

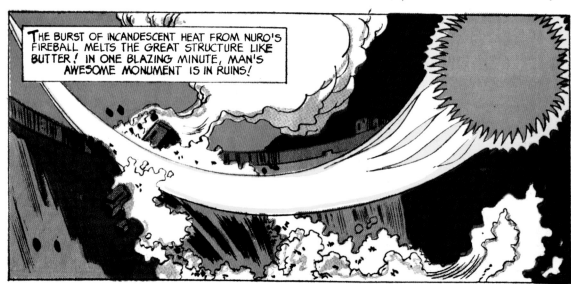

THE BURST OF INCANDESCENT HEAT FROM NURO'S FIREBALL MELTS THE GREAT STRUCTURE LIKE BUTTER! IN ONE BLAZING MINUTE, MAN'S AWESOME MONUMENT IS IN RUINS!

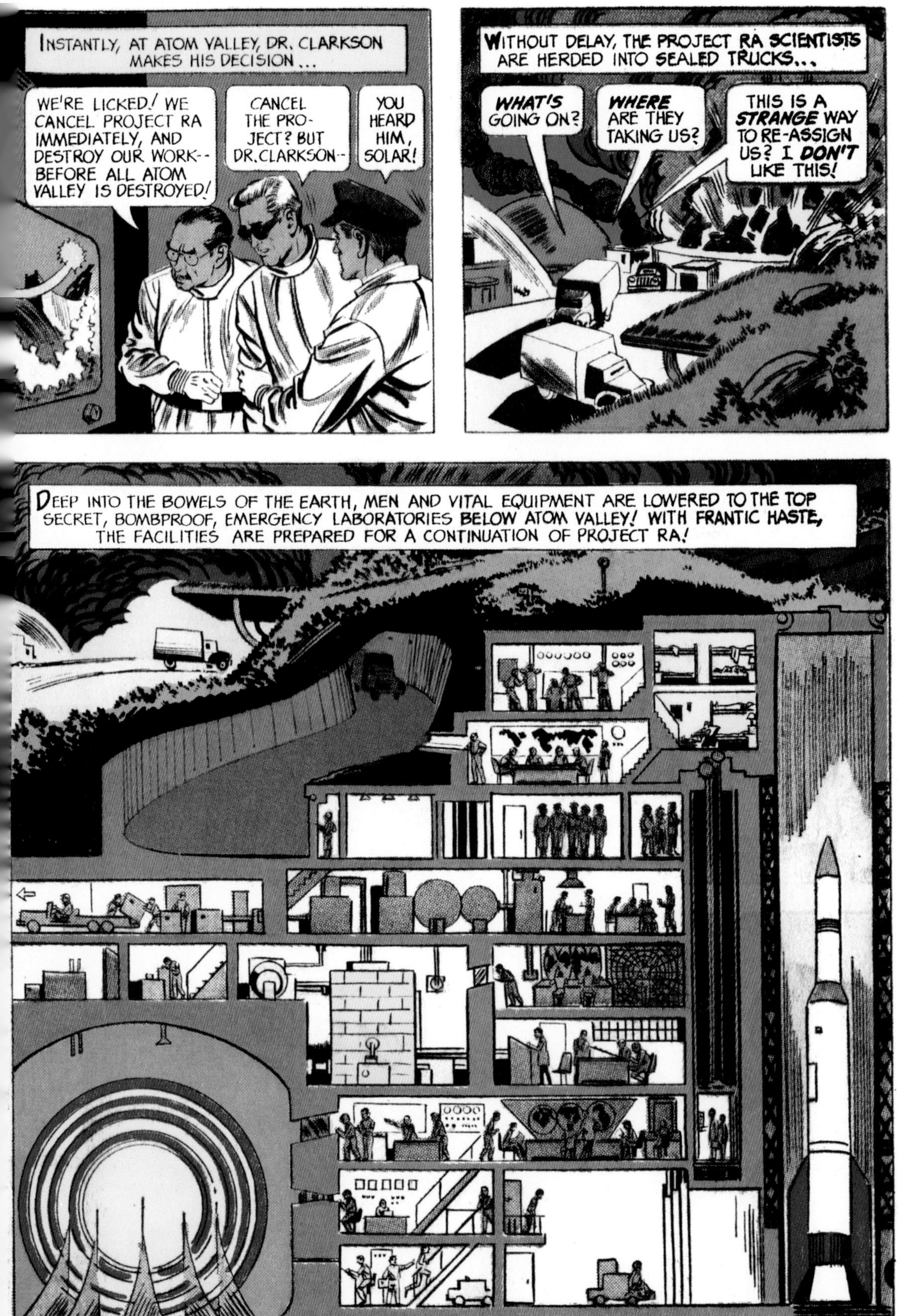
INSTANTLY, AT ATOM VALLEY, DR. CLARKSON MAKES HIS DECISION...
WE'RE LICKED! WE CANCEL PROJECT RA IMMEDIATELY, AND DESTROY OUR WORK--BEFORE ALL ATOM VALLEY IS DESTROYED!
CANCEL THE PROJECT? BUT DR. CLARKSON--
YOU HEARD HIM, SOLAR!
WITHOUT DELAY, THE PROJECT RA SCIENTISTS ARE HERDED INTO SEALED TRUCKS...
WHAT'S GOING ON?
WHERE ARE THEY TAKING US?
THIS IS A STRANGE WAY TO RE-ASSIGN US? I DON'T LIKE THIS!
DEEP INTO THE BOWELS OF THE EARTH, MEN AND VITAL EQUIPMENT ARE LOWERED TO THE TOP SECRET, BOMBPROOF, EMERGENCY LABORATORIES BELOW ATOM VALLEY! WITH FRANTIC HASTE, THE FACILITIES ARE PREPARED FOR A CONTINUATION OF PROJECT RA!

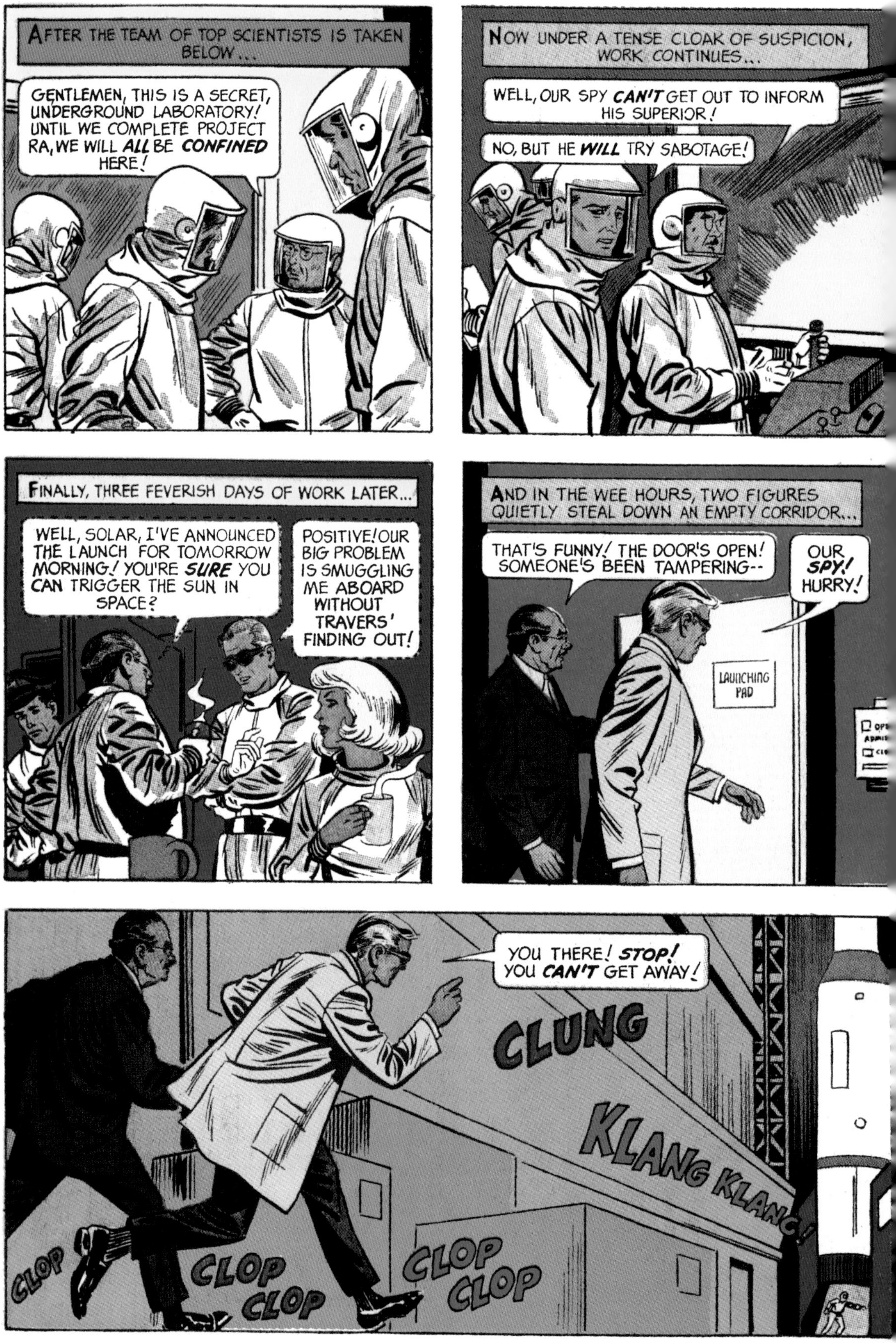
AFTER THE TEAM OF TOP SCIENTISTS IS TAKEN BELOW...
GENTLEMEN, THIS IS A SECRET, UNDERGROUND LABORATORY! UNTIL WE COMPLETE PROJECT RA, WE WILL ALL BE CONFINED HERE!
NOW UNDER A TENSE CLOAK OF SUSPICION, WORK CONTINUES...
WELL, OUR SPY CAN'T GET OUT TO INFORM HIS SUPERIOR!
NO, BUT HE WILL TRY SABOTAGE!
FINALLY, THREE FEVERISH DAYS OF WORK LATER...
WELL, SOLAR, I'VE ANNOUNCED THE LAUNCH FOR TOMORROW MORNING! YOU'RE SURE YOU CAN TRIGGER THE SUN IN SPACE?
POSITIVE! OUR BIG PROBLEM IS SMUGGLING ME ABOARD WITHOUT TRAVERS' FINDING OUT!
AND IN THE WEE HOURS, TWO FIGURES QUIETLY STEAL DOWN AN EMPTY CORRIDOR...
THAT'S FUNNY! THE DOOR'S OPEN! SOMEONE'S BEEN TAMPERING--
OUR SPY! HURRY!
LAUNCHING PAD
YOU THERE! STOP! YOU CAN'T GET AWAY!
CLUNG
KLANG KLANG KLANG!
CLOP
CLOP CLOP
CLOP CLOP

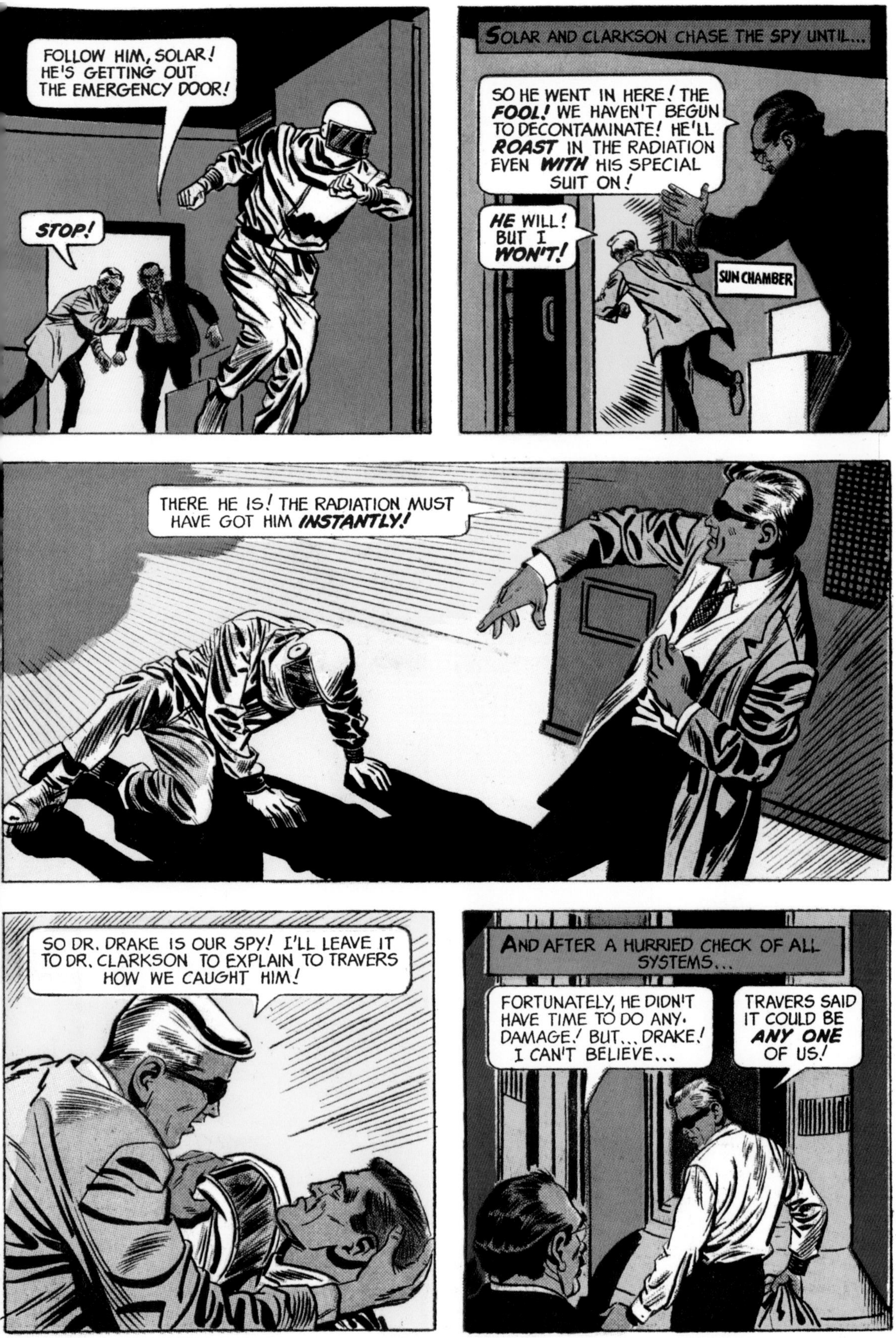
FOLLOW HIM, SOLAR! HE'S GETTING OUT THE EMERGENCY DOOR!
STOP!
SOLAR AND CLARKSON CHASE THE SPY UNTIL...
SO HE WENT IN HERE! THE FOOL! WE HAVEN'T BEGUN TO DECONTAMINATE! HE'LL ROAST IN THE RADIATION EVEN WITH HIS SPECIAL SUIT ON!
HE WILL! BUT I WON'T!
SUN CHAMBER
THERE HE IS! THE RADIATION MUST HAVE GOT HIM INSTANTLY!
SO DR. DRAKE IS OUR SPY! I'LL LEAVE IT TO DR. CLARKSON TO EXPLAIN TO TRAVERS HOW WE CAUGHT HIM!
AND AFTER A HURRIED CHECK OF ALL SYSTEMS...
FORTUNATELY, HE DIDN'T HAVE TIME TO DO ANY. DAMAGE! BUT... DRAKE! I CAN'T BELIEVE...
TRAVERS SAID IT COULD BE ANY ONE OF US!

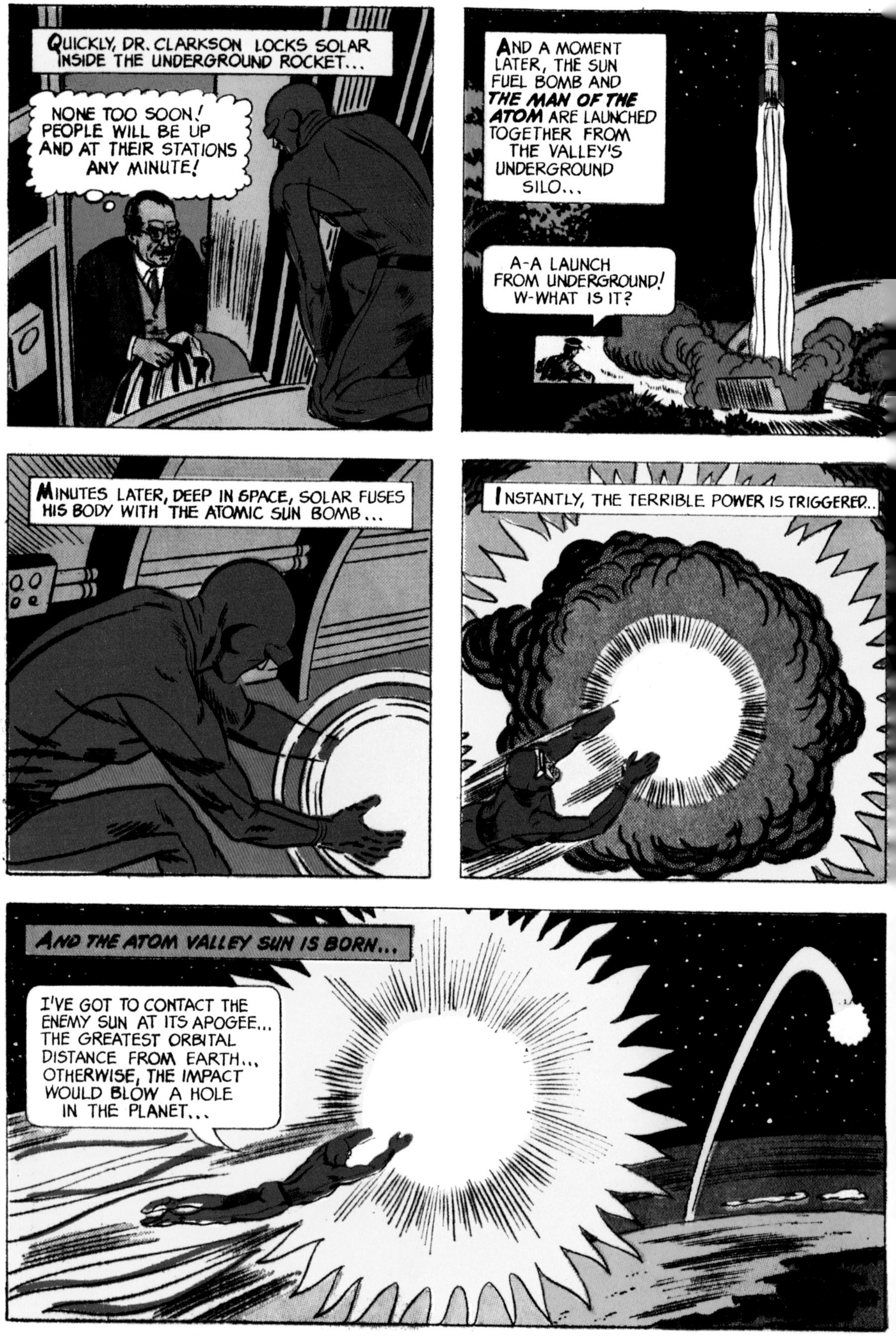
QUICKLY, DR. CLARKSON LOCKS SOLAR INSIDE THE UNDERGROUND ROCKET...
NONE TOO SOON! PEOPLE WILL BE UP AND AT THEIR STATIONS ANY MINUTE!
AND A MOMENT LATER, THE SUN FUEL BOMB AND THE MAN OF THE ATOM ARE LAUNCHED TOGETHER FROM THE VALLEY'S UNDERGROUND SILO...
A-A LAUNCH FROM UNDERGROUND! W-WHAT IS IT?
MINUTES LATER, DEEP IN SPACE, SOLAR FUSES HIS BODY WITH THE ATOMIC SUN BOMB...
INSTANTLY, THE TERRIBLE POWER IS TRIGGERED...
AND THE ATOM VALLEY SUN IS BORN...
I'VE GOT TO CONTACT THE ENEMY SUN AT ITS APOGEE... THE GREATEST ORBITAL DISTANCE FROM EARTH... OTHERWISE, THE IMPACT WOULD BLOW A HOLE IN THE PLANET...

SKILLFULLY, *THE MAN OF THE ATOM* MANEUVERS THE GLOWING MASS THROUGH SPACE LIKE SOME INCREDIBLE VOLLEY BALL...

I'M IN LUCK... ITS APOGEE IS ABOUT 200 MILES HIGH... THAT'S SAFE ENOUGH... GOT TO MAKE A DIRECT HIT...

WHEN THE TWO MEET THEY SHOULD FORM A CRITICAL MASS,... ERUPT IN A NOVA EXPLOSION! HERE WE GO... *DEAD ON TARGET!*

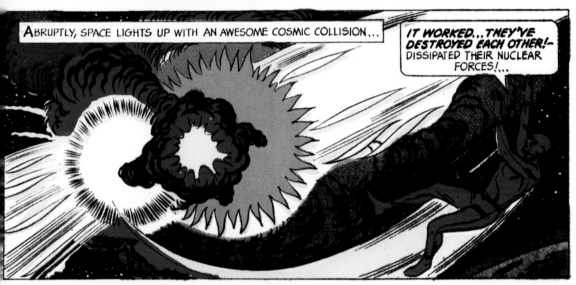

ABRUPTLY, SPACE LIGHTS UP WITH AN AWESOME COSMIC COLLISION...

*IT WORKED...THEY'VE DESTROYED EACH OTHER!* - DISSIPATED THEIR NUCLEAR FORCES!...

BUT LATER AT ATOM VALLEY, THE MAN THE WORLD KNOWS MERELY AS DR. SOLAR CAN NOT RELAX ...

...IF YOU REFUSE, MY SUN WILL INCINERATE ATOM VALLEY!

A MAN CUNNING ENOUGH TO LAUNCH SUCH A FORCE, EVEN *WITH* OUR PLANS, IS A TERRIBLE MENACE TO THE WORLD, SOLAR! WHO CAN HE BE?

I'M GOING TO PLAY HIS VOICE OVER A THOUSAND TIMES IF I HAVE TO! IT'S OUR *ONLY* CLUE... AND *ONE DAY* I'LL *HEAR* THAT MONSTER IN PERSON... AND *KNOW* WHO HE IS!

CLICK!

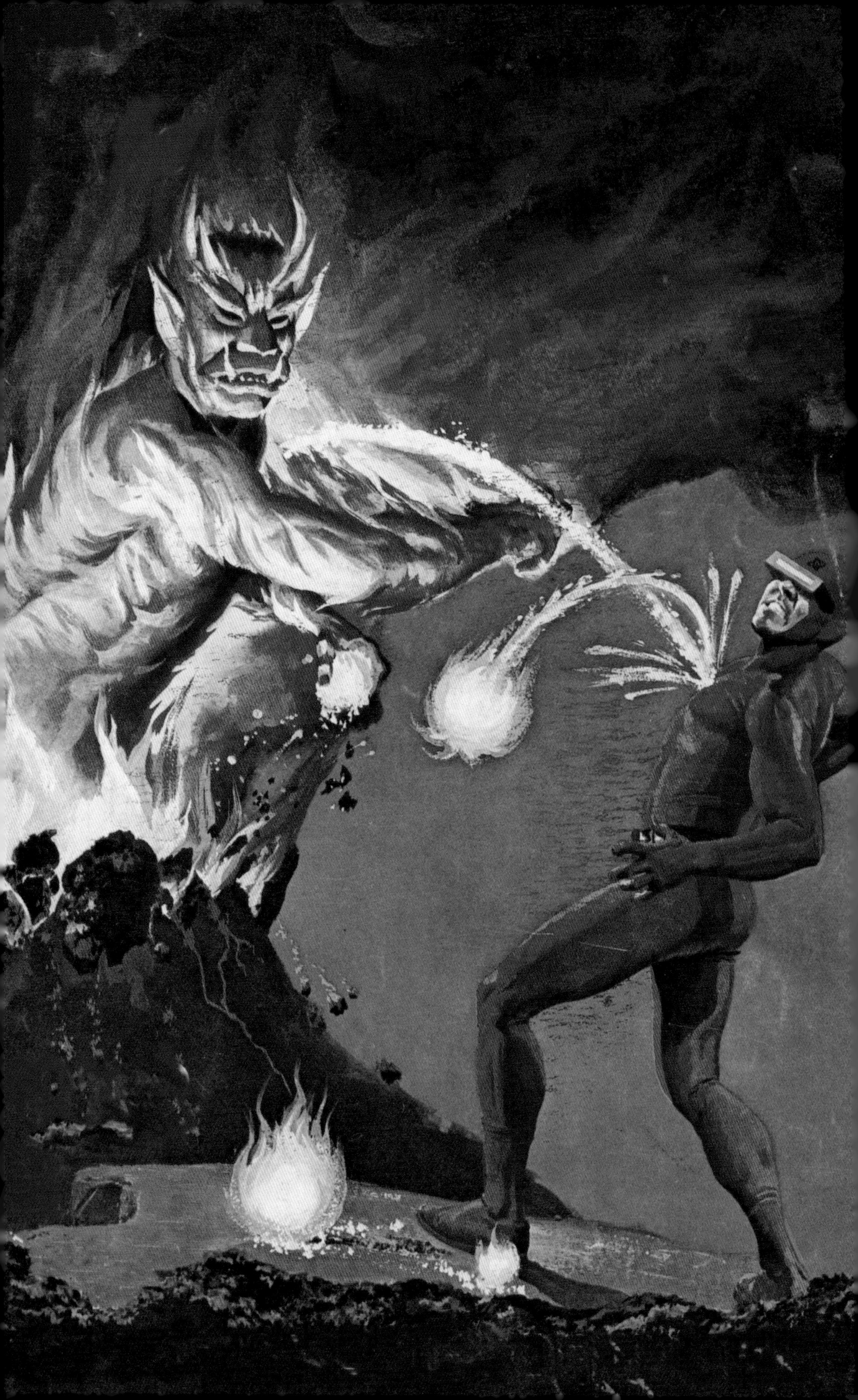

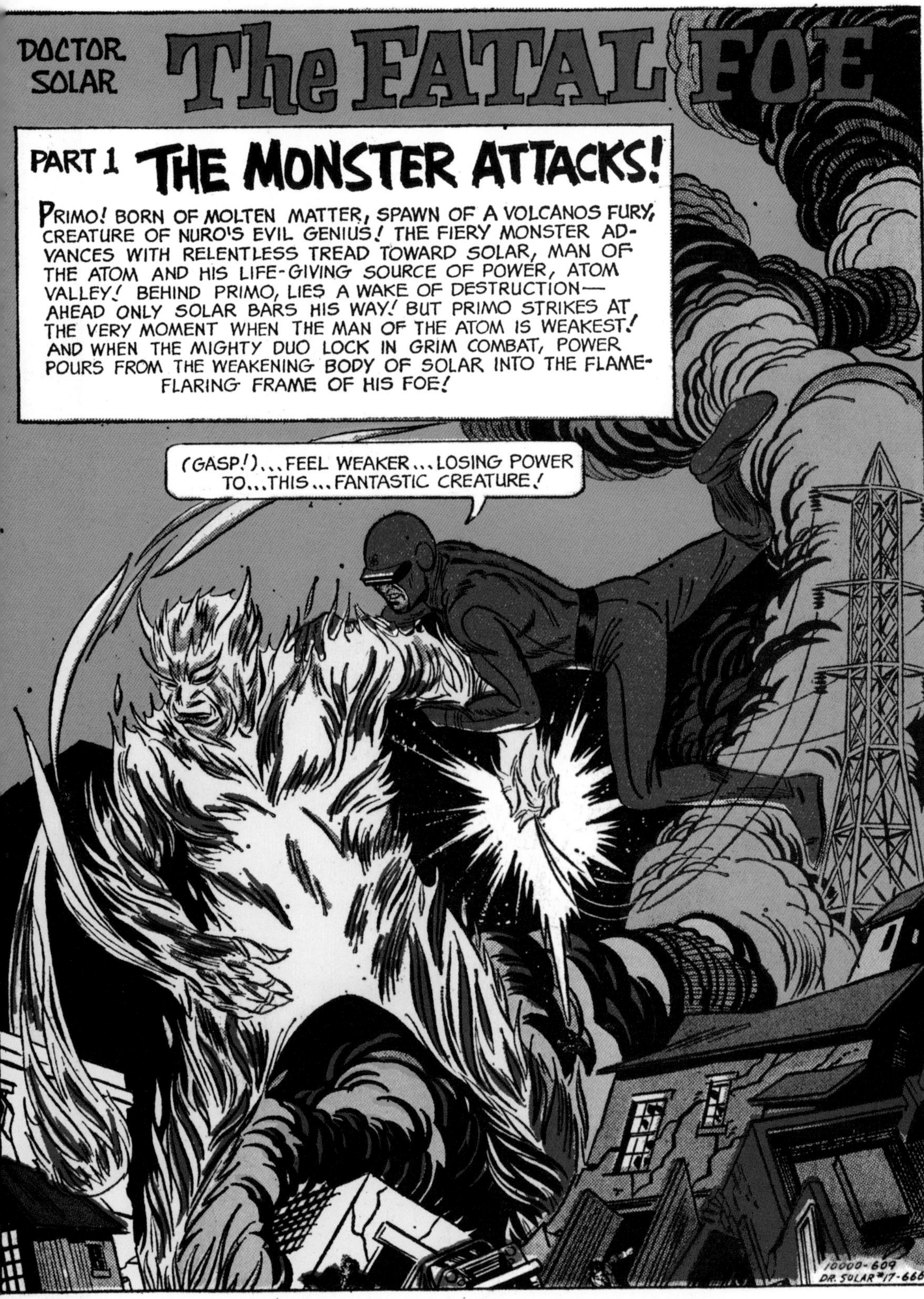
DOCTOR SOLAR
The FATAL FOE
PART 1 THE MONSTER ATTACKS!
PRIMO! BORN OF MOLTEN MATTER, SPAWN OF A VOLCANOS FURY, CREATURE OF NURO'S EVIL GENIUS! THE FIERY MONSTER ADVANCES WITH RELENTLESS TREAD TOWARD SOLAR, MAN OF THE ATOM AND HIS LIFE-GIVING SOURCE OF POWER, ATOM VALLEY! BEHIND PRIMO, LIES A WAKE OF DESTRUCTION— AHEAD ONLY SOLAR BARS HIS WAY! BUT PRIMO STRIKES AT THE VERY MOMENT WHEN THE MAN OF THE ATOM IS WEAKEST! AND WHEN THE MIGHTY DUO LOCK IN GRIM COMBAT, POWER POURS FROM THE WEAKENING BODY OF SOLAR INTO THE FLAME-FLARING FRAME OF HIS FOE!
(GASP!)...FEEL WEAKER...LOSING POWER TO...THIS...FANTASTIC CREATURE!
10000-609
DR. SOLAR #17-666

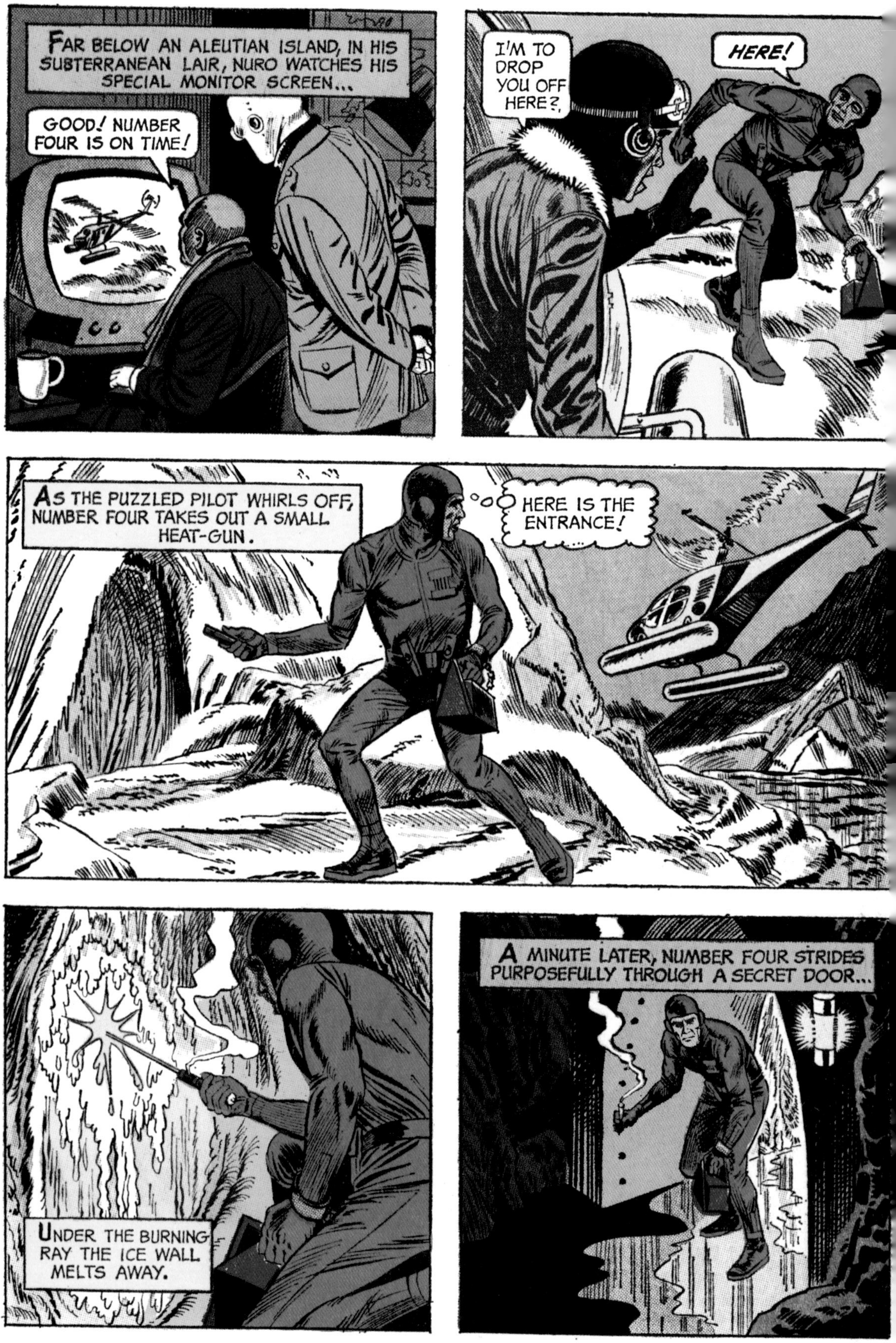
FAR BELOW AN ALEUTIAN ISLAND, IN HIS SUBTERRANEAN LAIR, NURO WATCHES HIS SPECIAL MONITOR SCREEN...
GOOD! NUMBER FOUR IS ON TIME!
I'M TO DROP YOU OFF HERE?
HERE!
AS THE PUZZLED PILOT WHIRLS OFF, NUMBER FOUR TAKES OUT A SMALL HEAT-GUN.
HERE IS THE ENTRANCE!
UNDER THE BURNING RAY THE ICE WALL MELTS AWAY.
A MINUTE LATER, NUMBER FOUR STRIDES PURPOSEFULLY THROUGH A SECRET DOOR...

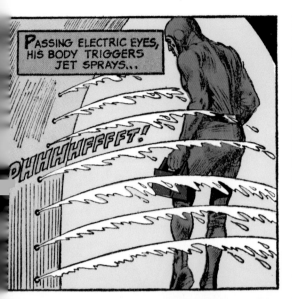

PASSING ELECTRIC EYES, HIS BODY TRIGGERS JET SPRAYS...

PHHHHFFFFT!

AND AS HE HURRIES DOWN THE PASSAGE, A NEW DOOR OF ICE IS FORMED BEHIND HIM...

QUICKLY, HE ENTERS A WAITING TRANSPORT CAPSULE...

AS THE CAPSULE DOOR SLIDES SHUT, NUMBER FOUR SWALLOWS A PILL...AND WITHIN SECONDS SLIPS INTO DEEP SLEEP...

SOON THE CAPSULE HURTLES LIKE A BULLET. DOWN, DOWN, DEEP INTO THE DARK FASTNESS OF EARTH...

WHOOOOSH!

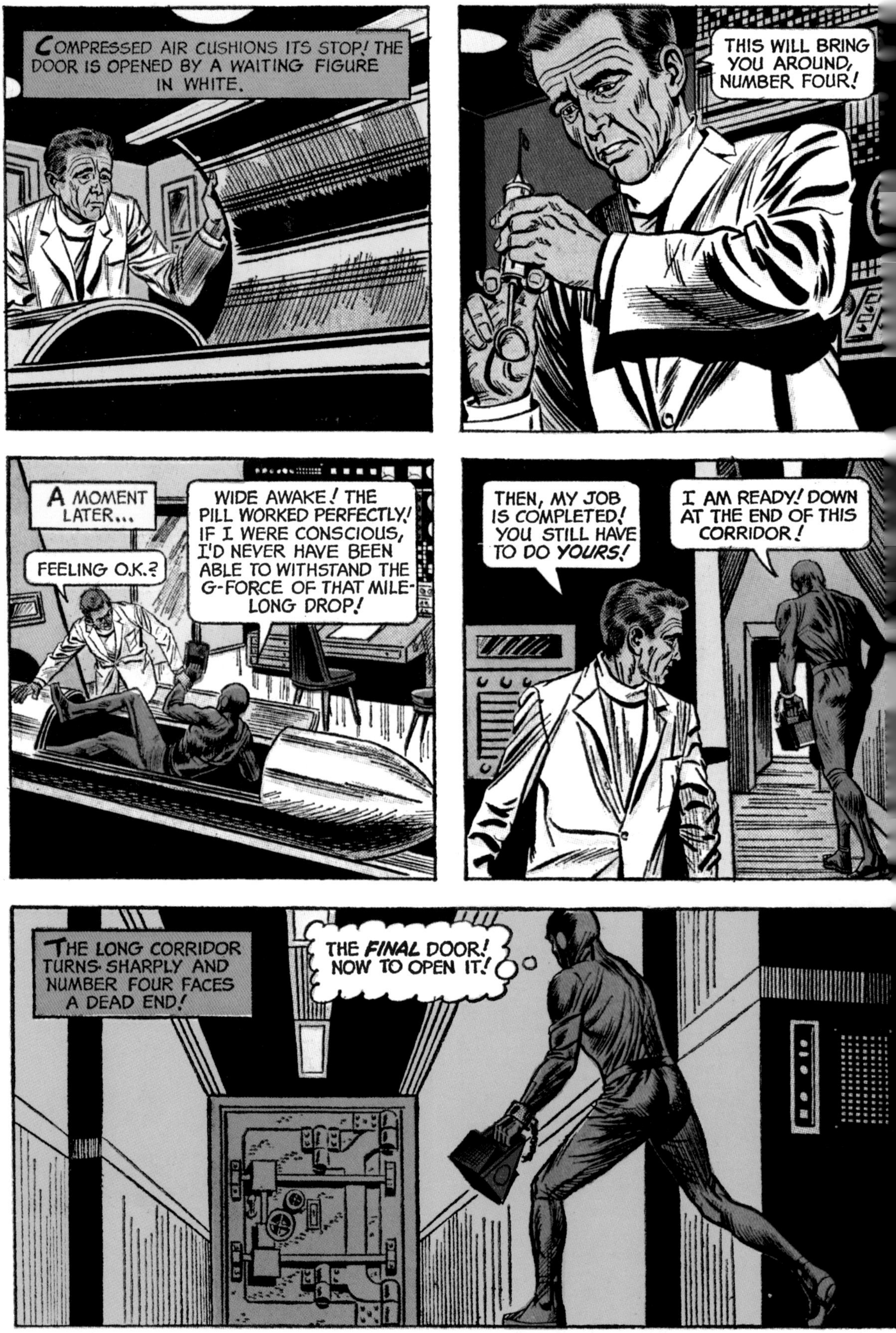
COMPRESSED AIR CUSHIONS ITS STOP! THE DOOR IS OPENED BY A WAITING FIGURE IN WHITE.
THIS WILL BRING YOU AROUND, NUMBER FOUR!
A MOMENT LATER...
FEELING O.K.?
WIDE AWAKE! THE PILL WORKED PERFECTLY! IF I WERE CONSCIOUS, I'D NEVER HAVE BEEN ABLE TO WITHSTAND THE G-FORCE OF THAT MILE-LONG DROP!
THEN, MY JOB IS COMPLETED! YOU STILL HAVE TO DO YOURS!
I AM READY! DOWN AT THE END OF THIS CORRIDOR!
THE LONG CORRIDOR TURNS SHARPLY AND NUMBER FOUR FACES A DEAD END!
THE FINAL DOOR! NOW TO OPEN IT!

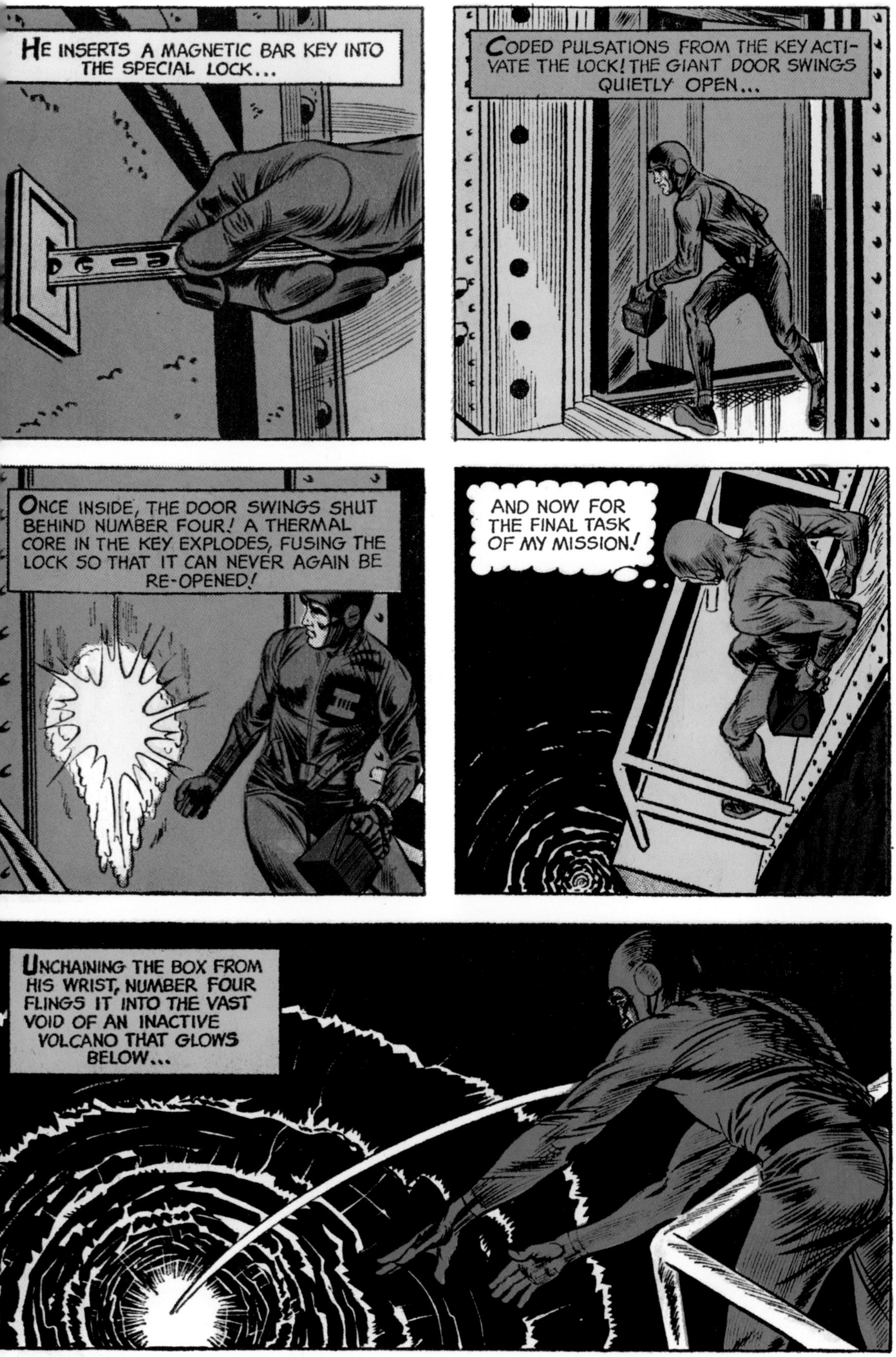
HE INSERTS A MAGNETIC BAR KEY INTO THE SPECIAL LOCK...
CODED PULSATIONS FROM THE KEY ACTIVATE THE LOCK! THE GIANT DOOR SWINGS QUIETLY OPEN...
ONCE INSIDE, THE DOOR SWINGS SHUT BEHIND NUMBER FOUR! A THERMAL CORE IN THE KEY EXPLODES, FUSING THE LOCK SO THAT IT CAN NEVER AGAIN BE RE-OPENED!
AND NOW FOR THE FINAL TASK OF MY MISSION!
UNCHAINING THE BOX FROM HIS WRIST, NUMBER FOUR FLINGS IT INTO THE VAST VOID OF AN INACTIVE VOLCANO THAT GLOWS BELOW...

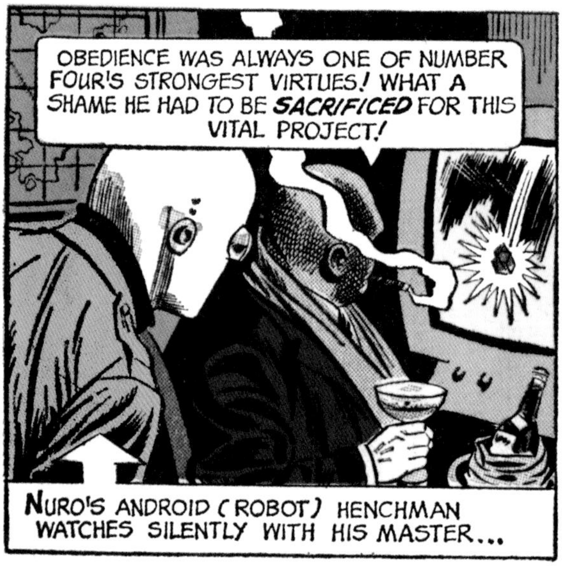
OBEDIENCE WAS ALWAYS ONE OF NUMBER FOUR'S STRONGEST VIRTUES! WHAT A SHAME HE HAD TO BE SACRIFICED FOR THIS VITAL PROJECT!
NURO'S ANDROID (ROBOT) HENCHMAN WATCHES SILENTLY WITH HIS MASTER...

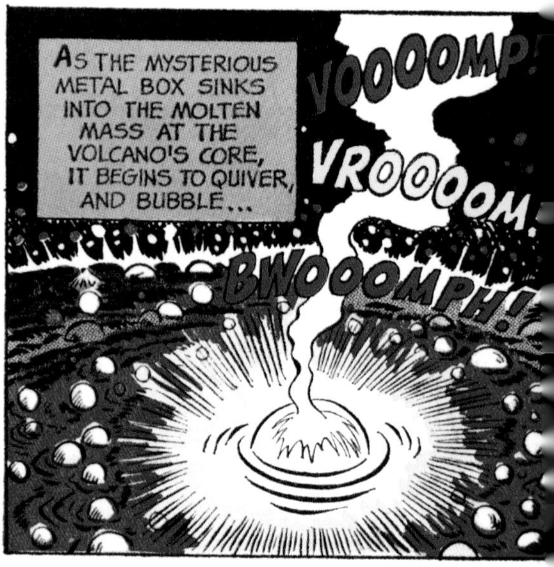
AS THE MYSTERIOUS METAL BOX SINKS INTO THE MOLTEN MASS AT THE VOLCANO'S CORE, IT BEGINS TO QUIVER, AND BUBBLE...
VOOOOMP!
VROOOOOM!
BWOOOMPH!!

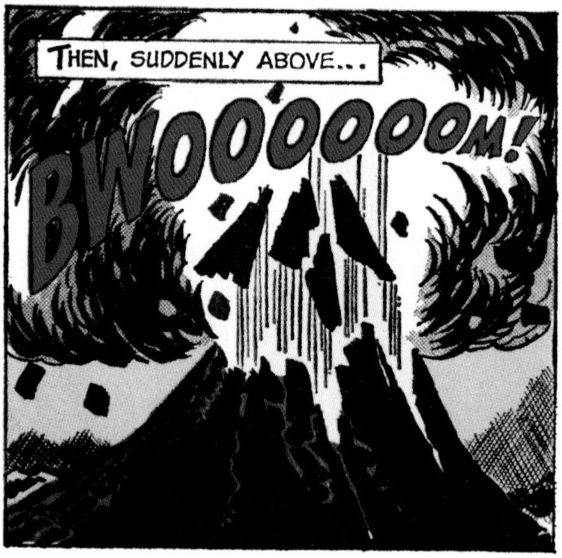
THEN, SUDDENLY ABOVE...
BWOOOOOOM!

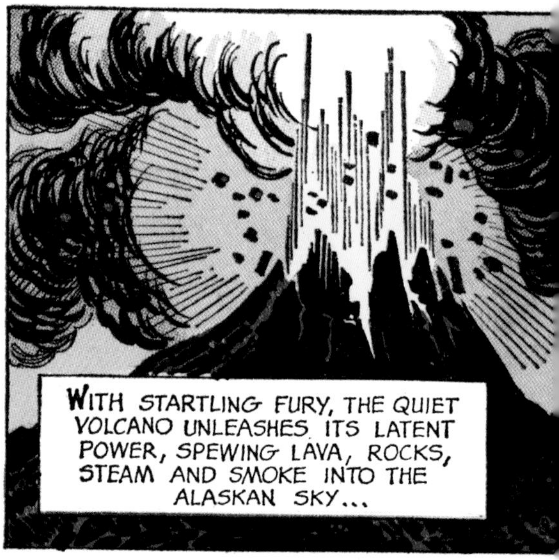
WITH STARTLING FURY, THE QUIET VOLCANO UNLEASHES ITS LATENT POWER, SPEWING LAVA, ROCKS, STEAM AND SMOKE INTO THE ALASKAN SKY...

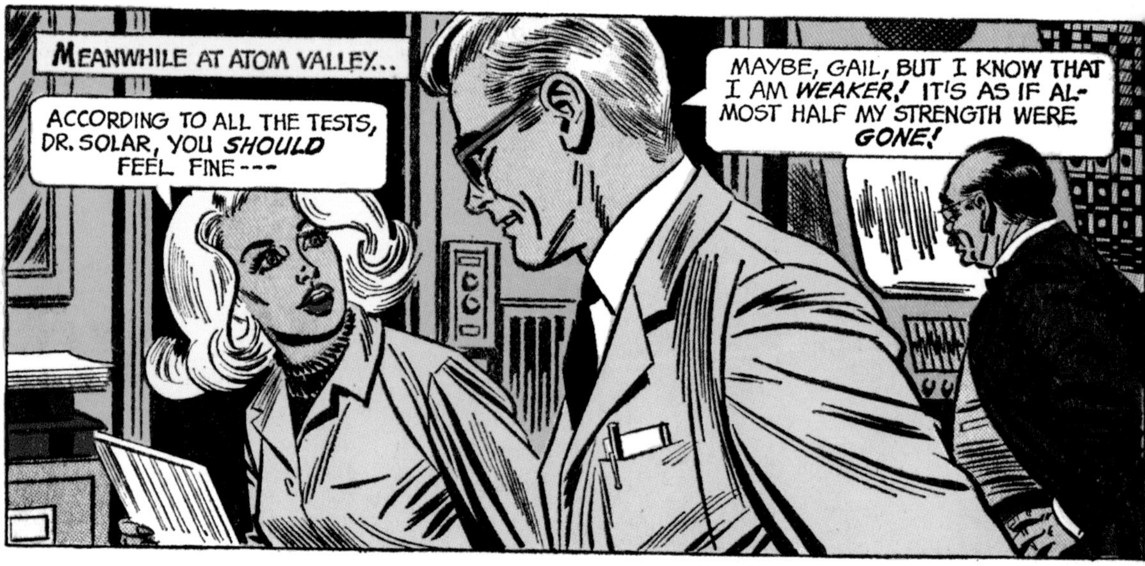
MEANWHILE AT ATOM VALLEY...
ACCORDING TO ALL THE TESTS, DR. SOLAR, YOU SHOULD FEEL FINE---
MAYBE, GAIL, BUT I KNOW THAT I AM WEAKER! IT'S AS IF AL-MOST HALF MY STRENGTH WERE GONE!

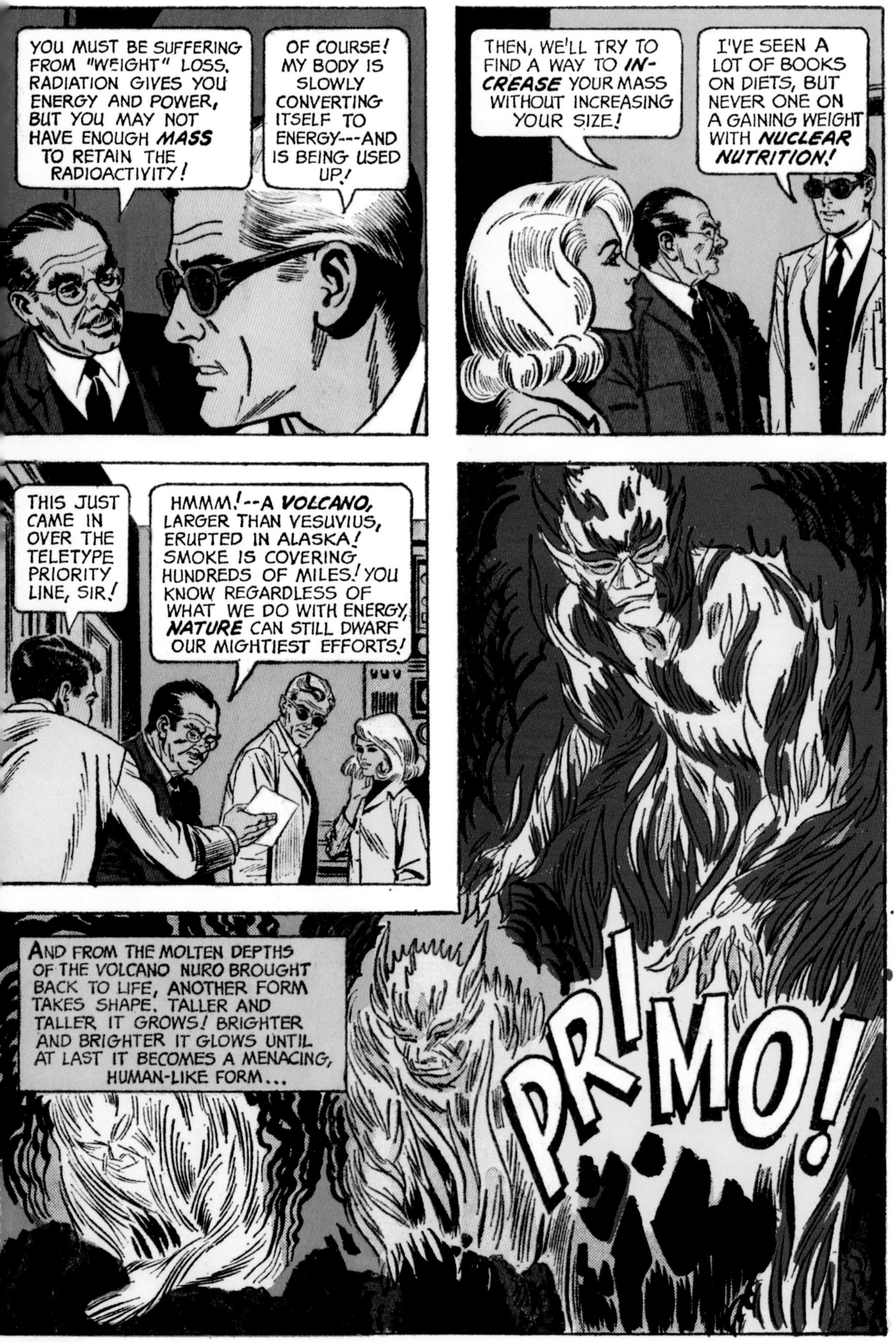
YOU MUST BE SUFFERING FROM "WEIGHT" LOSS. RADIATION GIVES YOU ENERGY AND POWER, BUT YOU MAY NOT HAVE ENOUGH MASS TO RETAIN THE RADIOACTIVITY!
OF COURSE! MY BODY IS SLOWLY CONVERTING ITSELF TO ENERGY---AND IS BEING USED UP!
THEN, WE'LL TRY TO FIND A WAY TO INCREASE YOUR MASS WITHOUT INCREASING YOUR SIZE!
I'VE SEEN A LOT OF BOOKS ON DIETS, BUT NEVER ONE ON A GAINING WEIGHT WITH NUCLEAR NUTRITION!
THIS JUST CAME IN OVER THE TELETYPE PRIORITY LINE, SIR!
HMMM!--A VOLCANO, LARGER THAN VESUVIUS, ERUPTED IN ALASKA! SMOKE IS COVERING HUNDREDS OF MILES! YOU KNOW REGARDLESS OF WHAT WE DO WITH ENERGY, NATURE CAN STILL DWARF OUR MIGHTIEST EFFORTS!
AND FROM THE MOLTEN DEPTHS OF THE VOLCANO NURO BROUGHT BACK TO LIFE, ANOTHER FORM TAKES SHAPE. TALLER AND TALLER IT GROWS! BRIGHTER AND BRIGHTER IT GLOWS UNTIL AT LAST IT BECOMES A MENACING, HUMAN-LIKE FORM...
PRIMO!

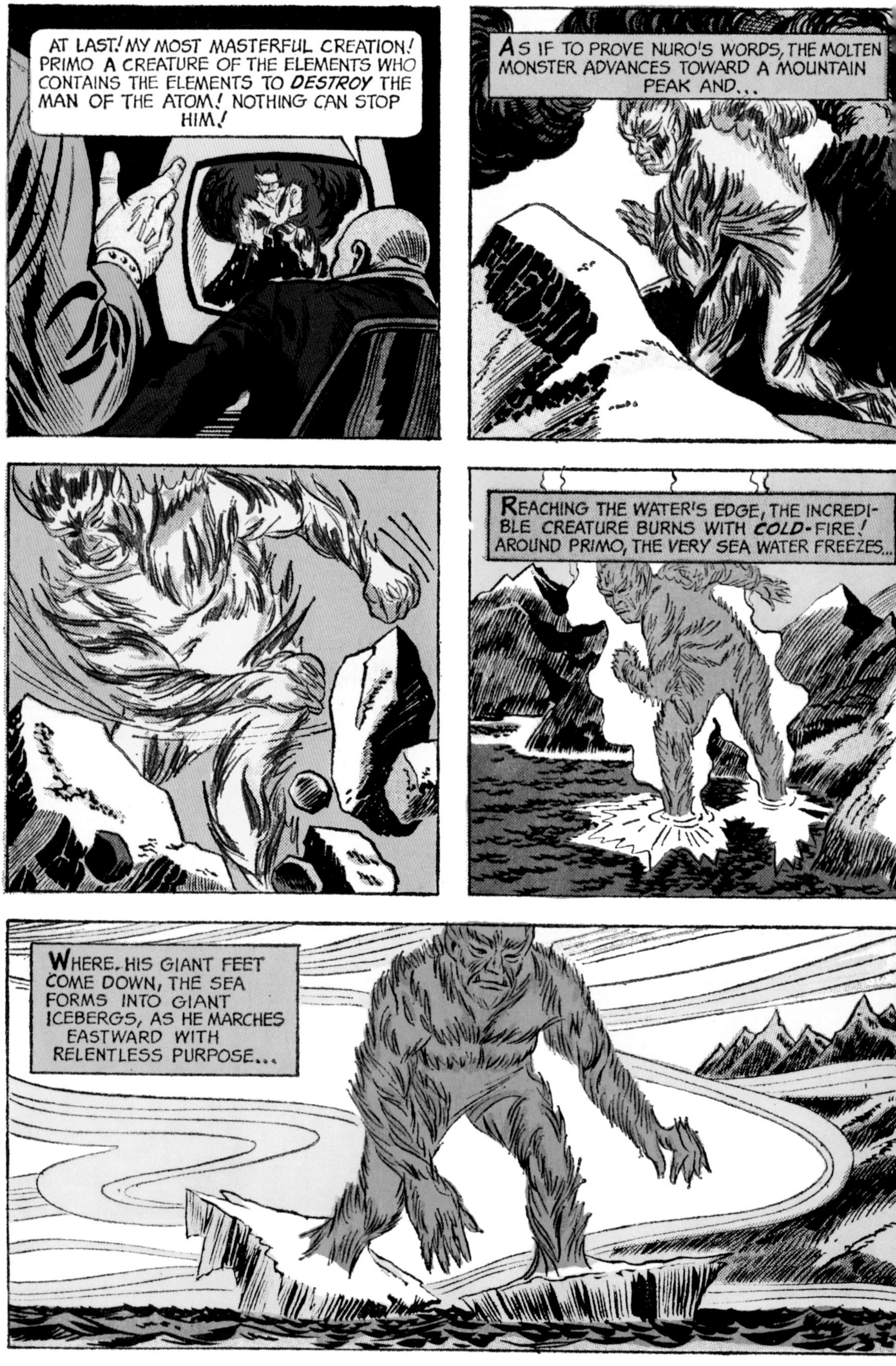
AT LAST! MY MOST MASTERFUL CREATION! PRIMO A CREATURE OF THE ELEMENTS WHO CONTAINS THE ELEMENTS TO DESTROY THE MAN OF THE ATOM! NOTHING CAN STOP HIM!
AS IF TO PROVE NURO'S WORDS, THE MOLTEN MONSTER ADVANCES TOWARD A MOUNTAIN PEAK AND...
REACHING THE WATER'S EDGE, THE INCREDIBLE CREATURE BURNS WITH COLD-FIRE! AROUND PRIMO, THE VERY SEA WATER FREEZES...
WHERE HIS GIANT FEET COME DOWN, THE SEA FORMS INTO GIANT ICEBERGS, AS HE MARCHES EASTWARD WITH RELENTLESS PURPOSE...

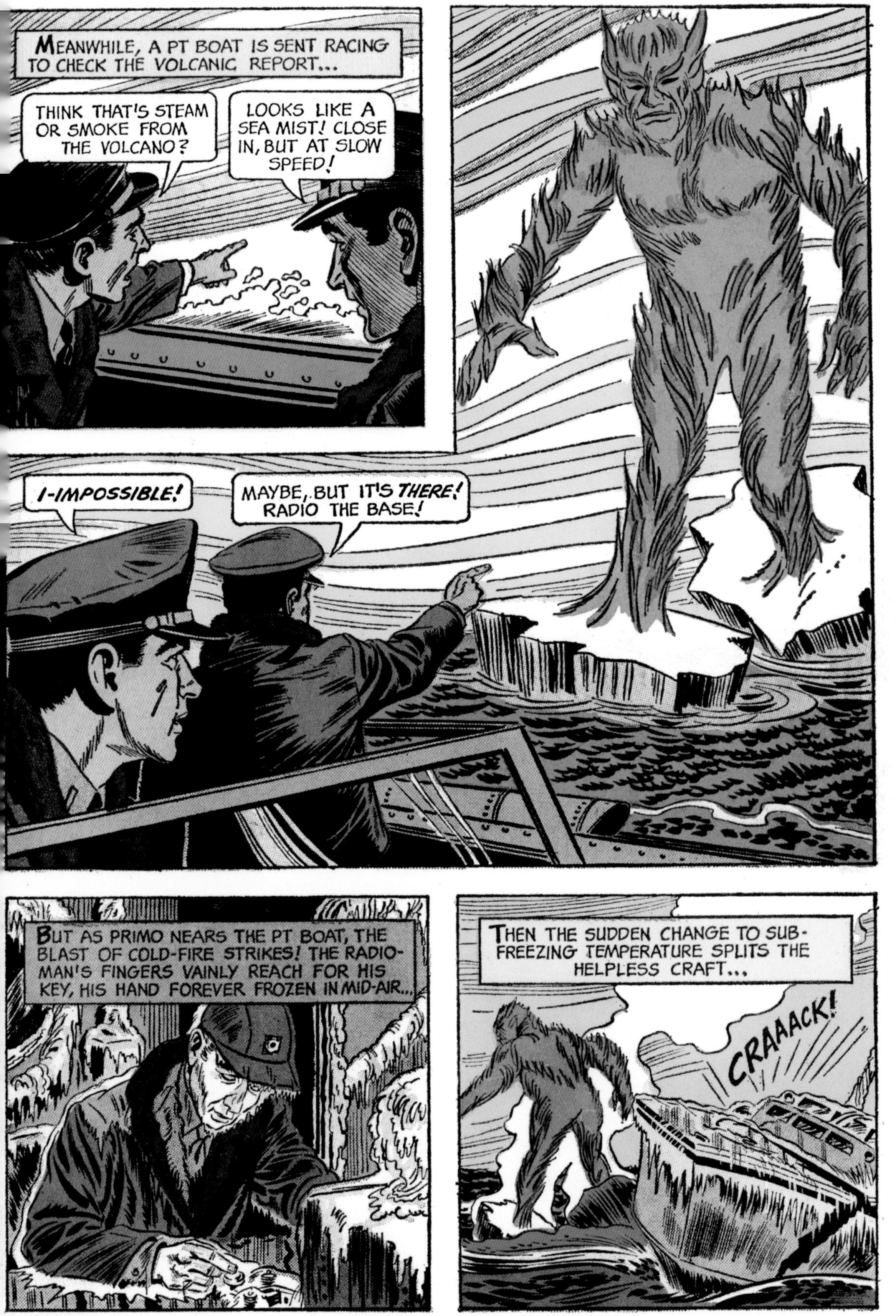
MEANWHILE, A PT BOAT IS SENT RACING TO CHECK THE VOLCANIC REPORT...
THINK THAT'S STEAM OR SMOKE FROM THE VOLCANO?
LOOKS LIKE A SEA MIST! CLOSE IN, BUT AT SLOW SPEED!
I-IMPOSSIBLE!
MAYBE, BUT IT'S THERE! RADIO THE BASE!
BUT AS PRIMO NEARS THE PT BOAT, THE BLAST OF COLD-FIRE STRIKES! THE RADIO-MAN'S FINGERS VAINLY REACH FOR HIS KEY, HIS HAND FOREVER FROZEN IN MID-AIR...
THEN THE SUDDEN CHANGE TO SUB-FREEZING TEMPERATURE SPLITS THE HELPLESS CRAFT...
CRAAACK!

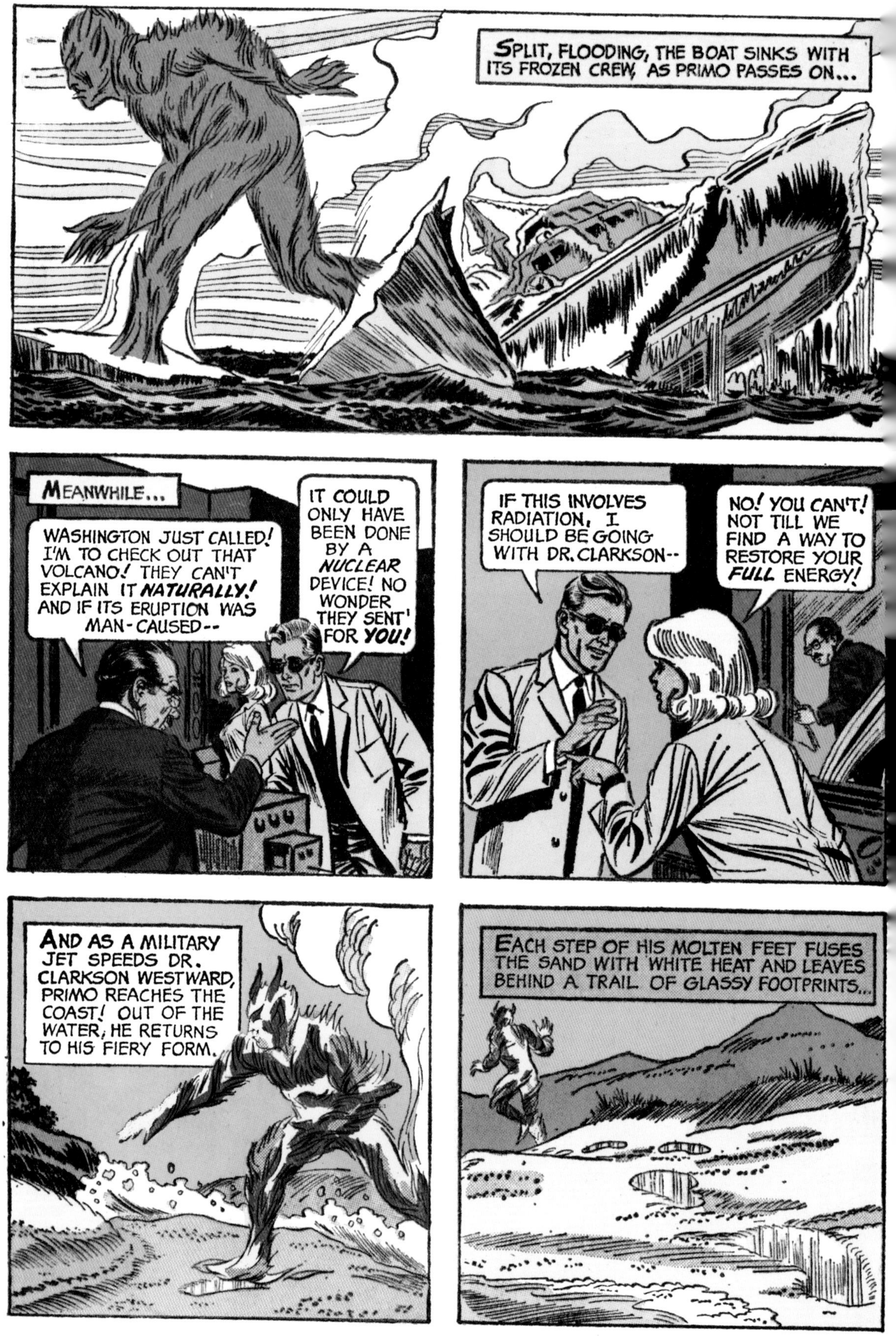
SPLIT, FLOODING, THE BOAT SINKS WITH ITS FROZEN CREW, AS PRIMO PASSES ON...
MEANWHILE...
WASHINGTON JUST CALLED! I'M TO CHECK OUT THAT VOLCANO! THEY CAN'T EXPLAIN IT NATURALLY! AND IF ITS ERUPTION WAS MAN-CAUSED--
IT COULD ONLY HAVE BEEN DONE BY A NUCLEAR DEVICE! NO WONDER THEY SENT FOR YOU!
IF THIS INVOLVES RADIATION, I SHOULD BE GOING WITH DR. CLARKSON--
NO! YOU CAN'T! NOT TILL WE FIND A WAY TO RESTORE YOUR FULL ENERGY!
AND AS A MILITARY JET SPEEDS DR. CLARKSON WESTWARD, PRIMO REACHES THE COAST! OUT OF THE WATER, HE RETURNS TO HIS FIERY FORM.
EACH STEP OF HIS MOLTEN FEET FUSES THE SAND WITH WHITE HEAT AND LEAVES BEHIND A TRAIL OF GLASSY FOOTPRINTS...

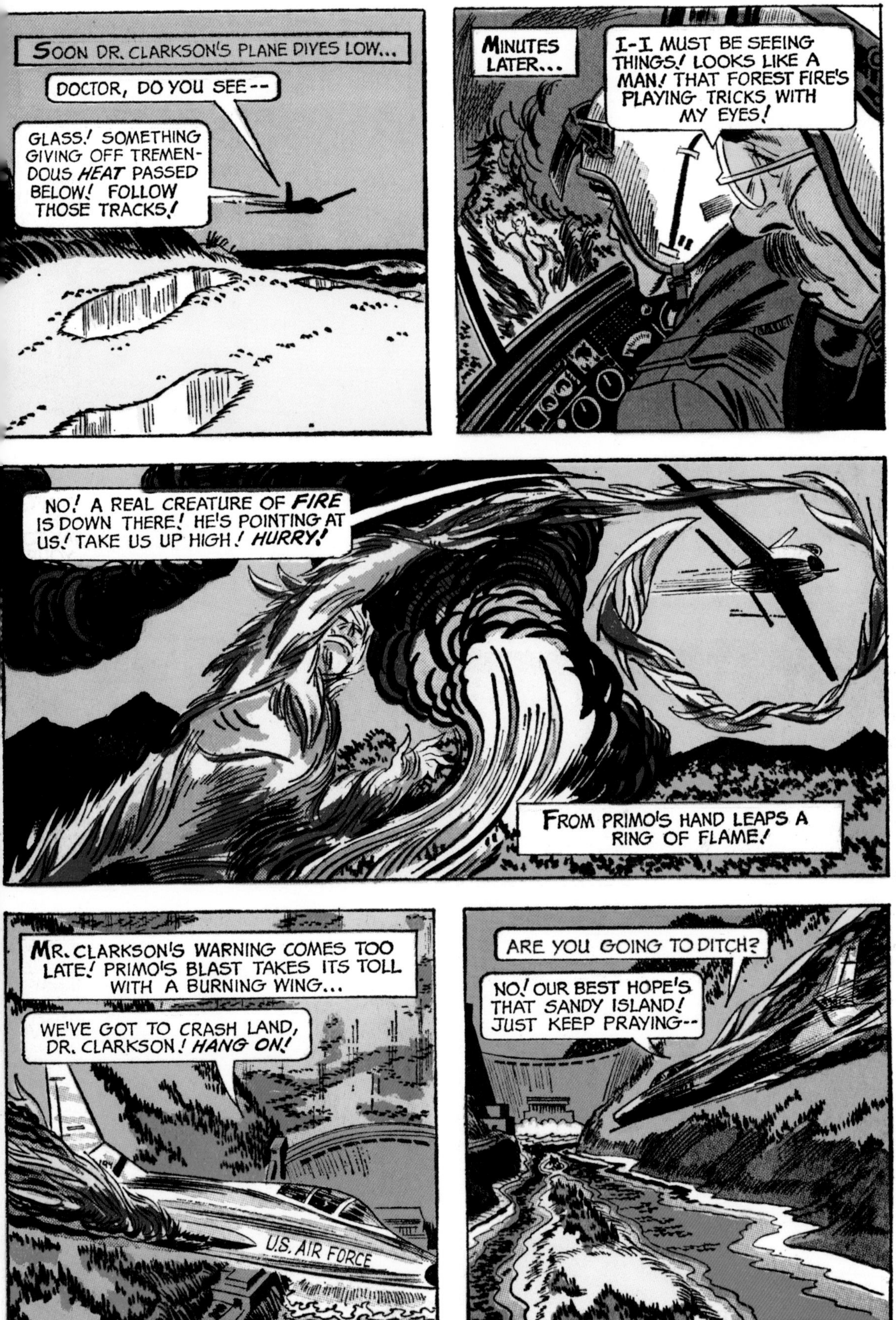

SOON DR. CLARKSON'S PLANE DIVES LOW...
DOCTOR, DO YOU SEE--
GLASS! SOMETHING GIVING OFF TREMENDOUS HEAT PASSED BELOW! FOLLOW THOSE TRACKS!
MINUTES LATER...
I-I MUST BE SEEING THINGS! LOOKS LIKE A MAN! THAT FOREST FIRE'S PLAYING TRICKS WITH MY EYES!
NO! A REAL CREATURE OF FIRE IS DOWN THERE! HE'S POINTING AT US! TAKE US UP HIGH! HURRY!
FROM PRIMO'S HAND LEAPS A RING OF FLAME!
MR. CLARKSON'S WARNING COMES TOO LATE! PRIMO'S BLAST TAKES ITS TOLL WITH A BURNING WING...
WE'VE GOT TO CRASH LAND, DR. CLARKSON! HANG ON!
U.S. AIR FORCE
ARE YOU GOING TO DITCH?
NO! OUR BEST HOPE'S THAT SANDY ISLAND! JUST KEEP PRAYING--

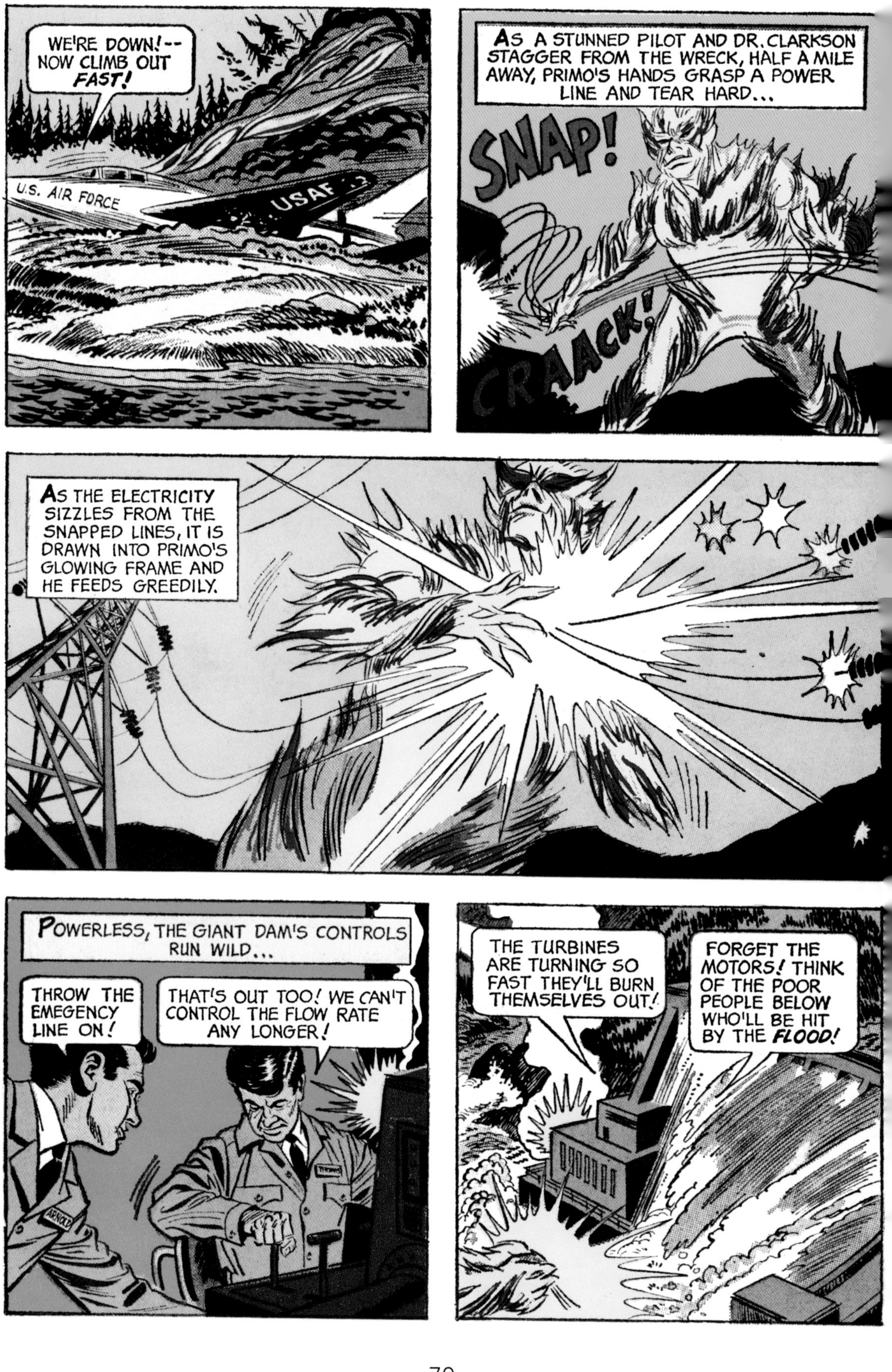
WE'RE DOWN! -- NOW CLIMB OUT FAST!
U.S. AIR FORCE
USAF
AS A STUNNED PILOT AND DR. CLARKSON STAGGER FROM THE WRECK, HALF A MILE AWAY, PRIMO'S HANDS GRASP A POWER LINE AND TEAR HARD...
SNAP!
CRAACK!
AS THE ELECTRICITY SIZZLES FROM THE SNAPPED LINES, IT IS DRAWN INTO PRIMO'S GLOWING FRAME AND HE FEEDS GREEDILY.
POWERLESS, THE GIANT DAM'S CONTROLS RUN WILD...
THROW THE EMEGENCY LINE ON!
THAT'S OUT TOO! WE CAN'T CONTROL THE FLOW RATE ANY LONGER!
ARNOLD
THE TURBINES ARE TURNING SO FAST THEY'LL BURN THEMSELVES OUT!
FORGET THE MOTORS! THINK OF THE POOR PEOPLE BELOW WHO'LL BE HIT BY THE FLOOD!

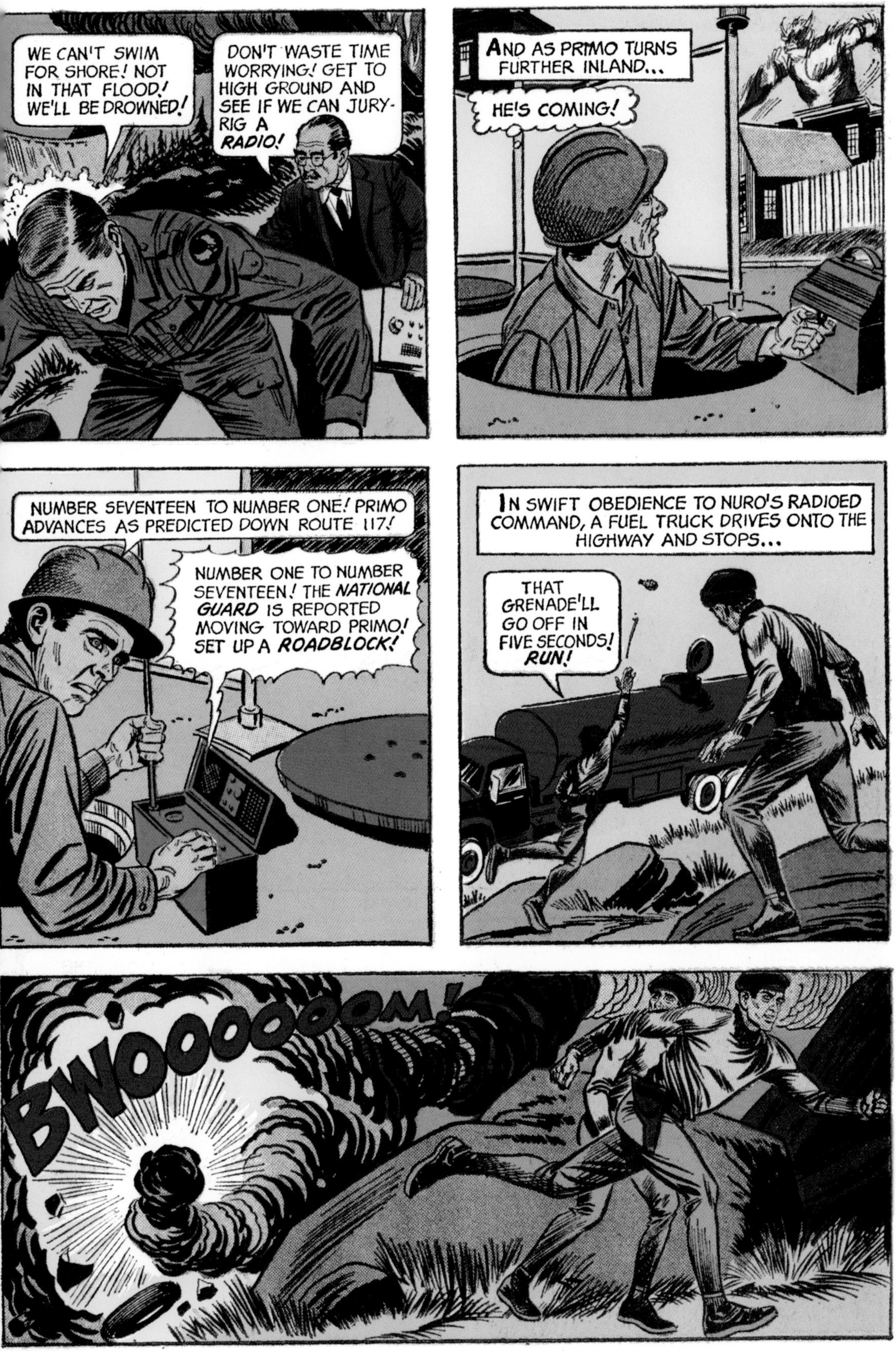
WE CAN'T SWIM FOR SHORE! NOT IN THAT FLOOD! WE'LL BE DROWNED!
DON'T WASTE TIME WORRYING! GET TO HIGH GROUND AND SEE IF WE CAN JURY-RIG A RADIO!
AND AS PRIMO TURNS FURTHER INLAND...
HE'S COMING!
NUMBER SEVENTEEN TO NUMBER ONE! PRIMO ADVANCES AS PREDICTED DOWN ROUTE 117!
NUMBER ONE TO NUMBER SEVENTEEN! THE NATIONAL GUARD IS REPORTED MOVING TOWARD PRIMO! SET UP A ROADBLOCK!
IN SWIFT OBEDIENCE TO NURO'S RADIOED COMMAND, A FUEL TRUCK DRIVES ONTO THE HIGHWAY AND STOPS...
THAT GRENADE'LL GO OFF IN FIVE SECONDS! RUN!
BWOOOOOOOM!

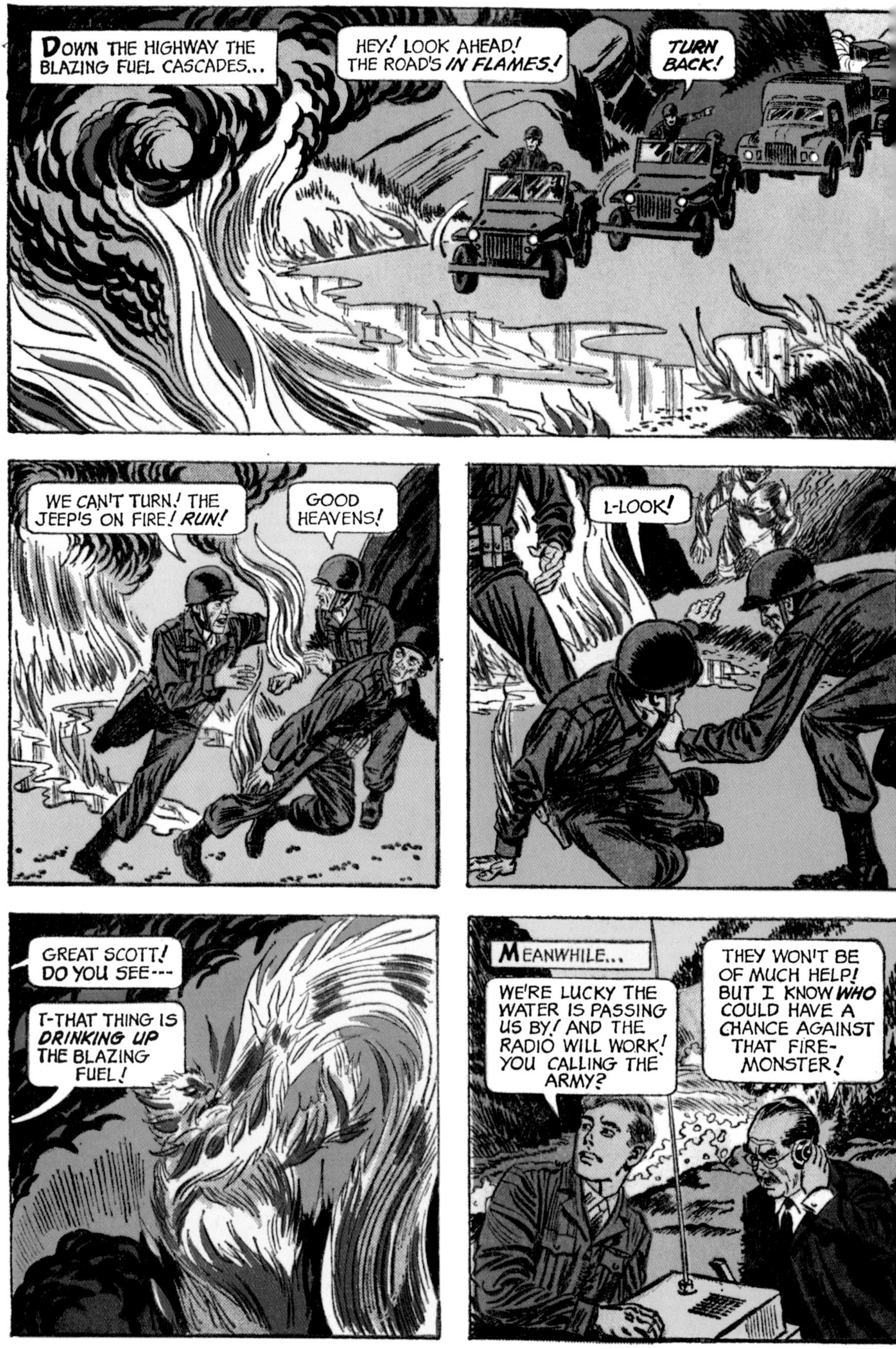
DOWN THE HIGHWAY THE BLAZING FUEL CASCADES...
HEY! LOOK AHEAD! THE ROAD'S *IN FLAMES!*
*TURN BACK!*
WE CAN'T TURN! THE JEEP'S ON FIRE! *RUN!*
GOOD HEAVENS!
L-LOOK!
GREAT SCOTT! DO YOU SEE---
T-THAT THING IS *DRINKING UP* THE BLAZING FUEL!
MEANWHILE...
WE'RE LUCKY THE WATER IS PASSING US BY! AND THE RADIO WILL WORK! YOU CALLING THE ARMY?
THEY WON'T BE OF MUCH HELP! BUT I KNOW *WHO* COULD HAVE A CHANCE AGAINST THAT FIRE-MONSTER!

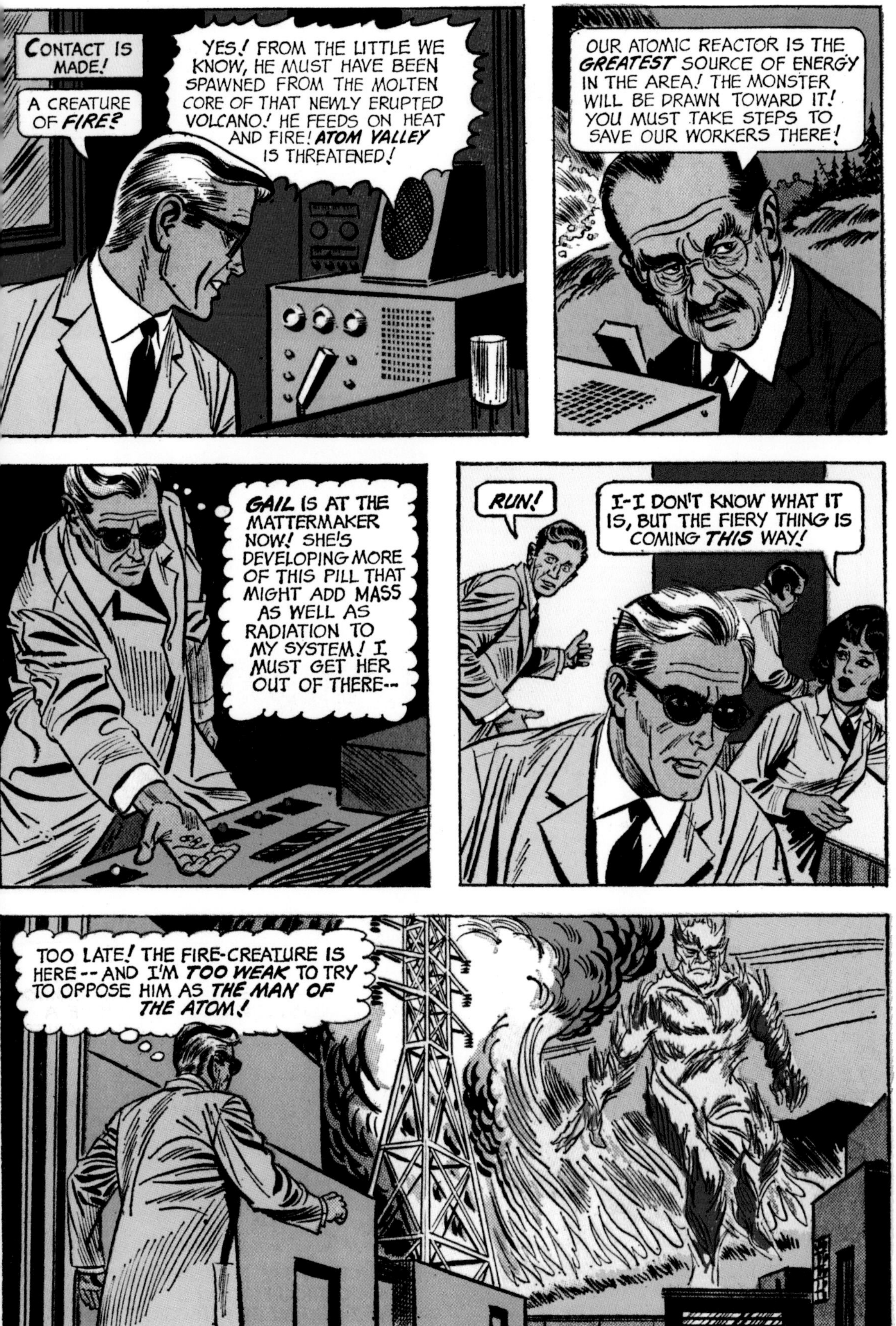

CONTACT IS MADE!
A CREATURE OF FIRE?
YES! FROM THE LITTLE WE KNOW, HE MUST HAVE BEEN SPAWNED FROM THE MOLTEN CORE OF THAT NEWLY ERUPTED VOLCANO! HE FEEDS ON HEAT AND FIRE! ATOM VALLEY IS THREATENED!
OUR ATOMIC REACTOR IS THE GREATEST SOURCE OF ENERGY IN THE AREA! THE MONSTER WILL BE DRAWN TOWARD IT! YOU MUST TAKE STEPS TO SAVE OUR WORKERS THERE!
GAIL IS AT THE MATTERMAKER NOW! SHE'S DEVELOPING MORE OF THIS PILL THAT MIGHT ADD MASS AS WELL AS RADIATION TO MY SYSTEM! I MUST GET HER OUT OF THERE--
RUN!
I-I DON'T KNOW WHAT IT IS, BUT THE FIERY THING IS COMING THIS WAY!
TOO LATE! THE FIRE-CREATURE IS HERE -- AND I'M TOO WEAK TO TRY TO OPPOSE HIM AS THE MAN OF THE ATOM!

DOCTOR SOLAR. PART II — DUEL TO DISINTEGRATION

PANIC GRIPS THE TOP SECRET NUCLEAR BASE, AS THE BLAZING FORM STALKS ONWARD! ONE FIGURE HESITATES, SEEKING A WAY TO COMBAT AND DEFEAT THE UNDEFEATABLE! DR. SOLAR STAYS, AS THE SEARING HEAT STRIKES THE BASE IN WITHERING WAVES! ONLY AS THE MAN OF THE ATOM CAN HE RISK COMBAT, BUT THEN, HE KNOWS HE WILL FIGHT WITH ONLY HALF HIS POWERS... AND IS EVEN HIS FULL STRENGTH ENOUGH TO DEFEAT NURO'S DESTRUCTIVE MASTERPIECE?

HE'LL REACH THE REACTOR BUILDING BEFORE I CAN! BUT MY BEST HOPE ISN'T THERE-- IT'S GETTING TO THE ENERGY-MATTER CONVERTER! AND THAT MEANS LEAVING GAIL IN THE REACTOR CHAMBER!

THESE NEW PILLS GAIL STARTED TO MAKE UP FOR ME WILL INCREASE MY MASS, BUT WHAT HAPPENS IF I CONVERT THEIR MATTER INTO ENERGY? WILL THAT GIVE ME MASS *AND* POWER, TOO?

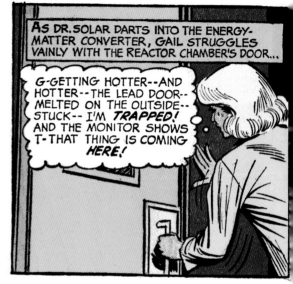

AS DR. SOLAR DARTS INTO THE ENERGY-MATTER CONVERTER, GAIL STRUGGLES VAINLY WITH THE REACTOR CHAMBER'S DOOR...

G-GETTING HOTTER--AND HOTTER--THE LEAD DOOR-- MELTED ON THE OUTSIDE-- STUCK-- I'M *TRAPPED!* AND THE MONITOR SHOWS T-THAT THING IS COMING *HERE!*

WITH DESPERATE SPEED, DR. SOLAR WORKS...

THERE! PART OF THEIR MASS IS BEING CHANGED INTO ENERGY!

BUT JUST *HOW* THESE NEW PILLS WILL HELP OR CHANGE MY IMBALANCE REMAINS TO BE SEEN.!--I'LL TAKE ONE FOR A START!

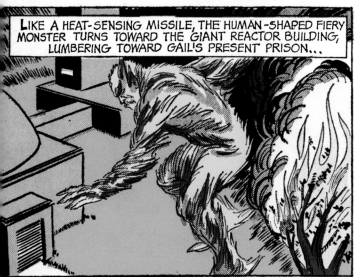

LIKE A HEAT-SENSING MISSILE, THE HUMAN-SHAPED FIERY MONSTER TURNS TOWARD THE GIANT REACTOR BUILDING, LUMBERING TOWARD GAIL'S PRESENT PRISON...

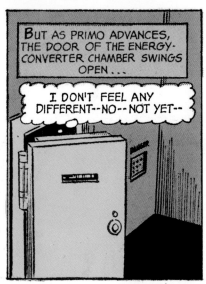

BUT AS PRIMO ADVANCES, THE DOOR OF THE ENERGY-CONVERTER CHAMBER SWINGS OPEN ...

I DON'T FEEL ANY DIFFERENT--NO--NOT YET--

THEN, SUDDENLY, AS THE MAN OF THE ATOM EMERGES, HE BEGINS TO GROW AND GROW...

NOW THE MASS-ADDITIVE IS WORKING! BUT IT'S INCREASING MY *SIZE!*

INSTINCTIVELY, PRIMO TURNS...

OF COURSE, HE SWUNG TOWARD ME! NOW *I* AM A GREATER SOURCE OF *HEAT* THAN THE CLOSED REACTOR CHAMBER!

ELSEWHERE...

IF MY PLAN IS CONTINUING TO RUN IDEALLY, BY NOW PRIMO SHOULD HAVE LOCATED *THE MAN OF THE ATOM!* AND ONCE HE DOES, THE MEDDLING OF THAT ATOMIC ANNOYANCE WILL *END!*

THE BLAZING CREATURE'S HANDS WHIRL FORWARD! FIREBALLS SPIN TOWARD THE ONCOMING MAN OF THE ATOM...

ONE THING CAN STOP FIRE--

*ICE!* AND THAT IS AN EASY ENERGY CHANGE FOR ME TO MAKE!

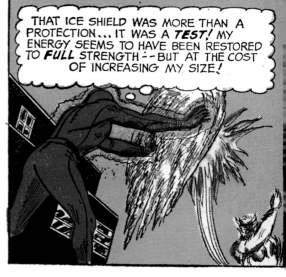

THAT ICE SHIELD WAS MORE THAN A PROTECTION... IT WAS A *TEST!* MY ENERGY SEEMS TO HAVE BEEN RESTORED TO *FULL* STRENGTH -- BUT AT THE COST OF INCREASING MY SIZE!

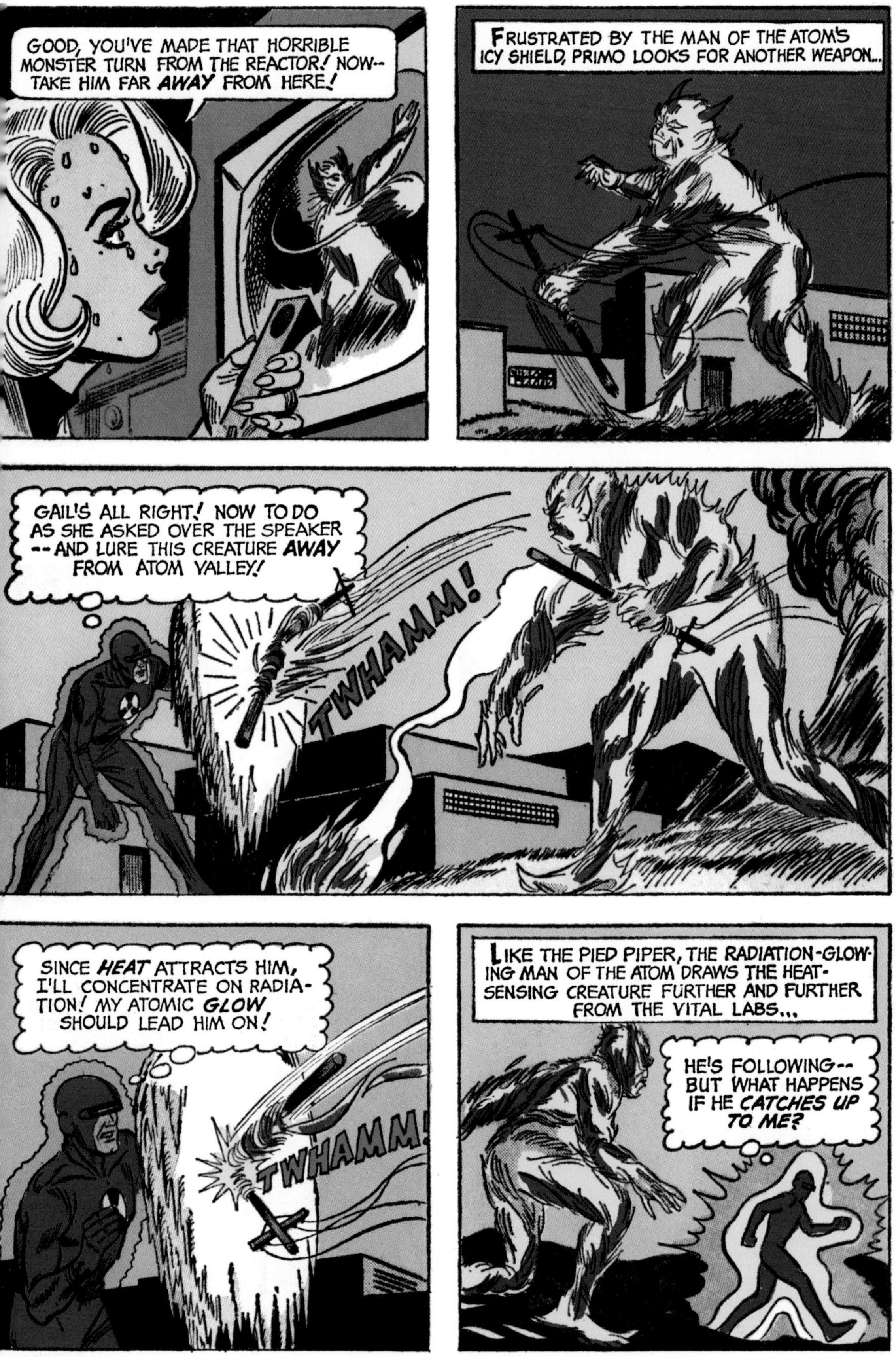
GOOD, YOU'VE MADE THAT HORRIBLE MONSTER TURN FROM THE REACTOR! NOW-- TAKE HIM FAR AWAY FROM HERE!
FRUSTRATED BY THE MAN OF THE ATOM'S ICY SHIELD, PRIMO LOOKS FOR ANOTHER WEAPON...
GAIL'S ALL RIGHT! NOW TO DO AS SHE ASKED OVER THE SPEAKER --AND LURE THIS CREATURE AWAY FROM ATOM VALLEY!
TWHAMM!
SINCE HEAT ATTRACTS HIM, I'LL CONCENTRATE ON RADIATION! MY ATOMIC GLOW SHOULD LEAD HIM ON!
TWHAMM!
LIKE THE PIED PIPER, THE RADIATION-GLOWING MAN OF THE ATOM DRAWS THE HEAT-SENSING CREATURE FURTHER AND FURTHER FROM THE VITAL LABS...
HE'S FOLLOWING-- BUT WHAT HAPPENS IF HE CATCHES UP TO ME?

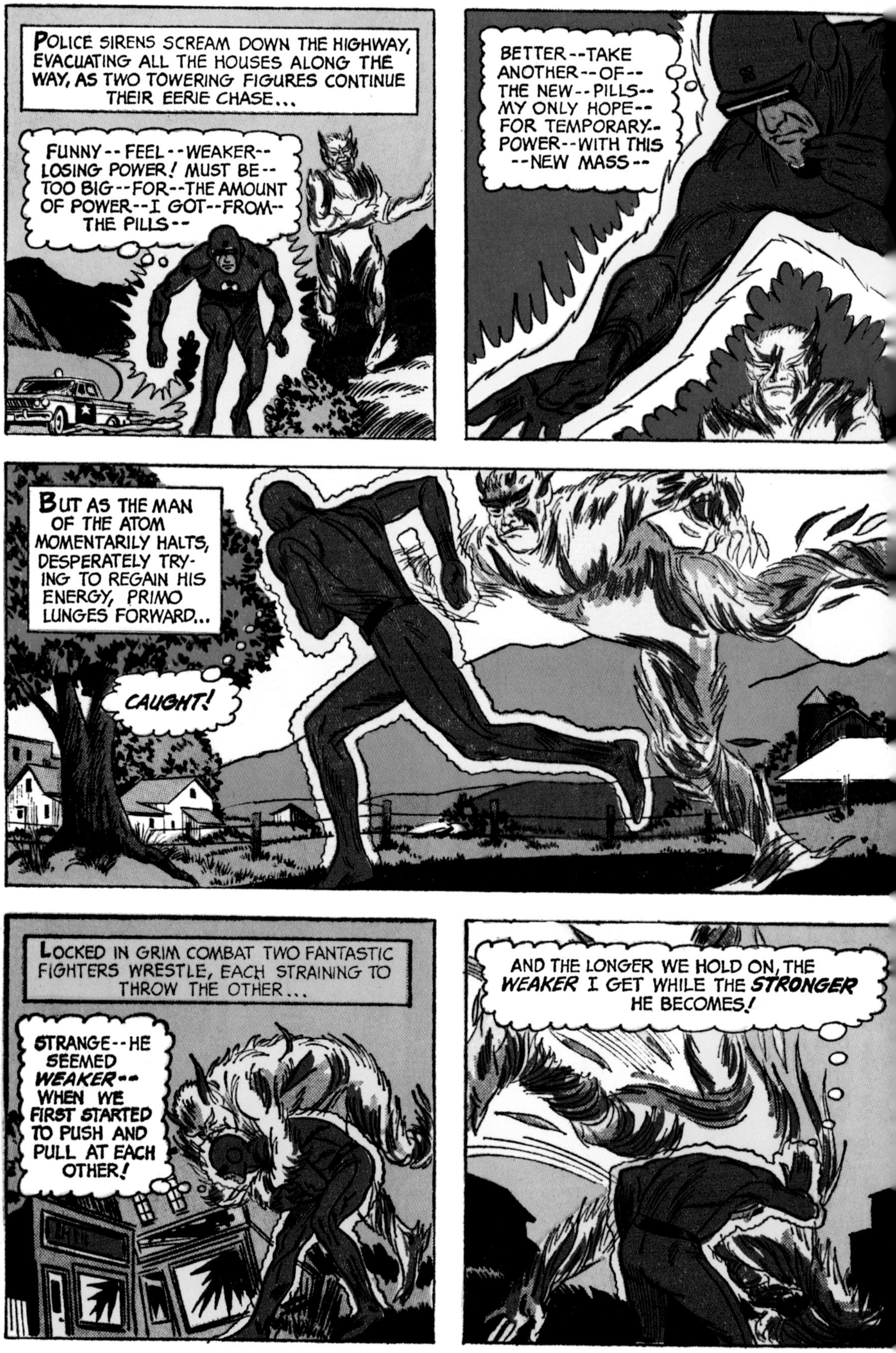
POLICE SIRENS SCREAM DOWN THE HIGHWAY, EVACUATING ALL THE HOUSES ALONG THE WAY, AS TWO TOWERING FIGURES CONTINUE THEIR EERIE CHASE...
FUNNY--FEEL--WEAKER--LOSING POWER! MUST BE--TOO BIG--FOR--THE AMOUNT OF POWER--I GOT--FROM--THE PILLS--
BETTER--TAKE ANOTHER--OF--THE NEW--PILLS--MY ONLY HOPE--FOR TEMPORARY--POWER--WITH THIS--NEW MASS--
BUT AS THE MAN OF THE ATOM MOMENTARILY HALTS, DESPERATELY TRYING TO REGAIN HIS ENERGY, PRIMO LUNGES FORWARD...
CAUGHT!
LOCKED IN GRIM COMBAT TWO FANTASTIC FIGHTERS WRESTLE, EACH STRAINING TO THROW THE OTHER...
STRANGE--HE SEEMED WEAKER--WHEN WE FIRST STARTED TO PUSH AND PULL AT EACH OTHER!
AND THE LONGER WE HOLD ON, THE WEAKER I GET WHILE THE STRONGER HE BECOMES!

OF COURSE! THAT'S WHY HE IS DRAWN TO HEAT--CONTACT WITH HEAT, THE SOURCE OF HIS OWN BIRTH, **STRENGTHENS** HIM! AND RIGHT NOW, WHILE HE HOLDS ME, *I* AM STRENGTHENING HIM!

WITH A FIERCE, FINAL EFFORT, THE MAN OF THE ATOM BREAKS FREE...

THERE! AND I KNOW ONE THING THAT ENDS FIRE--**WATER!**

CONCENTRATING DEEPLY, THE MAN OF THE ATOM CHANGES HIS ENERGY INTO A PULSATING MAGNETIC FORCE, AS HE RACES FOR THE CLOUDS OVERHEAD...

THEN, WEAVING FROM CLOUD TO CLOUD, HE FLASHES ABOVE...

ONE POSITIVELY CHARGED--THE OTHER NEGATIVELY! NOW, NATURE WILL DO THE REST!

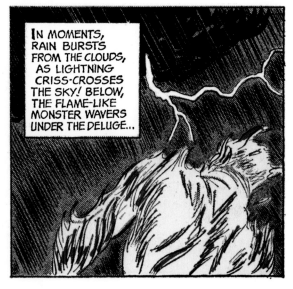

IN MOMENTS, RAIN BURSTS FROM THE CLOUDS, AS LIGHTNING CRISS-CROSSES THE SKY! BELOW, THE FLAME-LIKE MONSTER WAVERS UNDER THE DELUGE...

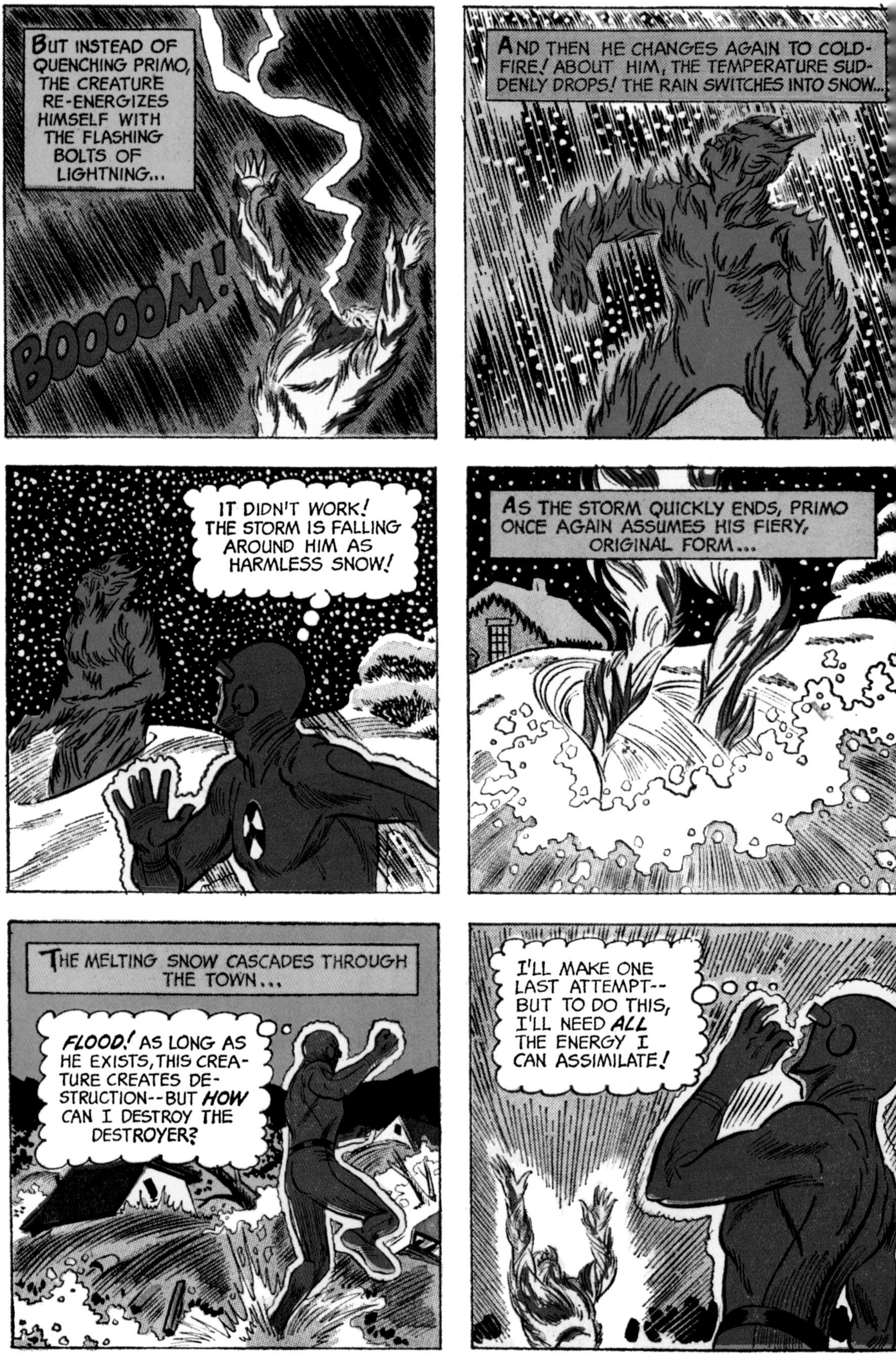
BUT INSTEAD OF QUENCHING PRIMO, THE CREATURE RE-ENERGIZES HIMSELF WITH THE FLASHING BOLTS OF LIGHTNING...
BOOOOOM!
AND THEN HE CHANGES AGAIN TO COLD-FIRE! ABOUT HIM, THE TEMPERATURE SUDDENLY DROPS! THE RAIN SWITCHES INTO SNOW...
IT DIDN'T WORK! THE STORM IS FALLING AROUND HIM AS HARMLESS SNOW!
AS THE STORM QUICKLY ENDS, PRIMO ONCE AGAIN ASSUMES HIS FIERY, ORIGINAL FORM...
THE MELTING SNOW CASCADES THROUGH THE TOWN...
FLOOD! AS LONG AS HE EXISTS, THIS CREATURE CREATES DESTRUCTION--BUT HOW CAN I DESTROY THE DESTROYER?
I'LL MAKE ONE LAST ATTEMPT--BUT TO DO THIS, I'LL NEED ALL THE ENERGY I CAN ASSIMILATE!

CONCENTRATING, THE ASTOUNDING MAN OF THE ATOM ONCE AGAIN CONVERTS HIMSELF TO ANOTHER FORM OF NUCLEAR ENERGY-- THAT OF A WHIRLWIND FORCE...

FASTER AND FASTER, THE MAN OF THE ATOM SPINS ABOUT THE FIERY MONSTER! AND AS HE WHIRLS, HE SETS UP AN ELECTRICAL FIELD AROUND PRIMO...

THE ELECTRIC FIELD SUDDENLY SPLITS OXYGEN LOOSE FROM THE SURROUNDING AIR...

AS THE NASCENT OXYGEN COMBINES WITH PRIMO, THE GIANT VOLCANIC CREATURE BEGINS BURNING FASTER AND FASTER...

AT LAST! ONE WAY TO DEFEAT FIRE IS TO HELP IT *BURN ITSELF OUT!*

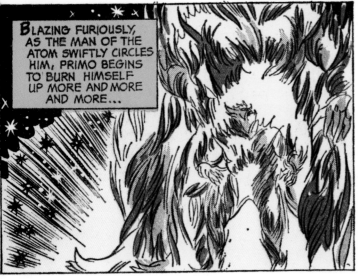

BLAZING FURIOUSLY, AS THE MAN OF THE ATOM SWIFTLY CIRCLES HIM, PRIMO BEGINS TO BURN HIMSELF UP MORE AND MORE AND MORE...

TILL FINALLY...

POOOOOOF!

GONE! BURNED OUT!--AND I--WHY THIS ACTION, REDUCED MY SIZE! BUT DID IT ALSO REDUCE MY STRENGTH?
LATER...
RATEMETER READING CHECKS OUT--YOUR FULL RADIATION ENERGY COMPONENT HAS BEEN REACHED!
GAIL'S ADDITIVE PILLS MUST HAVE HELPED DO THE TRICK! THEY INCREASED YOUR MASS SO YOU COULD RETAIN A GREATER RADIATION CHARGE!
BUT THEY ALSO GREATLY INCREASED HIS SIZE!
TRUE, BUT WHOEVER CREATED THAT CREATURE FROM THE DEPTHS OF A VOLCANO HELPED ME! IN FIGHTING THAT MOLTEN MONSTER, MY SYSTEM WAS RESTORED TO ITS CORRECT BALANCE WHEN I REDUCED MY SIZE! BUT I STILL HAVE TO LEARN WHO I HAVE TO THANK--AND FEAR!

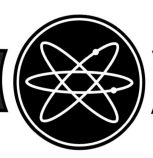

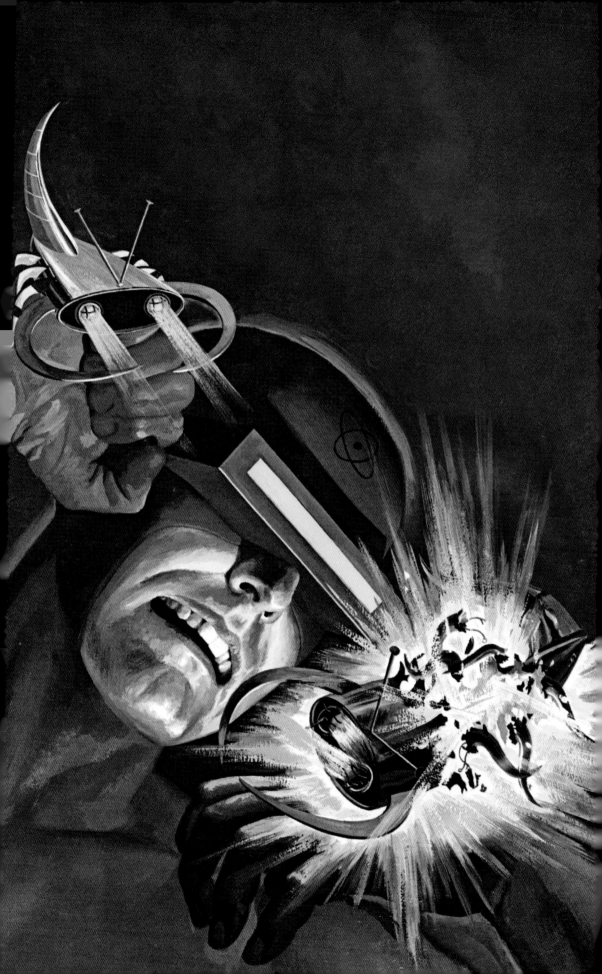

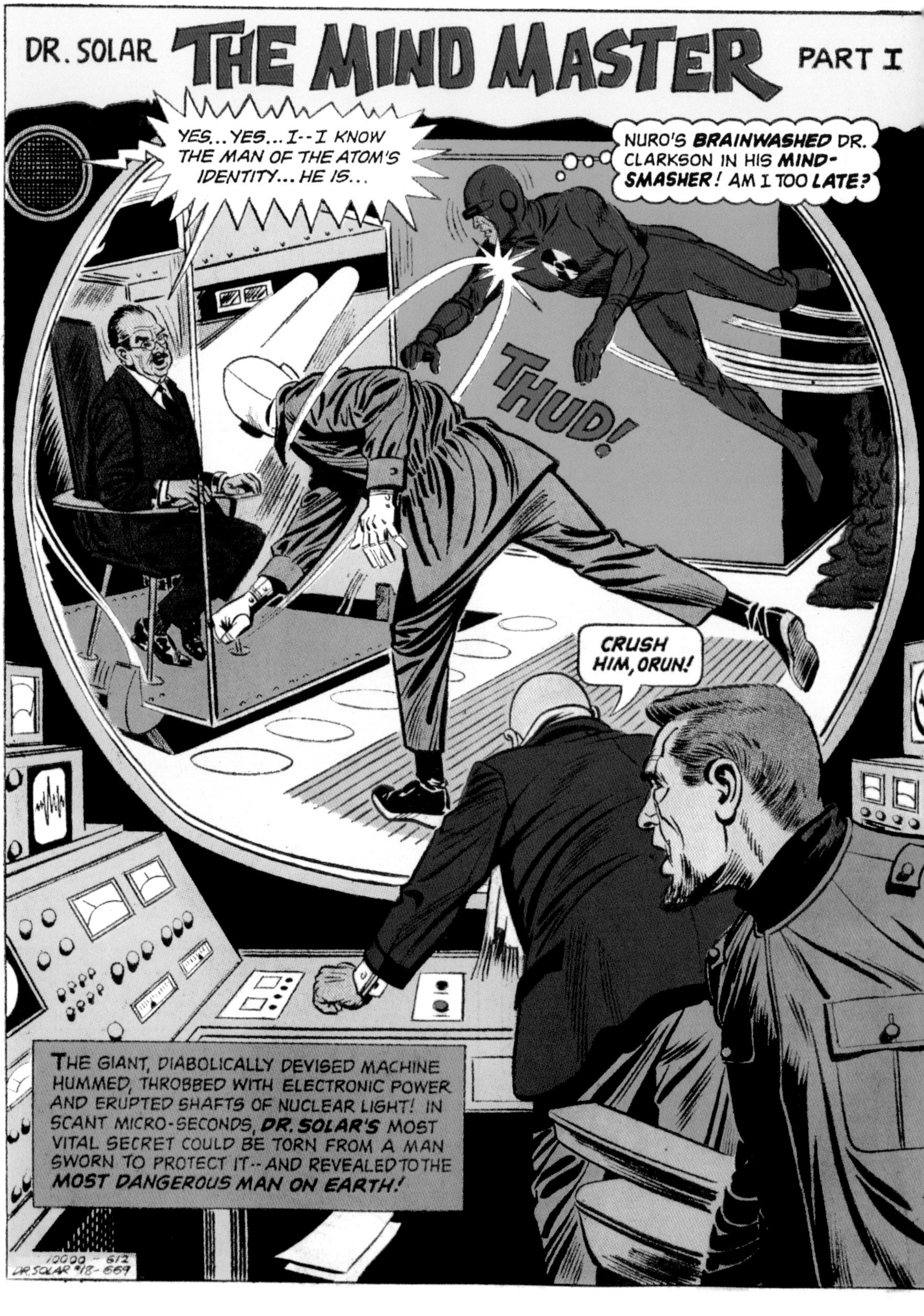
DR. SOLAR
THE MIND MASTER
PART I
YES... YES... I--I KNOW THE MAN OF THE ATOM'S IDENTITY... HE IS...
NURO'S BRAINWASHED DR. CLARKSON IN HIS MIND-SMASHER! AM I TOO LATE?
THUD!
CRUSH HIM, ORUN!
THE GIANT, DIABOLICALLY DEVISED MACHINE HUMMED, THROBBED WITH ELECTRONIC POWER AND ERUPTED SHAFTS OF NUCLEAR LIGHT! IN SCANT MICRO-SECONDS, DR. SOLAR'S MOST VITAL SECRET COULD BE TORN FROM A MAN SWORN TO PROTECT IT-- AND REVEALED TO THE MOST DANGEROUS MAN ON EARTH!
10000 - 612
DR. SOLAR #18 - 669

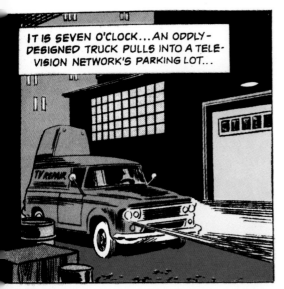

IT IS SEVEN O'CLOCK...AN ODDLY-DESIGNED TRUCK PULLS INTO A TELEVISION NETWORK'S PARKING LOT...

A SLIDING PANEL OPENS... AND A STRANGE FIGURE STEPS INTO THE SHADOWS OF A FIRE ESCAPE...

HE MOUNTS TO AN UPPER WINDOW AND BENDS THE WINDOW BARS OF A STORAGE ROOM LIKE SOFT TAFFY...

CREEAAK!

INSIDE, THE FORM MOVES WITH MECHANICAL GRACE TO A SPECIAL SECTION OF THE WALL... HE REMOVES A GLOVE AND HIS FINGERS CLOSE IN A CONE...

CLICK! CLICK!

AND AT THE WRIST, HIS FIST REVOLVES TEN TIMES A SECOND...

WHRRRRRRRR!

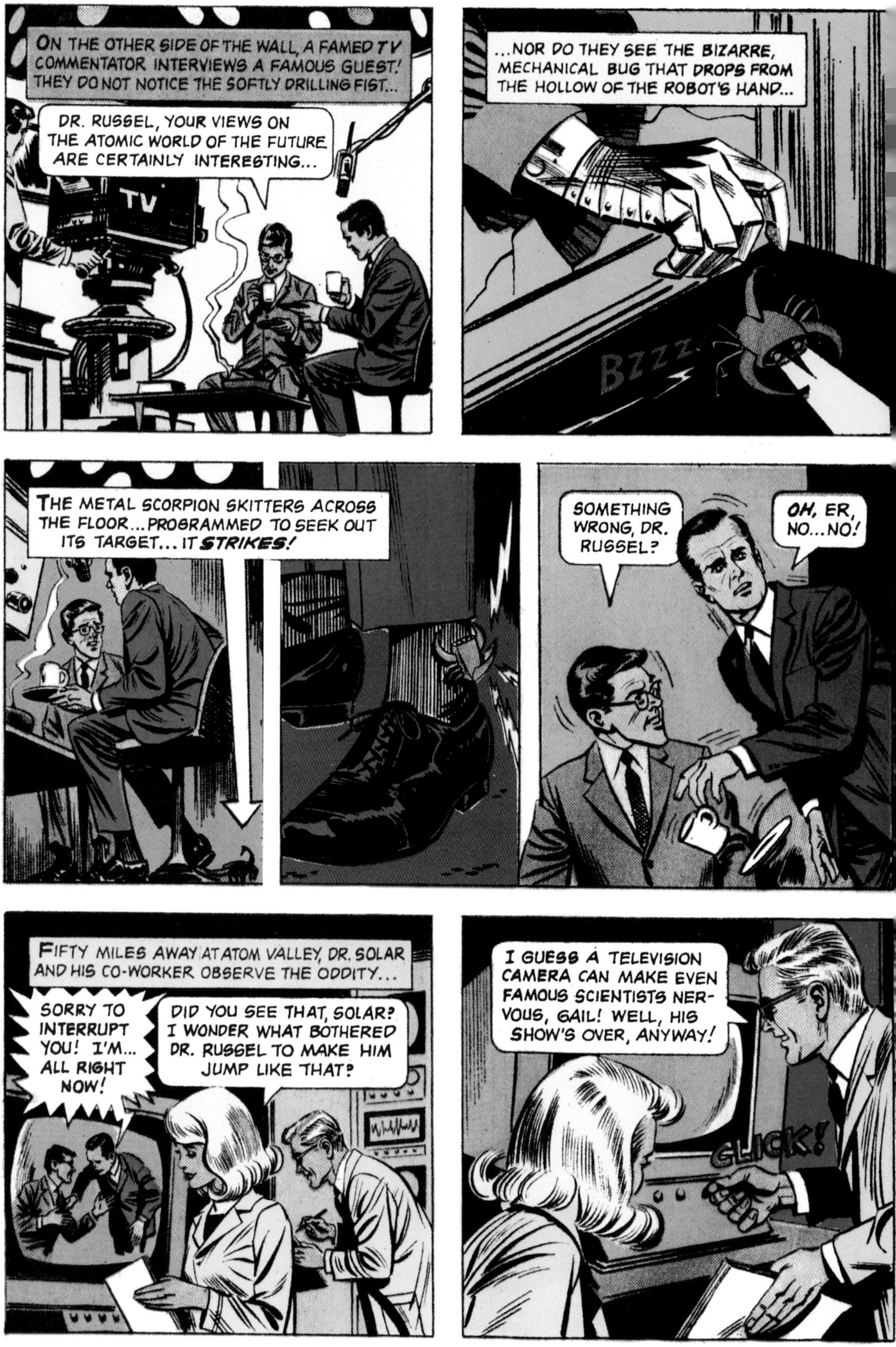
ON THE OTHER SIDE OF THE WALL, A FAMED TV COMMENTATOR INTERVIEWS A FAMOUS GUEST! THEY DO NOT NOTICE THE SOFTLY DRILLING FIST...
DR. RUSSEL, YOUR VIEWS ON THE ATOMIC WORLD OF THE FUTURE ARE CERTAINLY INTERESTING...
TV
...NOR DO THEY SEE THE BIZARRE, MECHANICAL BUG THAT DROPS FROM THE HOLLOW OF THE ROBOT'S HAND...
BZZZ
THE METAL SCORPION SKITTERS ACROSS THE FLOOR...PROGRAMMED TO SEEK OUT ITS TARGET... IT STRIKES!
SOMETHING WRONG, DR. RUSSEL?
OH, ER, NO...NO!
FIFTY MILES AWAY AT ATOM VALLEY, DR. SOLAR AND HIS CO-WORKER OBSERVE THE ODDITY...
SORRY TO INTERRUPT YOU! I'M... ALL RIGHT NOW!
DID YOU SEE THAT, SOLAR? I WONDER WHAT BOTHERED DR. RUSSEL TO MAKE HIM JUMP LIKE THAT?
I GUESS A TELEVISION CAMERA CAN MAKE EVEN FAMOUS SCIENTISTS NERVOUS, GAIL! WELL, HIS SHOW'S OVER, ANYWAY!
CLICK!

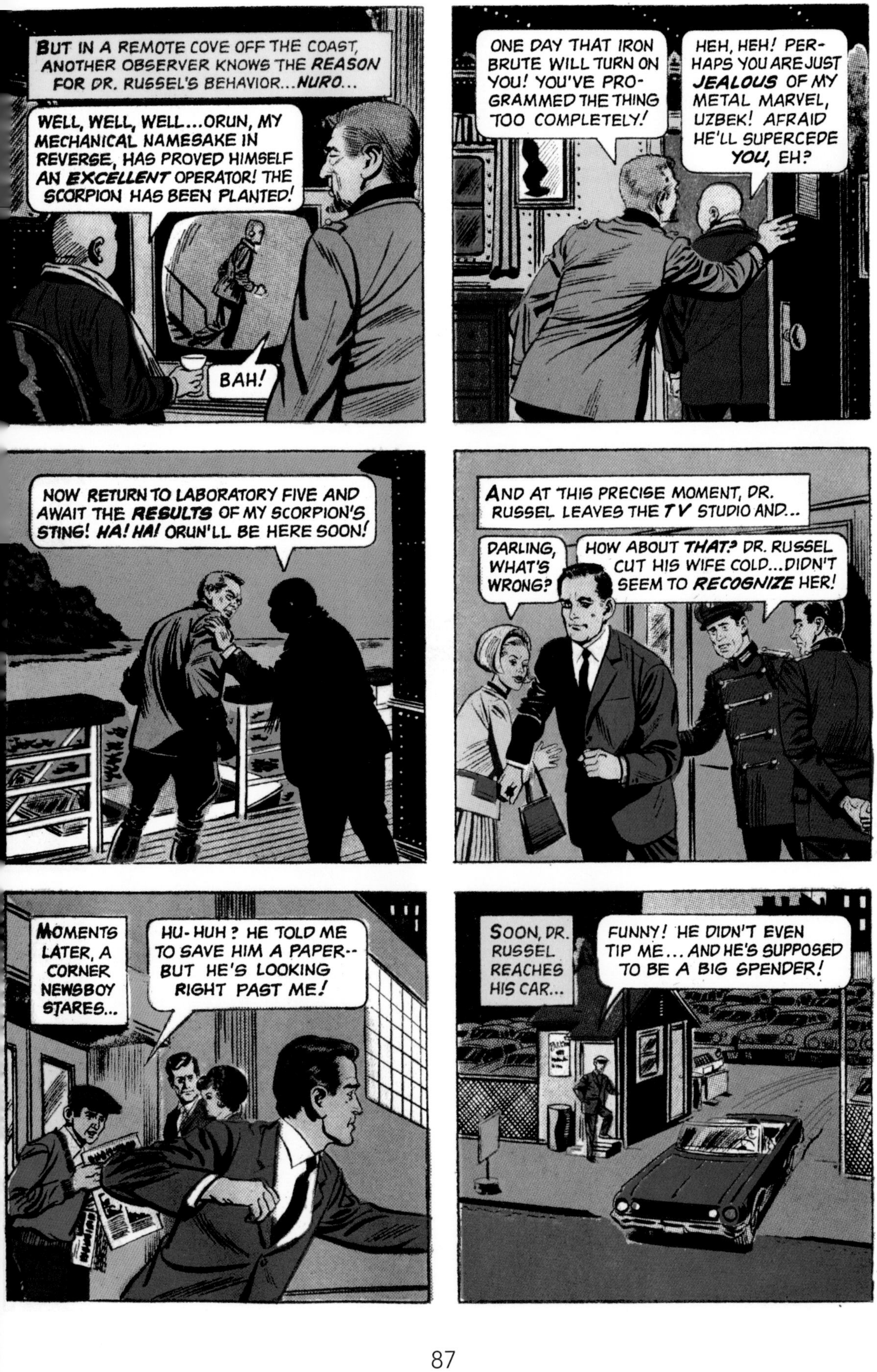
BUT IN A REMOTE COVE OFF THE COAST, ANOTHER OBSERVER KNOWS THE REASON FOR DR. RUSSEL'S BEHAVIOR...NURO...
WELL, WELL, WELL...ORUN, MY MECHANICAL NAMESAKE IN REVERSE, HAS PROVED HIMSELF AN EXCELLENT OPERATOR! THE SCORPION HAS BEEN PLANTED!
BAH!
ONE DAY THAT IRON BRUTE WILL TURN ON YOU! YOU'VE PROGRAMMED THE THING TOO COMPLETELY!
HEH, HEH! PERHAPS YOU ARE JUST JEALOUS OF MY METAL MARVEL, UZBEK! AFRAID HE'LL SUPERCEDE YOU, EH?
NOW RETURN TO LABORATORY FIVE AND AWAIT THE RESULTS OF MY SCORPION'S STING! HA! HA! ORUN'LL BE HERE SOON!
AND AT THIS PRECISE MOMENT, DR. RUSSEL LEAVES THE TV STUDIO AND...
DARLING, WHAT'S WRONG?
HOW ABOUT THAT? DR. RUSSEL CUT HIS WIFE COLD...DIDN'T SEEM TO RECOGNIZE HER!
MOMENTS LATER, A CORNER NEWSBOY STARES...
HU-HUH? HE TOLD ME TO SAVE HIM A PAPER-- BUT HE'S LOOKING RIGHT PAST ME!
SOON, DR. RUSSEL REACHES HIS CAR...
FUNNY! HE DIDN'T EVEN TIP ME... AND HE'S SUPPOSED TO BE A BIG SPENDER!

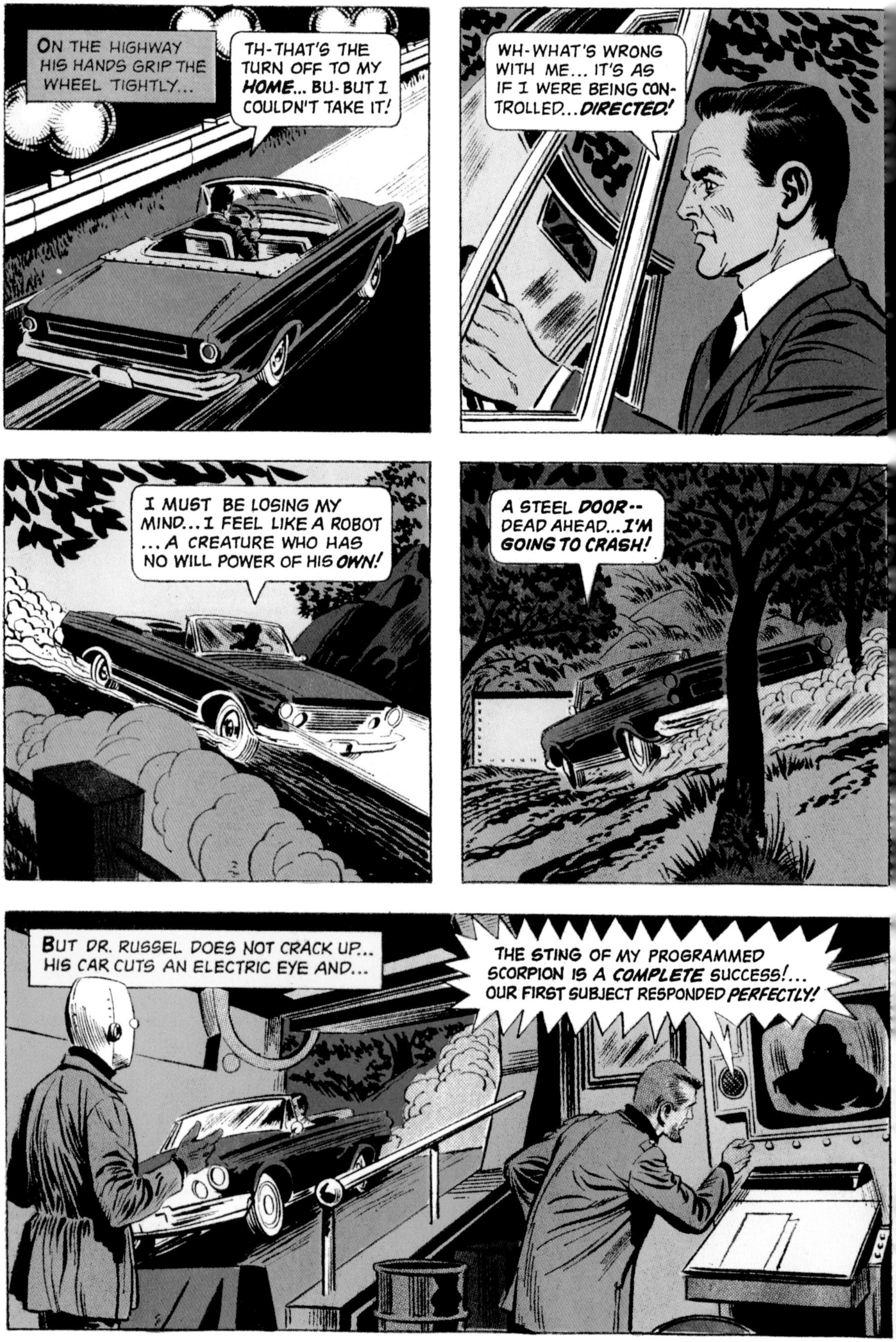

ON THE HIGHWAY HIS HANDS GRIP THE WHEEL TIGHTLY...
TH-THAT'S THE TURN OFF TO MY HOME... BU-BUT I COULDN'T TAKE IT!
WH-WHAT'S WRONG WITH ME... IT'S AS IF I WERE BEING CONTROLLED... DIRECTED!
I MUST BE LOSING MY MIND... I FEEL LIKE A ROBOT ...A CREATURE WHO HAS NO WILL POWER OF HIS OWN!
A STEEL DOOR-- DEAD AHEAD... I'M GOING TO CRASH!
BUT DR. RUSSEL DOES NOT CRACK UP... HIS CAR CUTS AN ELECTRIC EYE AND...
THE STING OF MY PROGRAMMED SCORPION IS A COMPLETE SUCCESS!... OUR FIRST SUBJECT RESPONDED PERFECTLY!

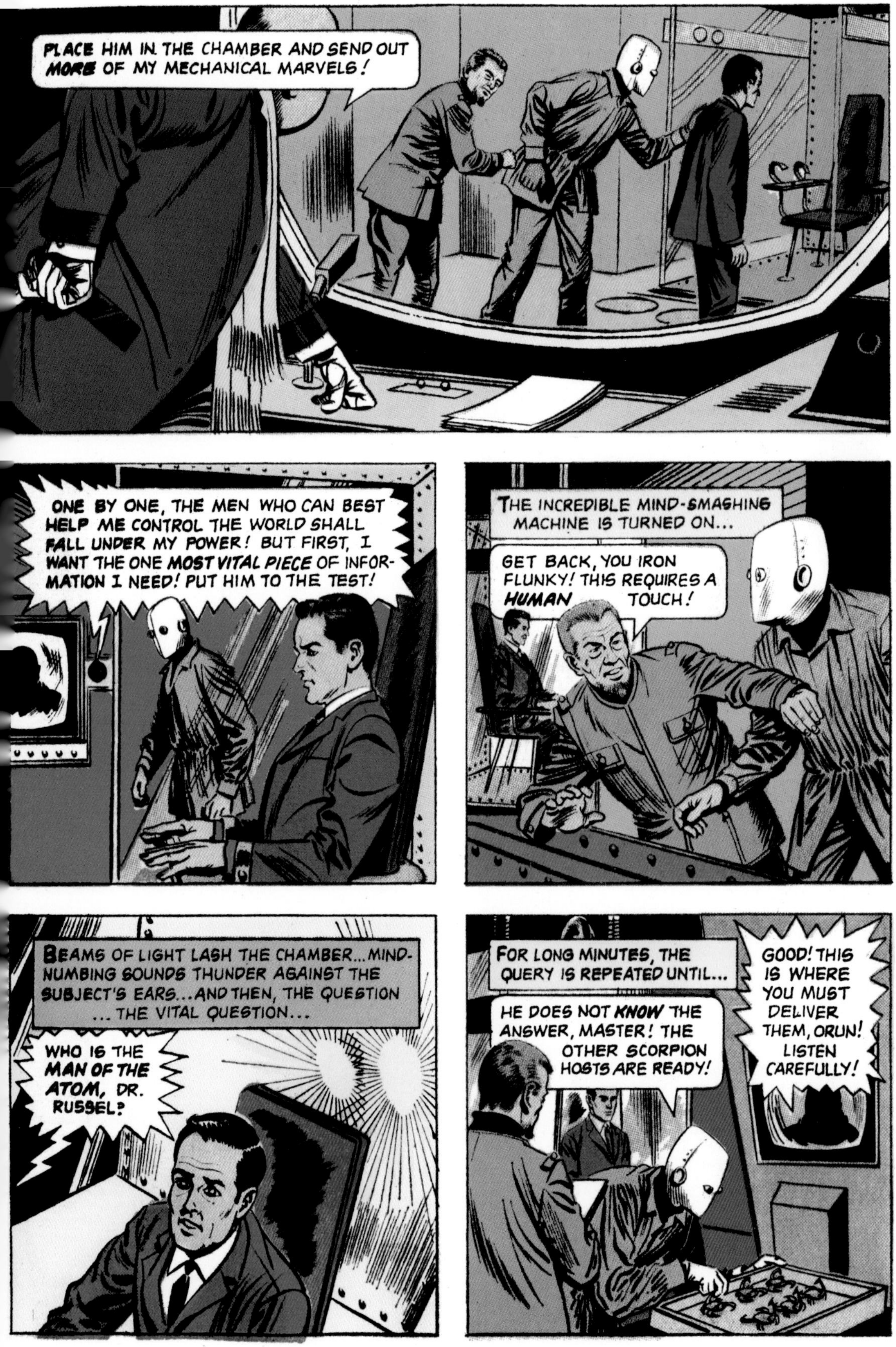
PLACE HIM IN THE CHAMBER AND SEND OUT MORE OF MY MECHANICAL MARVELS!
ONE BY ONE, THE MEN WHO CAN BEST HELP ME CONTROL THE WORLD SHALL FALL UNDER MY POWER! BUT FIRST, I WANT THE ONE MOST VITAL PIECE OF INFORMATION I NEED! PUT HIM TO THE TEST!
THE INCREDIBLE MIND-SMASHING MACHINE IS TURNED ON...
GET BACK, YOU IRON FLUNKY! THIS REQUIRES A HUMAN TOUCH!
BEAMS OF LIGHT LASH THE CHAMBER...MIND-NUMBING SOUNDS THUNDER AGAINST THE SUBJECT'S EARS...AND THEN, THE QUESTION ... THE VITAL QUESTION...
WHO IS THE MAN OF THE ATOM, DR. RUSSEL?
FOR LONG MINUTES, THE QUERY IS REPEATED UNTIL...
HE DOES NOT KNOW THE ANSWER, MASTER! THE OTHER SCORPION HOSTS ARE READY!
GOOD! THIS IS WHERE YOU MUST DELIVER THEM, ORUN! LISTEN CAREFULLY!

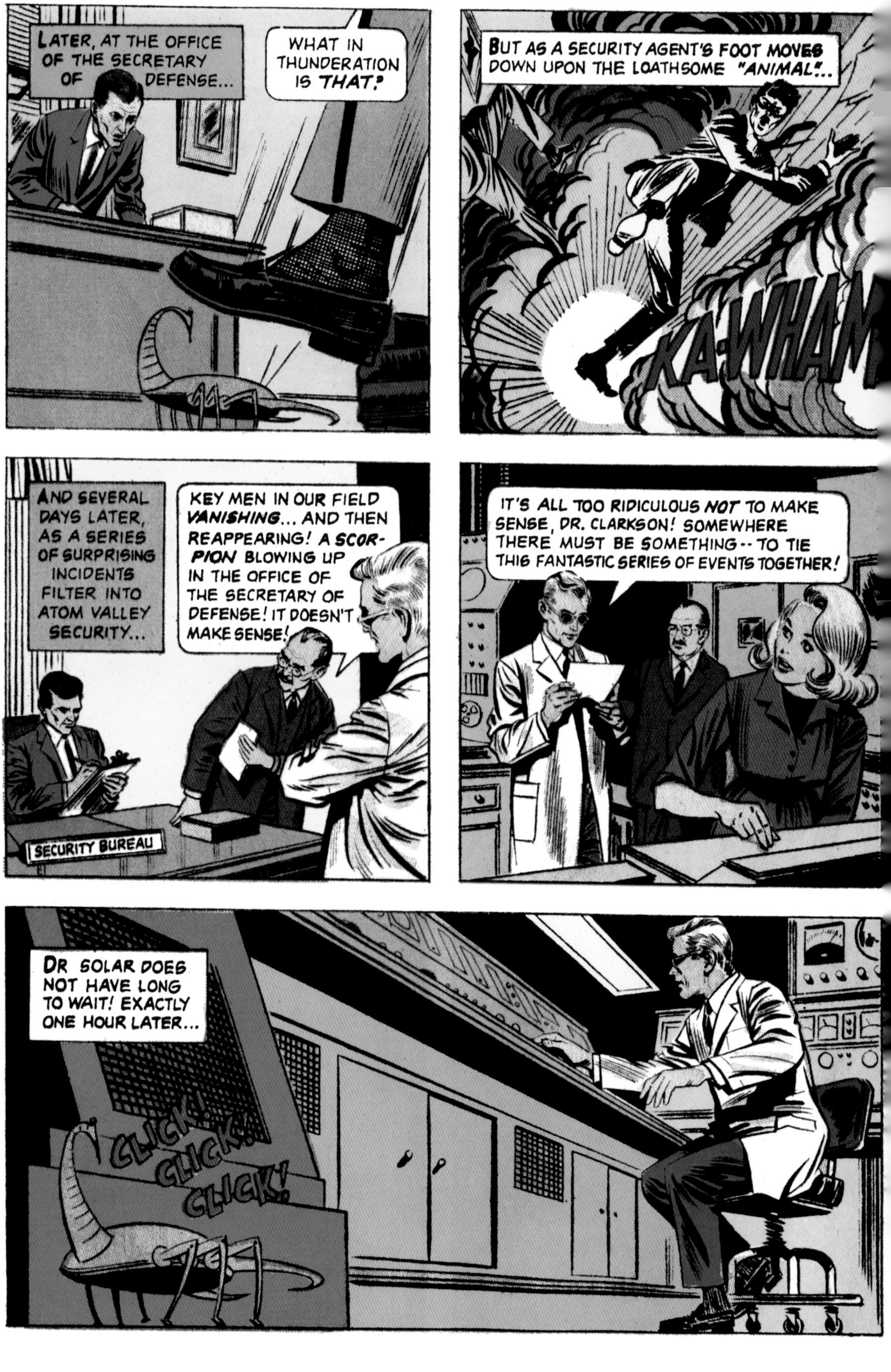

LATER, AT THE OFFICE OF THE SECRETARY OF DEFENSE...
WHAT IN THUNDERATION IS THAT?
BUT AS A SECURITY AGENT'S FOOT MOVES DOWN UPON THE LOATHSOME "ANIMAL"...
KA-WHAM
AND SEVERAL DAYS LATER, AS A SERIES OF SURPRISING INCIDENTS FILTER INTO ATOM VALLEY SECURITY...
KEY MEN IN OUR FIELD VANISHING... AND THEN REAPPEARING! A SCORPION BLOWING UP IN THE OFFICE OF THE SECRETARY OF DEFENSE! IT DOESN'T MAKE SENSE!
SECURITY BUREAU
IT'S ALL TOO RIDICULOUS NOT TO MAKE SENSE, DR. CLARKSON! SOMEWHERE THERE MUST BE SOMETHING -- TO TIE THIS FANTASTIC SERIES OF EVENTS TOGETHER!
DR SOLAR DOES NOT HAVE LONG TO WAIT! EXACTLY ONE HOUR LATER...
CLICK! CLICK! CLICK!

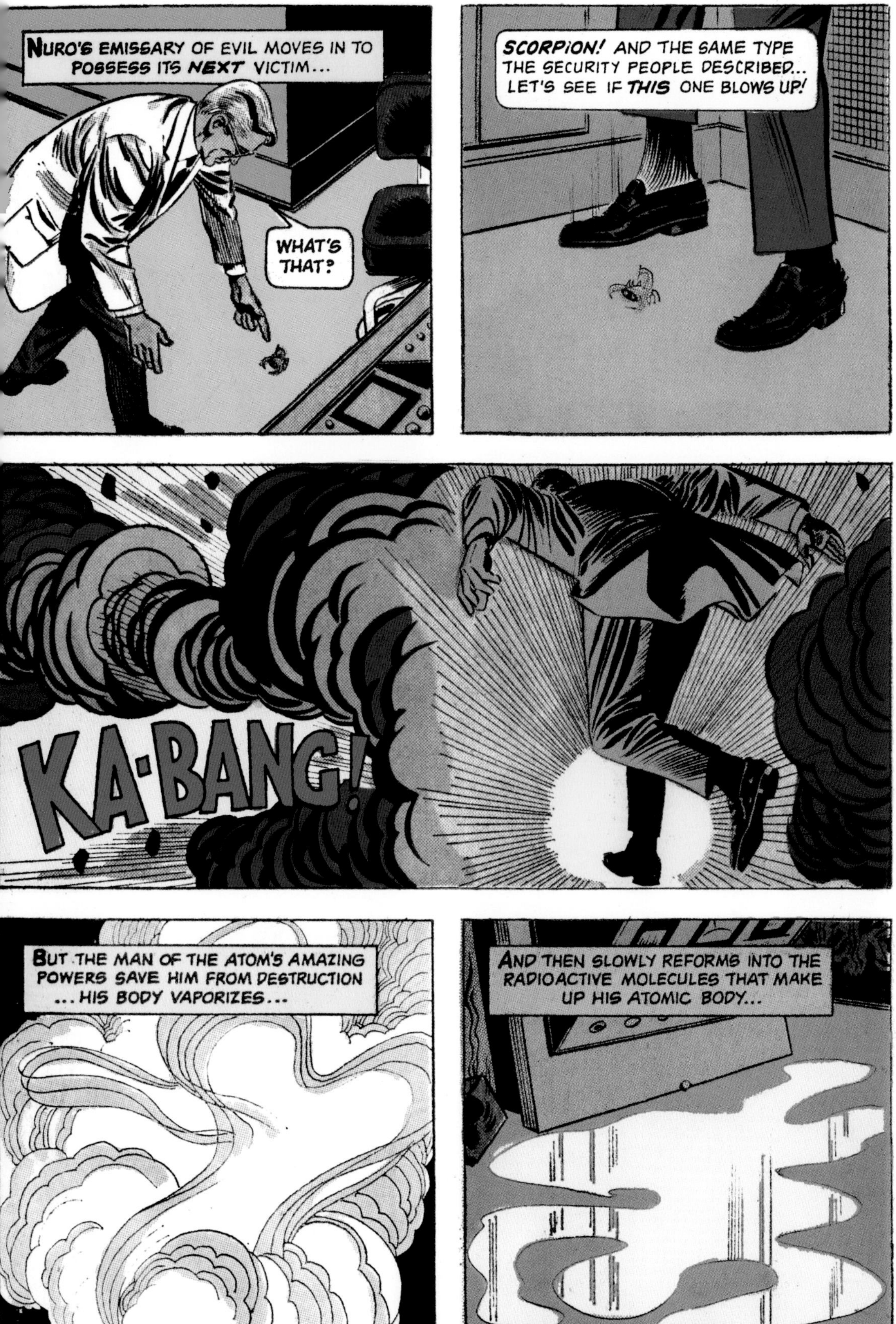
NURO'S EMISSARY OF EVIL MOVES IN TO POSSESS ITS NEXT VICTIM...
WHAT'S THAT?
SCORPION! AND THE SAME TYPE THE SECURITY PEOPLE DESCRIBED... LET'S SEE IF THIS ONE BLOWS UP!
KA-BANG!
BUT THE MAN OF THE ATOM'S AMAZING POWERS SAVE HIM FROM DESTRUCTION ...HIS BODY VAPORIZES...
AND THEN SLOWLY REFORMS INTO THE RADIOACTIVE MOLECULES THAT MAKE UP HIS ATOMIC BODY...

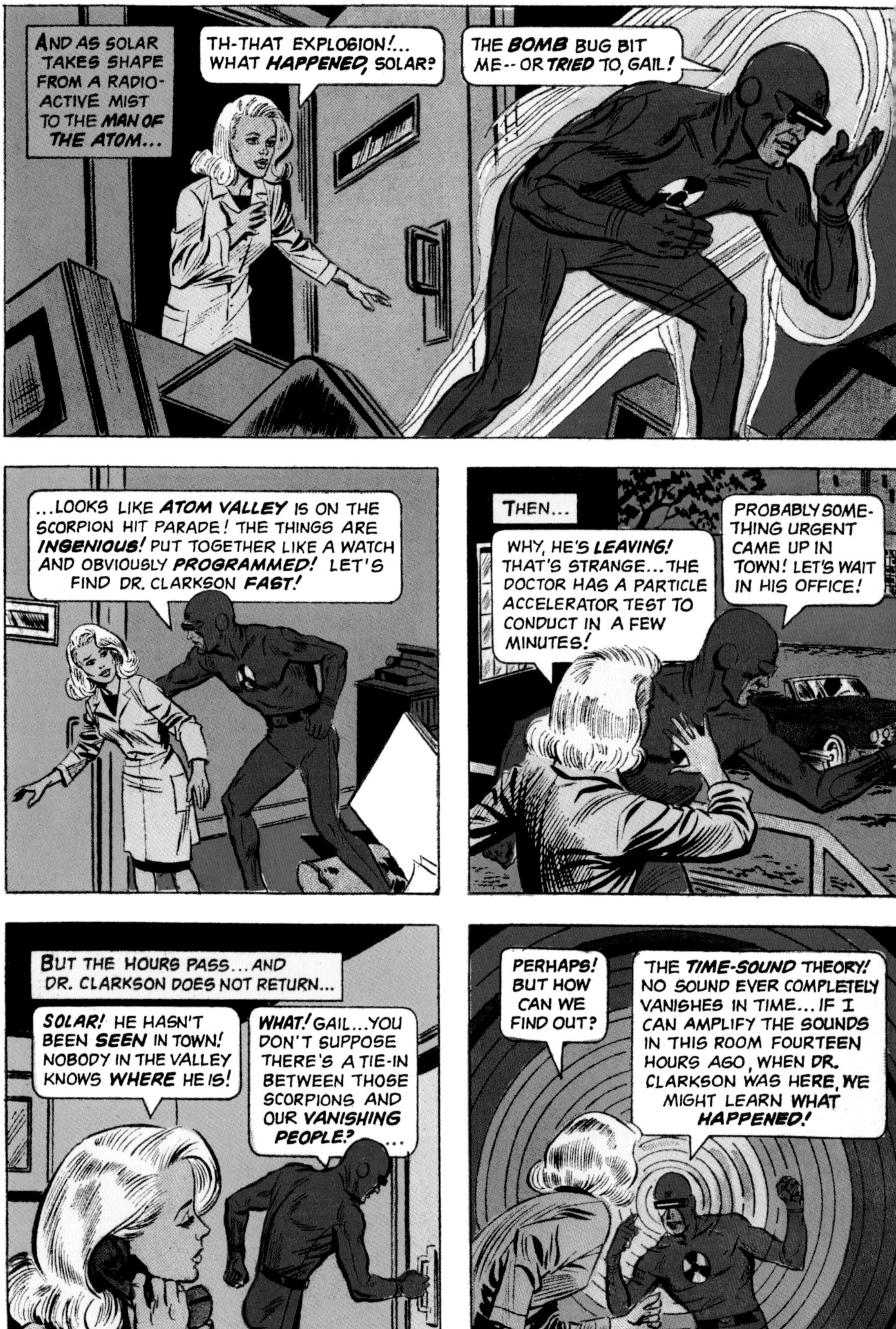
AND AS SOLAR TAKES SHAPE FROM A RADIO-ACTIVE MIST TO THE MAN OF THE ATOM...
TH-THAT EXPLOSION!... WHAT HAPPENED, SOLAR?
THE BOMB BUG BIT ME--OR TRIED TO, GAIL!
...LOOKS LIKE ATOM VALLEY IS ON THE SCORPION HIT PARADE! THE THINGS ARE INGENIOUS! PUT TOGETHER LIKE A WATCH AND OBVIOUSLY PROGRAMMED! LET'S FIND DR. CLARKSON FAST!
THEN...
WHY, HE'S LEAVING! THAT'S STRANGE...THE DOCTOR HAS A PARTICLE ACCELERATOR TEST TO CONDUCT IN A FEW MINUTES!
PROBABLY SOME-THING URGENT CAME UP IN TOWN! LET'S WAIT IN HIS OFFICE!
BUT THE HOURS PASS...AND DR. CLARKSON DOES NOT RETURN...
SOLAR! HE HASN'T BEEN SEEN IN TOWN! NOBODY IN THE VALLEY KNOWS WHERE HE IS!
WHAT! GAIL...YOU DON'T SUPPOSE THERE'S A TIE-IN BETWEEN THOSE SCORPIONS AND OUR VANISHING PEOPLE? ...
PERHAPS! BUT HOW CAN WE FIND OUT?
THE TIME-SOUND THEORY! NO SOUND EVER COMPLETELY VANISHES IN TIME...IF I CAN AMPLIFY THE SOUNDS IN THIS ROOM FOURTEEN HOURS AGO, WHEN DR. CLARKSON WAS HERE, WE MIGHT LEARN WHAT HAPPENED!

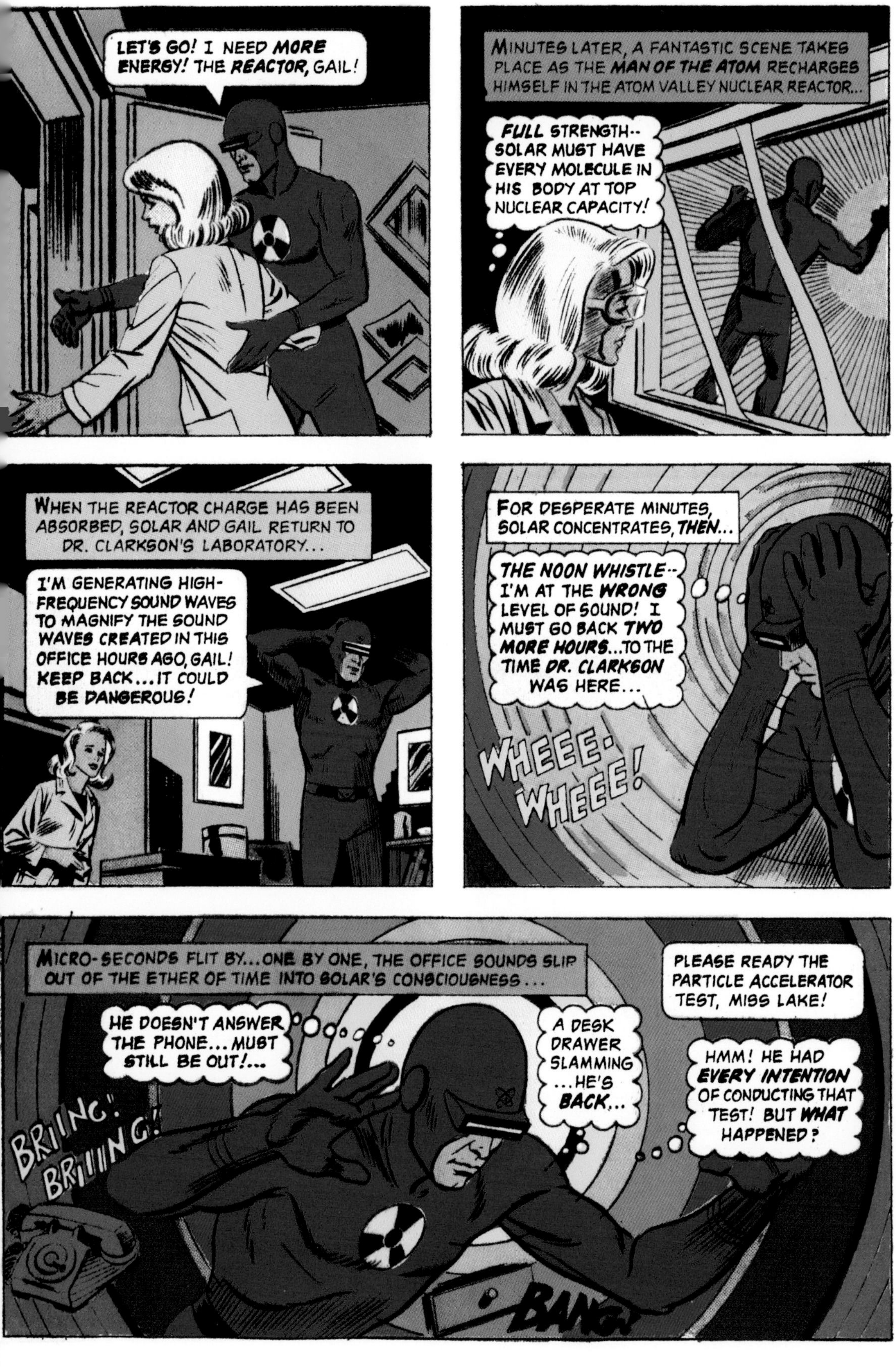
LET'S GO! I NEED MORE ENERGY! THE REACTOR, GAIL!
MINUTES LATER, A FANTASTIC SCENE TAKES PLACE AS THE MAN OF THE ATOM RECHARGES HIMSELF IN THE ATOM VALLEY NUCLEAR REACTOR...
FULL STRENGTH-- SOLAR MUST HAVE EVERY MOLECULE IN HIS BODY AT TOP NUCLEAR CAPACITY!
WHEN THE REACTOR CHARGE HAS BEEN ABSORBED, SOLAR AND GAIL RETURN TO DR. CLARKSON'S LABORATORY...
I'M GENERATING HIGH-FREQUENCY SOUND WAVES TO MAGNIFY THE SOUND WAVES CREATED IN THIS OFFICE HOURS AGO, GAIL! KEEP BACK...IT COULD BE DANGEROUS!
FOR DESPERATE MINUTES, SOLAR CONCENTRATES, THEN...
THE NOON WHISTLE-- I'M AT THE WRONG LEVEL OF SOUND! I MUST GO BACK TWO MORE HOURS...TO THE TIME DR. CLARKSON WAS HERE...
WHEEE-WHEEE!
MICRO-SECONDS FLIT BY...ONE BY ONE, THE OFFICE SOUNDS SLIP OUT OF THE ETHER OF TIME INTO SOLAR'S CONSCIOUSNESS...
HE DOESN'T ANSWER THE PHONE... MUST STILL BE OUT!...
BRIIING! BRIIING!
A DESK DRAWER SLAMMING ...HE'S BACK...
BANG!
PLEASE READY THE PARTICLE ACCELERATOR TEST, MISS LAKE!
HMM! HE HAD EVERY INTENTION OF CONDUCTING THAT TEST! BUT WHAT HAPPENED?

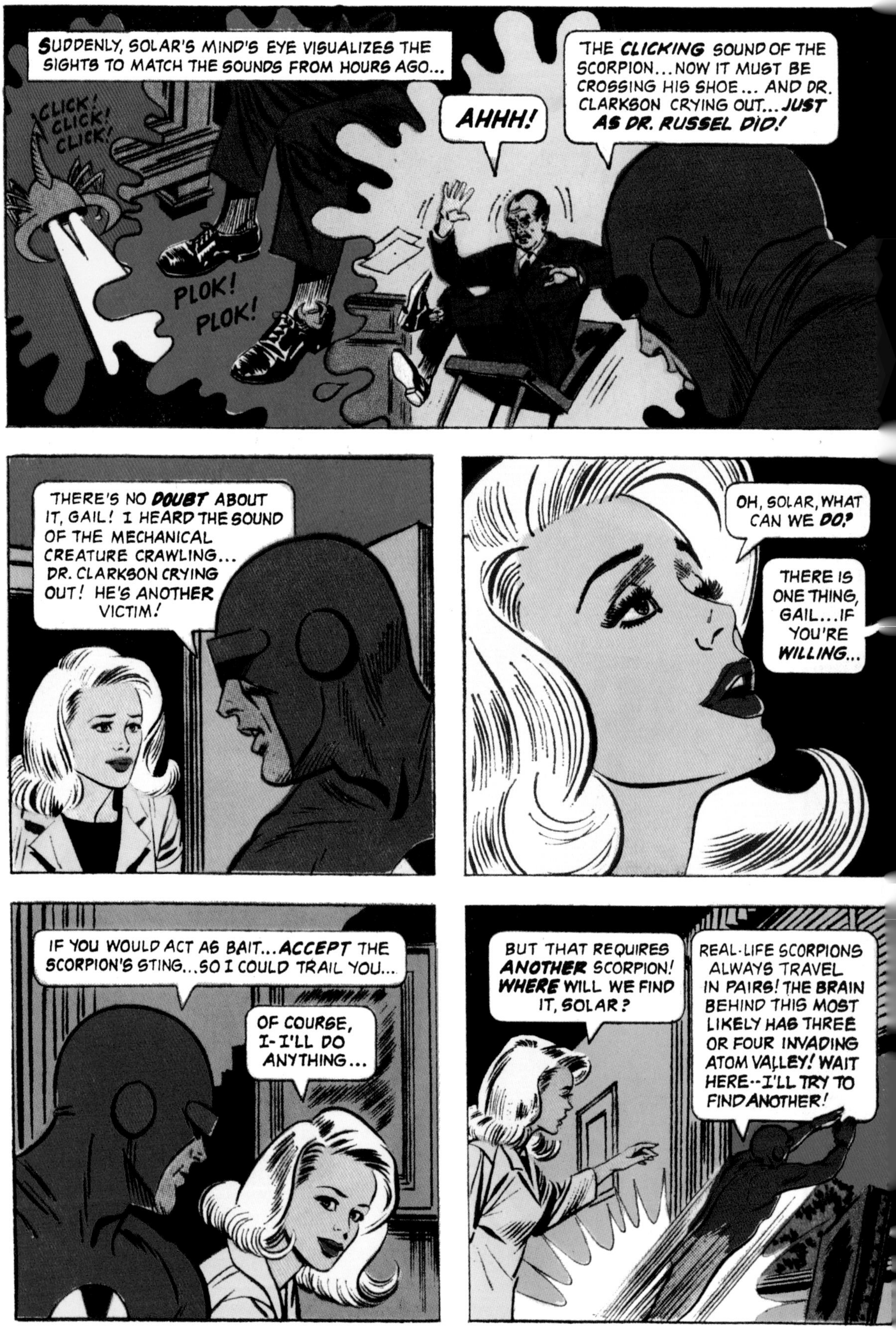
SUDDENLY, SOLAR'S MIND'S EYE VISUALIZES THE SIGHTS TO MATCH THE SOUNDS FROM HOURS AGO...
CLICK! CLICK! CLICK!
PLOK! PLOK!
AHHH!
THE CLICKING SOUND OF THE SCORPION... NOW IT MUST BE CROSSING HIS SHOE... AND DR. CLARKSON CRYING OUT... JUST AS DR. RUSSEL DID!
THERE'S NO DOUBT ABOUT IT, GAIL! I HEARD THE SOUND OF THE MECHANICAL CREATURE CRAWLING... DR. CLARKSON CRYING OUT! HE'S ANOTHER VICTIM!
OH, SOLAR, WHAT CAN WE DO?
THERE IS ONE THING, GAIL... IF YOU'RE WILLING...
IF YOU WOULD ACT AS BAIT... ACCEPT THE SCORPION'S STING... SO I COULD TRAIL YOU...
OF COURSE, I-I'LL DO ANYTHING...
BUT THAT REQUIRES ANOTHER SCORPION! WHERE WILL WE FIND IT, SOLAR?
REAL-LIFE SCORPIONS ALWAYS TRAVEL IN PAIRS! THE BRAIN BEHIND THIS MOST LIKELY HAS THREE OR FOUR INVADING ATOM VALLEY! WAIT HERE--I'LL TRY TO FIND ANOTHER!

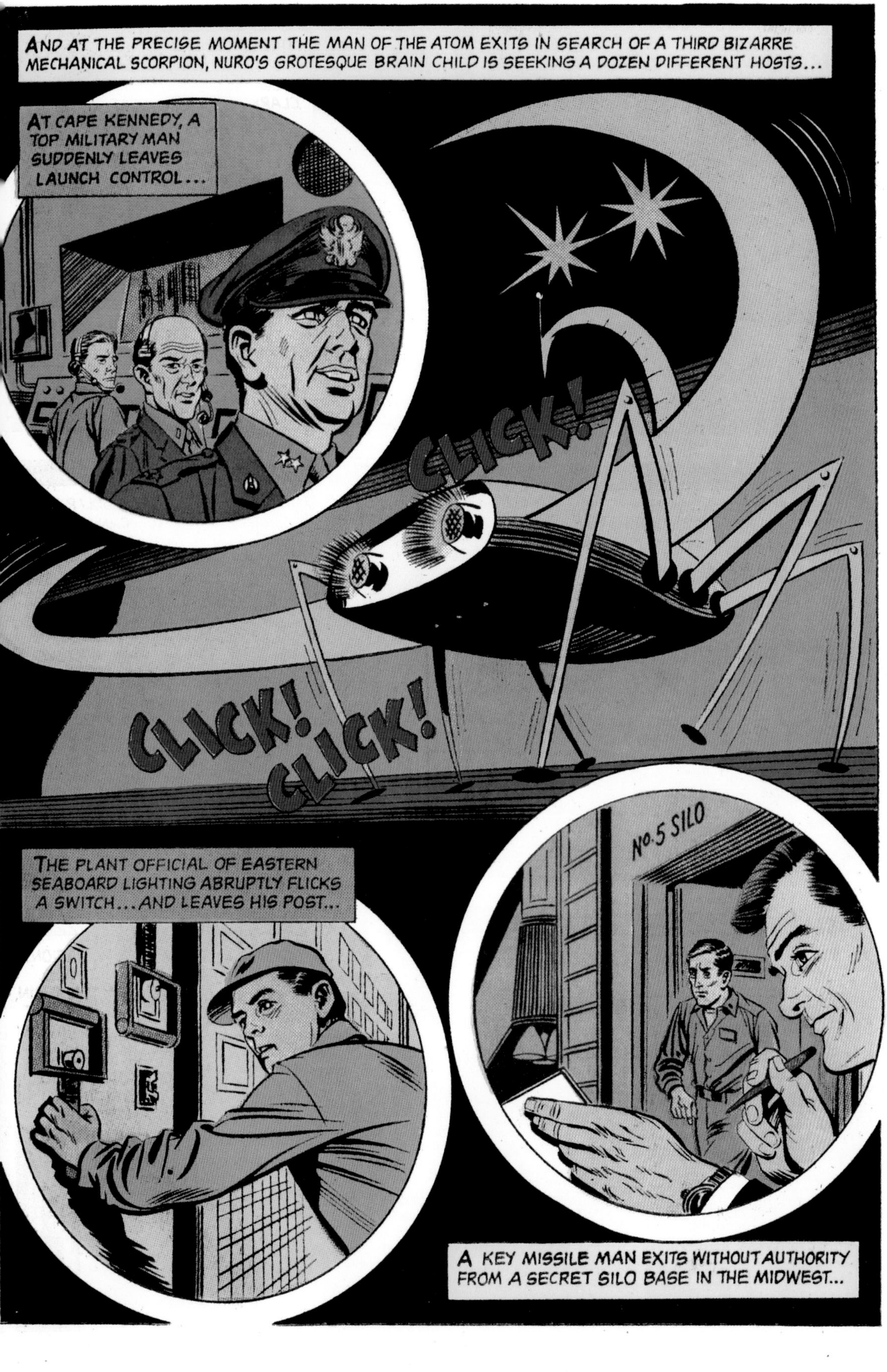
AND AT THE PRECISE MOMENT THE MAN OF THE ATOM EXITS IN SEARCH OF A THIRD BIZARRE MECHANICAL SCORPION, NURO'S GROTESQUE BRAIN CHILD IS SEEKING A DOZEN DIFFERENT HOSTS...
AT CAPE KENNEDY, A TOP MILITARY MAN SUDDENLY LEAVES LAUNCH CONTROL...
CLICK!
CLICK!
CLICK!
THE PLANT OFFICIAL OF EASTERN SEABOARD LIGHTING ABRUPTLY FLICKS A SWITCH...AND LEAVES HIS POST...
No. 5 SILO
A KEY MISSILE MAN EXITS WITHOUT AUTHORITY FROM A SECRET SILO BASE IN THE MIDWEST...

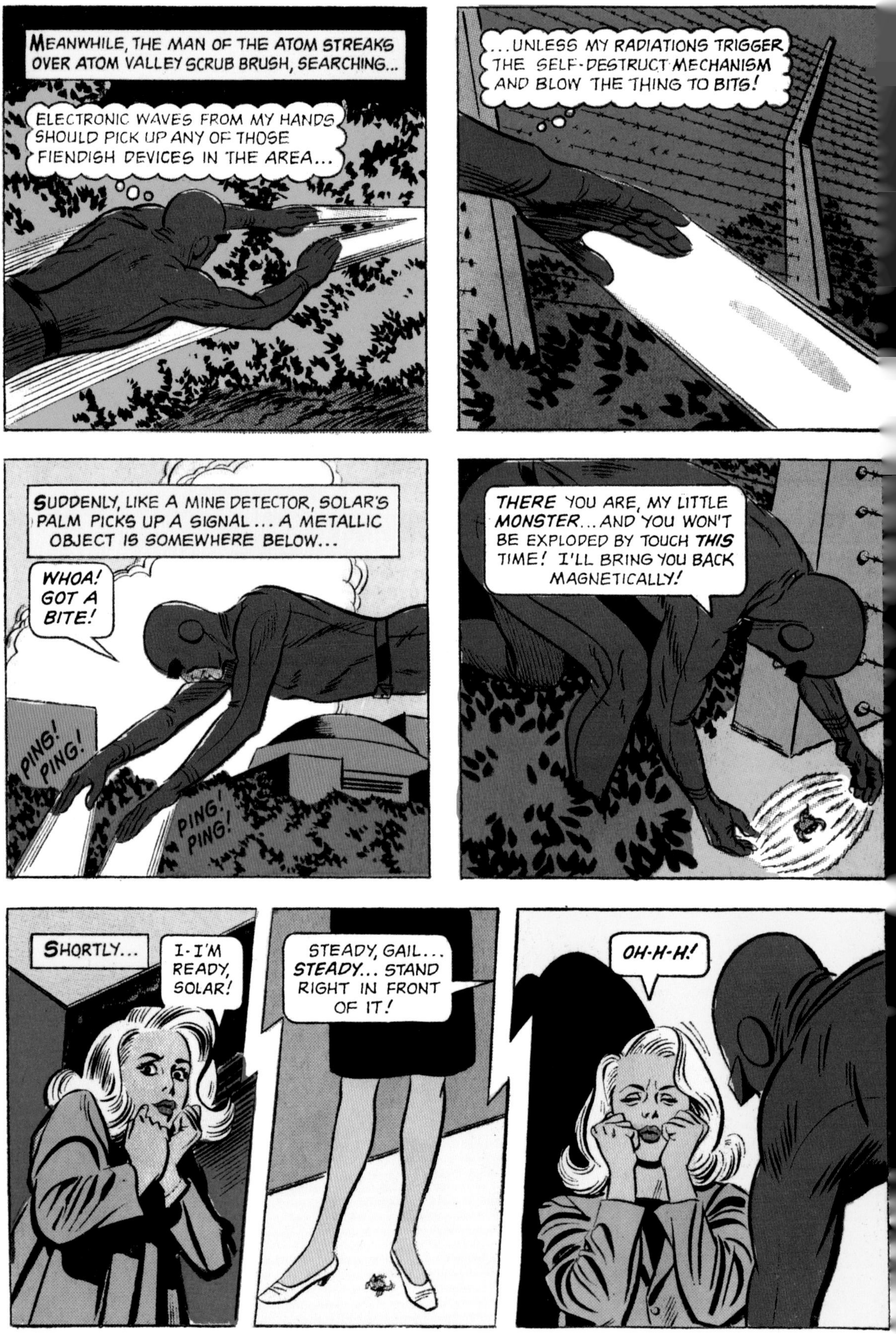
MEANWHILE, THE MAN OF THE ATOM STREAKS OVER ATOM VALLEY SCRUB BRUSH, SEARCHING...
ELECTRONIC WAVES FROM MY HANDS SHOULD PICK UP ANY OF THOSE FIENDISH DEVICES IN THE AREA...
...UNLESS MY RADIATIONS TRIGGER THE SELF-DESTRUCT MECHANISM AND BLOW THE THING TO BITS!
SUDDENLY, LIKE A MINE DETECTOR, SOLAR'S PALM PICKS UP A SIGNAL... A METALLIC OBJECT IS SOMEWHERE BELOW...
WHOA! GOT A BITE!
PING! PING!
PING! PING!
THERE YOU ARE, MY LITTLE MONSTER... AND YOU WON'T BE EXPLODED BY TOUCH THIS TIME! I'LL BRING YOU BACK MAGNETICALLY!
SHORTLY...
I-I'M READY, SOLAR!
STEADY, GAIL... STEADY... STAND RIGHT IN FRONT OF IT!
OH-H-H!

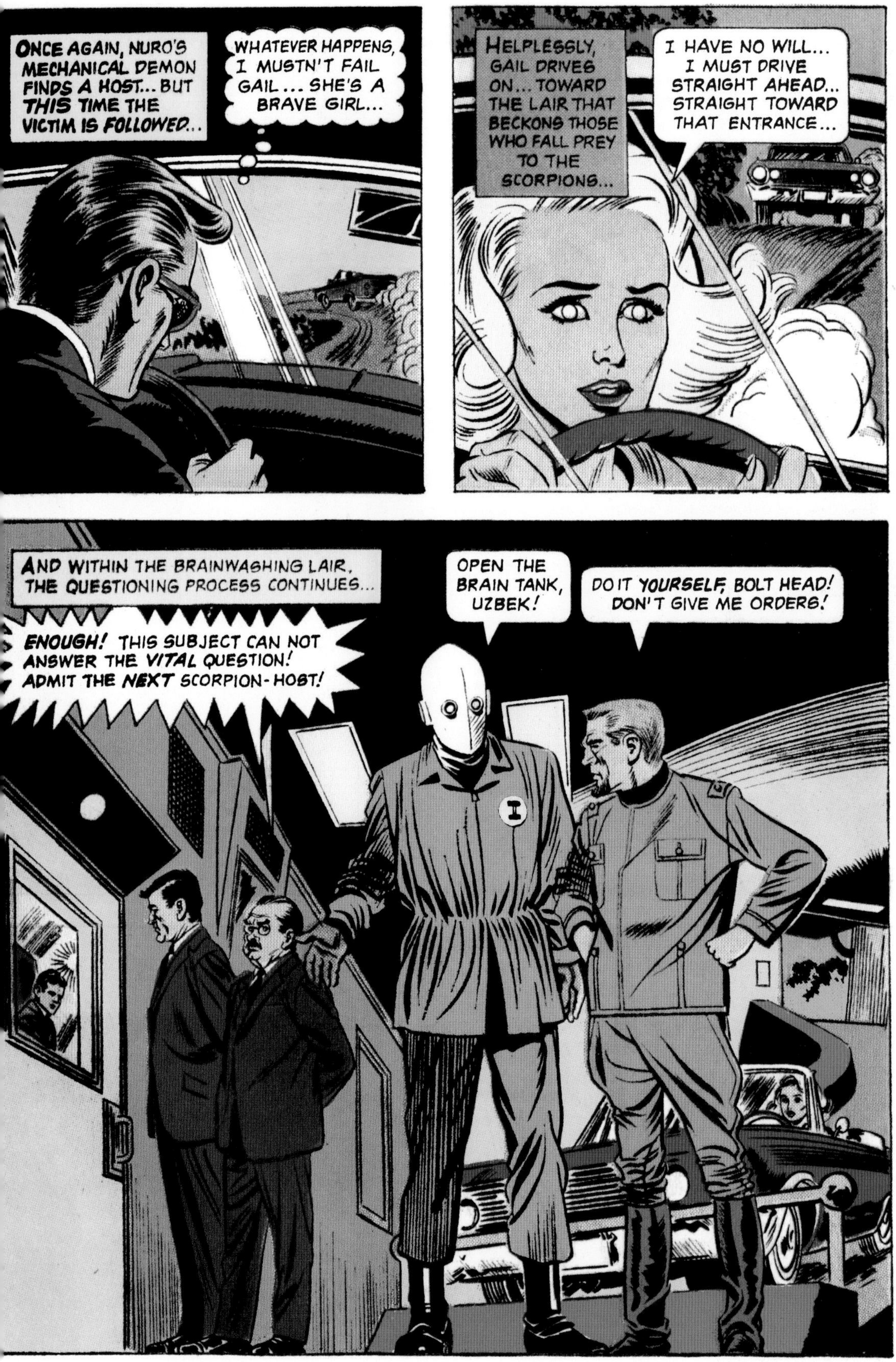
ONCE AGAIN, NURO'S MECHANICAL DEMON FINDS A HOST... BUT THIS TIME THE VICTIM IS FOLLOWED...
WHATEVER HAPPENS, I MUSTN'T FAIL GAIL... SHE'S A BRAVE GIRL...
HELPLESSLY, GAIL DRIVES ON... TOWARD THE LAIR THAT BECKONS THOSE WHO FALL PREY TO THE SCORPIONS...
I HAVE NO WILL... I MUST DRIVE STRAIGHT AHEAD... STRAIGHT TOWARD THAT ENTRANCE...
AND WITHIN THE BRAINWASHING LAIR, THE QUESTIONING PROCESS CONTINUES...
ENOUGH! THIS SUBJECT CAN NOT ANSWER THE VITAL QUESTION! ADMIT THE NEXT SCORPION-HOST!
OPEN THE BRAIN TANK, UZBEK!
DO IT YOURSELF, BOLT HEAD! DON'T GIVE ME ORDERS!

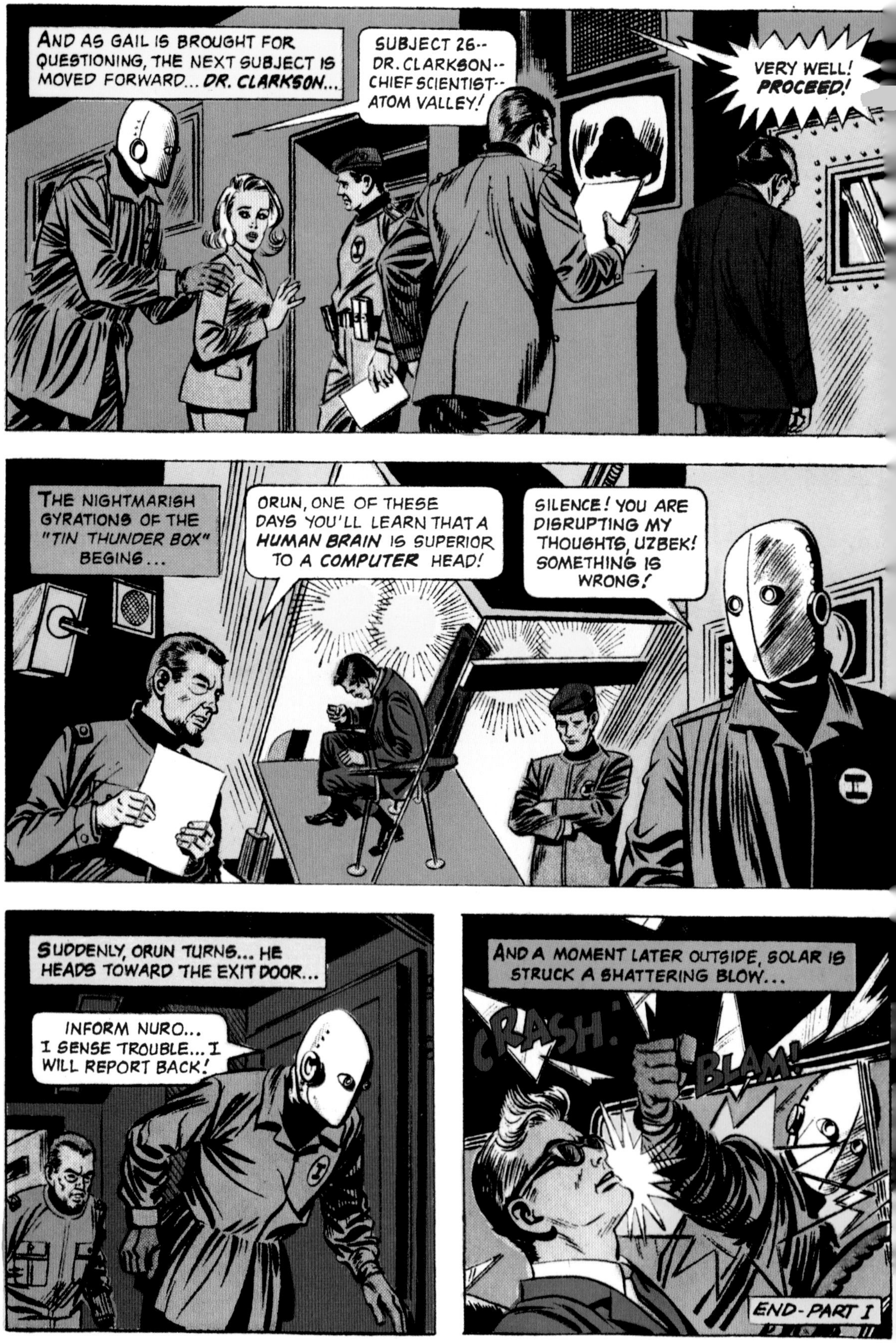
AND AS GAIL IS BROUGHT FOR QUESTIONING, THE NEXT SUBJECT IS MOVED FORWARD... DR. CLARKSON...
SUBJECT 26-- DR. CLARKSON-- CHIEF SCIENTIST-- ATOM VALLEY!
VERY WELL! PROCEED!
THE NIGHTMARISH GYRATIONS OF THE "TIN THUNDER BOX" BEGINS...
ORUN, ONE OF THESE DAYS YOU'LL LEARN THAT A HUMAN BRAIN IS SUPERIOR TO A COMPUTER HEAD!
SILENCE! YOU ARE DISRUPTING MY THOUGHTS, UZBEK! SOMETHING IS WRONG!
SUDDENLY, ORUN TURNS... HE HEADS TOWARD THE EXIT DOOR...
INFORM NURO... I SENSE TROUBLE... I WILL REPORT BACK!
AND A MOMENT LATER OUTSIDE, SOLAR IS STRUCK A SHATTERING BLOW...
CRASH!
BLAM!
END-PART I

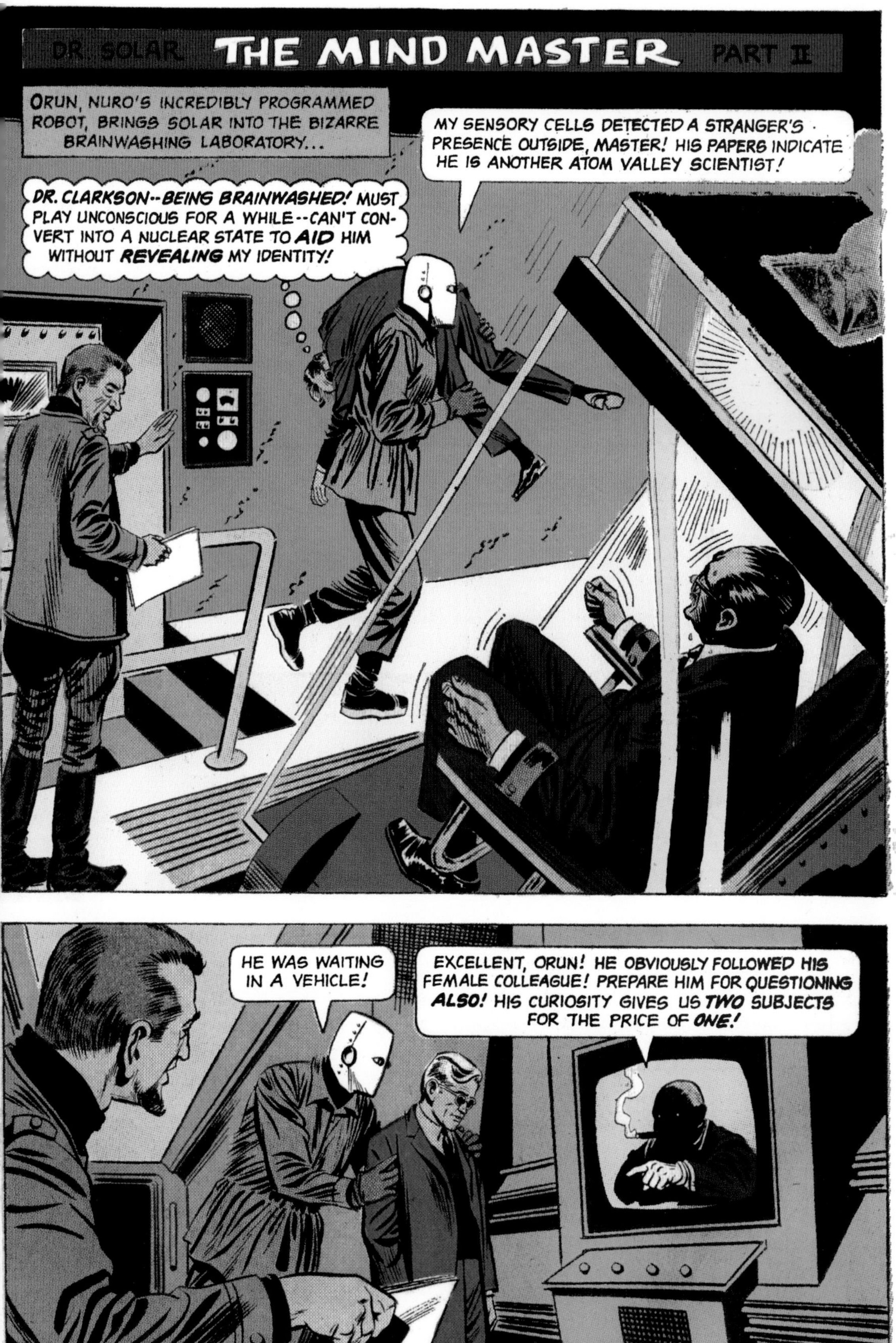
DR. SOLAR THE MIND MASTER PART II
ORUN, NURO'S INCREDIBLY PROGRAMMED ROBOT, BRINGS SOLAR INTO THE BIZARRE BRAINWASHING LABORATORY...
MY SENSORY CELLS DETECTED A STRANGER'S PRESENCE OUTSIDE, MASTER! HIS PAPERS INDICATE HE IS ANOTHER ATOM VALLEY SCIENTIST!
DR. CLARKSON--BEING BRAINWASHED! MUST PLAY UNCONSCIOUS FOR A WHILE--CAN'T CONVERT INTO A NUCLEAR STATE TO AID HIM WITHOUT REVEALING MY IDENTITY!
HE WAS WAITING IN A VEHICLE!
EXCELLENT, ORUN! HE OBVIOUSLY FOLLOWED HIS FEMALE COLLEAGUE! PREPARE HIM FOR QUESTIONING ALSO! HIS CURIOSITY GIVES US TWO SUBJECTS FOR THE PRICE OF ONE!

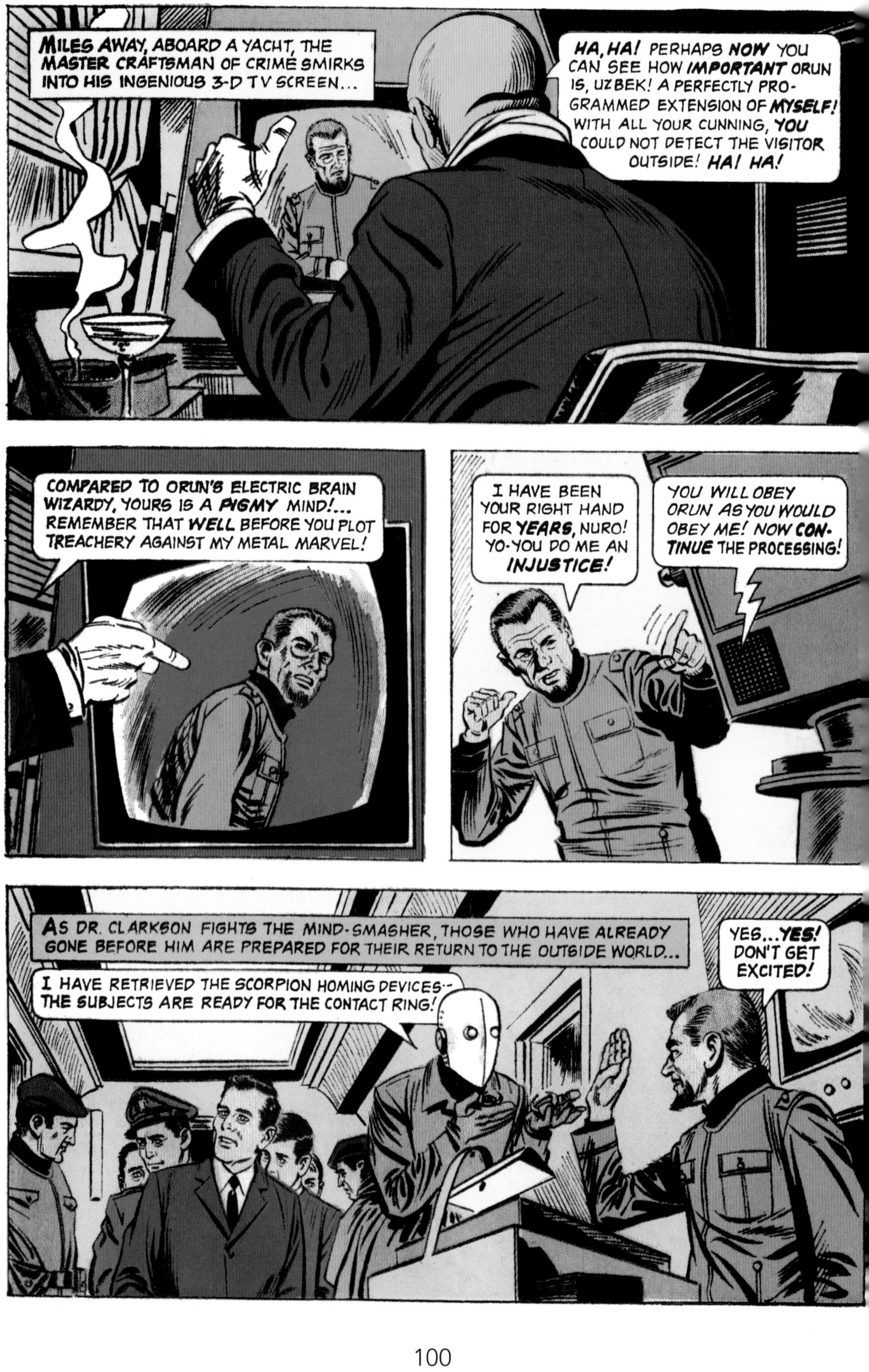
MILES AWAY, ABOARD A YACHT, THE MASTER CRAFTSMAN OF CRIME SMIRKS INTO HIS INGENIOUS 3-D TV SCREEN...
HA, HA! PERHAPS NOW YOU CAN SEE HOW IMPORTANT ORUN IS, UZBEK! A PERFECTLY PRO-GRAMMED EXTENSION OF MYSELF! WITH ALL YOUR CUNNING, YOU COULD NOT DETECT THE VISITOR OUTSIDE! HA! HA!
COMPARED TO ORUN'S ELECTRIC BRAIN WIZARDY, YOURS IS A PIGMY MIND!... REMEMBER THAT WELL BEFORE YOU PLOT TREACHERY AGAINST MY METAL MARVEL!
I HAVE BEEN YOUR RIGHT HAND FOR YEARS, NURO! YO-YOU DO ME AN INJUSTICE!
YOU WILL OBEY ORUN AS YOU WOULD OBEY ME! NOW CON-TINUE THE PROCESSING!
AS DR. CLARKSON FIGHTS THE MIND-SMASHER, THOSE WHO HAVE ALREADY GONE BEFORE HIM ARE PREPARED FOR THEIR RETURN TO THE OUTSIDE WORLD...
I HAVE RETRIEVED THE SCORPION HOMING DEVICES-- THE SUBJECTS ARE READY FOR THE CONTACT RING!
YES... YES! DON'T GET EXCITED!

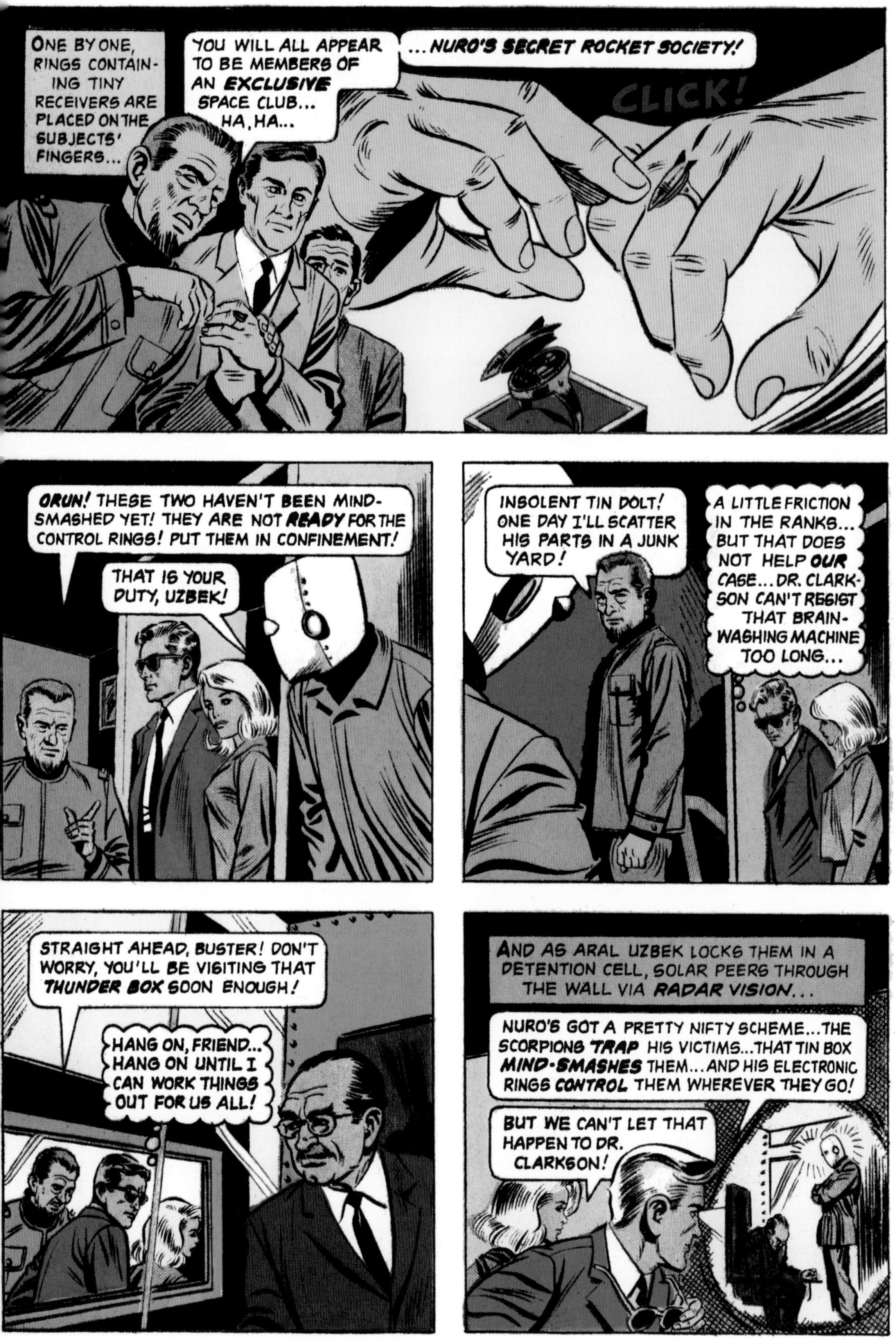
ONE BY ONE, RINGS CONTAINING TINY RECEIVERS ARE PLACED ON THE SUBJECTS' FINGERS...
YOU WILL ALL APPEAR TO BE MEMBERS OF AN EXCLUSIVE SPACE CLUB... HA, HA...
...NURO'S SECRET ROCKET SOCIETY!
CLICK!
ORUN! THESE TWO HAVEN'T BEEN MIND-SMASHED YET! THEY ARE NOT READY FOR THE CONTROL RINGS! PUT THEM IN CONFINEMENT!
THAT IS YOUR DUTY, UZBEK!
INSOLENT TIN DOLT! ONE DAY I'LL SCATTER HIS PARTS IN A JUNK YARD!
A LITTLE FRICTION IN THE RANKS... BUT THAT DOES NOT HELP OUR CASE... DR. CLARKSON CAN'T RESIST THAT BRAIN-WASHING MACHINE TOO LONG...
STRAIGHT AHEAD, BUSTER! DON'T WORRY, YOU'LL BE VISITING THAT THUNDER BOX SOON ENOUGH!
HANG ON, FRIEND... HANG ON UNTIL I CAN WORK THINGS OUT FOR US ALL!
AND AS ARAL UZBEK LOCKS THEM IN A DETENTION CELL, SOLAR PEERS THROUGH THE WALL VIA RADAR VISION...
NURO'S GOT A PRETTY NIFTY SCHEME... THE SCORPIONS TRAP HIS VICTIMS... THAT TIN BOX MIND-SMASHES THEM... AND HIS ELECTRONIC RINGS CONTROL THEM WHEREVER THEY GO!
BUT WE CAN'T LET THAT HAPPEN TO DR. CLARKSON!

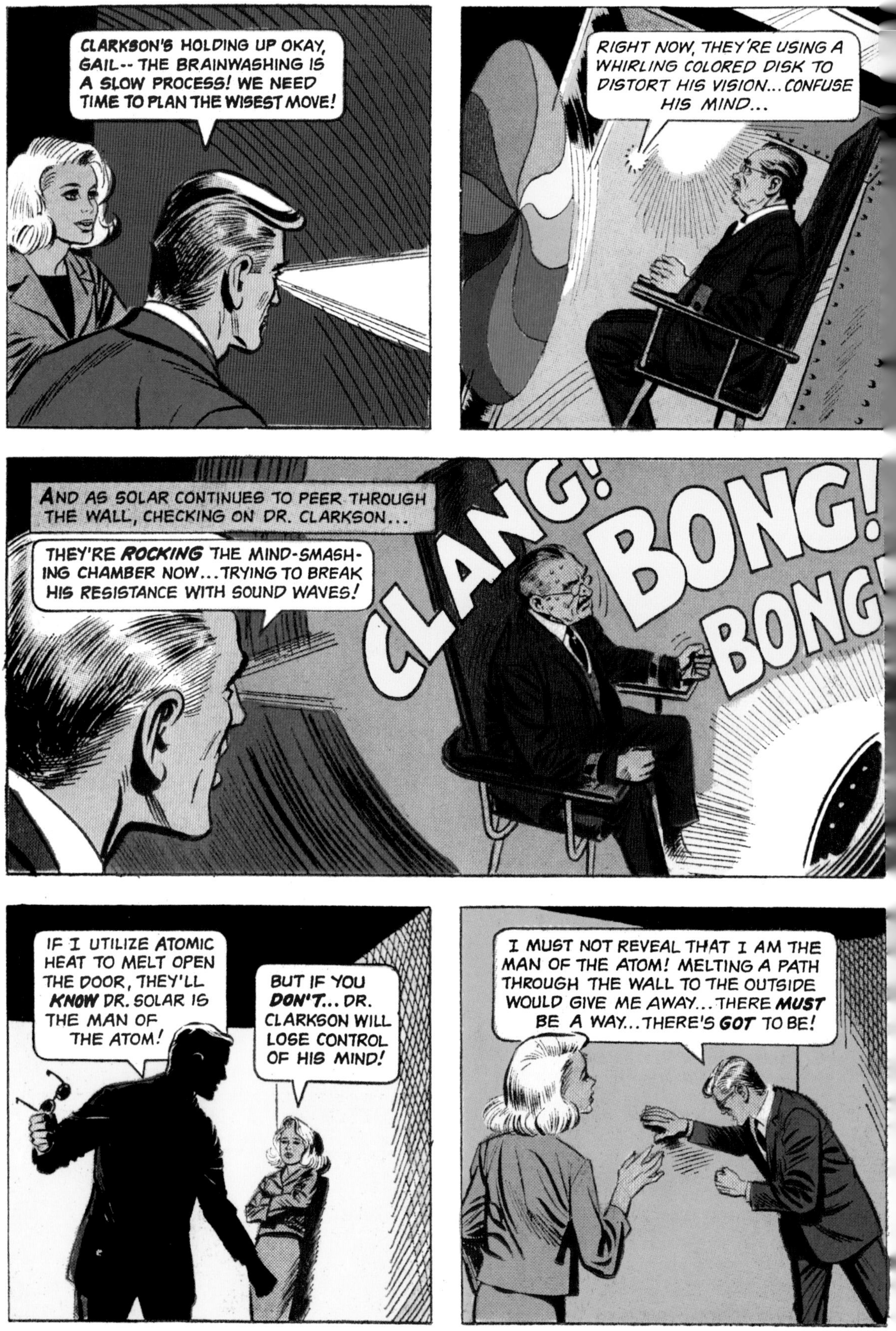
CLARKSON'S HOLDING UP OKAY, GAIL-- THE BRAINWASHING IS A SLOW PROCESS! WE NEED TIME TO PLAN THE WISEST MOVE!
RIGHT NOW, THEY'RE USING A WHIRLING COLORED DISK TO DISTORT HIS VISION... CONFUSE HIS MIND...
AND AS SOLAR CONTINUES TO PEER THROUGH THE WALL, CHECKING ON DR. CLARKSON...
THEY'RE ROCKING THE MIND-SMASHING CHAMBER NOW... TRYING TO BREAK HIS RESISTANCE WITH SOUND WAVES!
CLANG!
BONG!
BONG!
IF I UTILIZE ATOMIC HEAT TO MELT OPEN THE DOOR, THEY'LL KNOW DR. SOLAR IS THE MAN OF THE ATOM!
BUT IF YOU DON'T... DR. CLARKSON WILL LOSE CONTROL OF HIS MIND!
I MUST NOT REVEAL THAT I AM THE MAN OF THE ATOM! MELTING A PATH THROUGH THE WALL TO THE OUTSIDE WOULD GIVE ME AWAY... THERE MUST BE A WAY... THERE'S GOT TO BE!

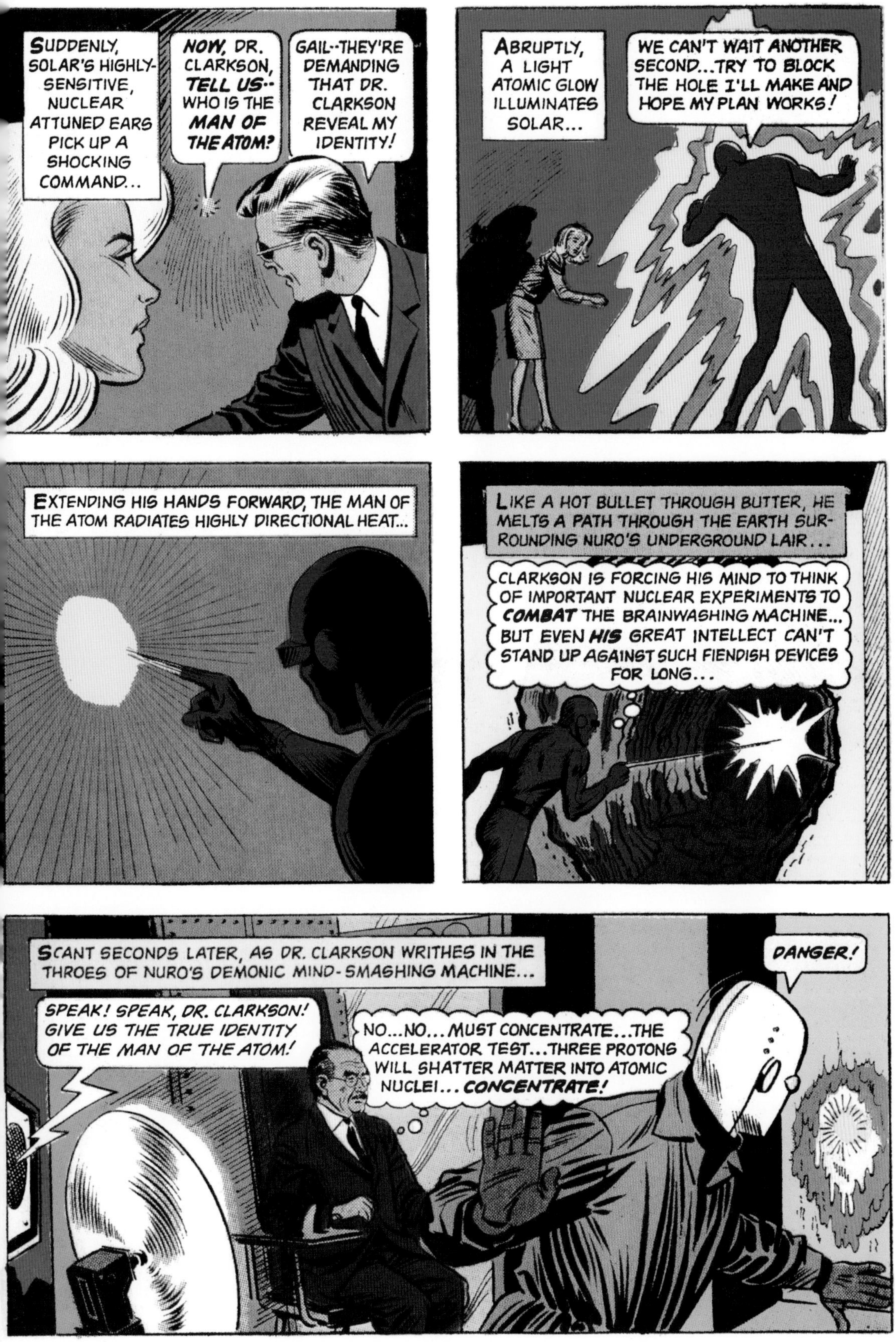
SUDDENLY, SOLAR'S HIGHLY-SENSITIVE, NUCLEAR ATTUNED EARS PICK UP A SHOCKING COMMAND...
NOW, DR. CLARKSON, TELL US-- WHO IS THE MAN OF THE ATOM?
GAIL--THEY'RE DEMANDING THAT DR. CLARKSON REVEAL MY IDENTITY!
ABRUPTLY, A LIGHT ATOMIC GLOW ILLUMINATES SOLAR...
WE CAN'T WAIT ANOTHER SECOND...TRY TO BLOCK THE HOLE I'LL MAKE AND HOPE MY PLAN WORKS!
EXTENDING HIS HANDS FORWARD, THE MAN OF THE ATOM RADIATES HIGHLY DIRECTIONAL HEAT...
LIKE A HOT BULLET THROUGH BUTTER, HE MELTS A PATH THROUGH THE EARTH SURROUNDING NURO'S UNDERGROUND LAIR...
CLARKSON IS FORCING HIS MIND TO THINK OF IMPORTANT NUCLEAR EXPERIMENTS TO COMBAT THE BRAINWASHING MACHINE... BUT EVEN HIS GREAT INTELLECT CAN'T STAND UP AGAINST SUCH FIENDISH DEVICES FOR LONG...
SCANT SECONDS LATER, AS DR. CLARKSON WRITHES IN THE THROES OF NURO'S DEMONIC MIND-SMASHING MACHINE...
SPEAK! SPEAK, DR. CLARKSON! GIVE US THE TRUE IDENTITY OF THE MAN OF THE ATOM!
NO...NO... MUST CONCENTRATE...THE ACCELERATOR TEST...THREE PROTONS WILL SHATTER MATTER INTO ATOMIC NUCLEI... CONCENTRATE!
DANGER!

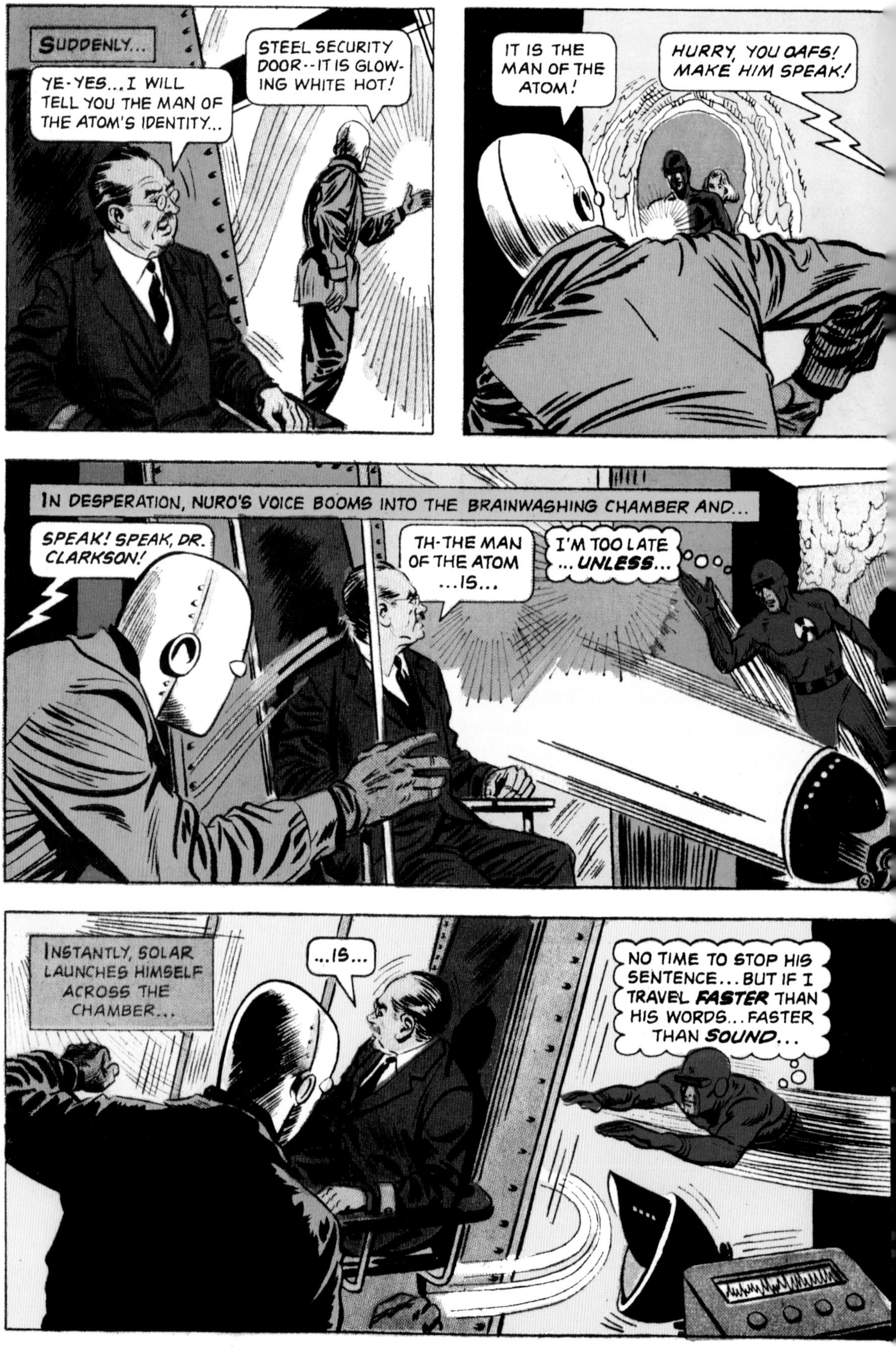
SUDDENLY...
YE-YES... I WILL TELL YOU THE MAN OF THE ATOM'S IDENTITY...
STEEL SECURITY DOOR--IT IS GLOWING WHITE HOT!
IT IS THE MAN OF THE ATOM!
HURRY, YOU OAFS! MAKE HIM SPEAK!
IN DESPERATION, NURO'S VOICE BOOMS INTO THE BRAINWASHING CHAMBER AND...
SPEAK! SPEAK, DR. CLARKSON!
TH-THE MAN OF THE ATOM ...IS...
I'M TOO LATE ...UNLESS...
INSTANTLY, SOLAR LAUNCHES HIMSELF ACROSS THE CHAMBER...
...IS...
NO TIME TO STOP HIS SENTENCE... BUT IF I TRAVEL FASTER THAN HIS WORDS... FASTER THAN SOUND...

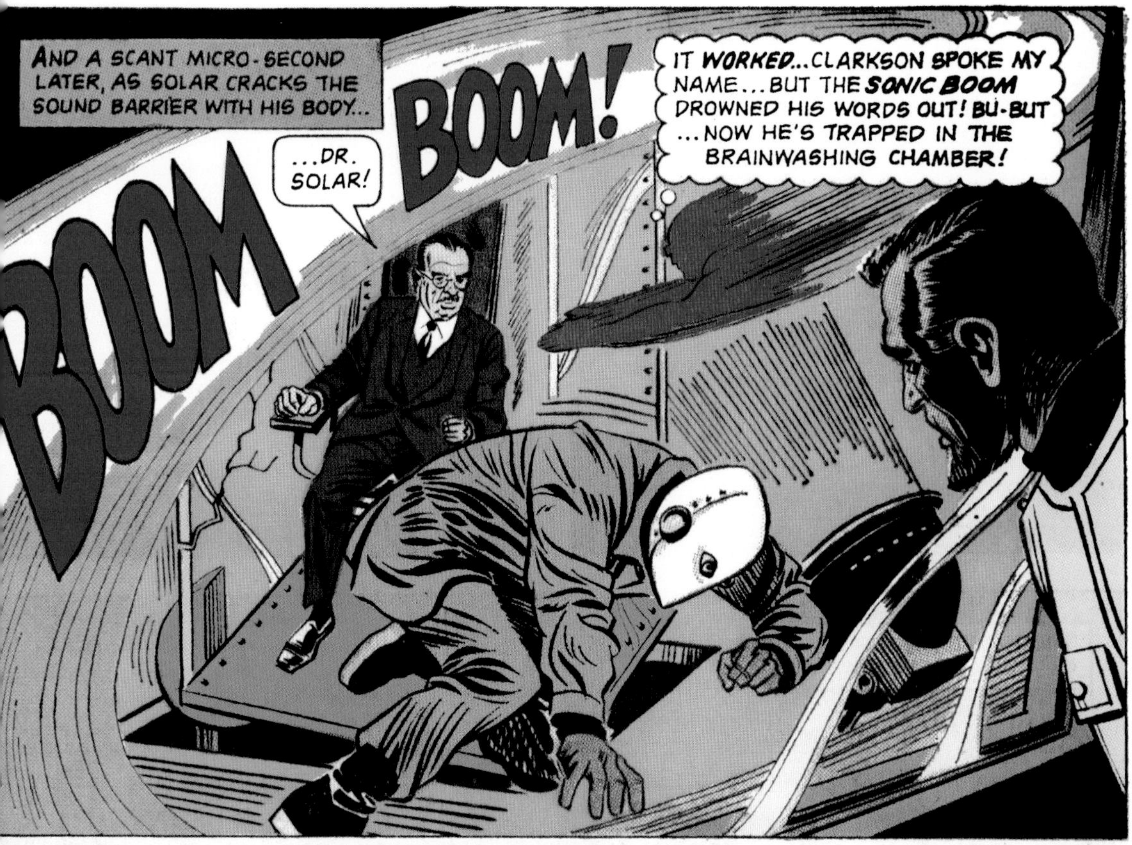
AND A SCANT MICRO-SECOND LATER, AS SOLAR CRACKS THE SOUND BARRIER WITH HIS BODY...
...DR. SOLAR!
BOOM BOOM!
IT WORKED...CLARKSON SPOKE MY NAME...BUT THE SONIC BOOM DROWNED HIS WORDS OUT! BU-BUT ...NOW HE'S TRAPPED IN THE BRAINWASHING CHAMBER!

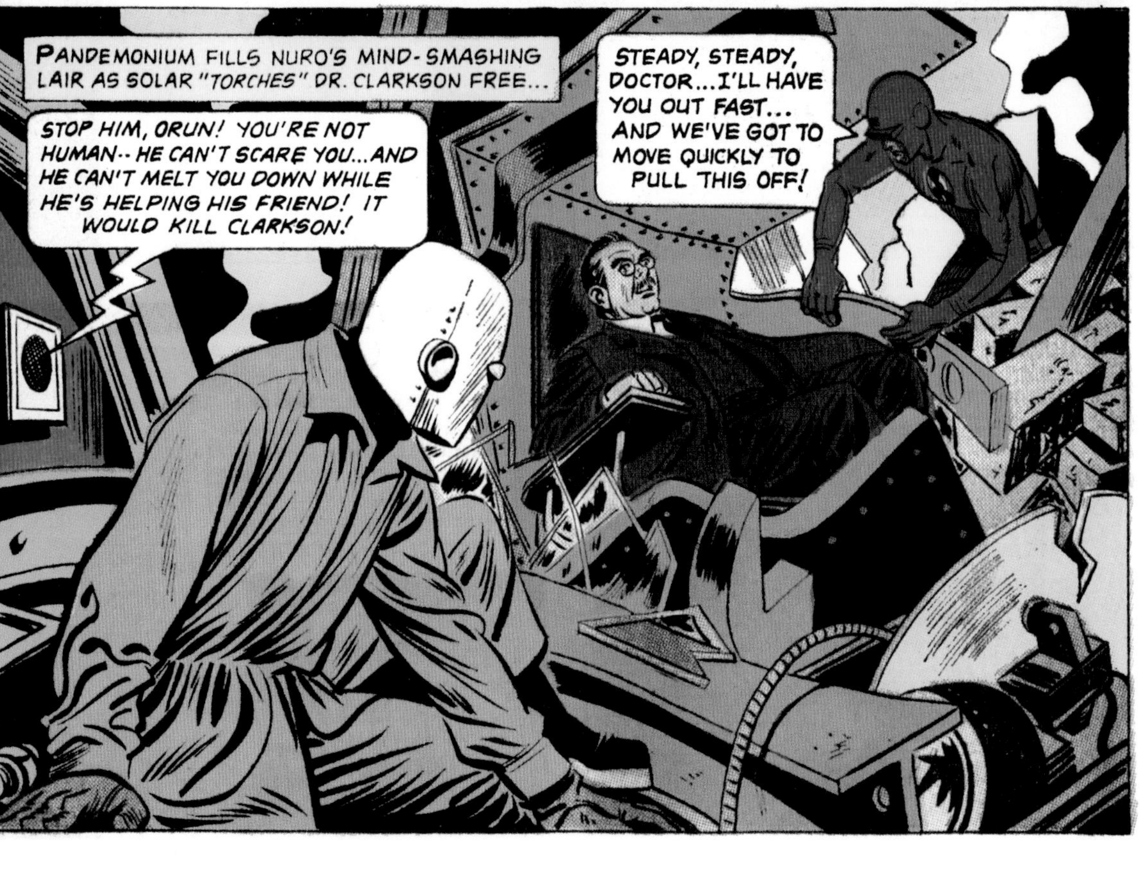
PANDEMONIUM FILLS NURO'S MIND-SMASHING LAIR AS SOLAR "TORCHES" DR. CLARKSON FREE...
STOP HIM, ORUN! YOU'RE NOT HUMAN-- HE CAN'T SCARE YOU...AND HE CAN'T MELT YOU DOWN WHILE HE'S HELPING HIS FRIEND! IT WOULD KILL CLARKSON!
STEADY, STEADY, DOCTOR...I'LL HAVE YOU OUT FAST... AND WE'VE GOT TO MOVE QUICKLY TO PULL THIS OFF!

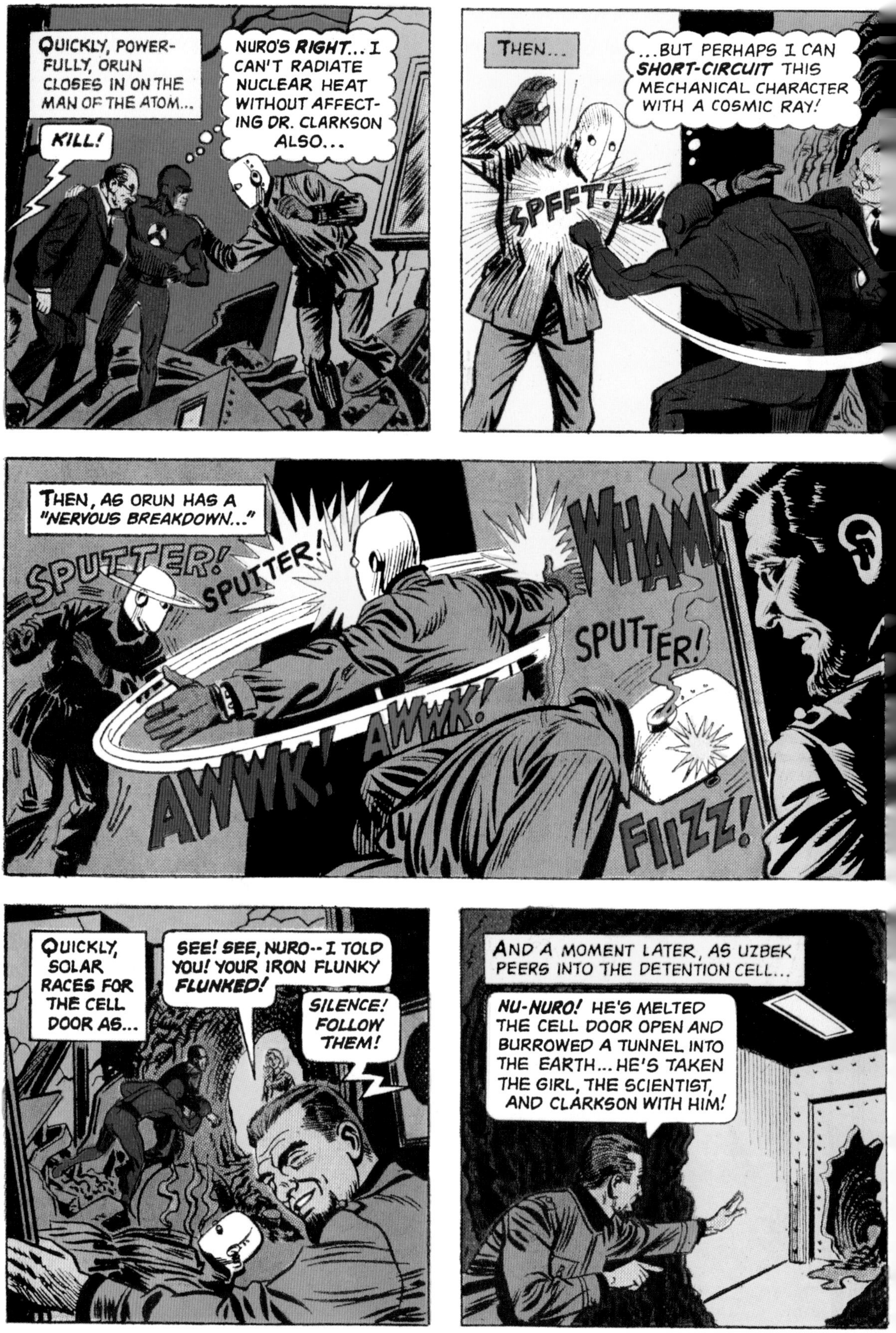
QUICKLY, POWERFULLY, ORUN CLOSES IN ON THE MAN OF THE ATOM...
KILL!
NURO'S RIGHT... I CAN'T RADIATE NUCLEAR HEAT WITHOUT AFFECTING DR. CLARKSON ALSO...
THEN...
...BUT PERHAPS I CAN SHORT-CIRCUIT THIS MECHANICAL CHARACTER WITH A COSMIC RAY!
SPFFT!
THEN, AS ORUN HAS A "NERVOUS BREAKDOWN..."
SPUTTER!
SPUTTER!
WHAM!
SPUTTER!
AWWK! AWWK!
FIIZZ!
QUICKLY, SOLAR RACES FOR THE CELL DOOR AS...
SEE! SEE, NURO-- I TOLD YOU! YOUR IRON FLUNKY FLUNKED!
SILENCE! FOLLOW THEM!
AND A MOMENT LATER, AS UZBEK PEERS INTO THE DETENTION CELL...
NU-NURO! HE'S MELTED THE CELL DOOR OPEN AND BURROWED A TUNNEL INTO THE EARTH... HE'S TAKEN THE GIRL, THE SCIENTIST, AND CLARKSON WITH HIM!

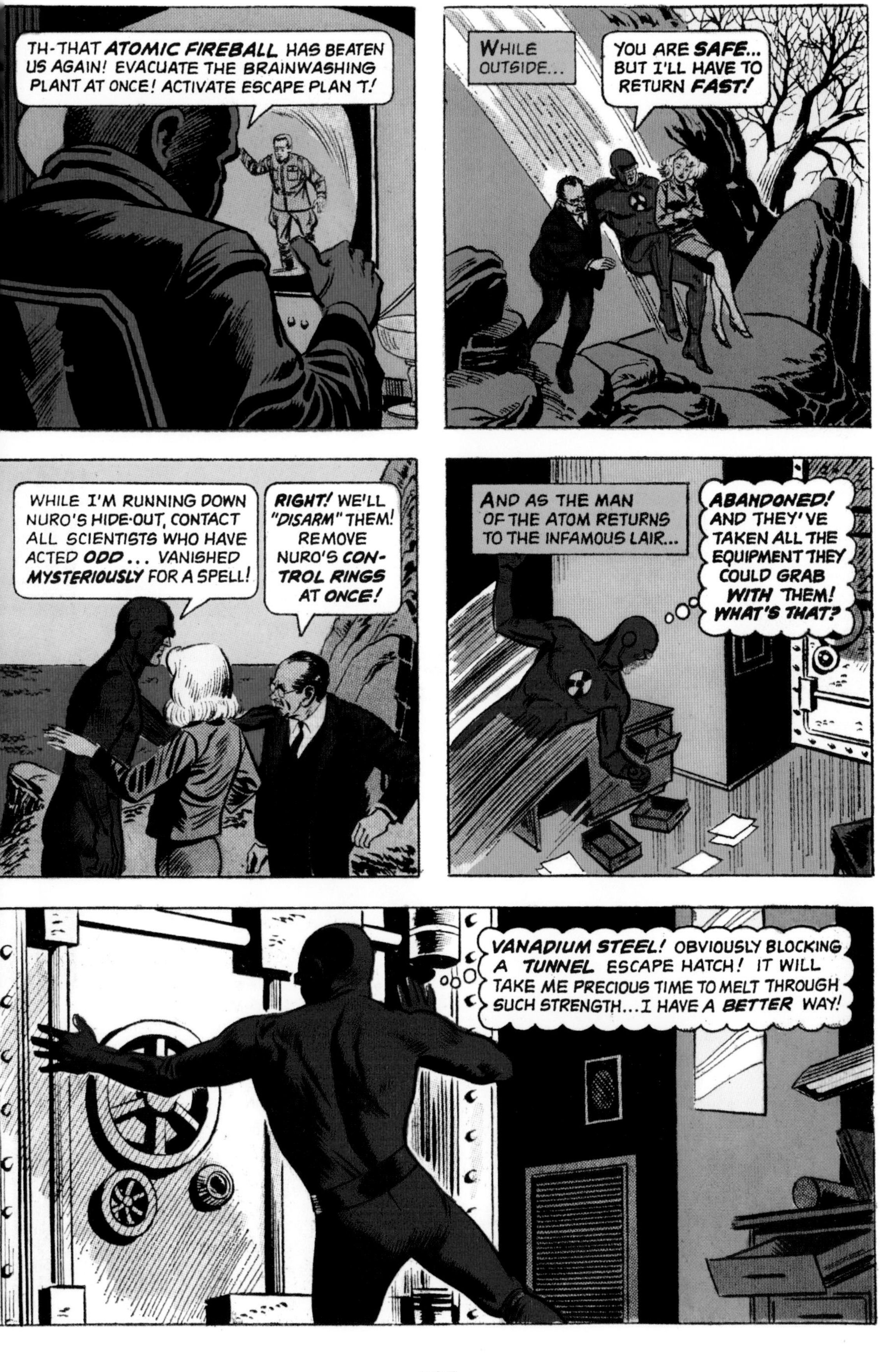
TH-THAT ATOMIC FIREBALL HAS BEATEN US AGAIN! EVACUATE THE BRAINWASHING PLANT AT ONCE! ACTIVATE ESCAPE PLAN T!
WHILE OUTSIDE...
YOU ARE SAFE... BUT I'LL HAVE TO RETURN FAST!
WHILE I'M RUNNING DOWN NURO'S HIDE-OUT, CONTACT ALL SCIENTISTS WHO HAVE ACTED ODD... VANISHED MYSTERIOUSLY FOR A SPELL!
RIGHT! WE'LL "DISARM" THEM! REMOVE NURO'S CONTROL RINGS AT ONCE!
AND AS THE MAN OF THE ATOM RETURNS TO THE INFAMOUS LAIR...
ABANDONED! AND THEY'VE TAKEN ALL THE EQUIPMENT THEY COULD GRAB WITH THEM! WHAT'S THAT?
VANADIUM STEEL! OBVIOUSLY BLOCKING A TUNNEL ESCAPE HATCH! IT WILL TAKE ME PRECIOUS TIME TO MELT THROUGH SUCH STRENGTH... I HAVE A BETTER WAY!

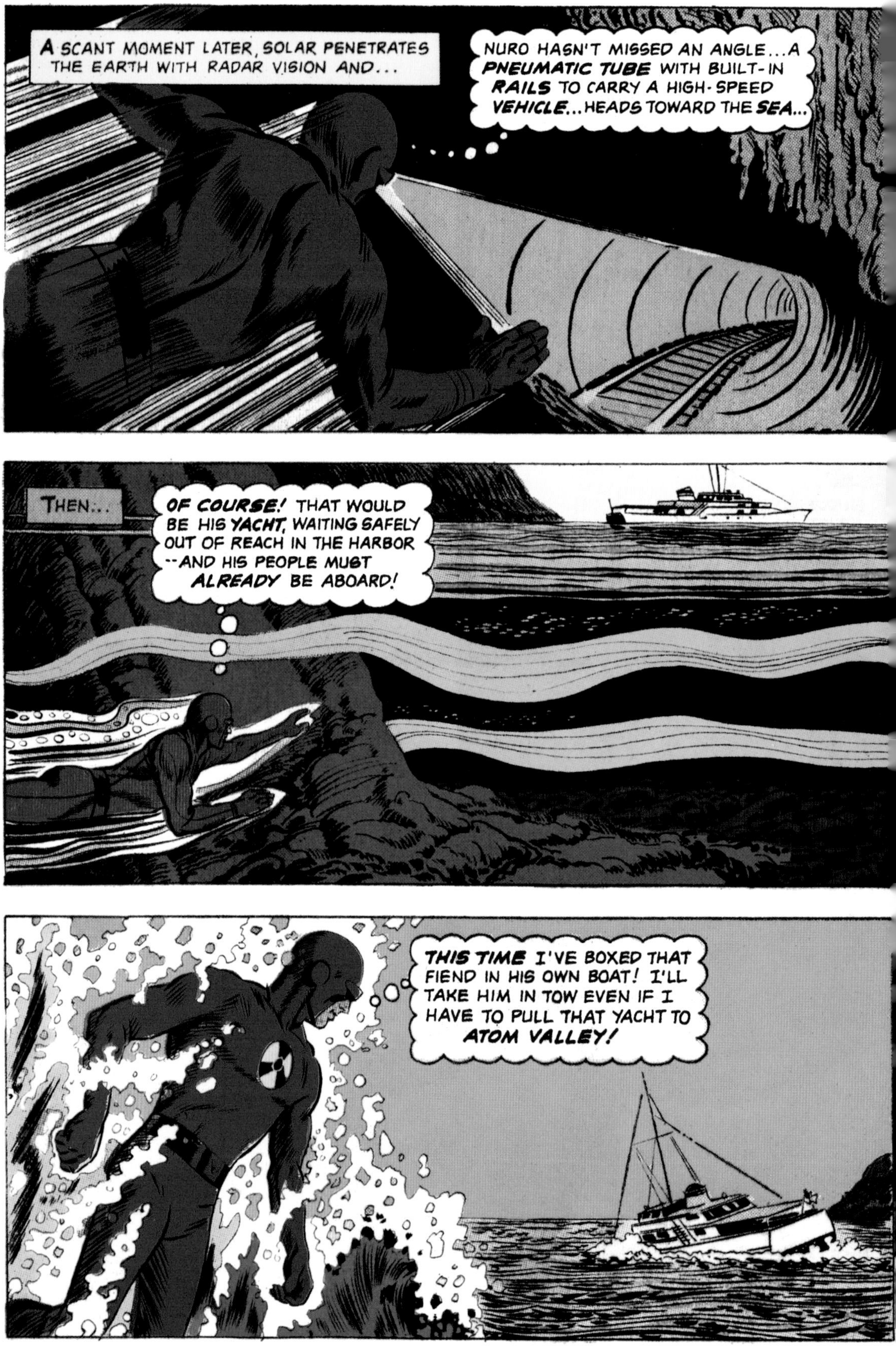
A SCANT MOMENT LATER, SOLAR PENETRATES THE EARTH WITH RADAR VISION AND...
NURO HASN'T MISSED AN ANGLE...A PNEUMATIC TUBE WITH BUILT-IN RAILS TO CARRY A HIGH-SPEED VEHICLE...HEADS TOWARD THE SEA...
THEN...
OF COURSE! THAT WOULD BE HIS YACHT, WAITING SAFELY OUT OF REACH IN THE HARBOR --AND HIS PEOPLE MUST ALREADY BE ABOARD!
THIS TIME I'VE BOXED THAT FIEND IN HIS OWN BOAT! I'LL TAKE HIM IN TOW EVEN IF I HAVE TO PULL THAT YACHT TO ATOM VALLEY!

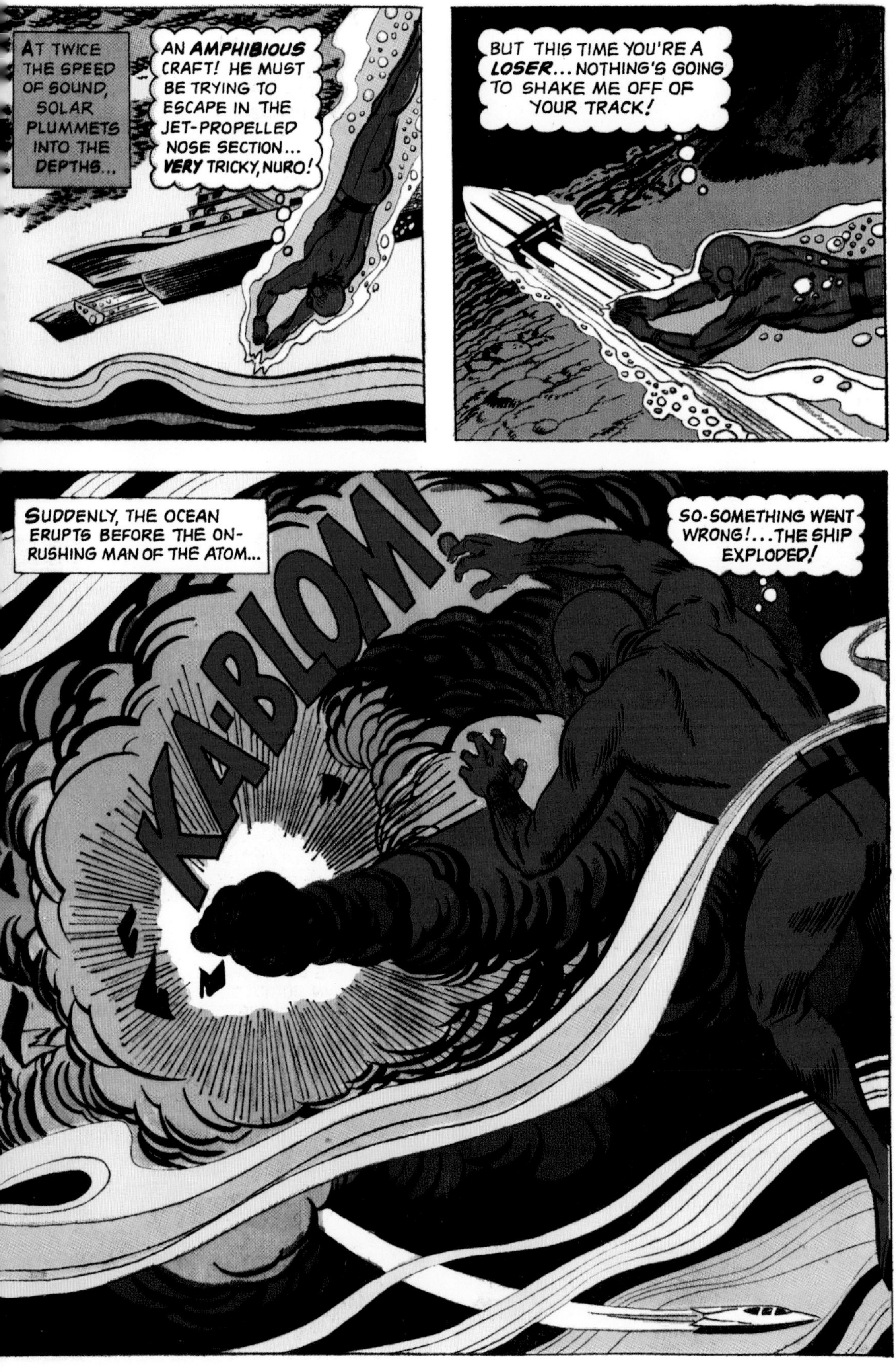
AT TWICE THE SPEED OF SOUND, SOLAR PLUMMETS INTO THE DEPTHS...
AN AMPHIBIOUS CRAFT! HE MUST BE TRYING TO ESCAPE IN THE JET-PROPELLED NOSE SECTION... VERY TRICKY, NURO!
BUT THIS TIME YOU'RE A LOSER... NOTHING'S GOING TO SHAKE ME OFF OF YOUR TRACK!
SUDDENLY, THE OCEAN ERUPTS BEFORE THE ON-RUSHING MAN OF THE ATOM...
SO-SOMETHING WENT WRONG!... THE SHIP EXPLODED!
KA-BLOM!

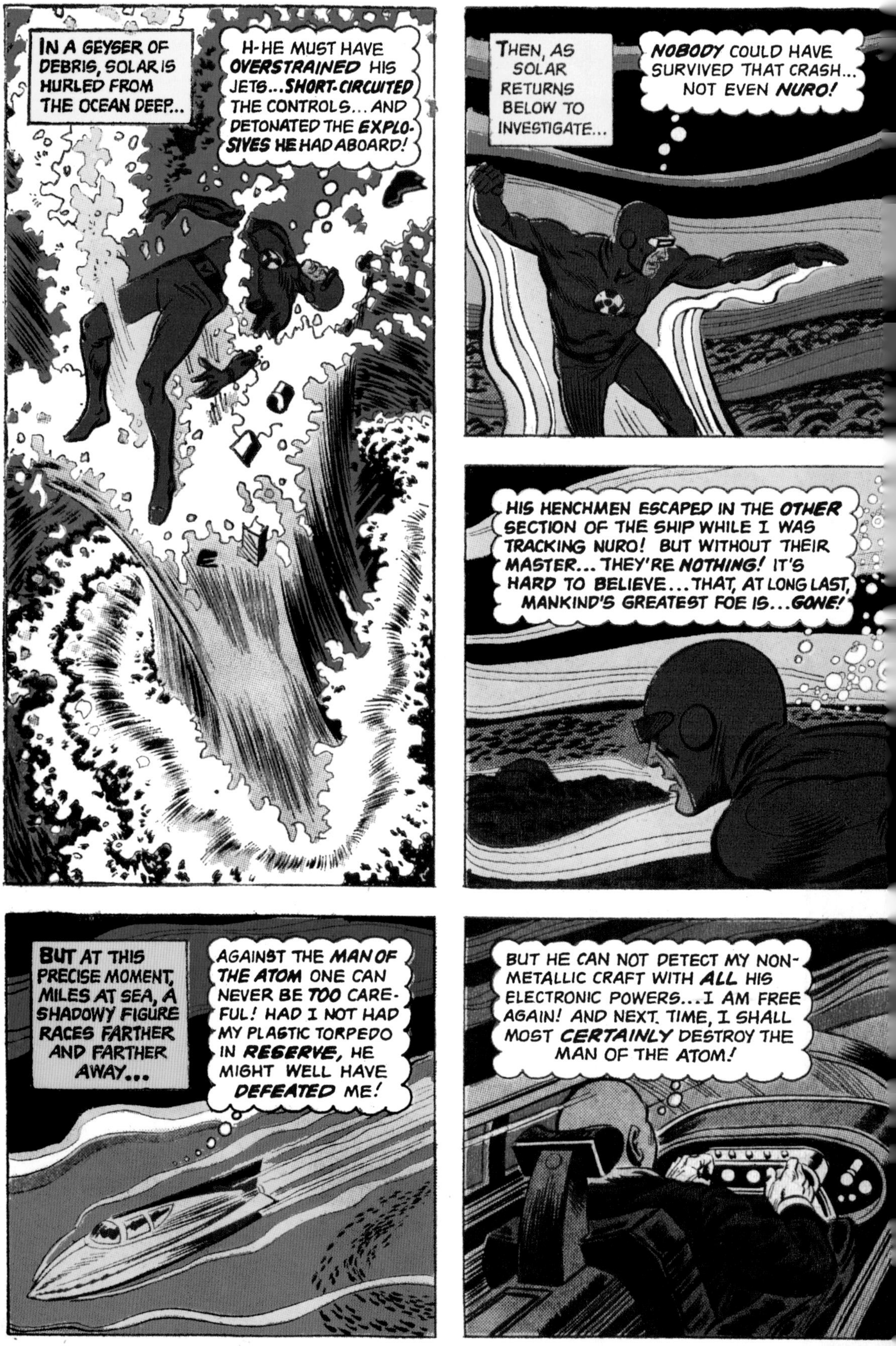
IN A GEYSER OF DEBRIS, SOLAR IS HURLED FROM THE OCEAN DEEP...
H-HE MUST HAVE OVERSTRAINED HIS JETS...SHORT-CIRCUITED THE CONTROLS... AND DETONATED THE EXPLOSIVES HE HAD ABOARD!
THEN, AS SOLAR RETURNS BELOW TO INVESTIGATE...
NOBODY COULD HAVE SURVIVED THAT CRASH... NOT EVEN NURO!
HIS HENCHMEN ESCAPED IN THE OTHER SECTION OF THE SHIP WHILE I WAS TRACKING NURO! BUT WITHOUT THEIR MASTER... THEY'RE NOTHING! IT'S HARD TO BELIEVE...THAT, AT LONG LAST, MANKIND'S GREATEST FOE IS...GONE!
BUT AT THIS PRECISE MOMENT, MILES AT SEA, A SHADOWY FIGURE RACES FARTHER AND FARTHER AWAY...
AGAINST THE MAN OF THE ATOM ONE CAN NEVER BE TOO CAREFUL! HAD I NOT HAD MY PLASTIC TORPEDO IN RESERVE, HE MIGHT WELL HAVE DEFEATED ME!
BUT HE CAN NOT DETECT MY NON-METALLIC CRAFT WITH ALL HIS ELECTRONIC POWERS...I AM FREE AGAIN! AND NEXT TIME, I SHALL MOST CERTAINLY DESTROY THE MAN OF THE ATOM!

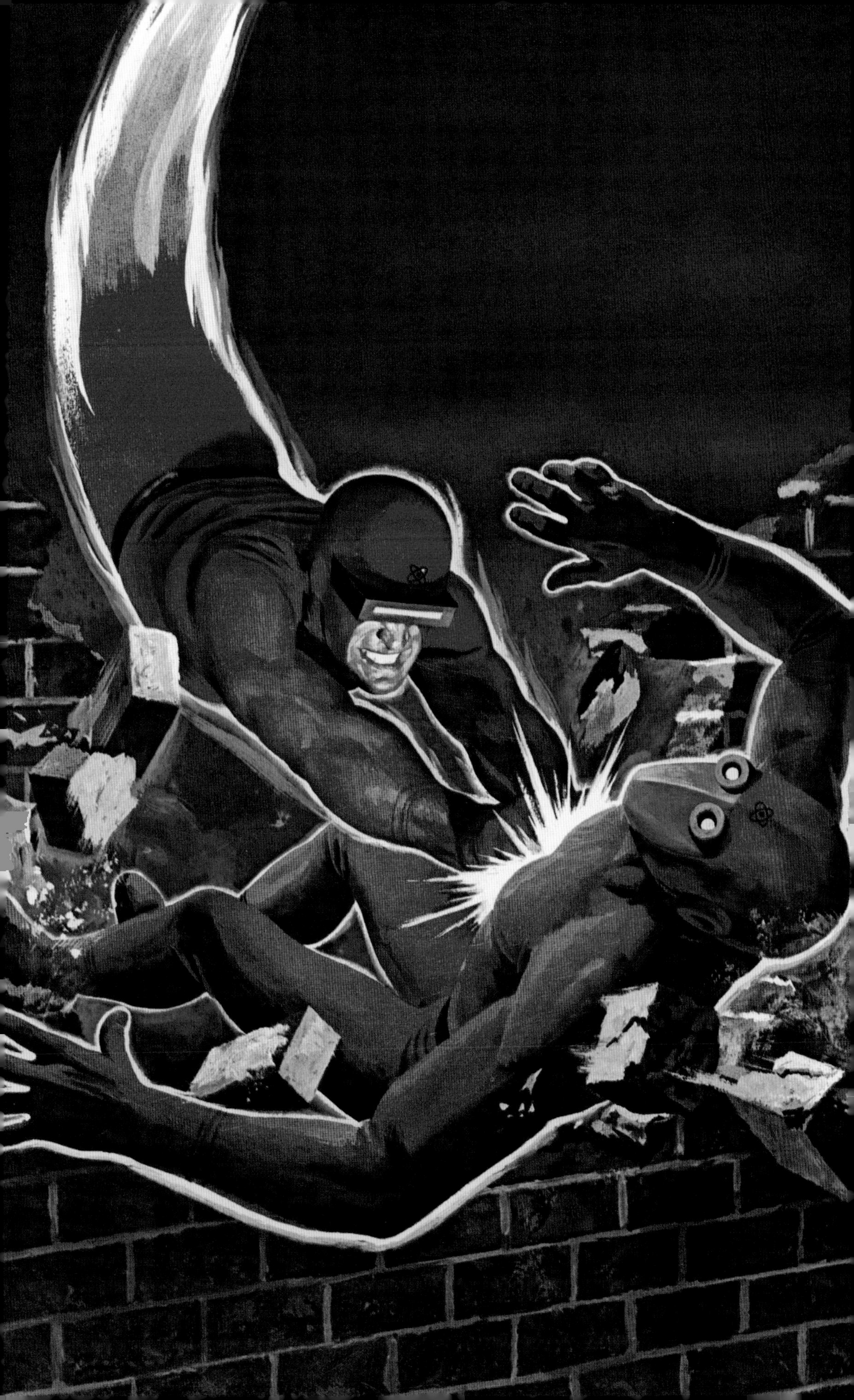

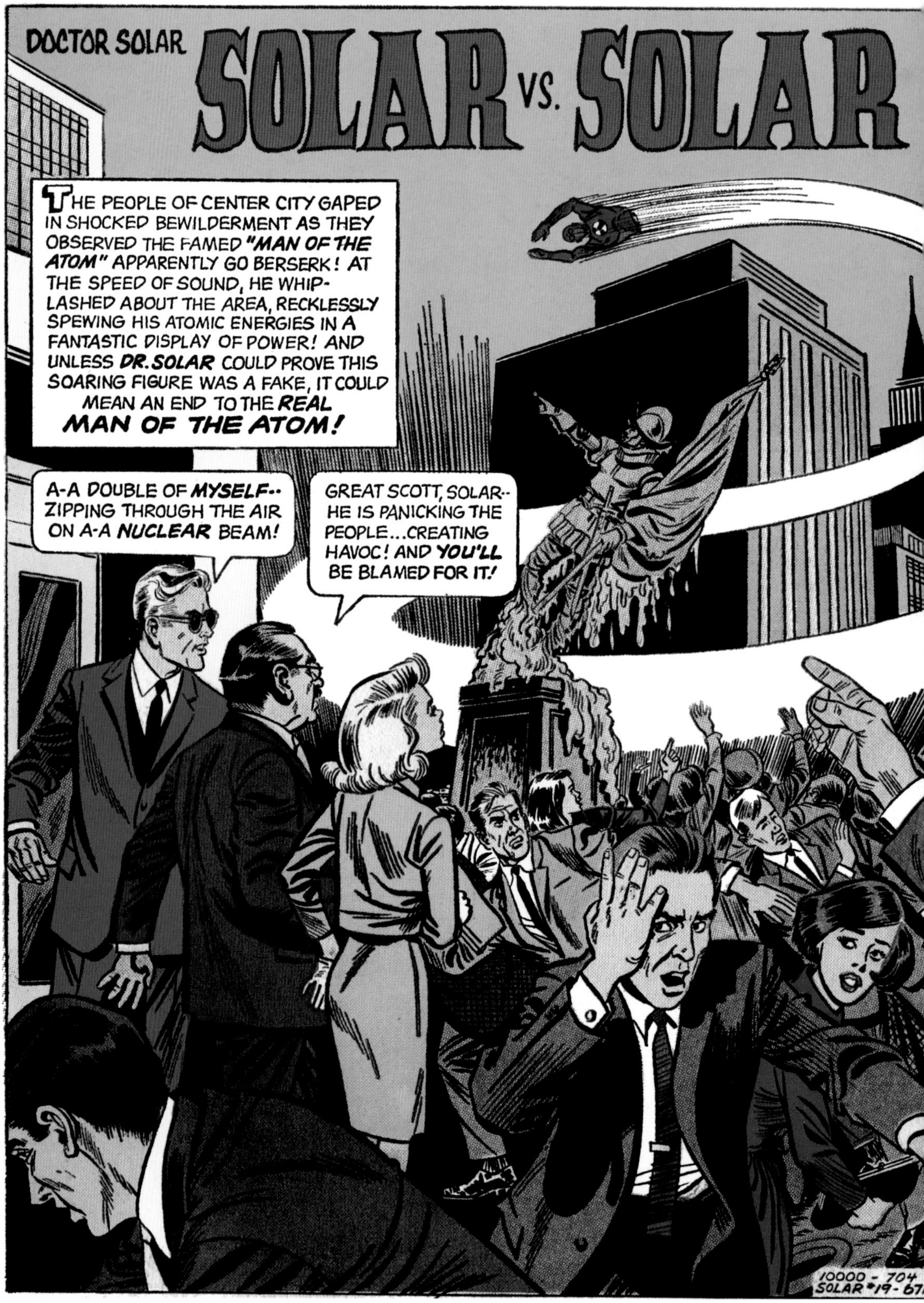
DOCTOR SOLAR
SOLAR VS. SOLAR
THE PEOPLE OF CENTER CITY GAPED IN SHOCKED BEWILDERMENT AS THEY OBSERVED THE FAMED "MAN OF THE ATOM" APPARENTLY GO BERSERK! AT THE SPEED OF SOUND, HE WHIPLASHED ABOUT THE AREA, RECKLESSLY SPEWING HIS ATOMIC ENERGIES IN A FANTASTIC DISPLAY OF POWER! AND UNLESS DR. SOLAR COULD PROVE THIS SOARING FIGURE WAS A FAKE, IT COULD MEAN AN END TO THE REAL MAN OF THE ATOM!
A-A DOUBLE OF MYSELF-- ZIPPING THROUGH THE AIR ON A-A NUCLEAR BEAM!
GREAT SCOTT, SOLAR-- HE IS PANICKING THE PEOPLE...CREATING HAVOC! AND YOU'LL BE BLAMED FOR IT!
10000 - 704
SOLAR #19 - 671

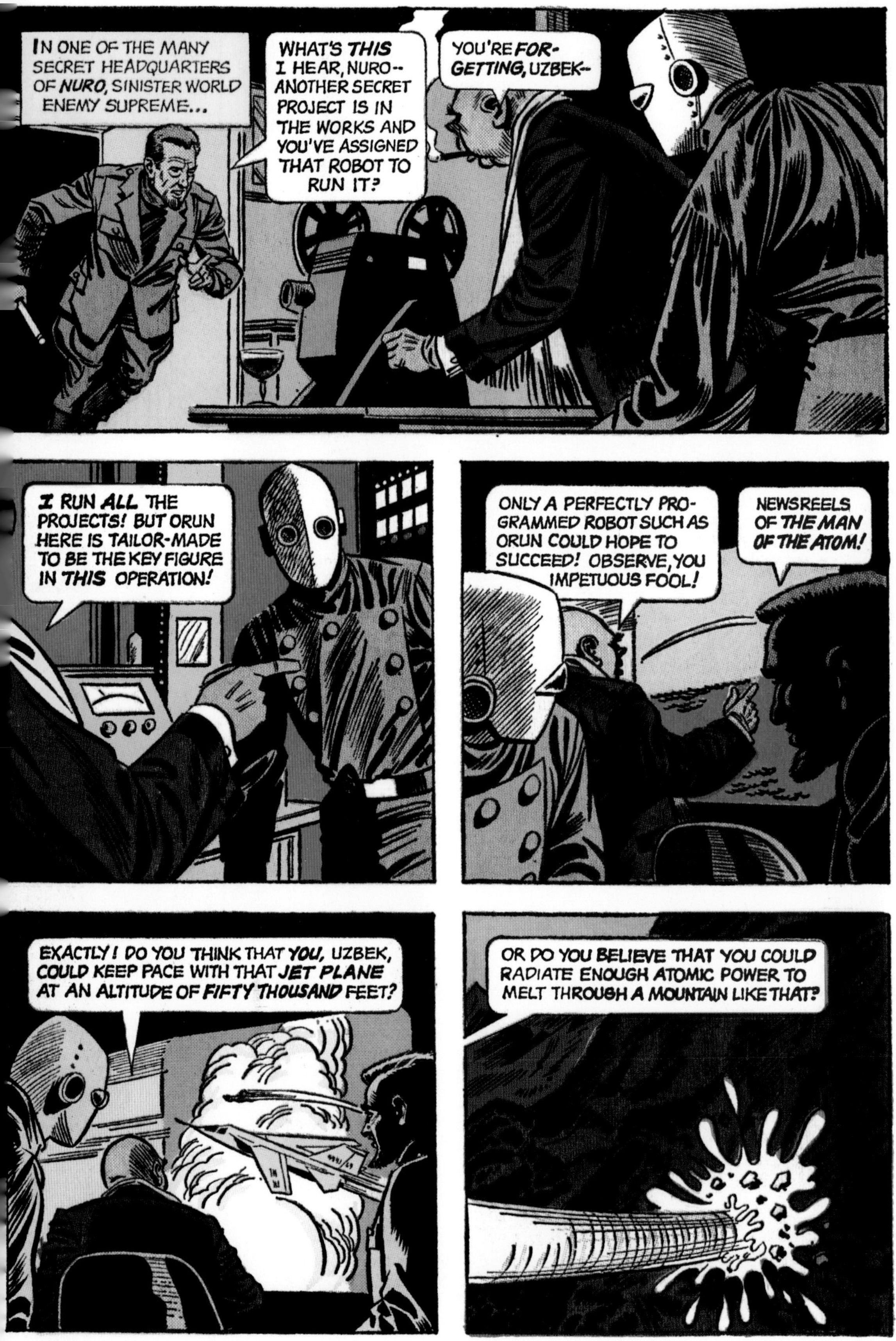
IN ONE OF THE MANY SECRET HEADQUARTERS OF NURO, SINISTER WORLD ENEMY SUPREME...
WHAT'S THIS I HEAR, NURO-- ANOTHER SECRET PROJECT IS IN THE WORKS AND YOU'VE ASSIGNED THAT ROBOT TO RUN IT?
YOU'RE FORGETTING, UZBEK--
I RUN ALL THE PROJECTS! BUT ORUN HERE IS TAILOR-MADE TO BE THE KEY FIGURE IN THIS OPERATION!
ONLY A PERFECTLY PROGRAMMED ROBOT SUCH AS ORUN COULD HOPE TO SUCCEED! OBSERVE, YOU IMPETUOUS FOOL!
NEWSREELS OF THE MAN OF THE ATOM!
EXACTLY! DO YOU THINK THAT YOU, UZBEK, COULD KEEP PACE WITH THAT JET PLANE AT AN ALTITUDE OF FIFTY THOUSAND FEET?
OR DO YOU BELIEVE THAT YOU COULD RADIATE ENOUGH ATOMIC POWER TO MELT THROUGH A MOUNTAIN LIKE THAT?

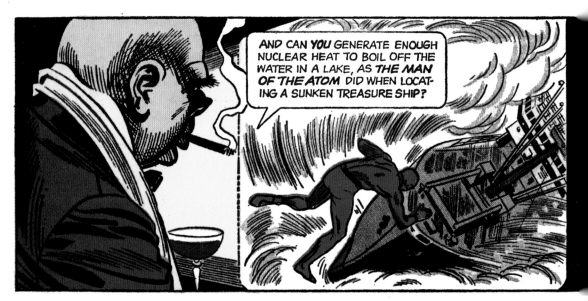

AND CAN *YOU* GENERATE ENOUGH NUCLEAR HEAT TO BOIL OFF THE WATER IN A LAKE, AS *THE MAN OF THE ATOM* DID WHEN LOCATING A SUNKEN TREASURE SHIP?

NO--BUT NEITHER CAN ANYONE ELSE ON EARTH!

I CAN, UZBEK!

CLICK!

YOU MEAN THIS SUPER-DUPER *TIN CAN* CAN DO ALL *THAT?*

PRECISELY! AND *MORE!*

IN THIS *MAN OF THE ATOM* COSTUME HE WILL DUPLICATE ALMOST TO THE LETTER A DOZEN FEATS OF THAT NUCLEAR AGE WONDER!

BUT ORUN IS JUST A HIGHLY-PRO-GRAMMED *THING-UMAJIG!* HE HASN'T ATOMIC POWERS LIKE *THE MAN OF THE ATOM!*

HE *WILL* HAVE WITHIN TWENTY-FOUR HOURS --WHEN I HAVE COMPLETED AN OPERATION ON HIS BODY! OBSERVE HIS NEW PARTS...A TINY *ATOMIC REACTOR* THAT'LL BE HIS *HEART!*

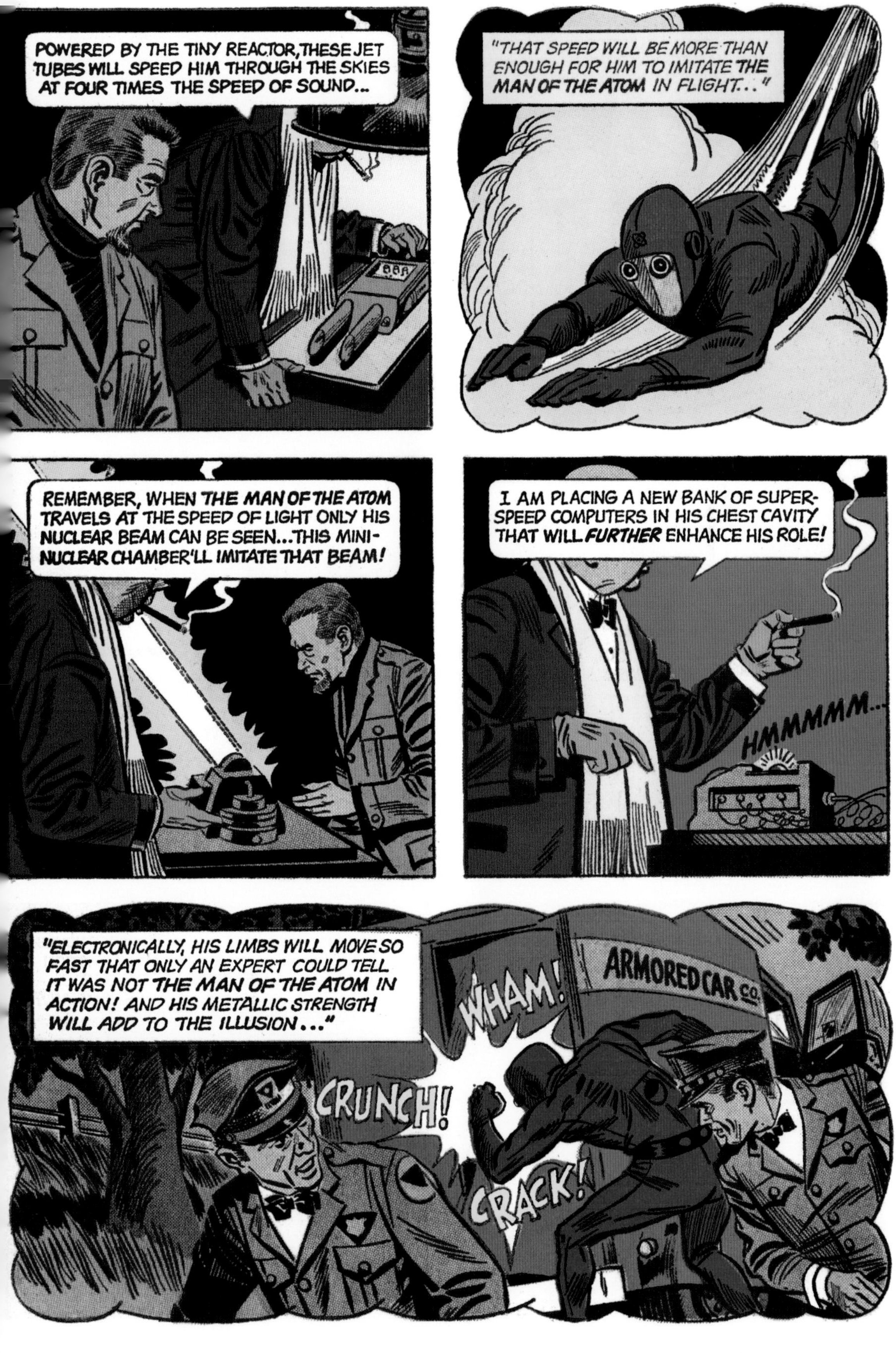

POWERED BY THE TINY REACTOR, THESE JET TUBES WILL SPEED HIM THROUGH THE SKIES AT FOUR TIMES THE SPEED OF SOUND...
"THAT SPEED WILL BE MORE THAN ENOUGH FOR HIM TO IMITATE THE MAN OF THE ATOM IN FLIGHT..."
REMEMBER, WHEN THE MAN OF THE ATOM TRAVELS AT THE SPEED OF LIGHT ONLY HIS NUCLEAR BEAM CAN BE SEEN...THIS MINI-NUCLEAR CHAMBER'LL IMITATE THAT BEAM!
I AM PLACING A NEW BANK OF SUPER-SPEED COMPUTERS IN HIS CHEST CAVITY THAT WILL FURTHER ENHANCE HIS ROLE!
HMMMMM...
"ELECTRONICALLY, HIS LIMBS WILL MOVE SO FAST THAT ONLY AN EXPERT COULD TELL IT WAS NOT THE MAN OF THE ATOM IN ACTION! AND HIS METALLIC STRENGTH WILL ADD TO THE ILLUSION..."
ARMORED CAR CO.
WHAM!
CRUNCH!
CRACK!

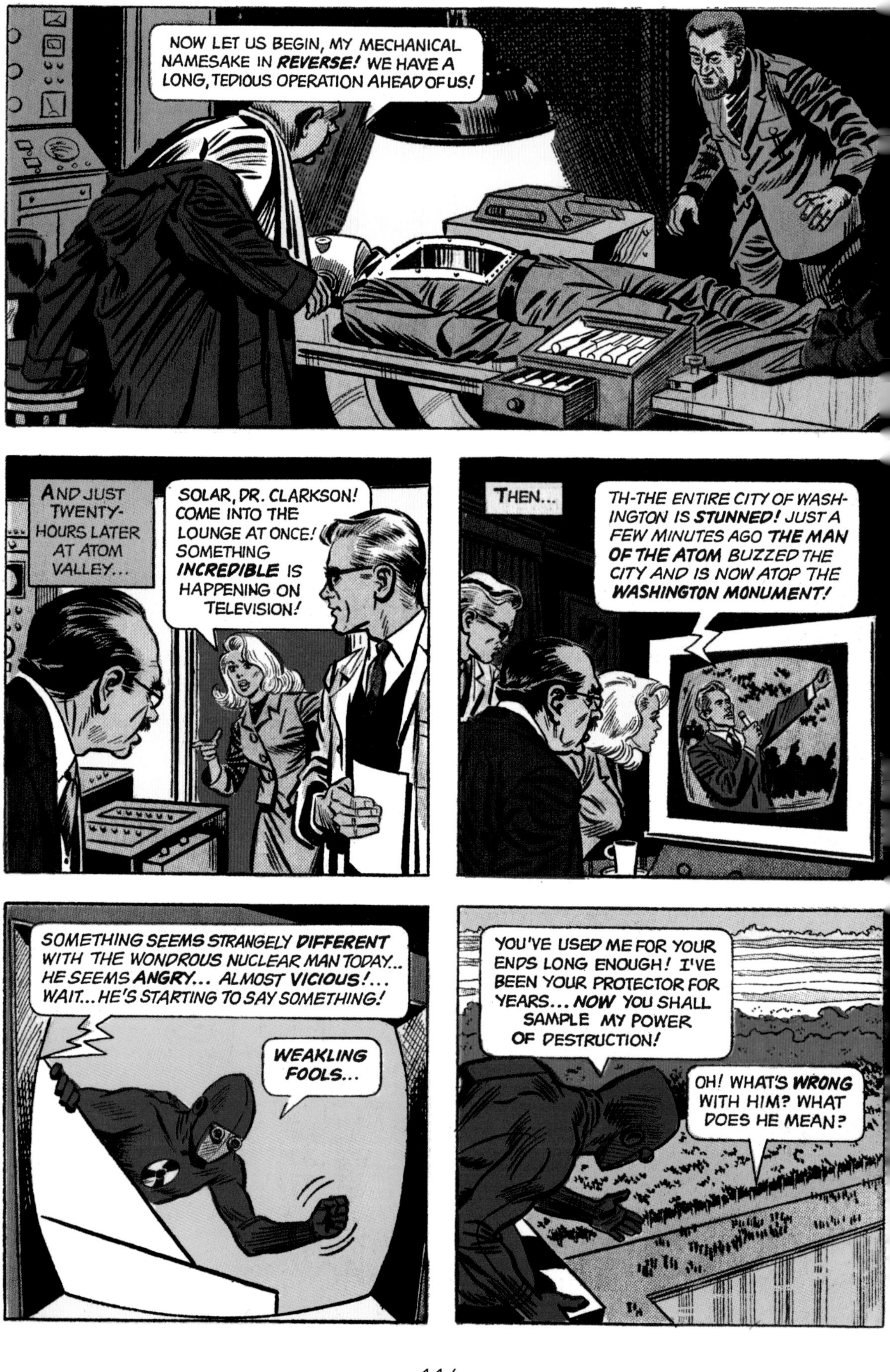
NOW LET US BEGIN, MY MECHANICAL NAMESAKE IN REVERSE! WE HAVE A LONG, TEDIOUS OPERATION AHEAD OF US!
AND JUST TWENTY-HOURS LATER AT ATOM VALLEY...
SOLAR, DR. CLARKSON! COME INTO THE LOUNGE AT ONCE! SOMETHING INCREDIBLE IS HAPPENING ON TELEVISION!
THEN...
TH-THE ENTIRE CITY OF WASHINGTON IS STUNNED! JUST A FEW MINUTES AGO THE MAN OF THE ATOM BUZZED THE CITY AND IS NOW ATOP THE WASHINGTON MONUMENT!
SOMETHING SEEMS STRANGELY DIFFERENT WITH THE WONDROUS NUCLEAR MAN TODAY... HE SEEMS ANGRY... ALMOST VICIOUS!... WAIT... HE'S STARTING TO SAY SOMETHING!
WEAKLING FOOLS...
YOU'VE USED ME FOR YOUR ENDS LONG ENOUGH! I'VE BEEN YOUR PROTECTOR FOR YEARS... NOW YOU SHALL SAMPLE MY POWER OF DESTRUCTION!
OH! WHAT'S WRONG WITH HIM? WHAT DOES HE MEAN?

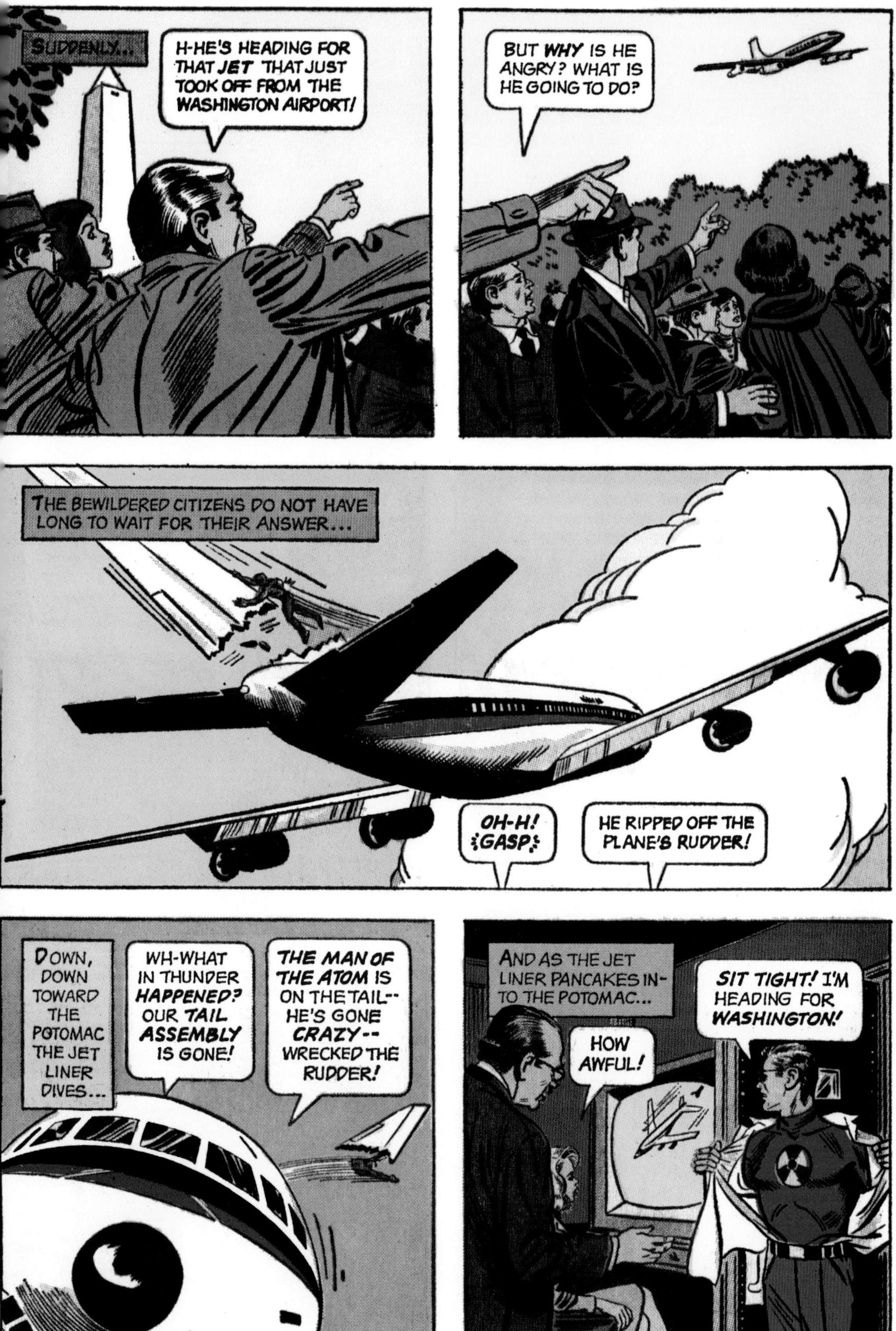
SUDDENLY...
H-HE'S HEADING FOR THAT JET THAT JUST TOOK OFF FROM THE WASHINGTON AIRPORT!
BUT WHY IS HE ANGRY? WHAT IS HE GOING TO DO?
THE BEWILDERED CITIZENS DO NOT HAVE LONG TO WAIT FOR THEIR ANSWER...
OH-H! GASP
HE RIPPED OFF THE PLANE'S RUDDER!
DOWN, DOWN TOWARD THE POTOMAC THE JET LINER DIVES...
WH-WHAT IN THUNDER HAPPENED? OUR TAIL ASSEMBLY IS GONE!
THE MAN OF THE ATOM IS ON THE TAIL-- HE'S GONE CRAZY-- WRECKED THE RUDDER!
AND AS THE JET LINER PANCAKES INTO THE POTOMAC...
HOW AWFUL!
SIT TIGHT! I'M HEADING FOR WASHINGTON!

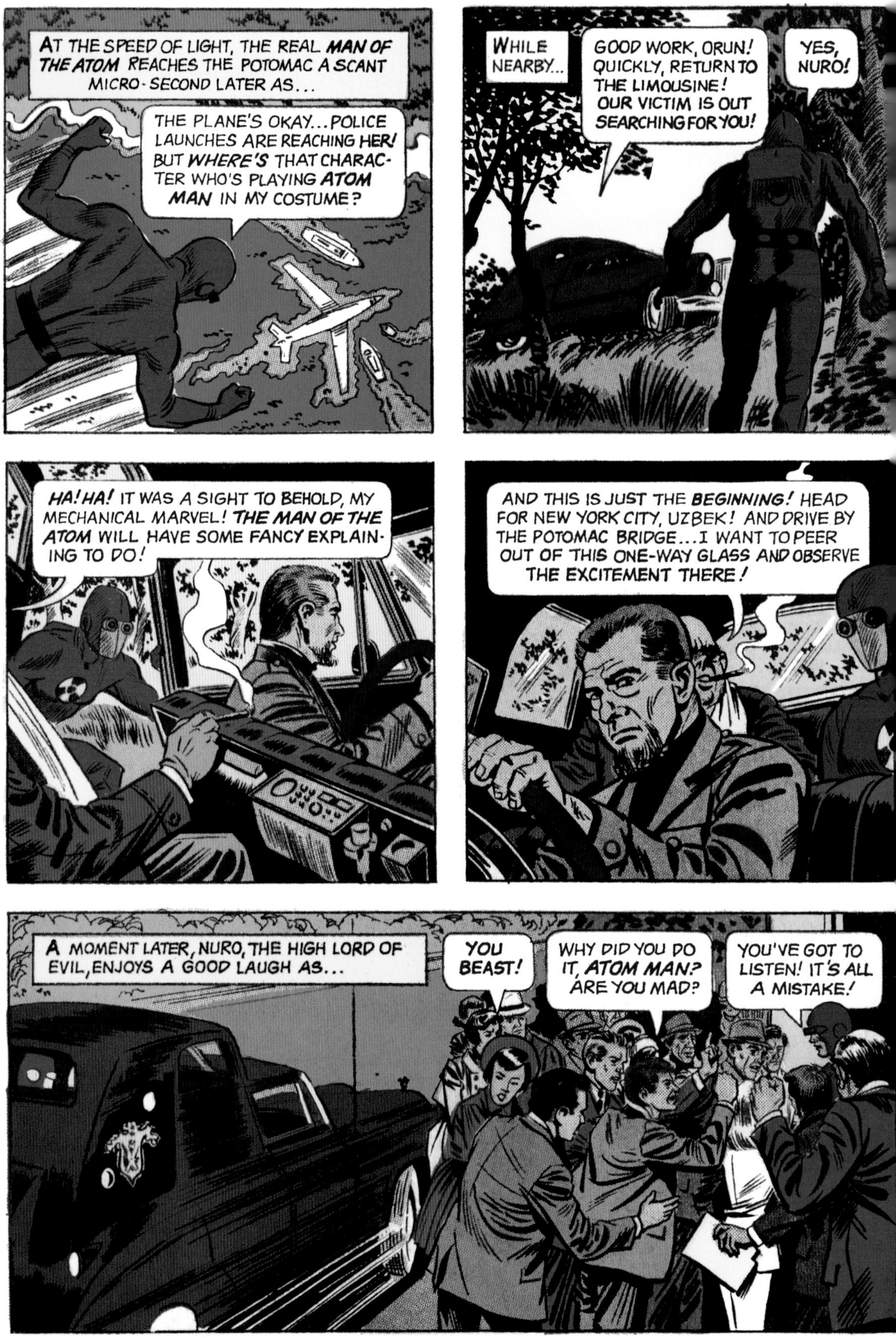
AT THE SPEED OF LIGHT, THE REAL MAN OF THE ATOM REACHES THE POTOMAC A SCANT MICRO-SECOND LATER AS...
THE PLANE'S OKAY...POLICE LAUNCHES ARE REACHING HER! BUT WHERE'S THAT CHARACTER WHO'S PLAYING ATOM MAN IN MY COSTUME?
WHILE NEARBY...
GOOD WORK, ORUN! QUICKLY, RETURN TO THE LIMOUSINE! OUR VICTIM IS OUT SEARCHING FOR YOU!
YES, NURO!
HA! HA! IT WAS A SIGHT TO BEHOLD, MY MECHANICAL MARVEL! THE MAN OF THE ATOM WILL HAVE SOME FANCY EXPLAINING TO DO!
AND THIS IS JUST THE BEGINNING! HEAD FOR NEW YORK CITY, UZBEK! AND DRIVE BY THE POTOMAC BRIDGE...I WANT TO PEER OUT OF THIS ONE-WAY GLASS AND OBSERVE THE EXCITEMENT THERE!
A MOMENT LATER, NURO, THE HIGH LORD OF EVIL, ENJOYS A GOOD LAUGH AS...
YOU BEAST!
WHY DID YOU DO IT, ATOM MAN? ARE YOU MAD?
YOU'VE GOT TO LISTEN! IT'S ALL A MISTAKE!

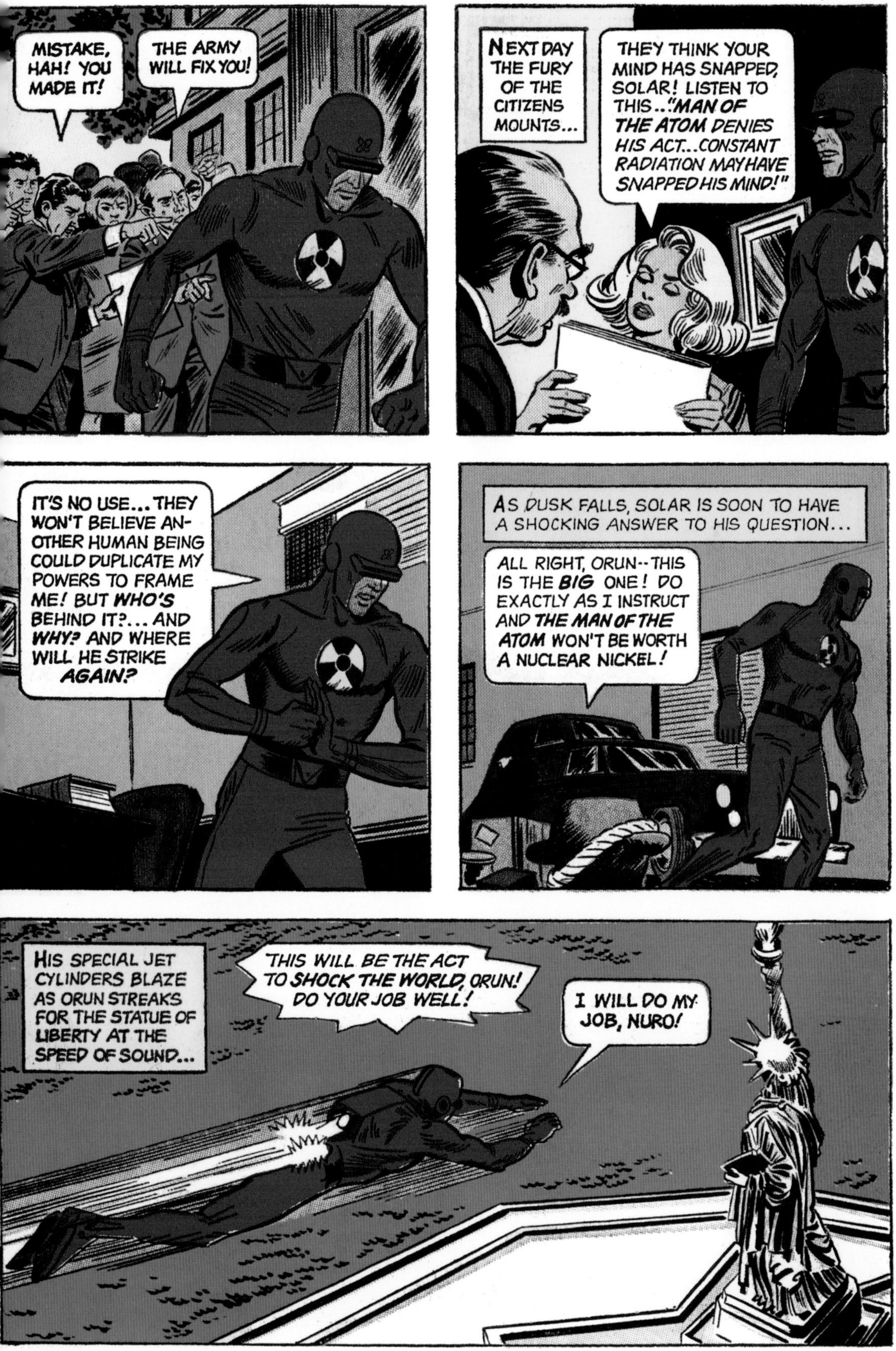
MISTAKE, HAH! YOU MADE IT!
THE ARMY WILL FIX YOU!
NEXT DAY THE FURY OF THE CITIZENS MOUNTS...
THEY THINK YOUR MIND HAS SNAPPED, SOLAR! LISTEN TO THIS..."MAN OF THE ATOM DENIES HIS ACT...CONSTANT RADIATION MAY HAVE SNAPPED HIS MIND!"
IT'S NO USE...THEY WON'T BELIEVE ANOTHER HUMAN BEING COULD DUPLICATE MY POWERS TO FRAME ME! BUT WHO'S BEHIND IT?... AND WHY? AND WHERE WILL HE STRIKE AGAIN?
AS DUSK FALLS, SOLAR IS SOON TO HAVE A SHOCKING ANSWER TO HIS QUESTION...
ALL RIGHT, ORUN--THIS IS THE BIG ONE! DO EXACTLY AS I INSTRUCT AND THE MAN OF THE ATOM WON'T BE WORTH A NUCLEAR NICKEL!
HIS SPECIAL JET CYLINDERS BLAZE AS ORUN STREAKS FOR THE STATUE OF LIBERTY AT THE SPEED OF SOUND...
THIS WILL BE THE ACT TO SHOCK THE WORLD, ORUN! DO YOUR JOB WELL!
I WILL DO MY JOB, NURO!

A STEEL-HARD HAND LASHES OUT AT THE FAMED LIBERTY TORCH...

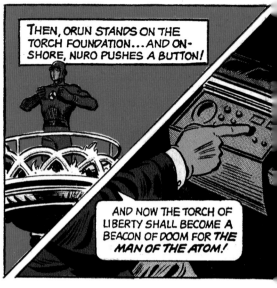

THEN, ORUN STANDS ON THE TORCH FOUNDATION...AND ON-SHORE, NURO PUSHES A BUTTON!

AND NOW THE TORCH OF LIBERTY SHALL BECOME A BEACON OF DOOM FOR *THE MAN OF THE ATOM!*

INSTANTLY, ATOMIC POWER IS LIBERATED WITHIN ORUN...HIS BODY GLOWS FIERCELY...

LO-LOOK! LO-LOOK! IT'S THE *MAN OF THE ATOM* AGAIN!

GREAT GRIEF! HE'S SMASHED THE LIBERTY TORCH -- HE'S REPLACING IT WITH HIS *OWN* GLOWING *NUCLEAR* ENERGY!

A FEARFUL CRY RINGS OUT ACROSS NEW YORK HARBOR...

*DEATH TO LIBERTY!* HEAR ME, WORLD! YOU SHALL BE ENSLAVED BY *THE MAN OF THE ATOM!*

ABRUPTLY, THE *ROBOT OF RUIN* PLUMMETS DOWNWARD...

GREAT NEPTUNE! HE'S COMING DEAD AT US!

H-HE'S CRAZED AS A HOOKED MARLIN! *EMERGENCY STATIONS!!*

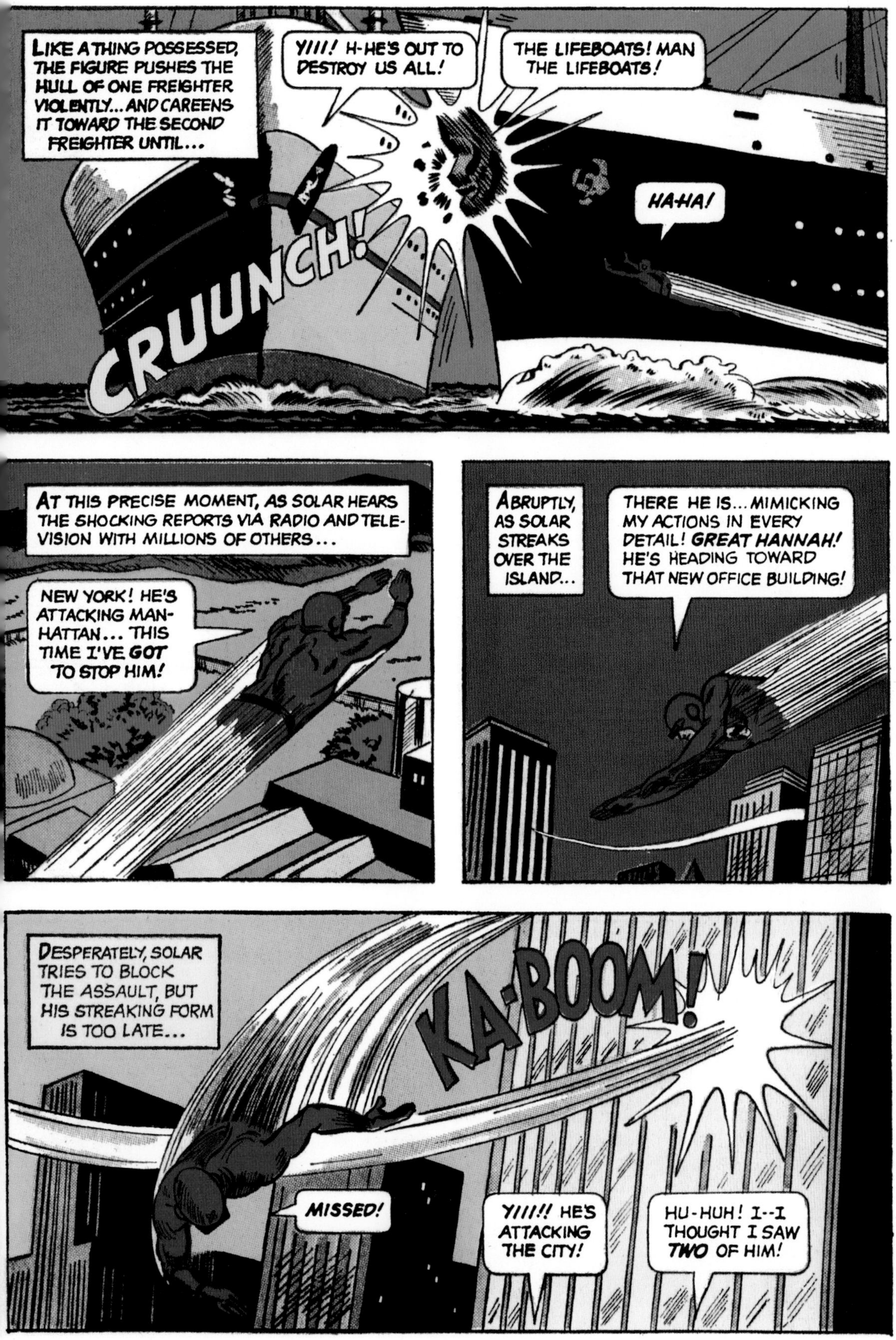
LIKE A THING POSSESSED, THE FIGURE PUSHES THE HULL OF ONE FREIGHTER VIOLENTLY... AND CAREENS IT TOWARD THE SECOND FREIGHTER UNTIL...
YIII! H-HE'S OUT TO DESTROY US ALL!
THE LIFEBOATS! MAN THE LIFEBOATS!
CRUUNCH!
HA-HA!
AT THIS PRECISE MOMENT, AS SOLAR HEARS THE SHOCKING REPORTS VIA RADIO AND TELE-VISION WITH MILLIONS OF OTHERS...
NEW YORK! HE'S ATTACKING MAN-HATTAN... THIS TIME I'VE GOT TO STOP HIM!
ABRUPTLY, AS SOLAR STREAKS OVER THE ISLAND...
THERE HE IS... MIMICKING MY ACTIONS IN EVERY DETAIL! GREAT HANNAH! HE'S HEADING TOWARD THAT NEW OFFICE BUILDING!
DESPERATELY, SOLAR TRIES TO BLOCK THE ASSAULT, BUT HIS STREAKING FORM IS TOO LATE...
KA-BOOM!
MISSED!
YIII!! HE'S ATTACKING THE CITY!
HU-HUH! I--I THOUGHT I SAW TWO OF HIM!

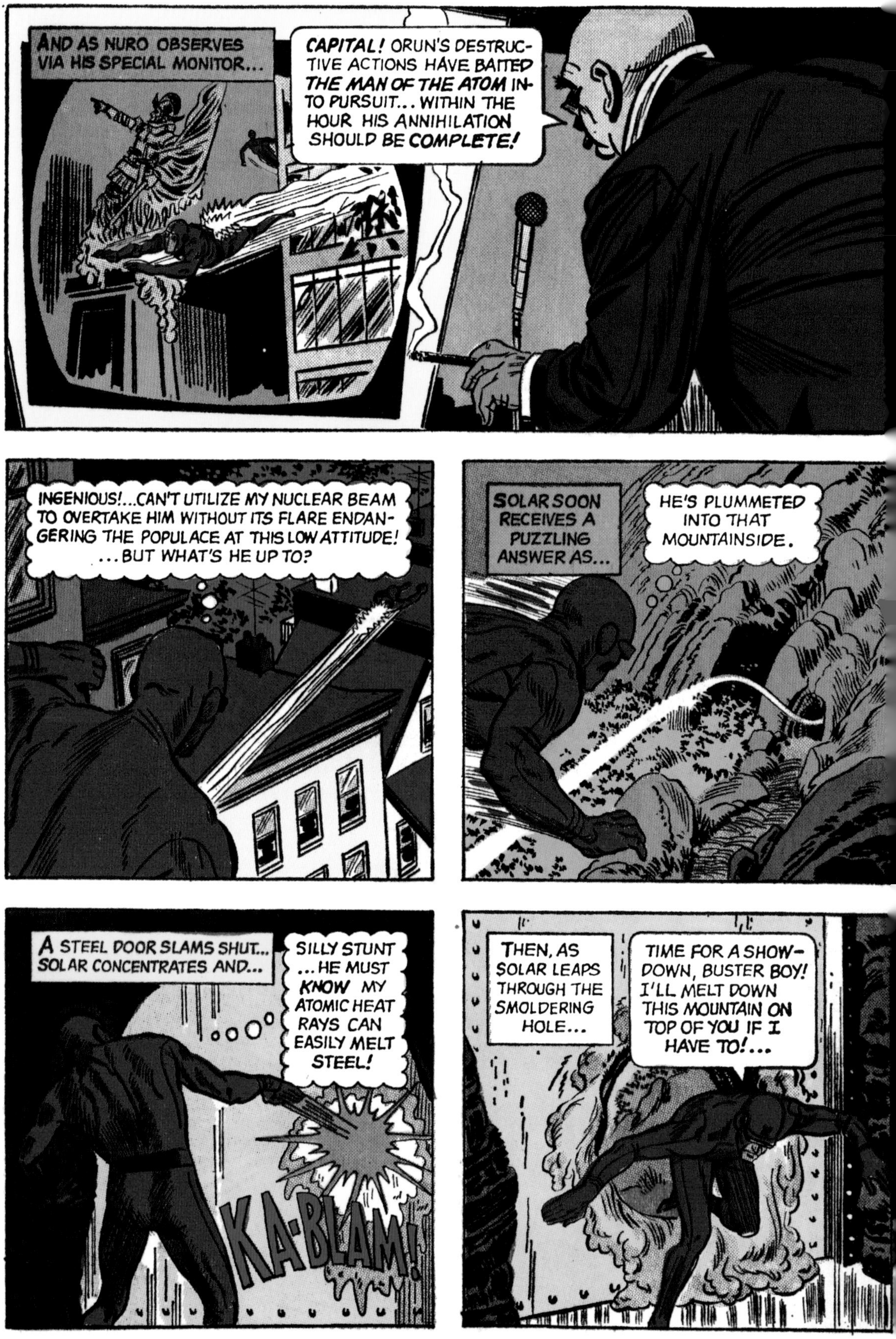
AND AS NURO OBSERVES VIA HIS SPECIAL MONITOR...
CAPITAL! ORUN'S DESTRUCTIVE ACTIONS HAVE BAITED THE MAN OF THE ATOM INTO PURSUIT... WITHIN THE HOUR HIS ANNIHILATION SHOULD BE COMPLETE!
INGENIOUS!...CAN'T UTILIZE MY NUCLEAR BEAM TO OVERTAKE HIM WITHOUT ITS FLARE ENDANGERING THE POPULACE AT THIS LOW ATTITUDE! ...BUT WHAT'S HE UP TO?
SOLAR SOON RECEIVES A PUZZLING ANSWER AS...
HE'S PLUMMETED INTO THAT MOUNTAINSIDE.
A STEEL DOOR SLAMS SHUT... SOLAR CONCENTRATES AND...
SILLY STUNT ...HE MUST KNOW MY ATOMIC HEAT RAYS CAN EASILY MELT STEEL!
KA-BLAM!
THEN, AS SOLAR LEAPS THROUGH THE SMOLDERING HOLE...
TIME FOR A SHOWDOWN, BUSTER BOY! I'LL MELT DOWN THIS MOUNTAIN ON TOP OF YOU IF I HAVE TO!...

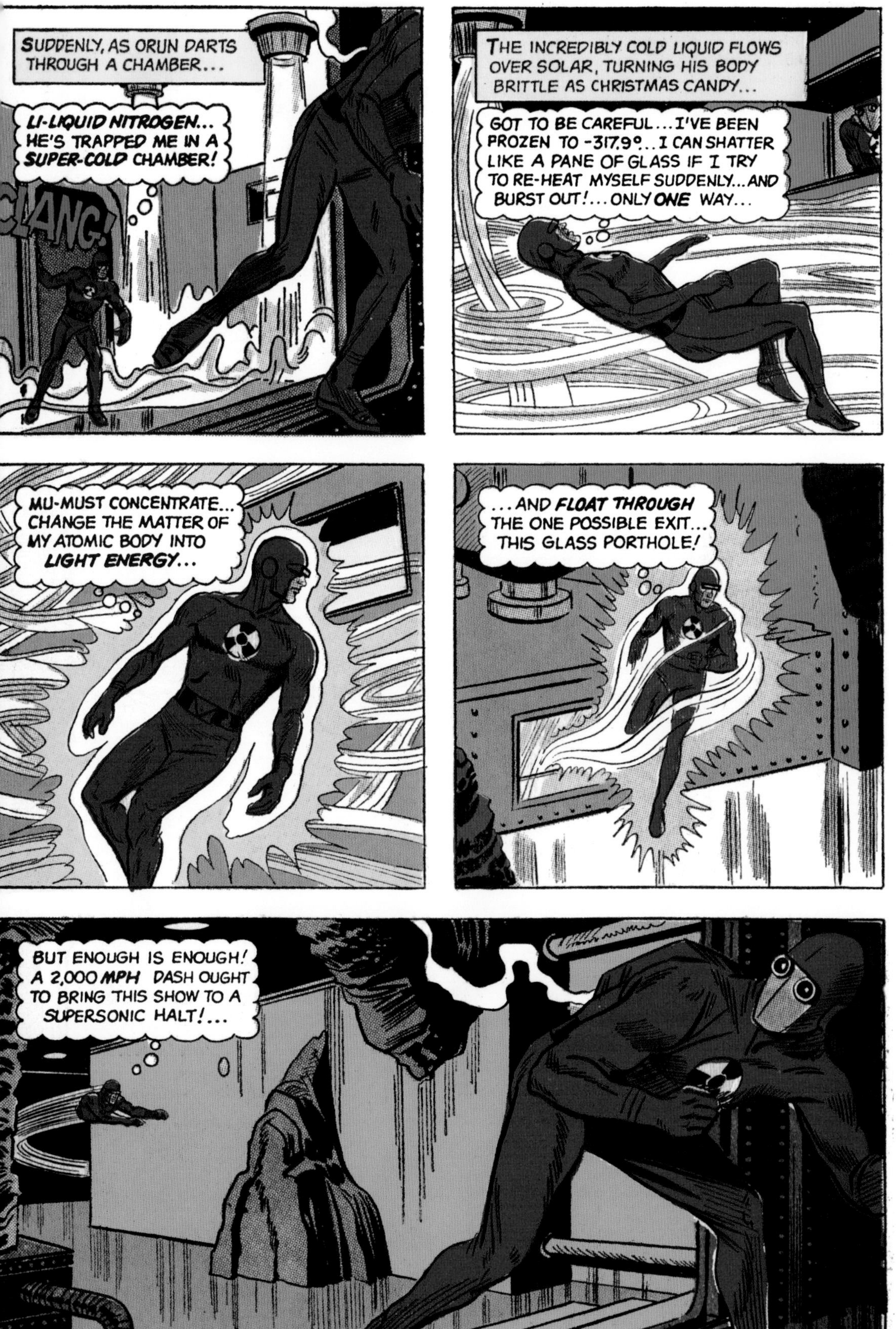
SUDDENLY, AS ORUN DARTS THROUGH A CHAMBER...
LI-LIQUID NITROGEN... HE'S TRAPPED ME IN A SUPER-COLD CHAMBER!
CLANG!
THE INCREDIBLY COLD LIQUID FLOWS OVER SOLAR, TURNING HIS BODY BRITTLE AS CHRISTMAS CANDY...
GOT TO BE CAREFUL... I'VE BEEN FROZEN TO -317.9°... I CAN SHATTER LIKE A PANE OF GLASS IF I TRY TO RE-HEAT MYSELF SUDDENLY... AND BURST OUT!... ONLY ONE WAY...
MU-MUST CONCENTRATE... CHANGE THE MATTER OF MY ATOMIC BODY INTO LIGHT ENERGY...
...AND FLOAT THROUGH THE ONE POSSIBLE EXIT... THIS GLASS PORTHOLE!
BUT ENOUGH IS ENOUGH! A 2,000 MPH DASH OUGHT TO BRING THIS SHOW TO A SUPERSONIC HALT!...

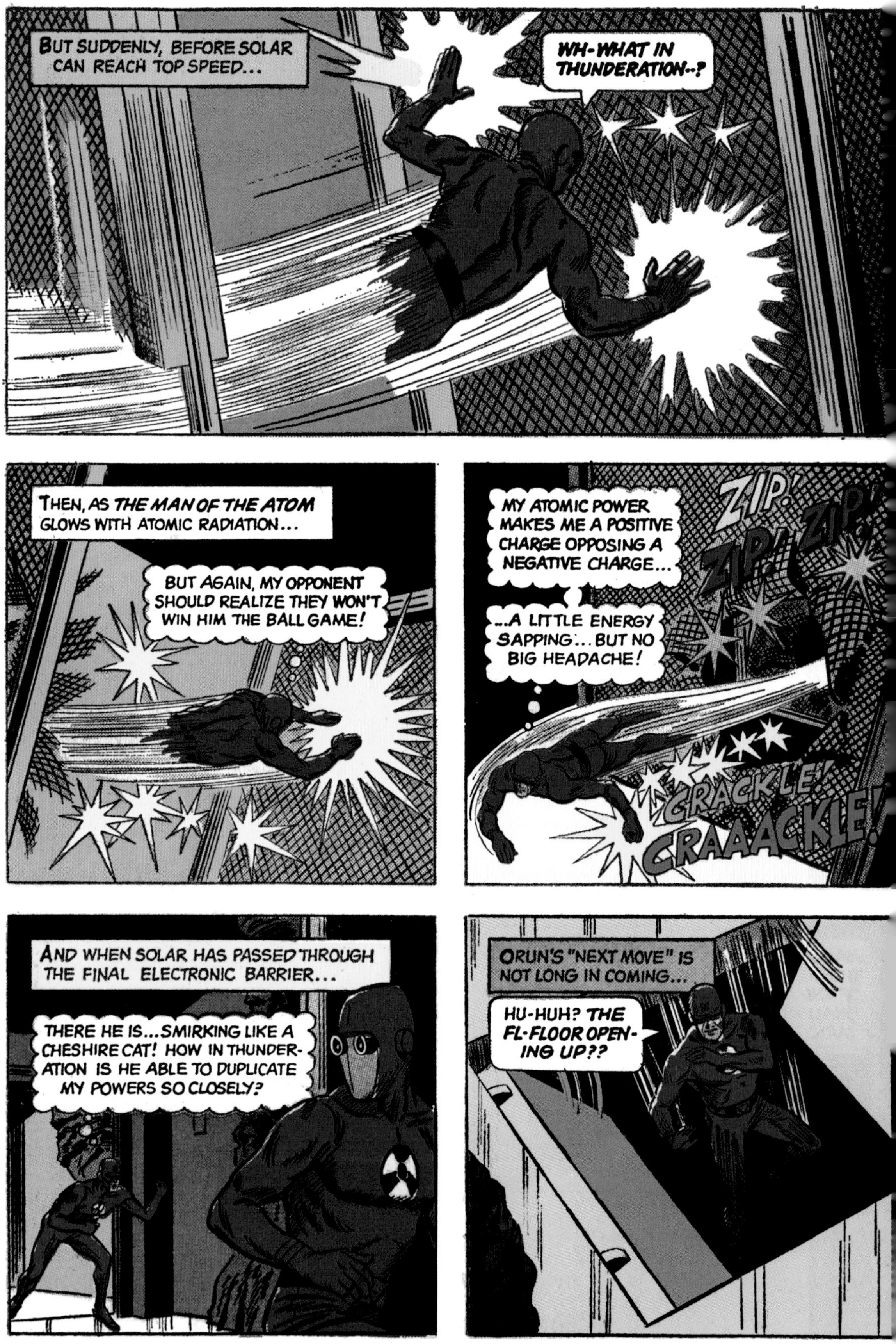
BUT SUDDENLY, BEFORE SOLAR CAN REACH TOP SPEED...
WH-WHAT IN THUNDERATION--?
THEN, AS THE MAN OF THE ATOM GLOWS WITH ATOMIC RADIATION...
BUT AGAIN, MY OPPONENT SHOULD REALIZE THEY WON'T WIN HIM THE BALL GAME!
MY ATOMIC POWER MAKES ME A POSITIVE CHARGE OPPOSING A NEGATIVE CHARGE...
...A LITTLE ENERGY SAPPING... BUT NO BIG HEADACHE!
ZIP! ZIP! ZIP!
CRACKLE! CRAAACKLE!
AND WHEN SOLAR HAS PASSED THROUGH THE FINAL ELECTRONIC BARRIER...
THERE HE IS...SMIRKING LIKE A CHESHIRE CAT! HOW IN THUNDERATION IS HE ABLE TO DUPLICATE MY POWERS SO CLOSELY?
ORUN'S "NEXT MOVE" IS NOT LONG IN COMING...
HU-HUH? THE FL-FLOOR OPENING UP??

ABRUPTLY, THE HEAVY SECTION OF FLOORING THUDS SHUT...

THUD!

AND BELOW, AS SOLAR GLOWS SOFTLY TO ILLUMINATE HIS POSITION...

*LEAD!* I'M TRAPPED IN A SOLID LEAD PRISON! ATOMIC RADIATION CAN'T PENETRATE THIS TRAP... I'M LIKE AN ISOTOPE IN ITS LEAD-LINED PROTECTIVE JAR!

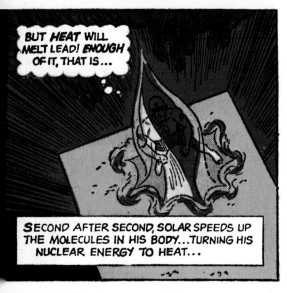

BUT *HEAT* WILL MELT LEAD! *ENOUGH* OF IT, THAT IS...

SECOND AFTER SECOND, SOLAR SPEEDS UP THE MOLECULES IN HIS BODY...TURNING HIS NUCLEAR ENERGY TO HEAT...

AND FINALLY...

LEAD WALLS DO NOT A PRISON MAKE...WHEN YOU'RE BUILT LIKE AN ATOMIC BOMB! BUT WHAT'S MY RINGER GOT WAITING FOR ME *NOW?*

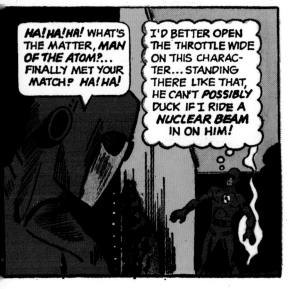

HA! HA! HA! WHAT'S THE MATTER, *MAN OF THE ATOM?*... FINALLY MET YOUR MATCH? HA! HA!

I'D BETTER OPEN THE THROTTLE WIDE ON THIS CHARACTER... STANDING THERE LIKE THAT, HE CAN'T *POSSIBLY* DUCK IF I RIDE A *NUCLEAR BEAM* IN ON HIM!

QUICKLY, SOLAR TRANSFORMS THE MATTER OF HIS ATOMIC BODY INTO LIGHT ENERGY...

BUT WHY IS HE *LAUGHING?*

*CONTINUED...*

125

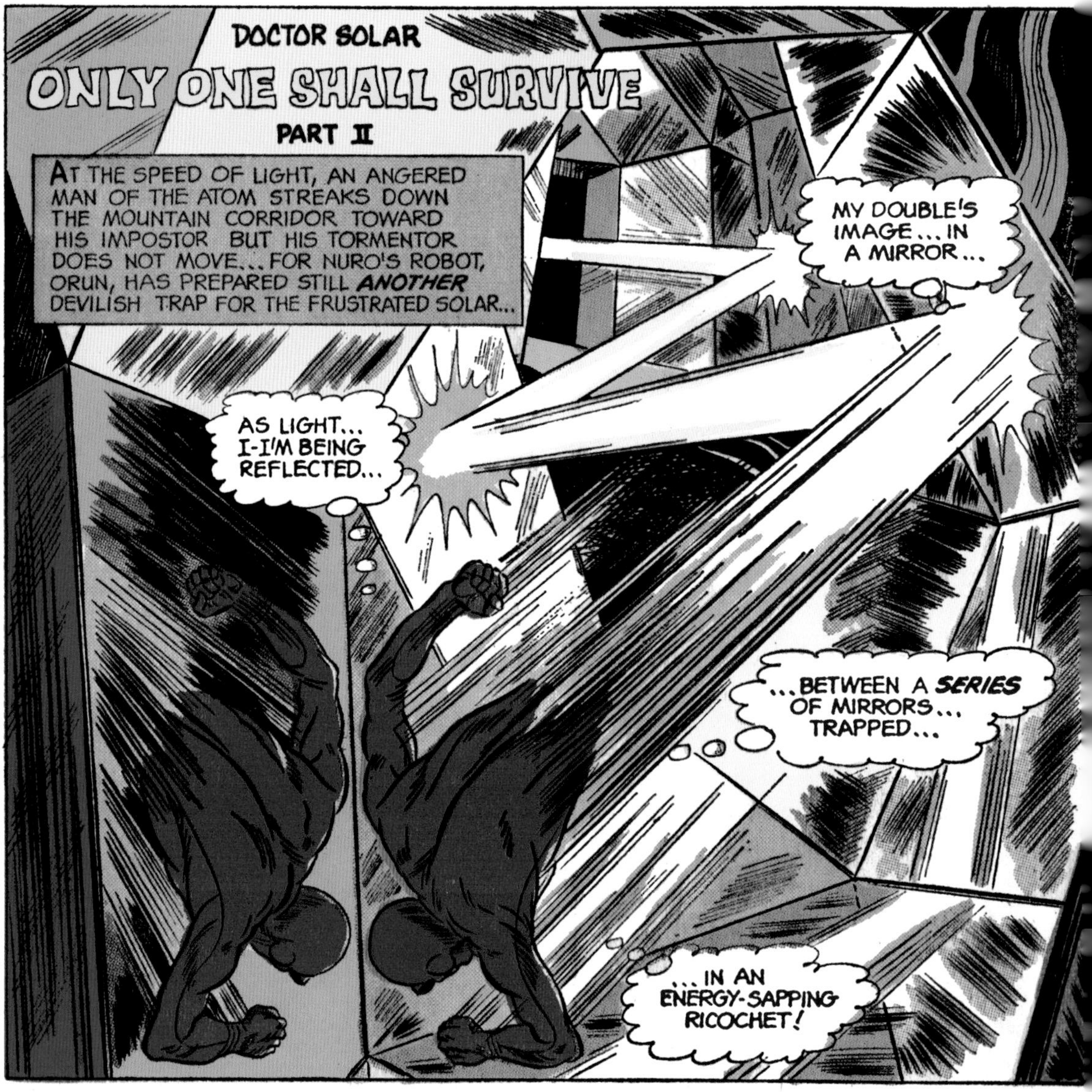
DOCTOR SOLAR
ONLY ONE SHALL SURVIVE
PART II
AT THE SPEED OF LIGHT, AN ANGERED MAN OF THE ATOM STREAKS DOWN THE MOUNTAIN CORRIDOR TOWARD HIS IMPOSTOR BUT HIS TORMENTOR DOES NOT MOVE... FOR NURO'S ROBOT, ORUN, HAS PREPARED STILL ANOTHER DEVILISH TRAP FOR THE FRUSTRATED SOLAR...
MY DOUBLE'S IMAGE... IN A MIRROR...
AS LIGHT... I-I'M BEING REFLECTED...
...BETWEEN A SERIES OF MIRRORS... TRAPPED...
...IN AN ENERGY-SAPPING RICOCHET!

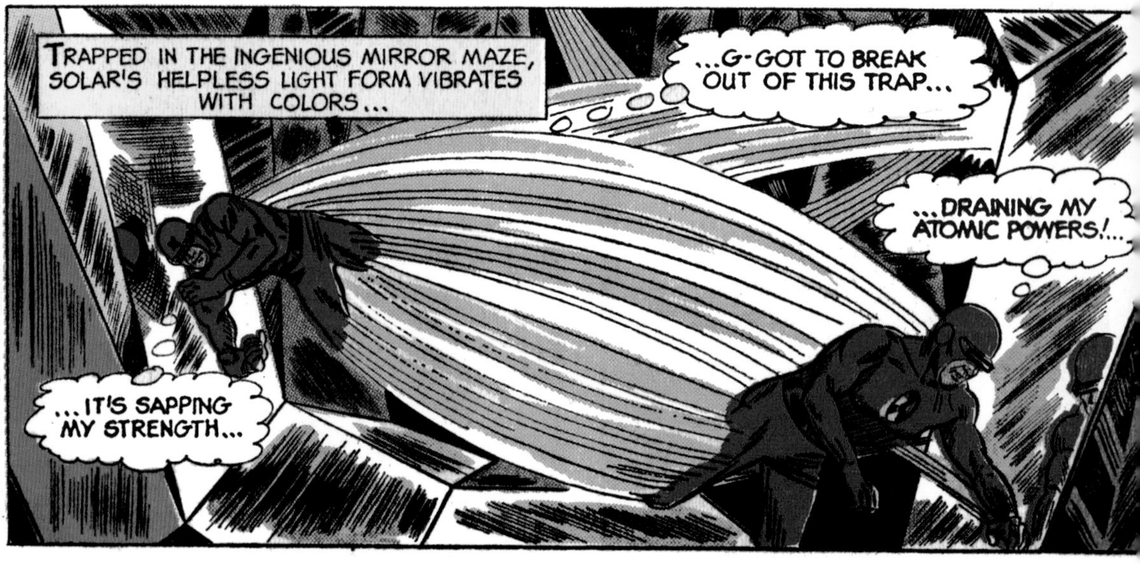
TRAPPED IN THE INGENIOUS MIRROR MAZE, SOLAR'S HELPLESS LIGHT FORM VIBRATES WITH COLORS...
...G-GOT TO BREAK OUT OF THIS TRAP...
...DRAINING MY ATOMIC POWERS!...
...IT'S SAPPING MY STRENGTH...

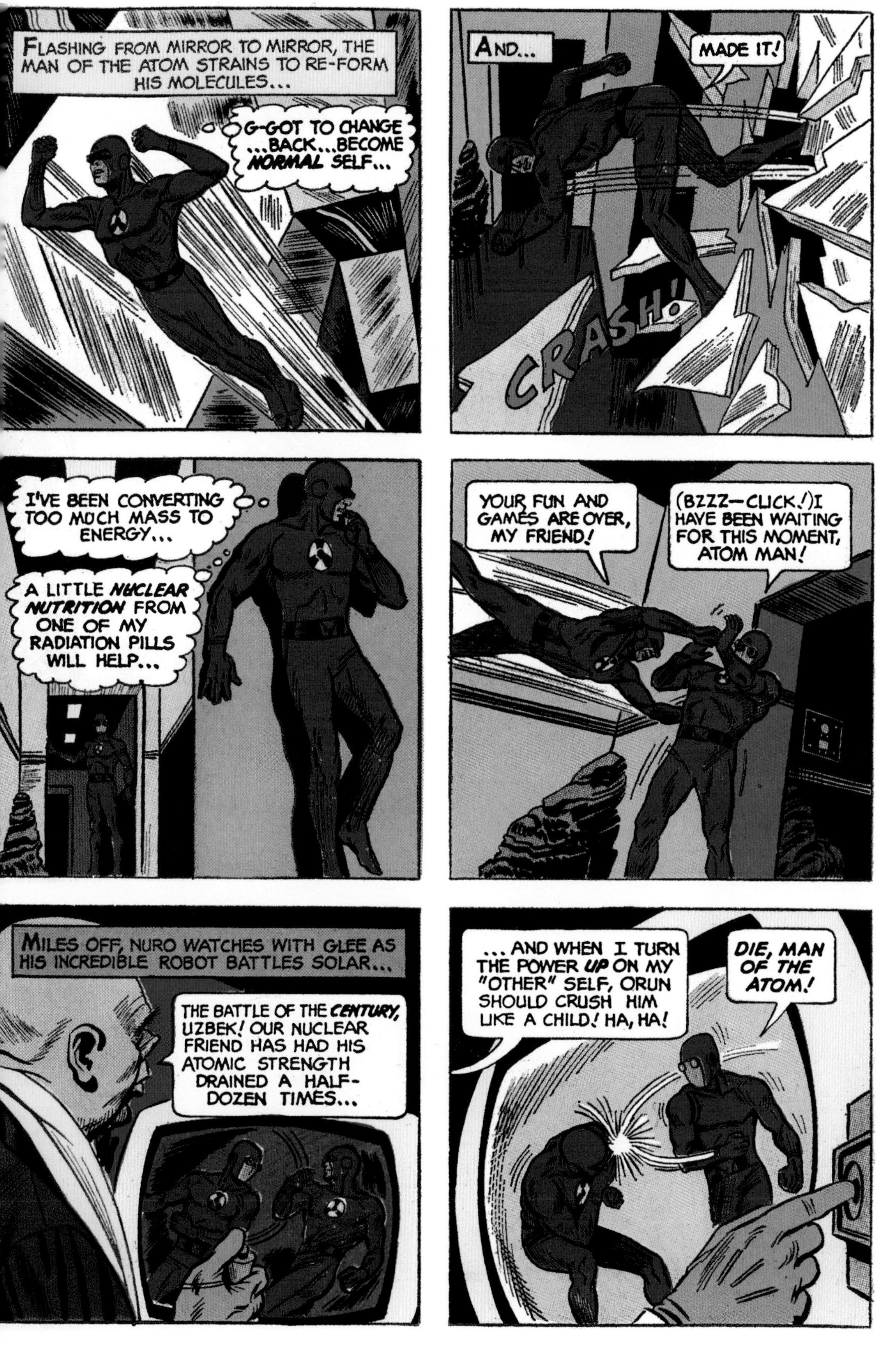
FLASHING FROM MIRROR TO MIRROR, THE MAN OF THE ATOM STRAINS TO RE-FORM HIS MOLECULES...
G-GOT TO CHANGE ...BACK...BECOME NORMAL SELF...
AND...
MADE IT!
CRASH!
I'VE BEEN CONVERTING TOO MUCH MASS TO ENERGY...
A LITTLE NUCLEAR NUTRITION FROM ONE OF MY RADIATION PILLS WILL HELP...
YOUR FUN AND GAMES ARE OVER, MY FRIEND!
(BZZZ—CLICK!) I HAVE BEEN WAITING FOR THIS MOMENT, ATOM MAN!
MILES OFF, NURO WATCHES WITH GLEE AS HIS INCREDIBLE ROBOT BATTLES SOLAR...
THE BATTLE OF THE CENTURY, UZBEK! OUR NUCLEAR FRIEND HAS HAD HIS ATOMIC STRENGTH DRAINED A HALF-DOZEN TIMES...
...AND WHEN I TURN THE POWER UP ON MY "OTHER" SELF, ORUN SHOULD CRUSH HIM LIKE A CHILD! HA, HA!
DIE, MAN OF THE ATOM!

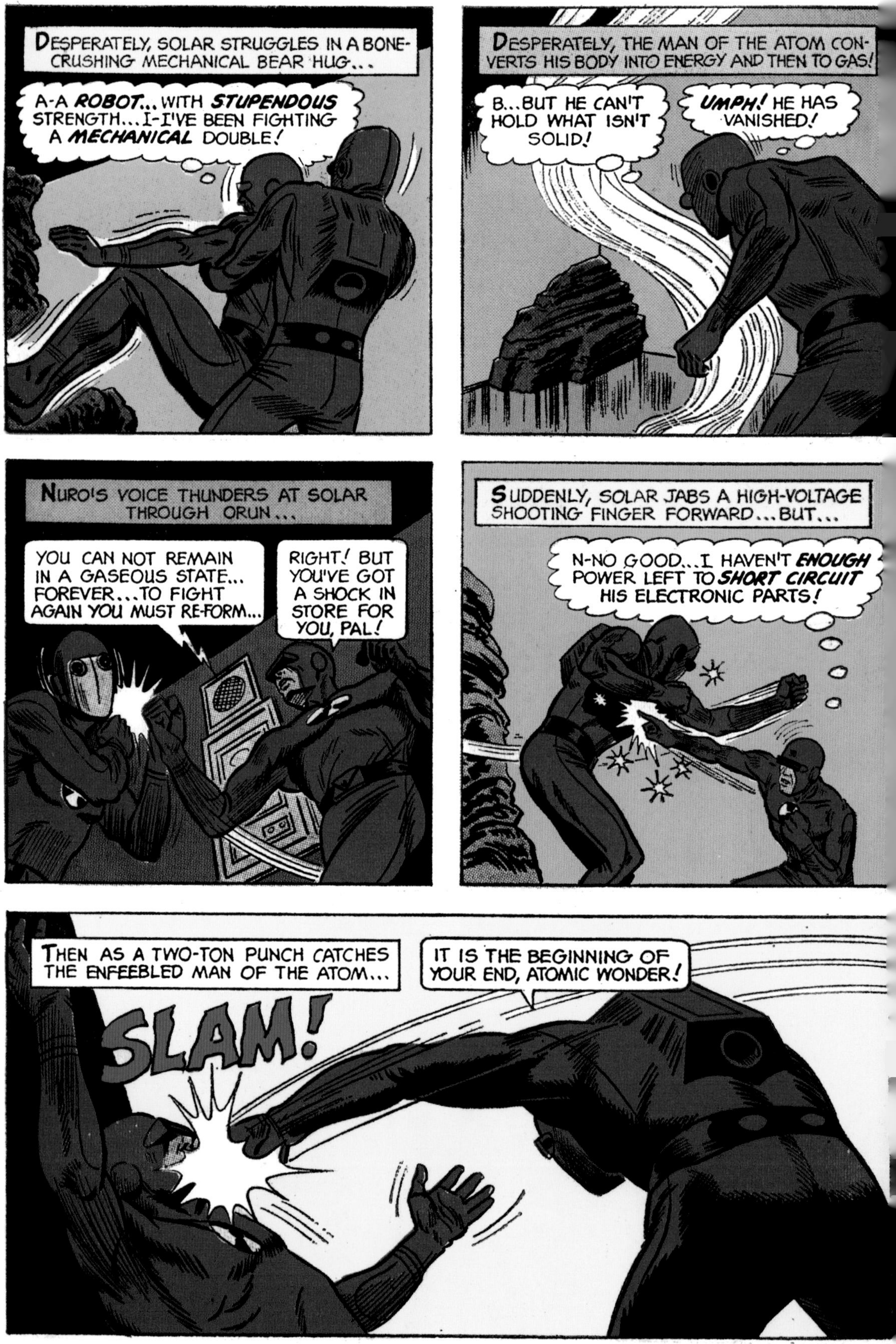
DESPERATELY, SOLAR STRUGGLES IN A BONE-CRUSHING MECHANICAL BEAR HUG...
A-A ROBOT... WITH STUPENDOUS STRENGTH... I-I'VE BEEN FIGHTING A MECHANICAL DOUBLE!
DESPERATELY, THE MAN OF THE ATOM CONVERTS HIS BODY INTO ENERGY AND THEN TO GAS!
B...BUT HE CAN'T HOLD WHAT ISN'T SOLID!
UMPH! HE HAS VANISHED!
NURO'S VOICE THUNDERS AT SOLAR THROUGH ORUN...
YOU CAN NOT REMAIN IN A GASEOUS STATE... FOREVER...TO FIGHT AGAIN YOU MUST RE-FORM...
RIGHT! BUT YOU'VE GOT A SHOCK IN STORE FOR YOU, PAL!
SUDDENLY, SOLAR JABS A HIGH-VOLTAGE SHOOTING FINGER FORWARD...BUT...
N-NO GOOD...I HAVEN'T ENOUGH POWER LEFT TO SHORT CIRCUIT HIS ELECTRONIC PARTS!
THEN AS A TWO-TON PUNCH CATCHES THE ENFEEBLED MAN OF THE ATOM...
IT IS THE BEGINNING OF YOUR END, ATOMIC WONDER!
SLAM!

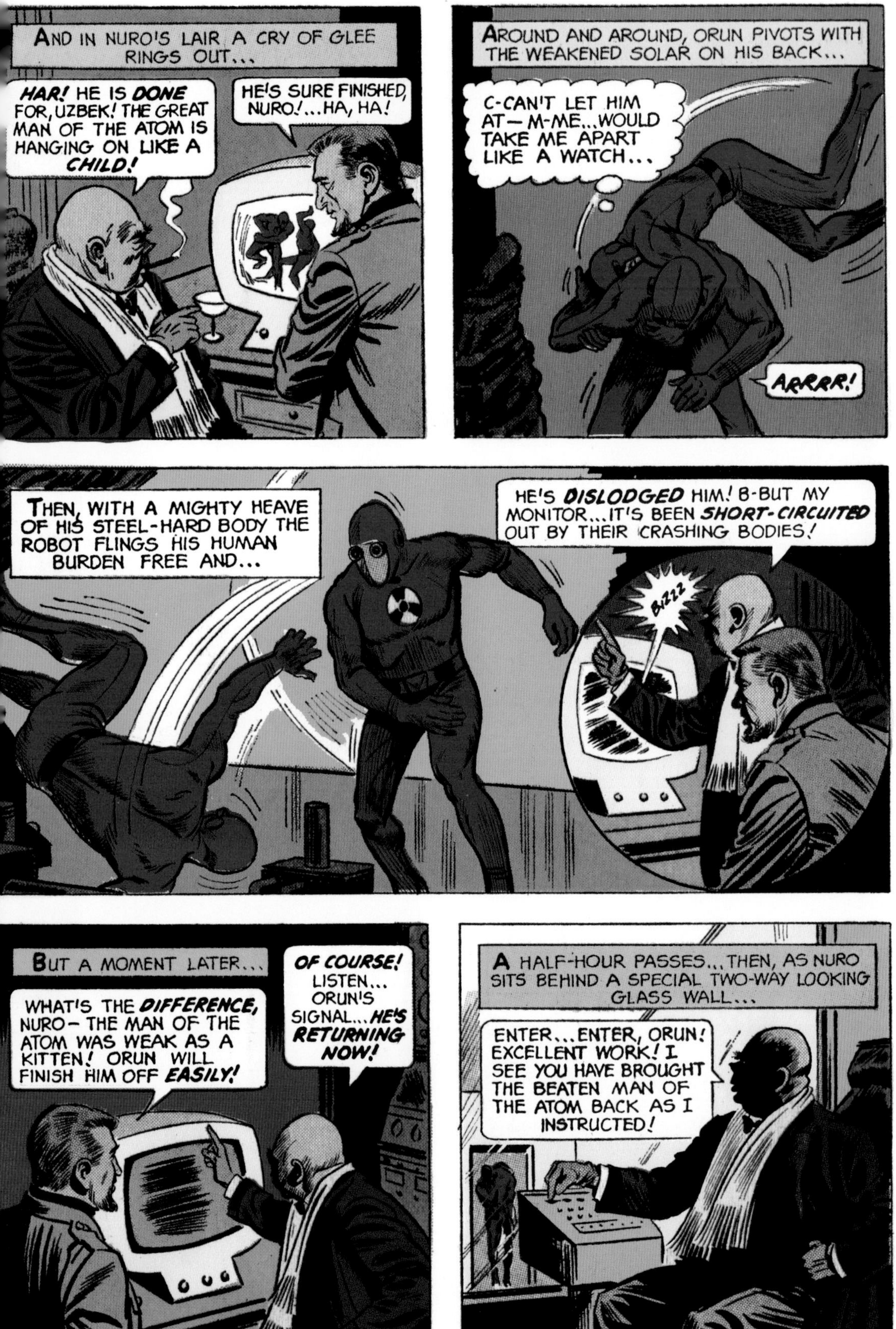
AND IN NURO'S LAIR A CRY OF GLEE RINGS OUT...
HAR! HE IS DONE FOR, UZBEK! THE GREAT MAN OF THE ATOM IS HANGING ON LIKE A CHILD!
HE'S SURE FINISHED, NURO!...HA, HA!
AROUND AND AROUND, ORUN PIVOTS WITH THE WEAKENED SOLAR ON HIS BACK...
C-CAN'T LET HIM AT—M-ME...WOULD TAKE ME APART LIKE A WATCH...
ARRRR!
THEN, WITH A MIGHTY HEAVE OF HIS STEEL-HARD BODY THE ROBOT FLINGS HIS HUMAN BURDEN FREE AND...
HE'S DISLODGED HIM! B-BUT MY MONITOR...IT'S BEEN SHORT-CIRCUITED OUT BY THEIR CRASHING BODIES!
BIZZZ
BUT A MOMENT LATER...
WHAT'S THE DIFFERENCE, NURO—THE MAN OF THE ATOM WAS WEAK AS A KITTEN! ORUN WILL FINISH HIM OFF EASILY!
OF COURSE! LISTEN... ORUN'S SIGNAL...HE'S RETURNING NOW!
A HALF-HOUR PASSES...THEN, AS NURO SITS BEHIND A SPECIAL TWO-WAY LOOKING GLASS WALL...
ENTER...ENTER, ORUN! EXCELLENT WORK! I SEE YOU HAVE BROUGHT THE BEATEN MAN OF THE ATOM BACK AS I INSTRUCTED!

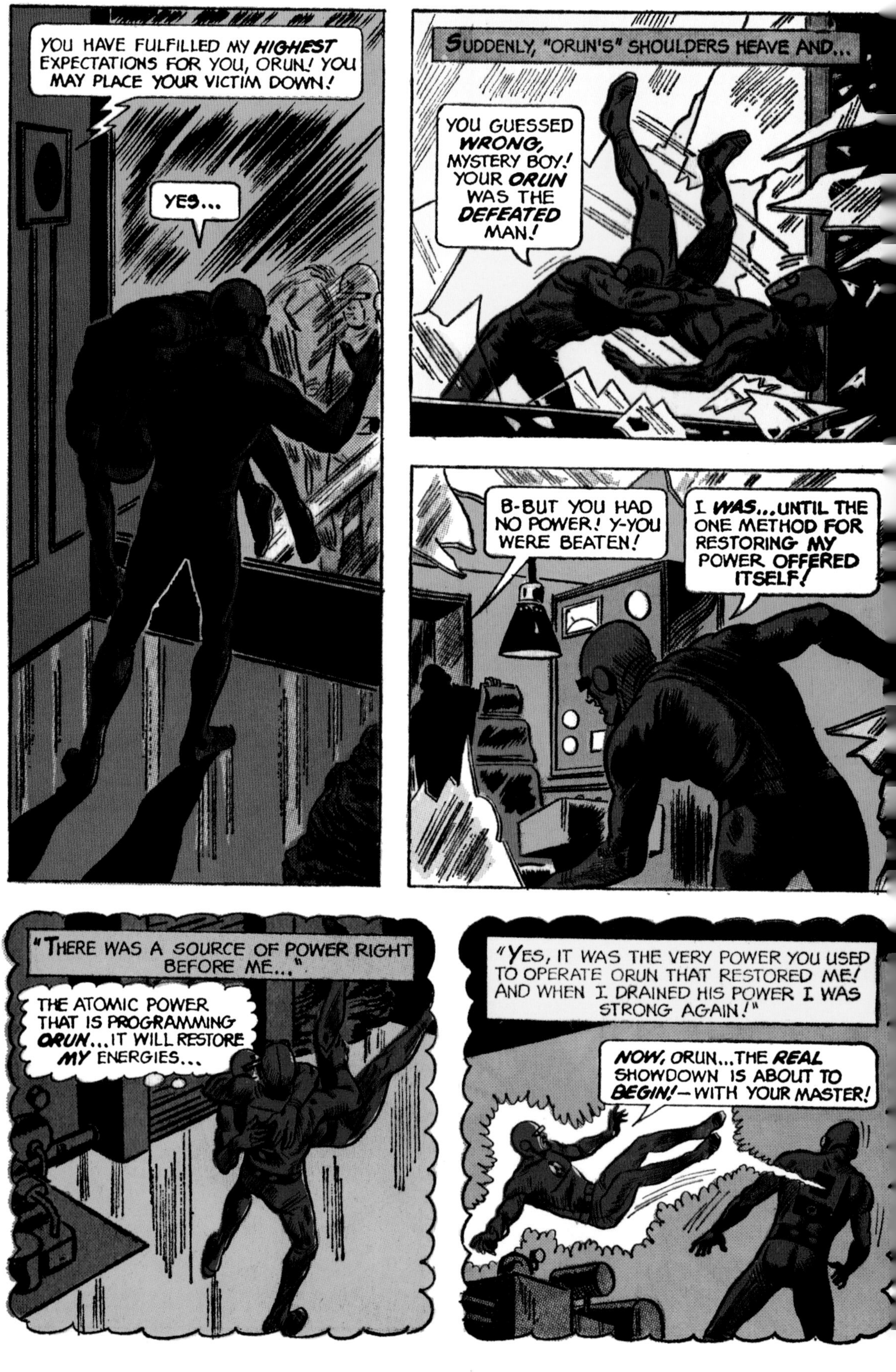
YOU HAVE FULFILLED MY HIGHEST EXPECTATIONS FOR YOU, ORUN! YOU MAY PLACE YOUR VICTIM DOWN!
YES...
SUDDENLY, "ORUN'S" SHOULDERS HEAVE AND...
YOU GUESSED WRONG, MYSTERY BOY! YOUR ORUN WAS THE DEFEATED MAN!
B-BUT YOU HAD NO POWER! Y-YOU WERE BEATEN!
I WAS... UNTIL THE ONE METHOD FOR RESTORING MY POWER OFFERED ITSELF!
"THERE WAS A SOURCE OF POWER RIGHT BEFORE ME..."
THE ATOMIC POWER THAT IS PROGRAMMING ORUN... IT WILL RESTORE MY ENERGIES...
"YES, IT WAS THE VERY POWER YOU USED TO OPERATE ORUN THAT RESTORED ME! AND WHEN I DRAINED HIS POWER I WAS STRONG AGAIN!"
NOW, ORUN... THE REAL SHOWDOWN IS ABOUT TO BEGIN! — WITH YOUR MASTER!

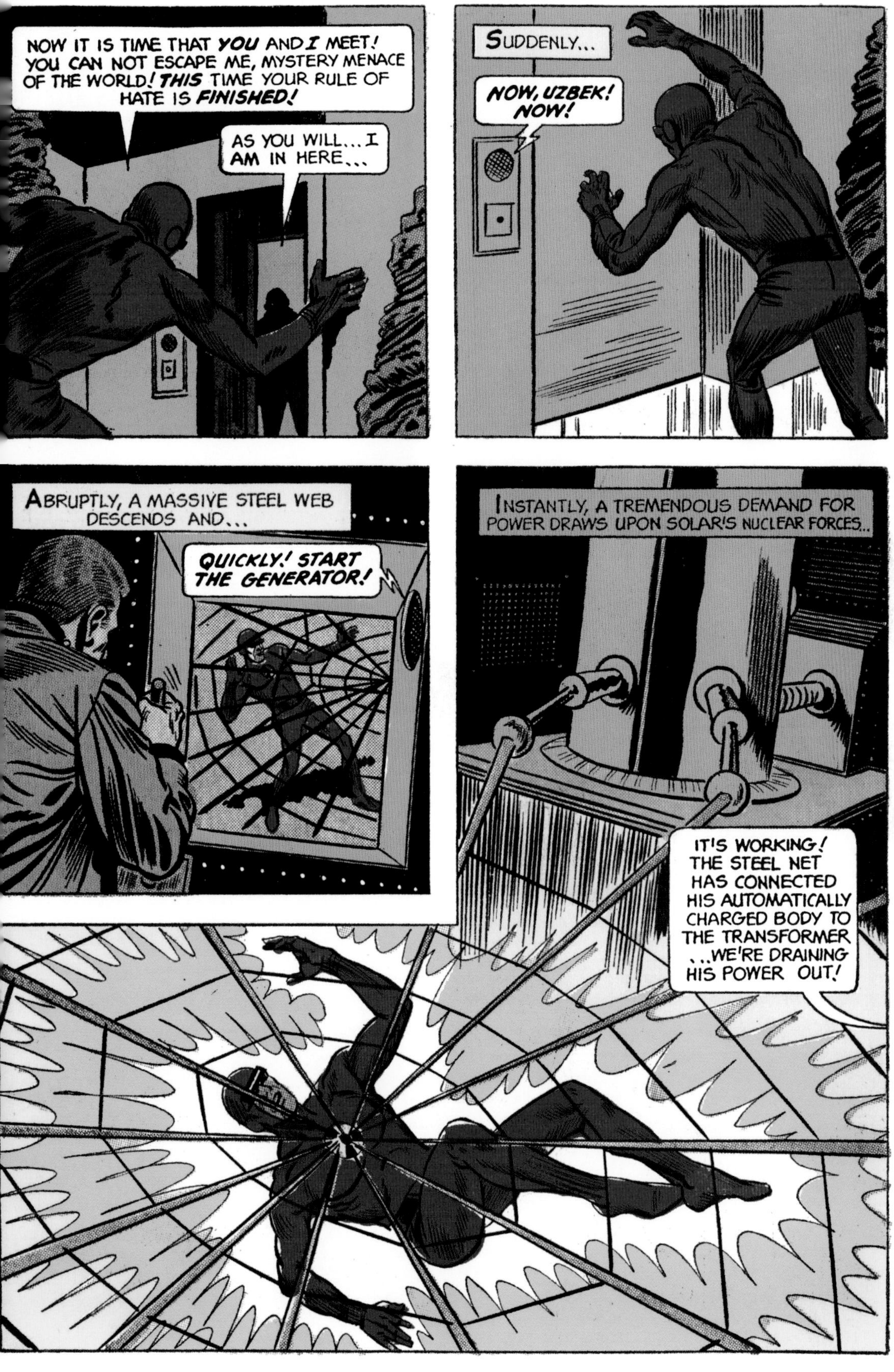
NOW IT IS TIME THAT YOU AND I MEET! YOU CAN NOT ESCAPE ME, MYSTERY MENACE OF THE WORLD! THIS TIME YOUR RULE OF HATE IS FINISHED!
AS YOU WILL... I AM IN HERE...
SUDDENLY...
NOW, UZBEK! NOW!
ABRUPTLY, A MASSIVE STEEL WEB DESCENDS AND...
QUICKLY! START THE GENERATOR!
INSTANTLY, A TREMENDOUS DEMAND FOR POWER DRAWS UPON SOLAR'S NUCLEAR FORCES...
IT'S WORKING! THE STEEL NET HAS CONNECTED HIS AUTOMATICALLY CHARGED BODY TO THE TRANSFORMER ...WE'RE DRAINING HIS POWER OUT!

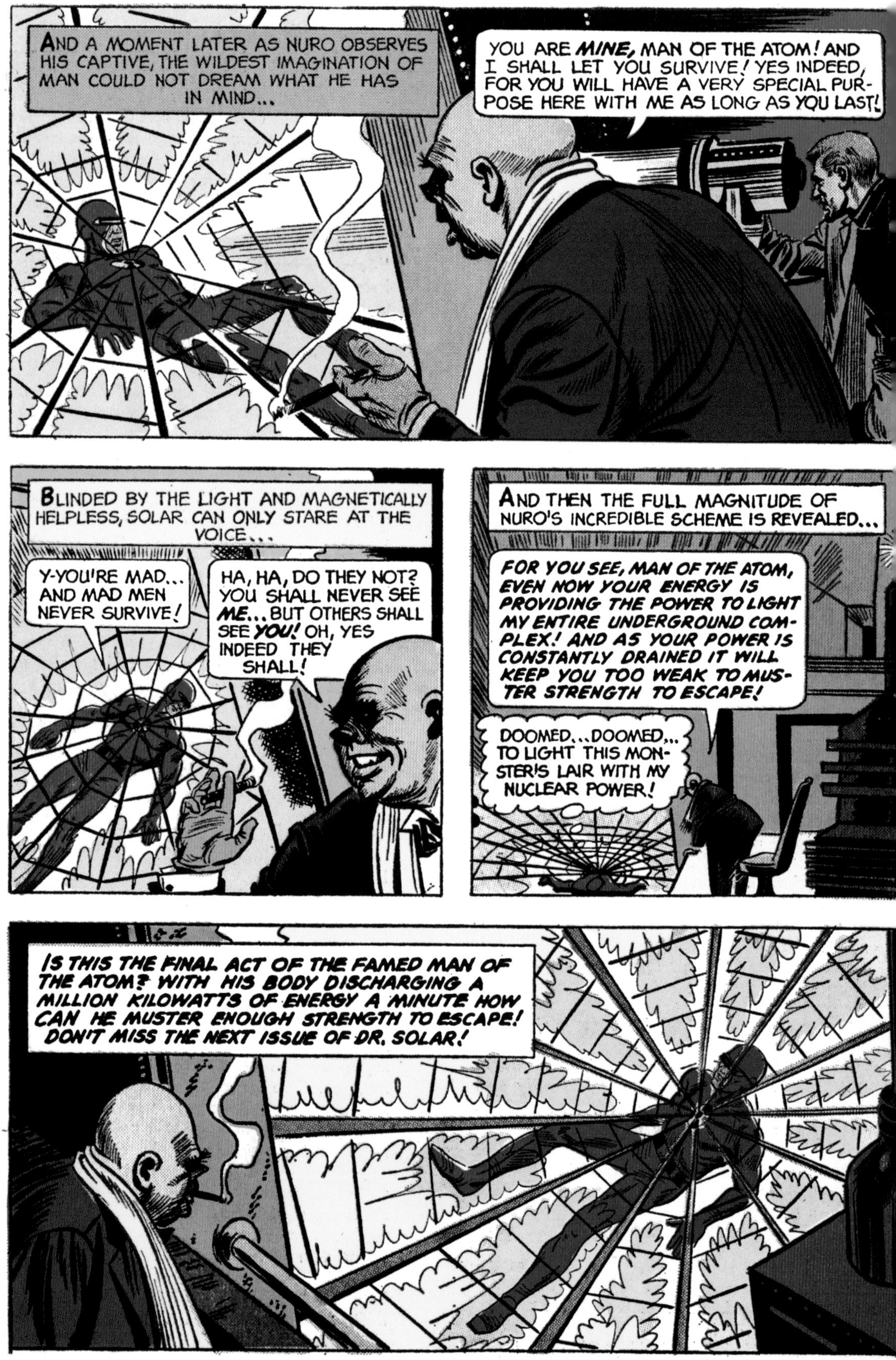
AND A MOMENT LATER AS NURO OBSERVES HIS CAPTIVE, THE WILDEST IMAGINATION OF MAN COULD NOT DREAM WHAT HE HAS IN MIND...
YOU ARE MINE, MAN OF THE ATOM! AND I SHALL LET YOU SURVIVE! YES INDEED, FOR YOU WILL HAVE A VERY SPECIAL PURPOSE HERE WITH ME AS LONG AS YOU LAST!
BLINDED BY THE LIGHT AND MAGNETICALLY HELPLESS, SOLAR CAN ONLY STARE AT THE VOICE...
Y-YOU'RE MAD... AND MAD MEN NEVER SURVIVE!
HA, HA, DO THEY NOT? YOU SHALL NEVER SEE ME... BUT OTHERS SHALL SEE YOU! OH, YES INDEED THEY SHALL!
AND THEN THE FULL MAGNITUDE OF NURO'S INCREDIBLE SCHEME IS REVEALED...
FOR YOU SEE, MAN OF THE ATOM, EVEN NOW YOUR ENERGY IS PROVIDING THE POWER TO LIGHT MY ENTIRE UNDERGROUND COMPLEX! AND AS YOUR POWER IS CONSTANTLY DRAINED IT WILL KEEP YOU TOO WEAK TO MUSTER STRENGTH TO ESCAPE!
DOOMED... DOOMED... TO LIGHT THIS MONSTER'S LAIR WITH MY NUCLEAR POWER!
IS THIS THE FINAL ACT OF THE FAMED MAN OF THE ATOM? WITH HIS BODY DISCHARGING A MILLION KILOWATTS OF ENERGY A MINUTE HOW CAN HE MUSTER ENOUGH STRENGTH TO ESCAPE! DON'T MISS THE NEXT ISSUE OF DR. SOLAR!

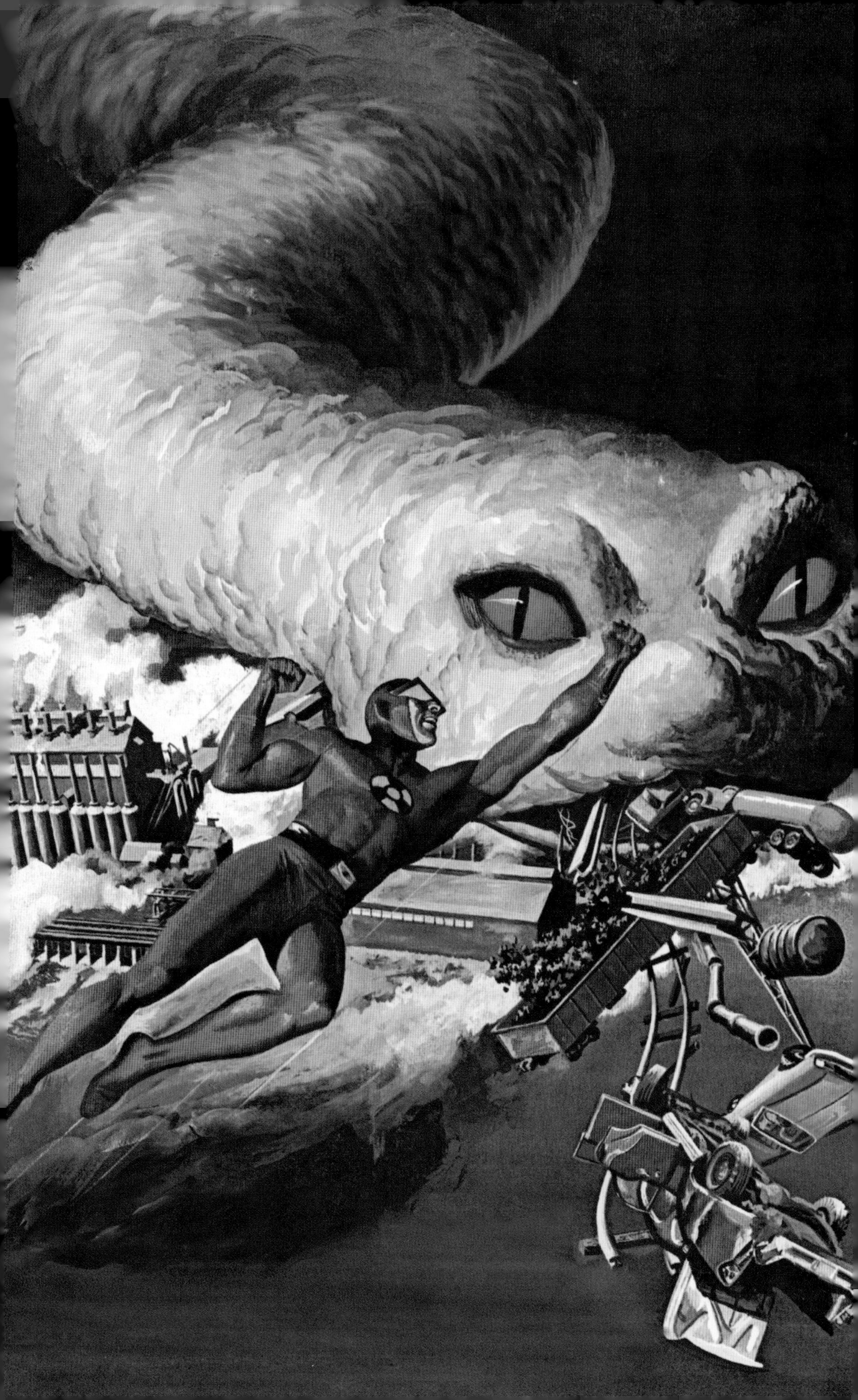

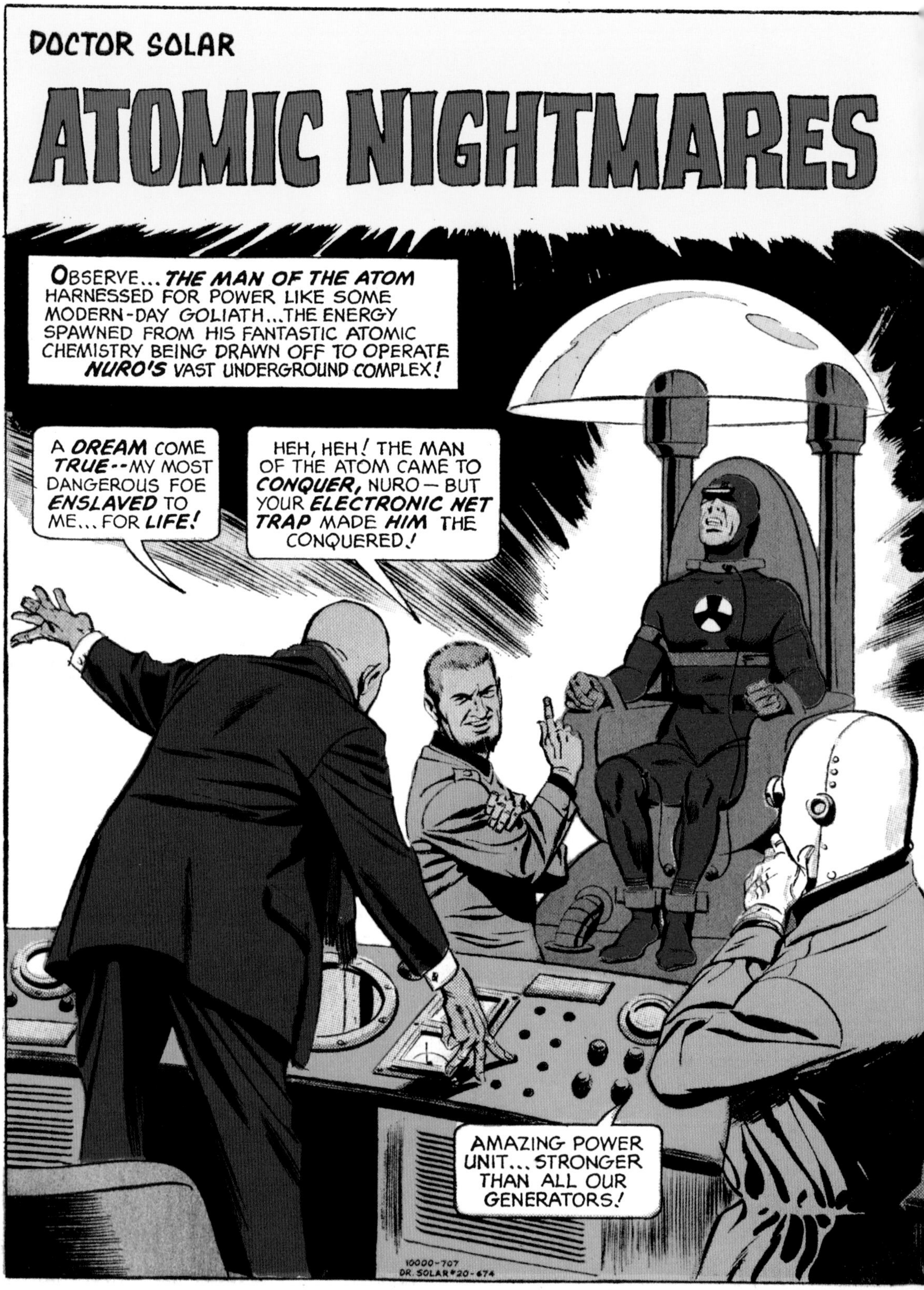
DOCTOR SOLAR
ATOMIC NIGHTMARES
OBSERVE... THE MAN OF THE ATOM HARNESSED FOR POWER LIKE SOME MODERN-DAY GOLIATH... THE ENERGY SPAWNED FROM HIS FANTASTIC ATOMIC CHEMISTRY BEING DRAWN OFF TO OPERATE NURO'S VAST UNDERGROUND COMPLEX!
A DREAM COME TRUE--MY MOST DANGEROUS FOE ENSLAVED TO ME... FOR LIFE!
HEH, HEH! THE MAN OF THE ATOM CAME TO CONQUER, NURO — BUT YOUR ELECTRONIC NET TRAP MADE HIM THE CONQUERED!
AMAZING POWER UNIT... STRONGER THAN ALL OUR GENERATORS!
10000-707
DR. SOLAR #20-674

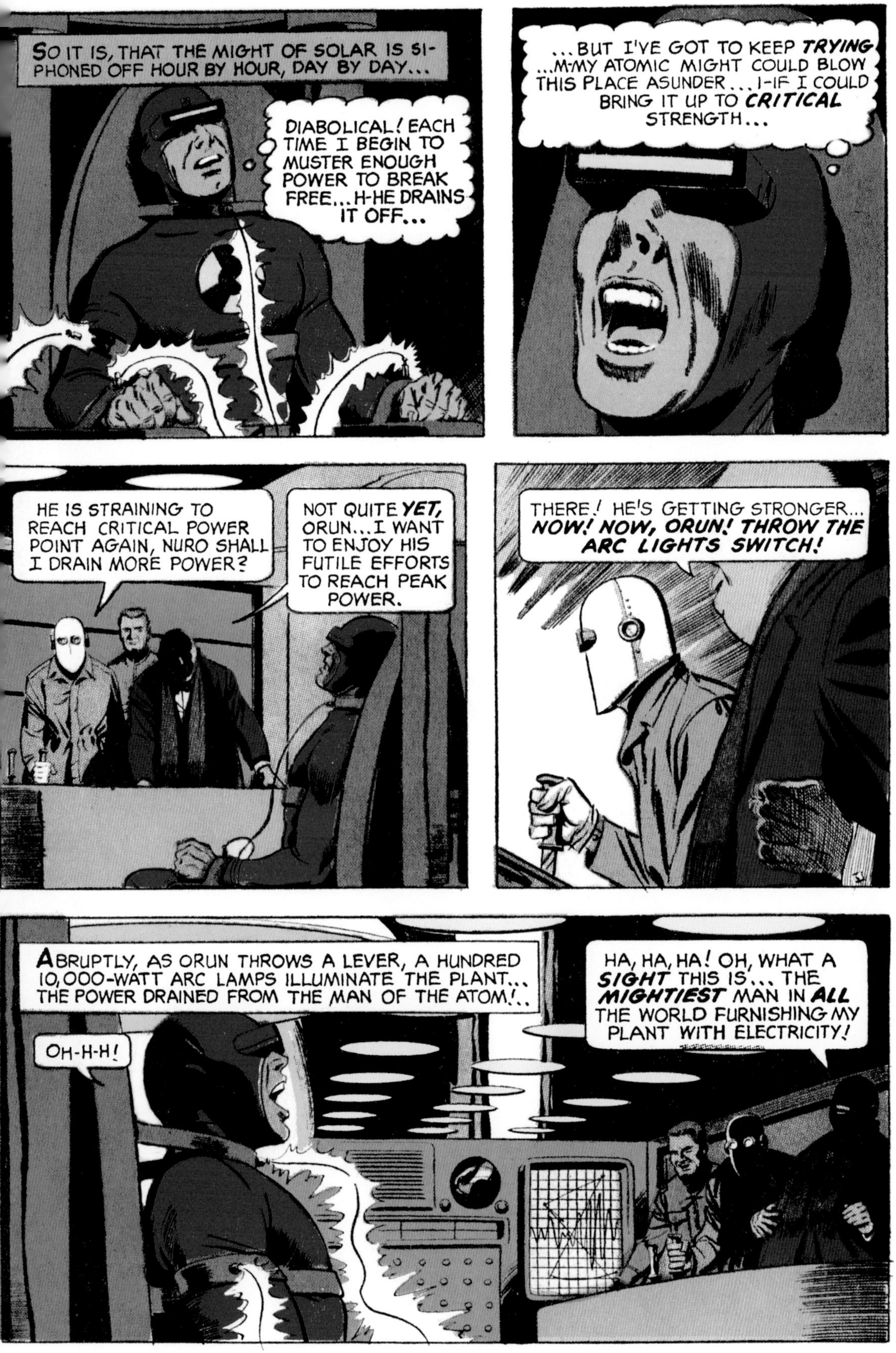

SO IT IS, THAT THE MIGHT OF SOLAR IS SIPHONED OFF HOUR BY HOUR, DAY BY DAY...
DIABOLICAL! EACH TIME I BEGIN TO MUSTER ENOUGH POWER TO BREAK FREE... H-HE DRAINS IT OFF...
...BUT I'VE GOT TO KEEP TRYING ...M-MY ATOMIC MIGHT COULD BLOW THIS PLACE ASUNDER... I-IF I COULD BRING IT UP TO CRITICAL STRENGTH...
HE IS STRAINING TO REACH CRITICAL POWER POINT AGAIN, NURO SHALL I DRAIN MORE POWER?
NOT QUITE YET, ORUN... I WANT TO ENJOY HIS FUTILE EFFORTS TO REACH PEAK POWER.
THERE! HE'S GETTING STRONGER... NOW! NOW, ORUN! THROW THE ARC LIGHTS SWITCH!
ABRUPTLY, AS ORUN THROWS A LEVER, A HUNDRED 10,000-WATT ARC LAMPS ILLUMINATE THE PLANT... THE POWER DRAINED FROM THE MAN OF THE ATOM!..
OH-H-H!
HA, HA, HA! OH, WHAT A SIGHT THIS IS... THE MIGHTIEST MAN IN ALL THE WORLD FURNISHING MY PLANT WITH ELECTRICITY!

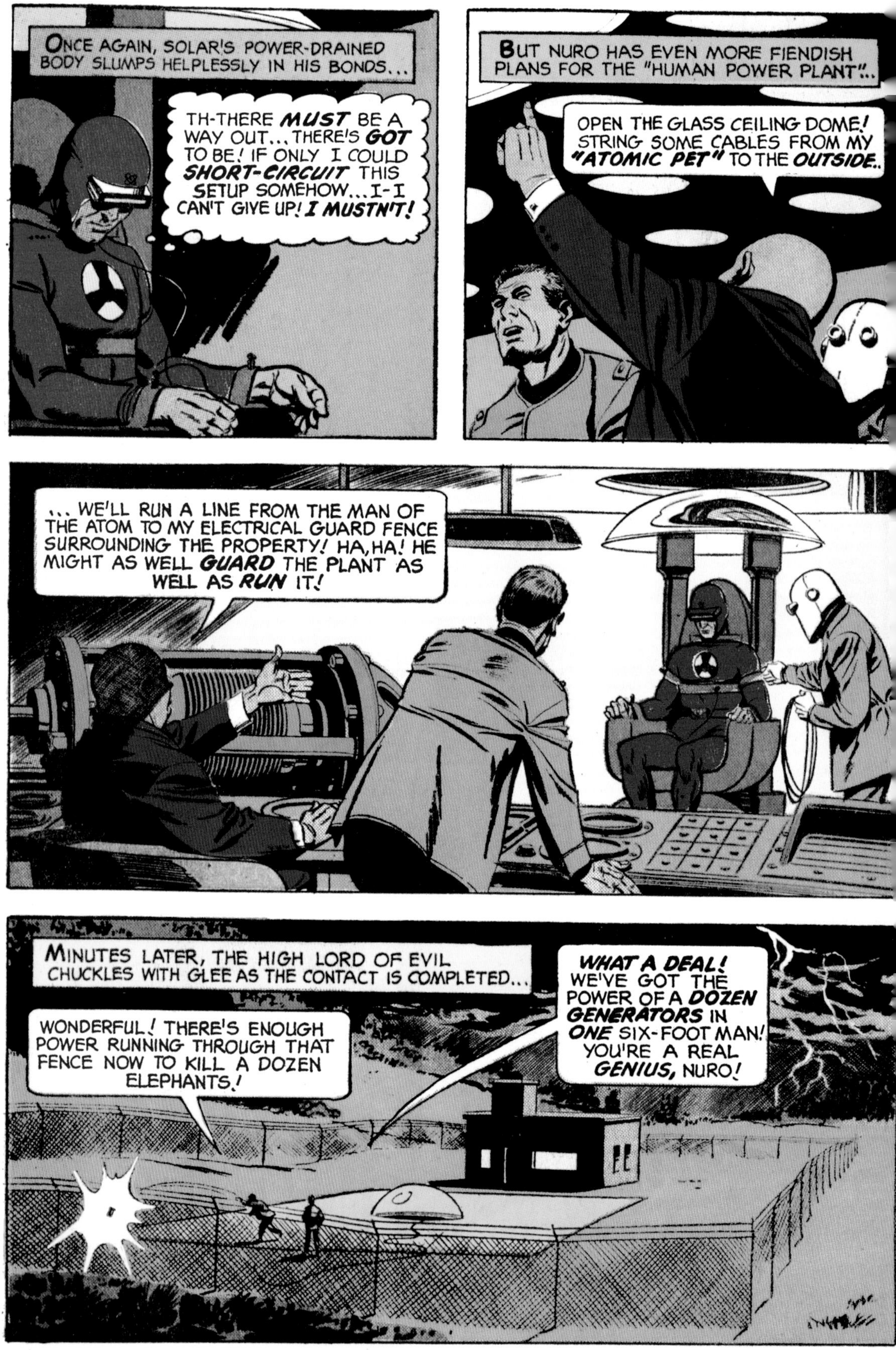
ONCE AGAIN, SOLAR'S POWER-DRAINED BODY SLUMPS HELPLESSLY IN HIS BONDS...
TH-THERE **MUST** BE A WAY OUT... THERE'S **GOT** TO BE! IF ONLY I COULD **SHORT-CIRCUIT** THIS SETUP SOMEHOW... I-I CAN'T GIVE UP! **I MUSTN'T!**
BUT NURO HAS EVEN MORE FIENDISH PLANS FOR THE "HUMAN POWER PLANT"...
OPEN THE GLASS CEILING DOME! STRING SOME CABLES FROM MY **"ATOMIC PET"** TO THE **OUTSIDE**..
... WE'LL RUN A LINE FROM THE MAN OF THE ATOM TO MY ELECTRICAL GUARD FENCE SURROUNDING THE PROPERTY! HA, HA! HE MIGHT AS WELL **GUARD** THE PLANT AS WELL AS **RUN** IT!
MINUTES LATER, THE HIGH LORD OF EVIL CHUCKLES WITH GLEE AS THE CONTACT IS COMPLETED...
WONDERFUL! THERE'S ENOUGH POWER RUNNING THROUGH THAT FENCE NOW TO KILL A DOZEN ELEPHANTS!
**WHAT A DEAL!** WE'VE GOT THE POWER OF A **DOZEN GENERATORS** IN **ONE** SIX-FOOT MAN! YOU'RE A REAL **GENIUS**, NURO!

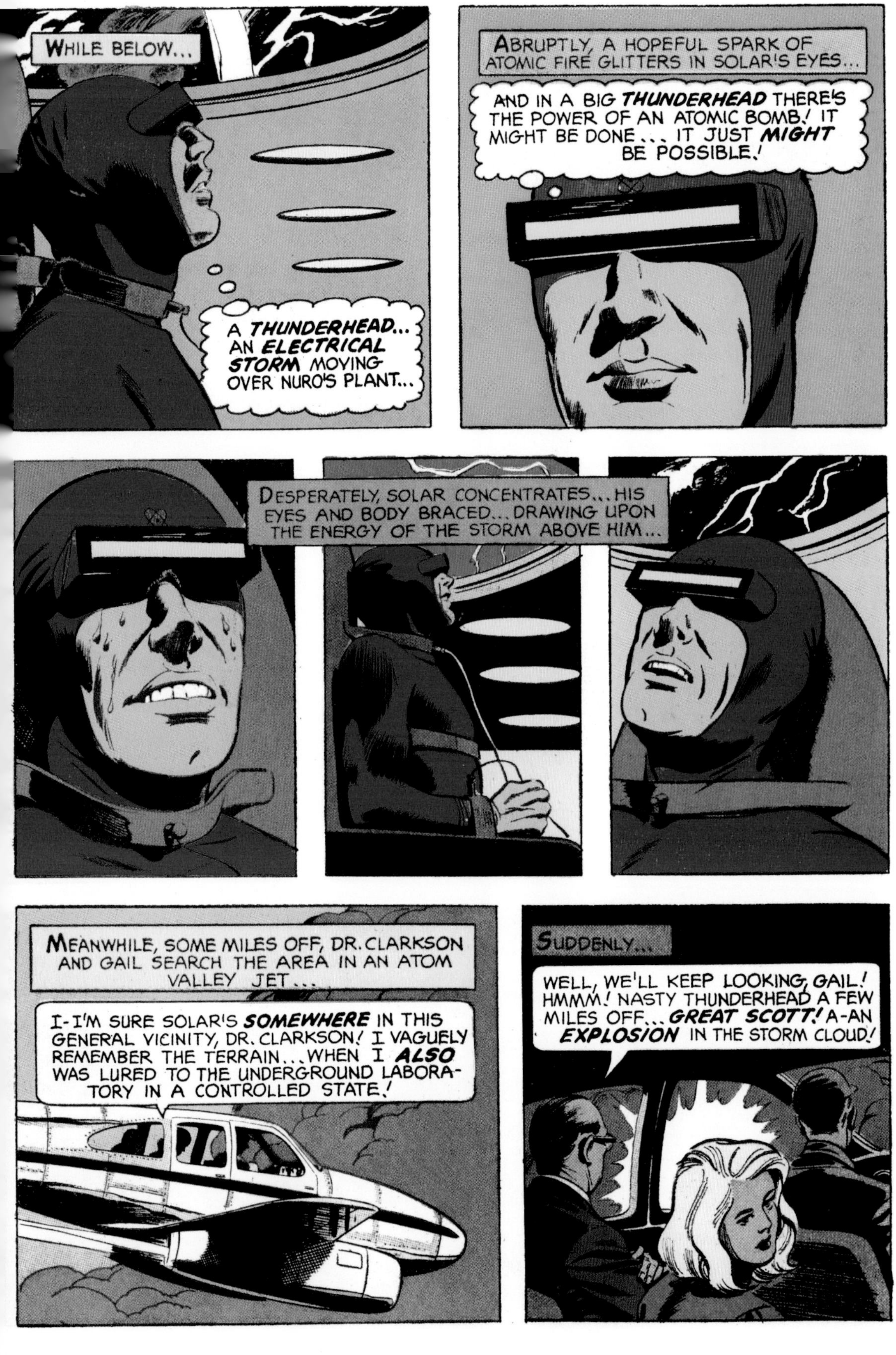
WHILE BELOW...
A THUNDERHEAD... AN ELECTRICAL STORM MOVING OVER NURO'S PLANT...
ABRUPTLY, A HOPEFUL SPARK OF ATOMIC FIRE GLITTERS IN SOLAR'S EYES...
AND IN A BIG THUNDERHEAD THERE'S THE POWER OF AN ATOMIC BOMB! IT MIGHT BE DONE... IT JUST MIGHT BE POSSIBLE!
DESPERATELY, SOLAR CONCENTRATES... HIS EYES AND BODY BRACED... DRAWING UPON THE ENERGY OF THE STORM ABOVE HIM...
MEANWHILE, SOME MILES OFF, DR. CLARKSON AND GAIL SEARCH THE AREA IN AN ATOM VALLEY JET...
I-I'M SURE SOLAR'S SOMEWHERE IN THIS GENERAL VICINITY, DR. CLARKSON! I VAGUELY REMEMBER THE TERRAIN... WHEN I ALSO WAS LURED TO THE UNDERGROUND LABORATORY IN A CONTROLLED STATE!
SUDDENLY...
WELL, WE'LL KEEP LOOKING, GAIL! HMMM! NASTY THUNDERHEAD A FEW MILES OFF... GREAT SCOTT! A-AN EXPLOSION IN THE STORM CLOUD!

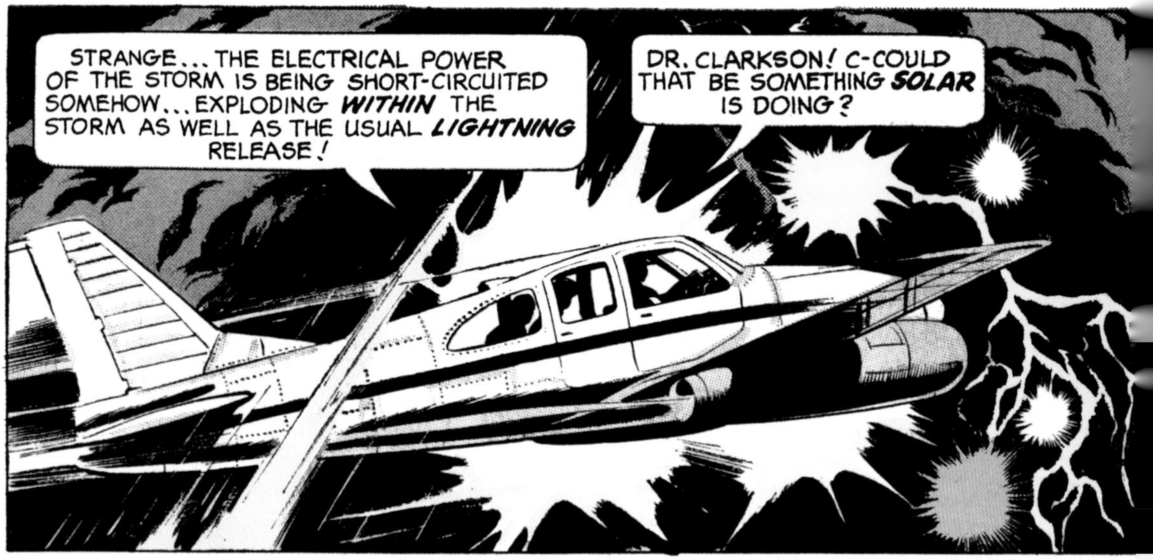
STRANGE... THE ELECTRICAL POWER OF THE STORM IS BEING SHORT-CIRCUITED SOMEHOW... EXPLODING WITHIN THE STORM AS WELL AS THE USUAL LIGHTNING RELEASE!
DR. CLARKSON! C-COULD THAT BE SOMETHING SOLAR IS DOING?

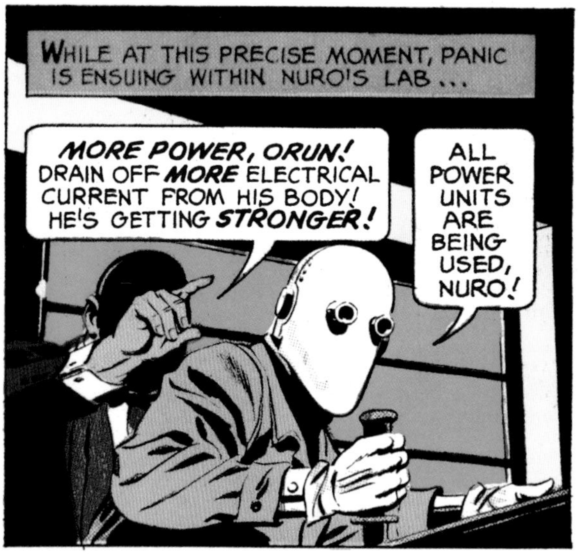
WHILE AT THIS PRECISE MOMENT, PANIC IS ENSUING WITHIN NURO'S LAB...
MORE POWER, ORUN! DRAIN OFF MORE ELECTRICAL CURRENT FROM HIS BODY! HE'S GETTING STRONGER!
ALL POWER UNITS ARE BEING USED, NURO!

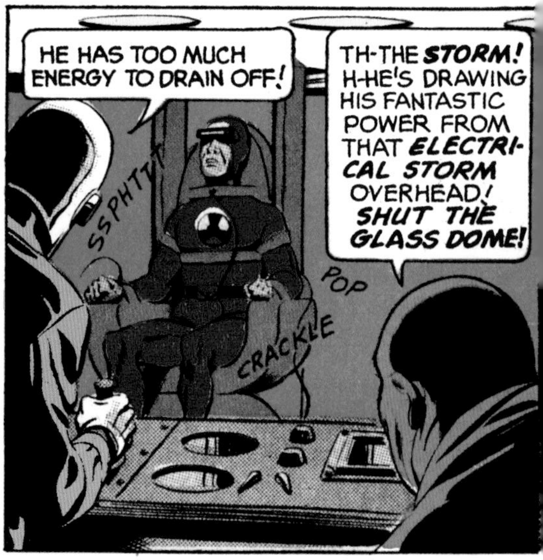
HE HAS TOO MUCH ENERGY TO DRAIN OFF!
TH-THE STORM! H-HE'S DRAWING HIS FANTASTIC POWER FROM THAT ELECTRICAL STORM OVERHEAD! SHUT THE GLASS DOME!
SSPHTTT
POP
CRACKLE

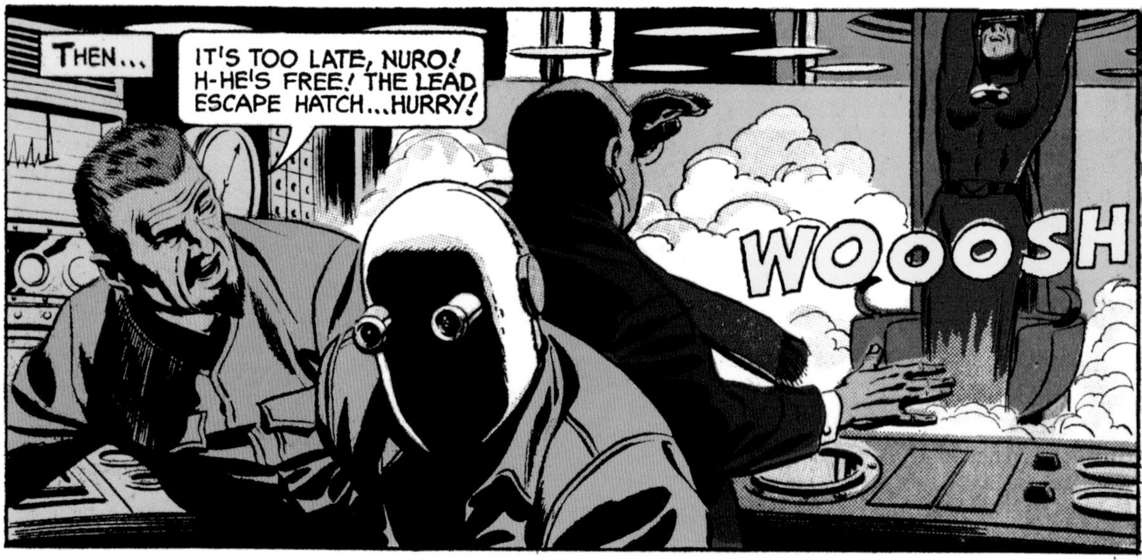
THEN...
IT'S TOO LATE, NURO! H-HE'S FREE! THE LEAD ESCAPE HATCH...HURRY!
WOOOSH

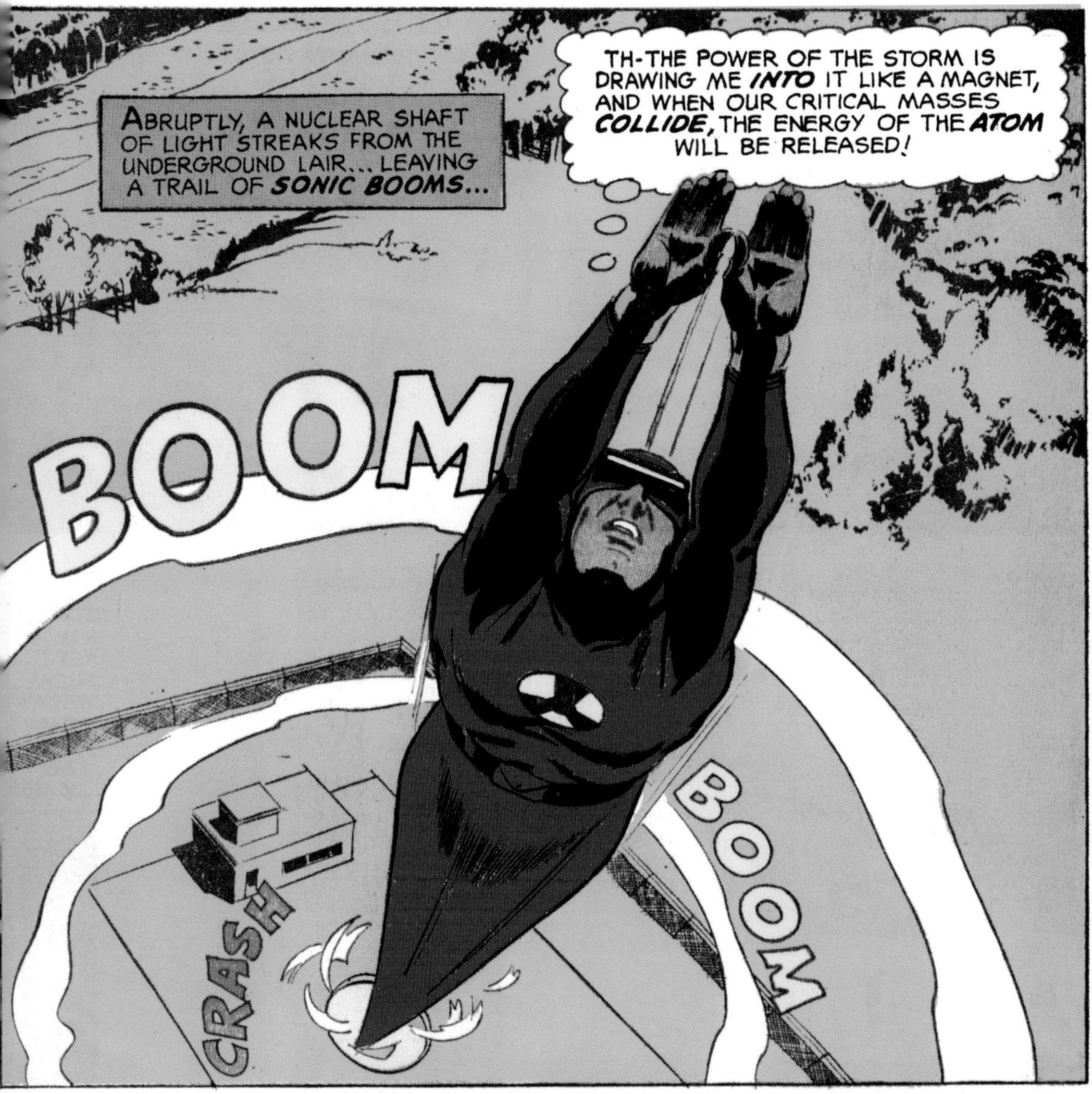
ABRUPTLY, A NUCLEAR SHAFT OF LIGHT STREAKS FROM THE UNDERGROUND LAIR... LEAVING A TRAIL OF SONIC BOOMS...
TH-THE POWER OF THE STORM IS DRAWING ME INTO IT LIKE A MAGNET, AND WHEN OUR CRITICAL MASSES COLLIDE, THE ENERGY OF THE ATOM WILL BE RELEASED!
BOOM
BOOM
CRASH

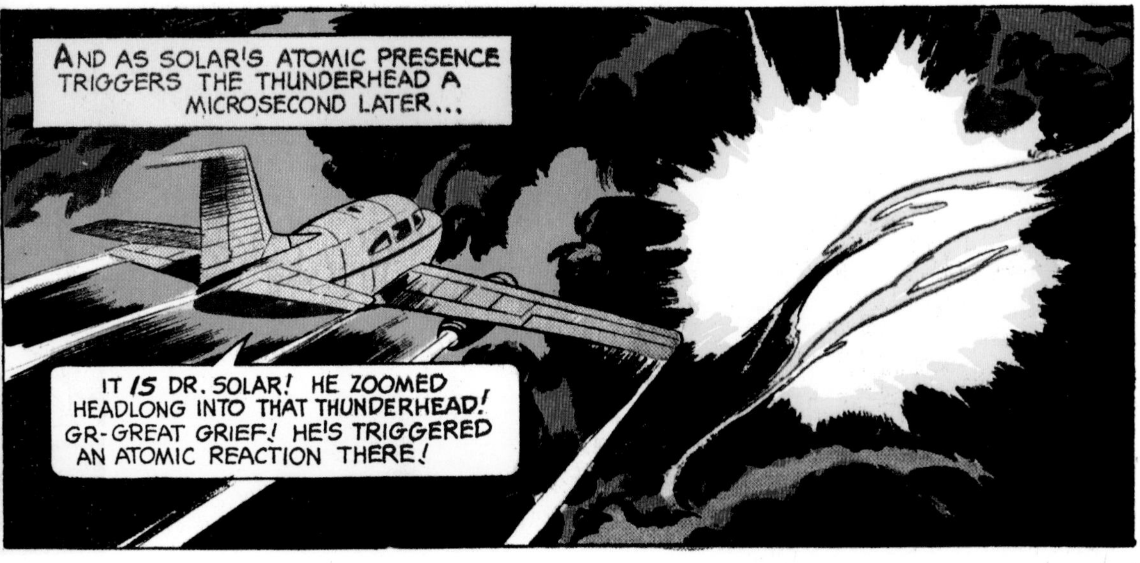
AND AS SOLAR'S ATOMIC PRESENCE TRIGGERS THE THUNDERHEAD A MICROSECOND LATER...
IT IS DR. SOLAR! HE ZOOMED HEADLONG INTO THAT THUNDERHEAD! GR-GREAT GRIEF! HE'S TRIGGERED AN ATOMIC REACTION THERE!

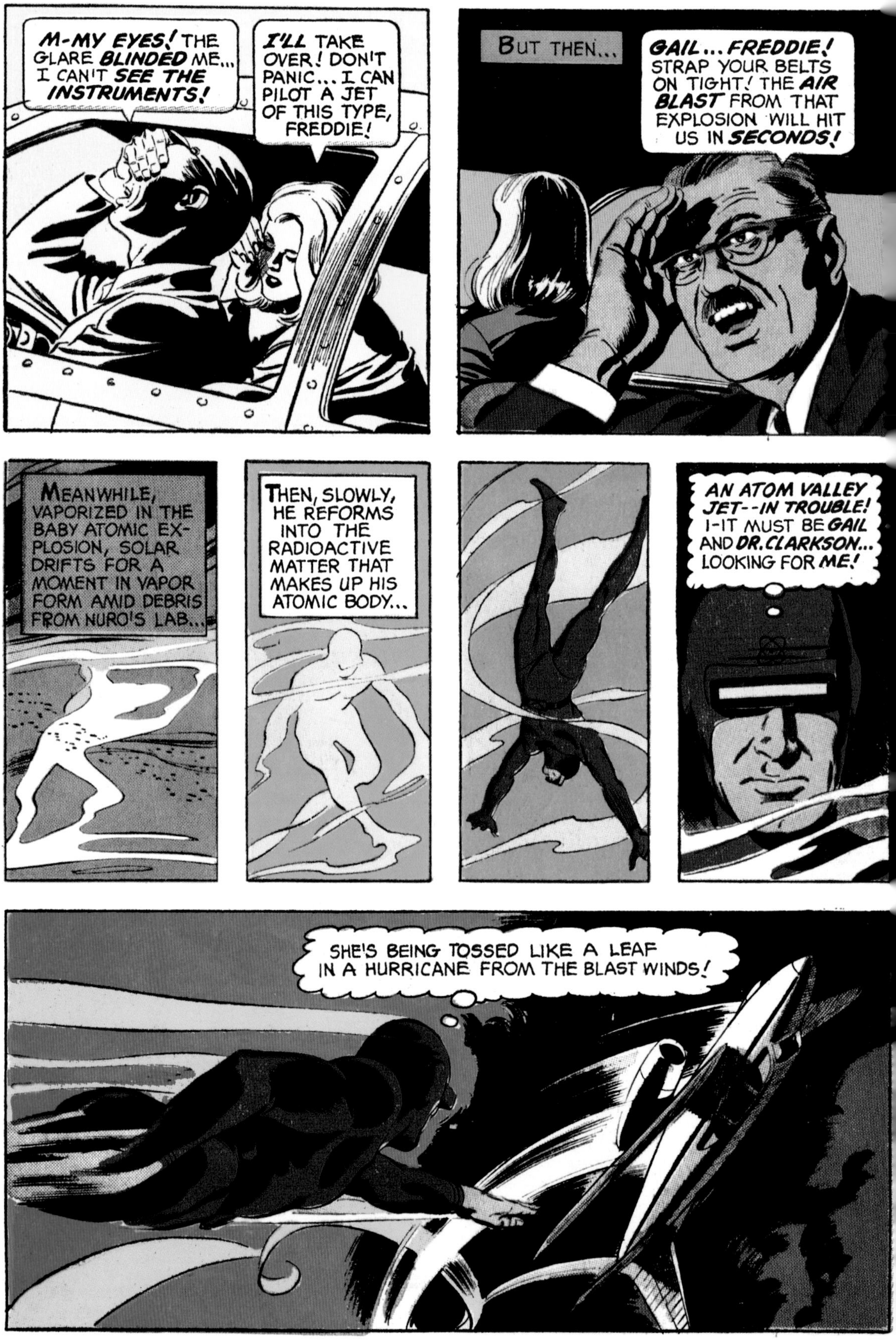

M-MY EYES! THE GLARE BLINDED ME... I CAN'T SEE THE INSTRUMENTS!
I'LL TAKE OVER! DON'T PANIC... I CAN PILOT A JET OF THIS TYPE, FREDDIE!
BUT THEN...
GAIL... FREDDIE! STRAP YOUR BELTS ON TIGHT! THE AIR BLAST FROM THAT EXPLOSION WILL HIT US IN SECONDS!
MEANWHILE, VAPORIZED IN THE BABY ATOMIC EXPLOSION, SOLAR DRIFTS FOR A MOMENT IN VAPOR FORM AMID DEBRIS FROM NURO'S LAB...
THEN, SLOWLY, HE REFORMS INTO THE RADIOACTIVE MATTER THAT MAKES UP HIS ATOMIC BODY...
AN ATOM VALLEY JET--IN TROUBLE! I-IT MUST BE GAIL AND DR. CLARKSON... LOOKING FOR ME!
SHE'S BEING TOSSED LIKE A LEAF IN A HURRICANE FROM THE BLAST WINDS!

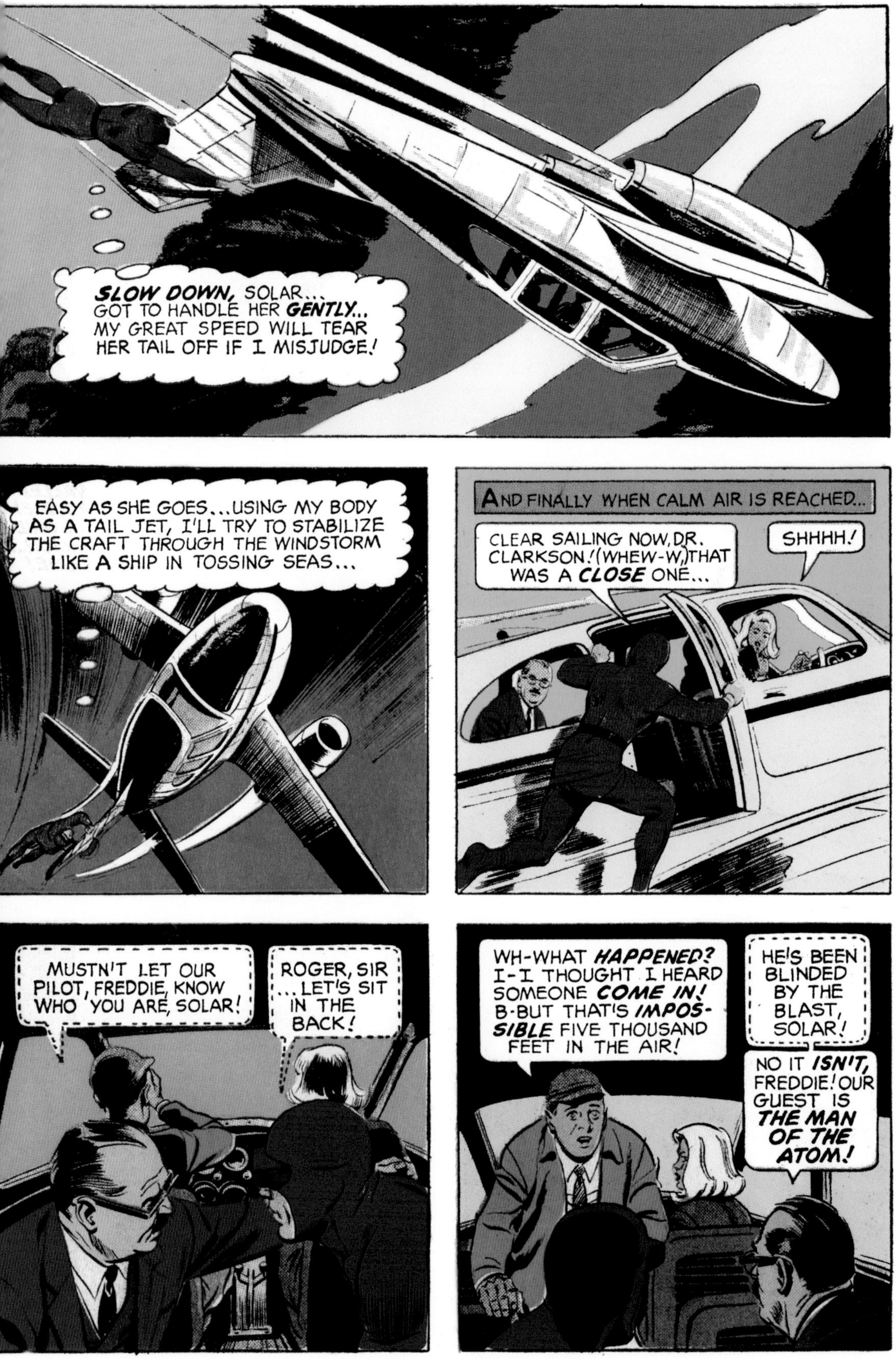
SLOW DOWN, SOLAR... GOT TO HANDLE HER GENTLY... MY GREAT SPEED WILL TEAR HER TAIL OFF IF I MISJUDGE!
EASY AS SHE GOES...USING MY BODY AS A TAIL JET, I'LL TRY TO STABILIZE THE CRAFT THROUGH THE WINDSTORM LIKE A SHIP IN TOSSING SEAS...
AND FINALLY WHEN CALM AIR IS REACHED...
CLEAR SAILING NOW, DR. CLARKSON! (WHEW-W) THAT WAS A CLOSE ONE...
SHHHH!
MUSTN'T LET OUR PILOT, FREDDIE, KNOW WHO YOU ARE, SOLAR!
ROGER, SIR ...LET'S SIT IN THE BACK!
WH-WHAT HAPPENED? I-I THOUGHT I HEARD SOMEONE COME IN! B-BUT THAT'S IMPOSSIBLE FIVE THOUSAND FEET IN THE AIR!
HE'S BEEN BLINDED BY THE BLAST, SOLAR!
NO IT ISN'T, FREDDIE! OUR GUEST IS THE MAN OF THE ATOM!

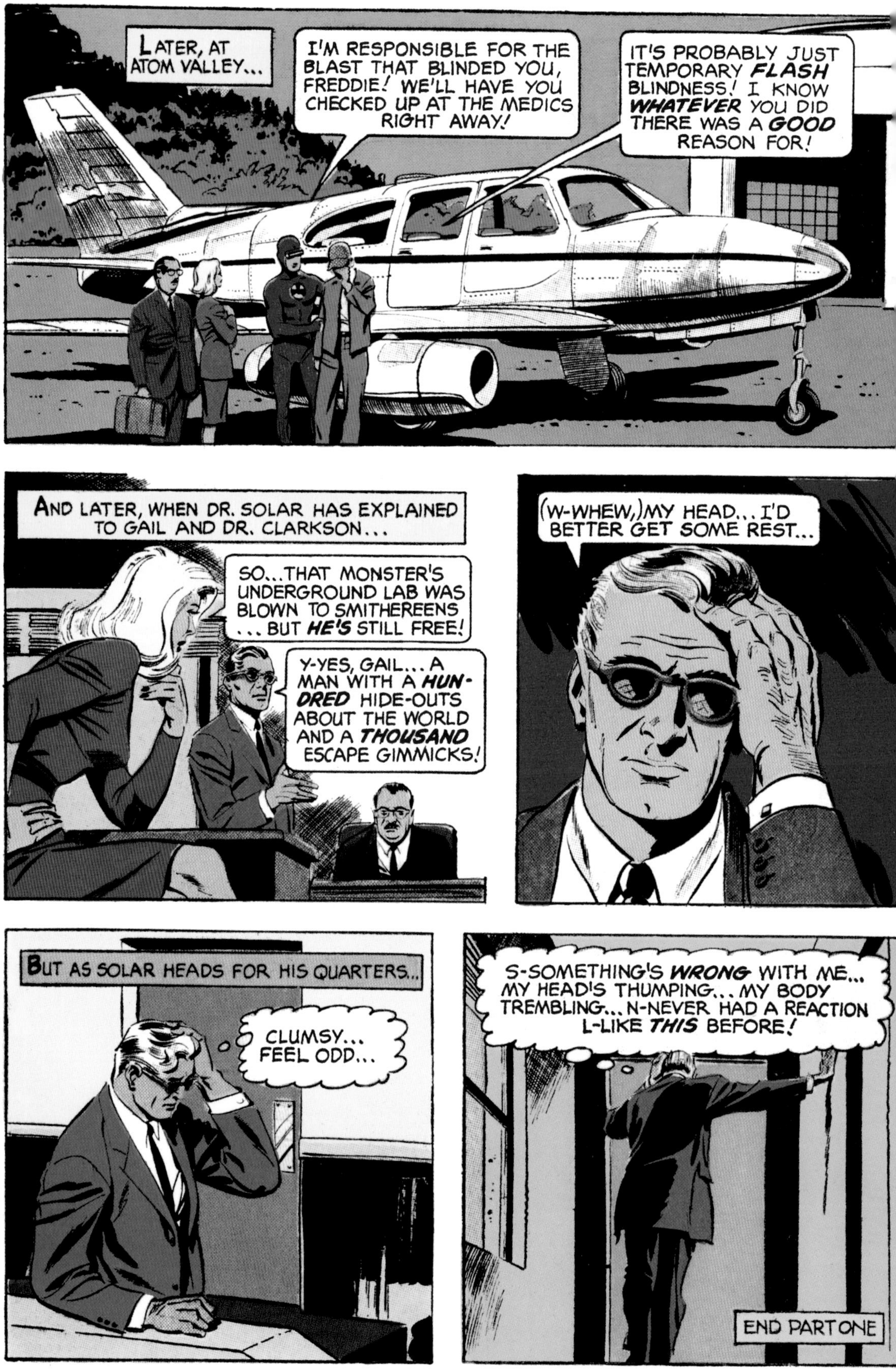
LATER, AT ATOM VALLEY...
I'M RESPONSIBLE FOR THE BLAST THAT BLINDED YOU, FREDDIE! WE'LL HAVE YOU CHECKED UP AT THE MEDICS RIGHT AWAY!
IT'S PROBABLY JUST TEMPORARY FLASH BLINDNESS! I KNOW WHATEVER YOU DID THERE WAS A GOOD REASON FOR!
AND LATER, WHEN DR. SOLAR HAS EXPLAINED TO GAIL AND DR. CLARKSON...
SO...THAT MONSTER'S UNDERGROUND LAB WAS BLOWN TO SMITHEREENS ...BUT HE'S STILL FREE!
Y-YES, GAIL... A MAN WITH A HUNDRED HIDE-OUTS ABOUT THE WORLD AND A THOUSAND ESCAPE GIMMICKS!
(W-WHEW,) MY HEAD... I'D BETTER GET SOME REST...
BUT AS SOLAR HEADS FOR HIS QUARTERS...
CLUMSY... FEEL ODD...
S-SOMETHING'S WRONG WITH ME... MY HEAD'S THUMPING... MY BODY TREMBLING... N-NEVER HAD A REACTION L-LIKE THIS BEFORE!
END PART ONE

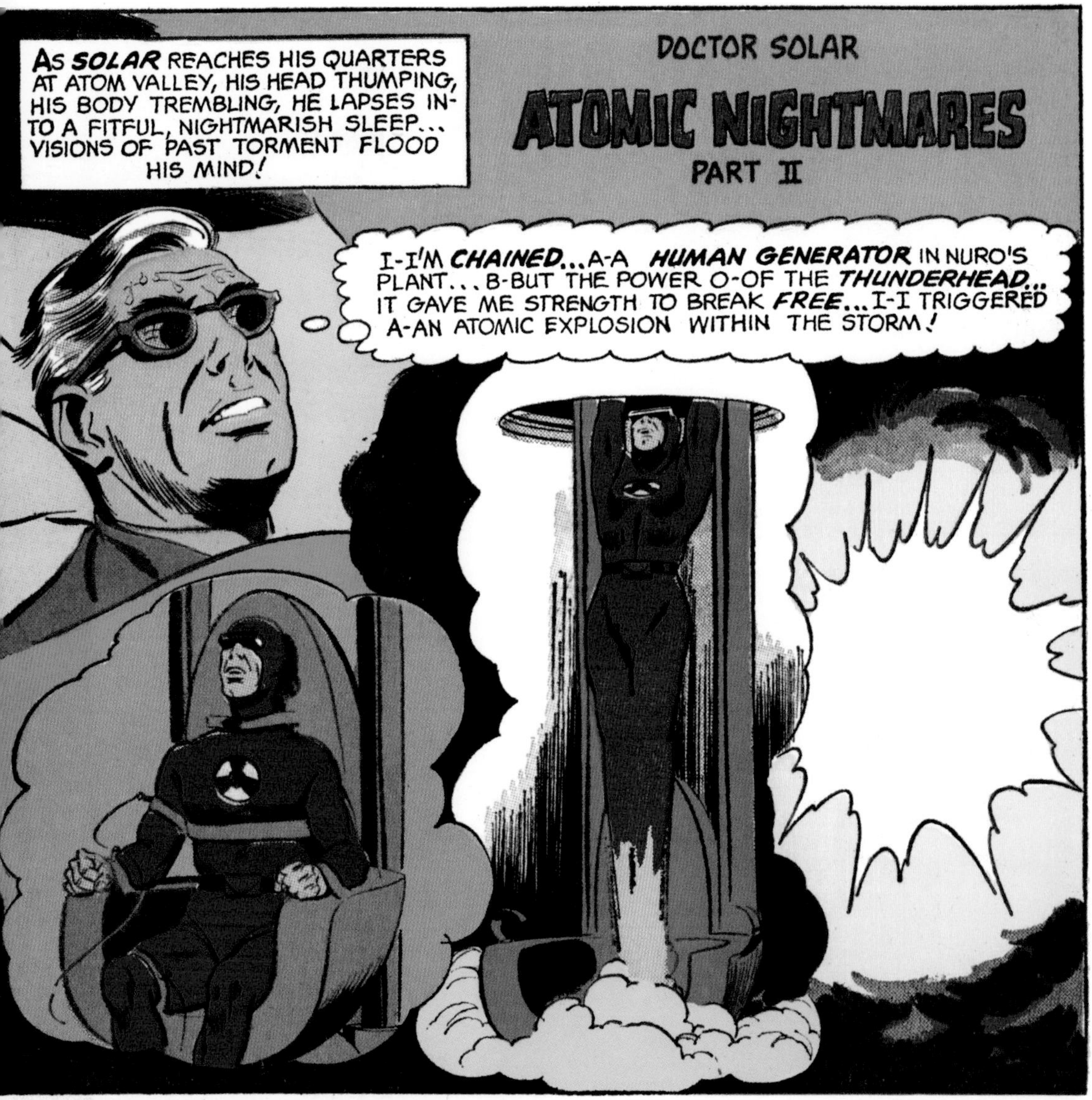
AS SOLAR REACHES HIS QUARTERS AT ATOM VALLEY, HIS HEAD THUMPING, HIS BODY TREMBLING, HE LAPSES INTO A FITFUL, NIGHTMARISH SLEEP... VISIONS OF PAST TORMENT FLOOD HIS MIND!
DOCTOR SOLAR
ATOMIC NIGHTMARES
PART II
I-I'M CHAINED...A-A HUMAN GENERATOR IN NURO'S PLANT... B-BUT THE POWER O-OF THE THUNDERHEAD.. IT GAVE ME STRENGTH TO BREAK FREE...I-I TRIGGERED A-AN ATOMIC EXPLOSION WITHIN THE STORM!

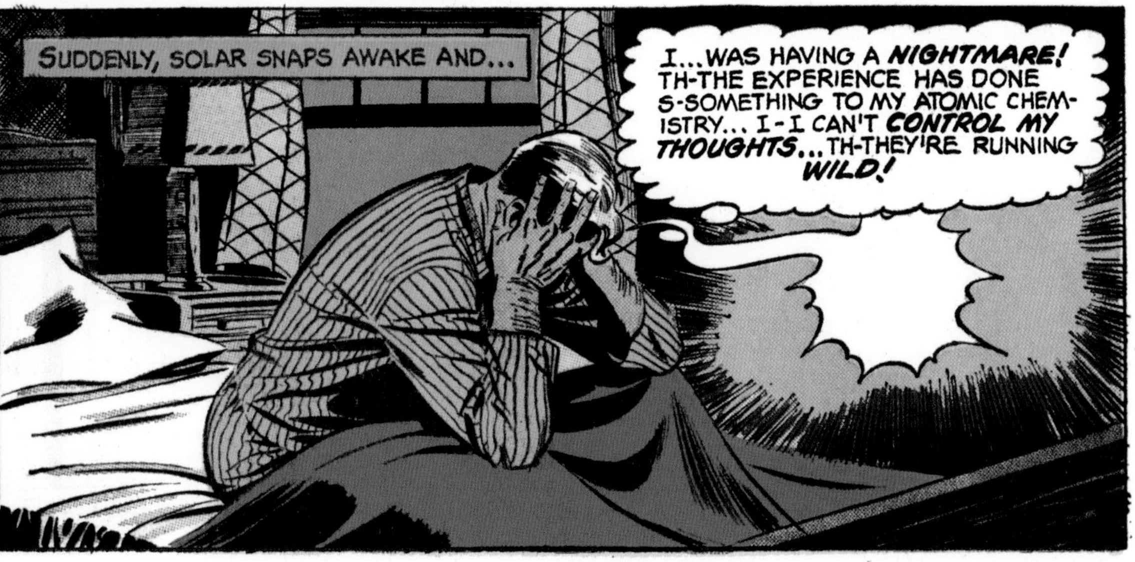
SUDDENLY, SOLAR SNAPS AWAKE AND...
I...WAS HAVING A NIGHTMARE! TH-THE EXPERIENCE HAS DONE S-SOMETHING TO MY ATOMIC CHEMISTRY... I-I CAN'T CONTROL MY THOUGHTS...TH-THEY'RE RUNNING WILD!

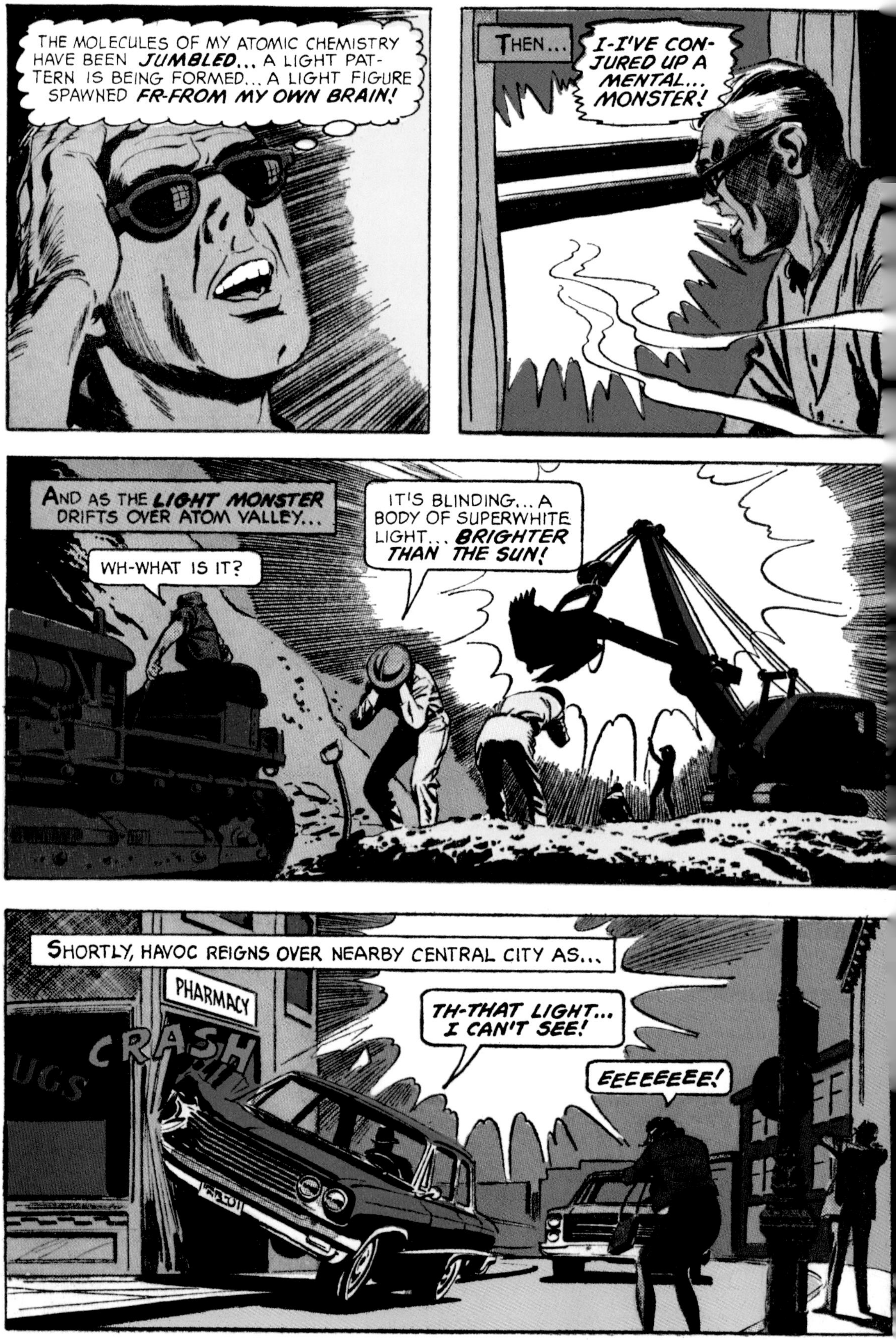
THE MOLECULES OF MY ATOMIC CHEMISTRY HAVE BEEN JUMBLED... A LIGHT PATTERN IS BEING FORMED... A LIGHT FIGURE SPAWNED FR-FROM MY OWN BRAIN!
THEN...
I-I'VE CONJURED UP A MENTAL... MONSTER!
AND AS THE LIGHT MONSTER DRIFTS OVER ATOM VALLEY...
WH-WHAT IS IT?
IT'S BLINDING... A BODY OF SUPERWHITE LIGHT... BRIGHTER THAN THE SUN!
SHORTLY, HAVOC REIGNS OVER NEARBY CENTRAL CITY AS...
PHARMACY
CRASH
TH-THAT LIGHT... I CAN'T SEE!
EEEEEEEE!

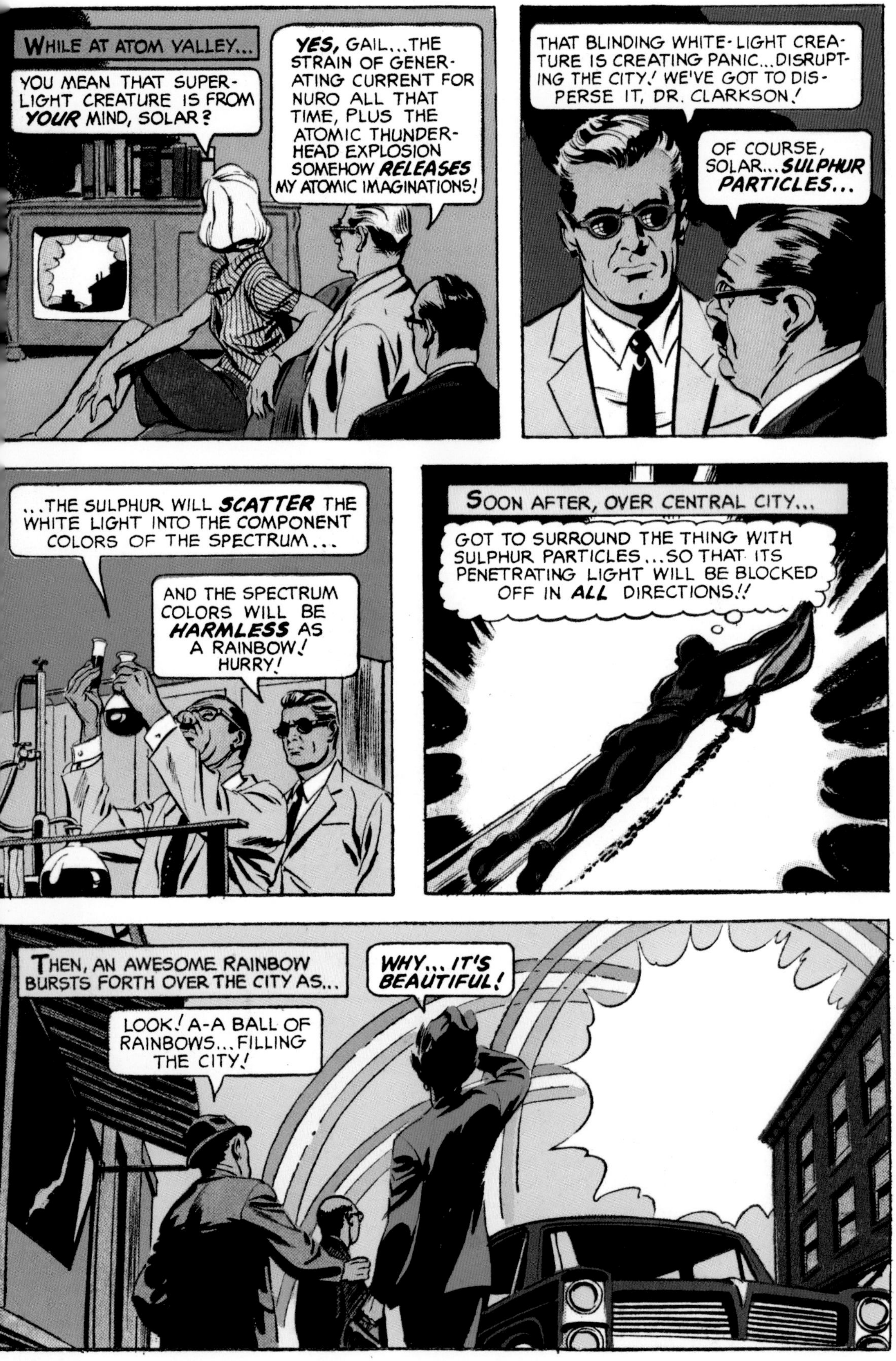
WHILE AT ATOM VALLEY...
YOU MEAN THAT SUPER-LIGHT CREATURE IS FROM YOUR MIND, SOLAR?
YES, GAIL...THE STRAIN OF GENERATING CURRENT FOR NURO ALL THAT TIME, PLUS THE ATOMIC THUNDERHEAD EXPLOSION SOMEHOW RELEASES MY ATOMIC IMAGINATIONS!
THAT BLINDING WHITE-LIGHT CREATURE IS CREATING PANIC...DISRUPTING THE CITY! WE'VE GOT TO DISPERSE IT, DR. CLARKSON!
OF COURSE, SOLAR...SULPHUR PARTICLES...
...THE SULPHUR WILL SCATTER THE WHITE LIGHT INTO THE COMPONENT COLORS OF THE SPECTRUM...
AND THE SPECTRUM COLORS WILL BE HARMLESS AS A RAINBOW! HURRY!
SOON AFTER, OVER CENTRAL CITY...
GOT TO SURROUND THE THING WITH SULPHUR PARTICLES...SO THAT ITS PENETRATING LIGHT WILL BE BLOCKED OFF IN ALL DIRECTIONS!!
THEN, AN AWESOME RAINBOW BURSTS FORTH OVER THE CITY AS...
WHY... IT'S BEAUTIFUL!
LOOK! A-A BALL OF RAINBOWS...FILLING THE CITY!

AND AS THE LIGHT MONSTER'S POWER IS DRAINED BY THE DIFFUSED RAYS...

JUST AS NURO DRAINED *MY* POWER, THE LIGHT CREATURE IS BEING SAPPED OF *ITS* ENERGY! PERHAPS IT'S WEAK ENOUGH NOW FOR MY MIND TO SMASH IT!

SOLAR CONCENTRATES... AND "KILLS" HIS MENTAL CREATURE...WITH *WILL POWER ALONE*...

BACK...BACK INSIDE MY MIND, MONSTER... YOU'RE NOTHING BUT A WARPED FIGMENT OF MY *OWN BRAIN!*

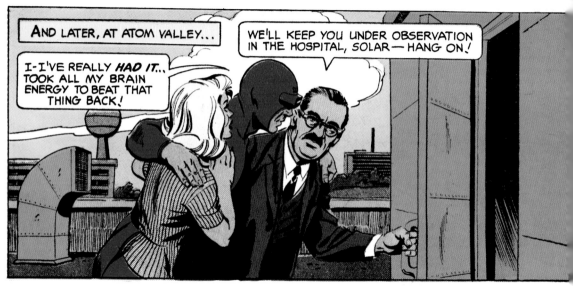

AND LATER, AT ATOM VALLEY...

I-I'VE REALLY *HAD IT*... TOOK ALL MY BRAIN ENERGY TO BEAT THAT THING BACK!

WE'LL KEEP YOU UNDER OBSERVATION IN THE HOSPITAL, SOLAR— HANG ON!

WHEN SOLAR HAS BEEN PLACED IN A TOP SECURITY ROOM...

IF ONLY I COULD STOP *THINKING*...

JUST REST, SOLAR... *REST!*

HE CAN'T BE LEFT ALONE FOR A *MOMENT*, GAIL! WE'LL WORK IN SHIFTS... I'LL TAKE THE FIRST ONE!

ALL RIGHT, DR. CLARKSON! I'LL RELIEVE YOU AT MIDNIGHT!

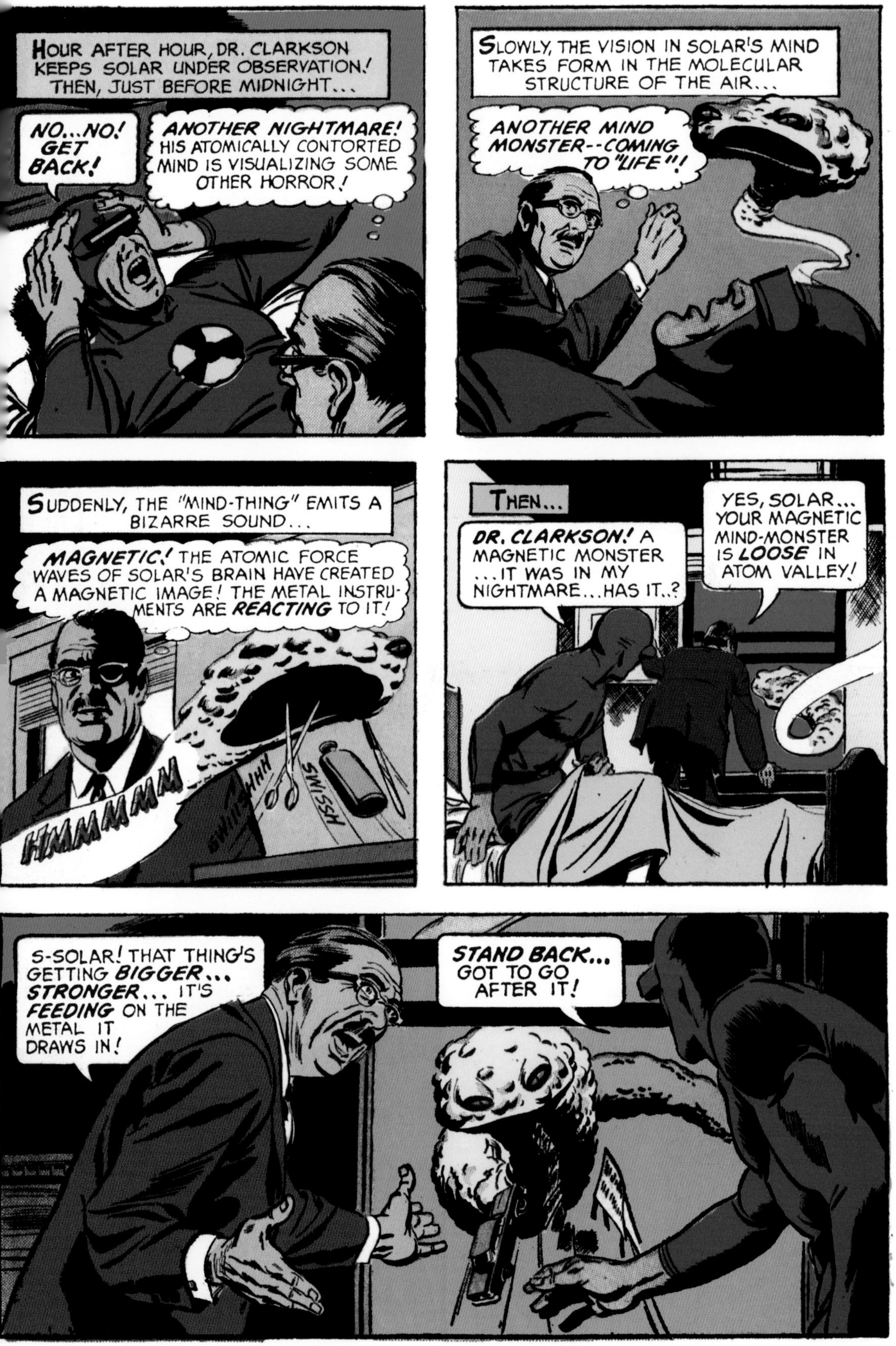
HOUR AFTER HOUR, DR. CLARKSON KEEPS SOLAR UNDER OBSERVATION! THEN, JUST BEFORE MIDNIGHT...
NO...NO! GET BACK!
ANOTHER NIGHTMARE! HIS ATOMICALLY CONTORTED MIND IS VISUALIZING SOME OTHER HORROR!
SLOWLY, THE VISION IN SOLAR'S MIND TAKES FORM IN THE MOLECULAR STRUCTURE OF THE AIR...
ANOTHER MIND MONSTER--COMING TO "LIFE"!
SUDDENLY, THE "MIND-THING" EMITS A BIZARRE SOUND...
MAGNETIC! THE ATOMIC FORCE WAVES OF SOLAR'S BRAIN HAVE CREATED A MAGNETIC IMAGE! THE METAL INSTRU-MENTS ARE REACTING TO IT!
HMMMMM
SWISSH
THEN...
DR. CLARKSON! A MAGNETIC MONSTER ...IT WAS IN MY NIGHTMARE...HAS IT..?
YES, SOLAR... YOUR MAGNETIC MIND-MONSTER IS LOOSE IN ATOM VALLEY!
S-SOLAR! THAT THING'S GETTING BIGGER... STRONGER... IT'S FEEDING ON THE METAL IT DRAWS IN!
STAND BACK... GOT TO GO AFTER IT!

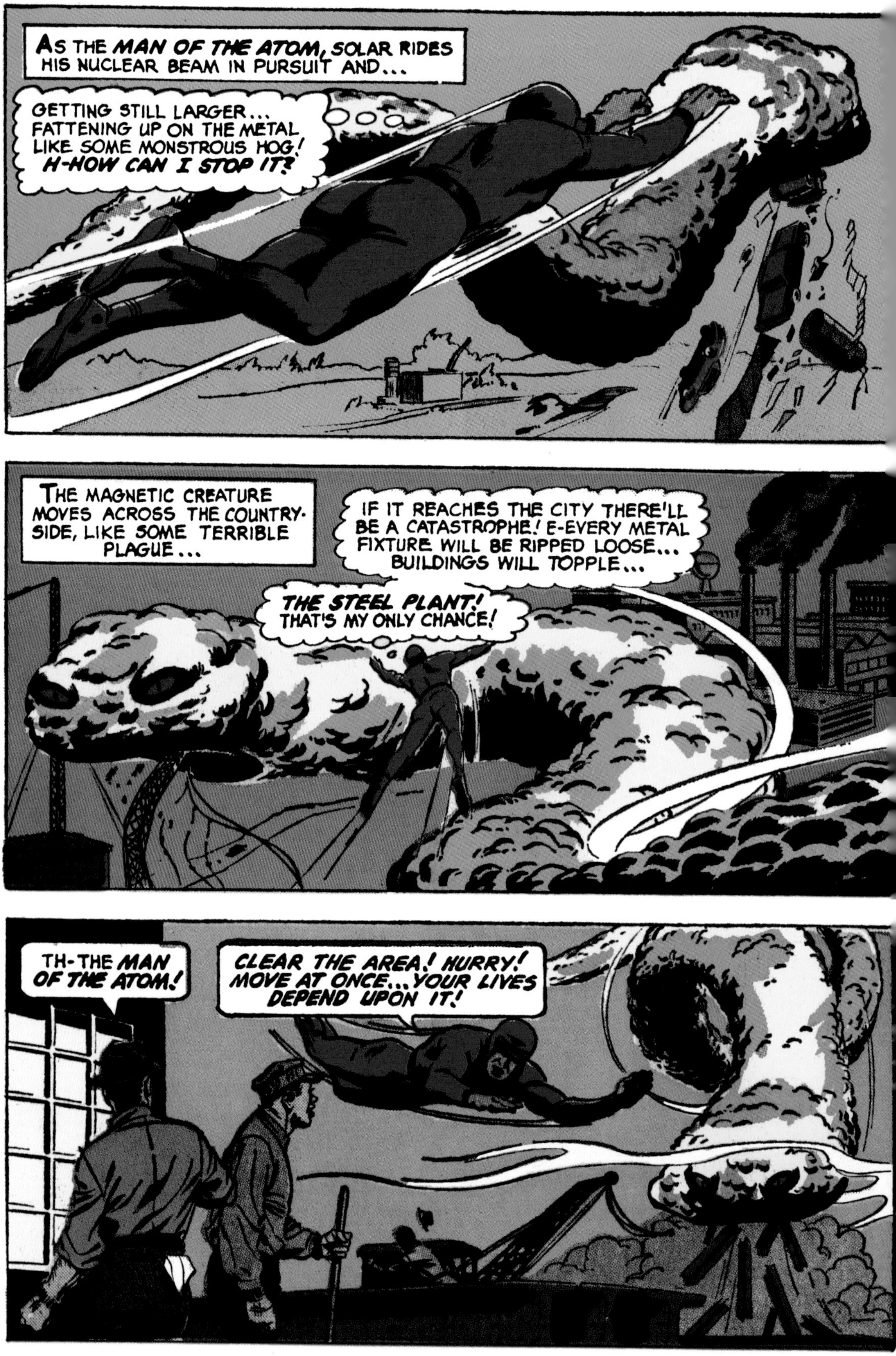

AS THE MAN OF THE ATOM, SOLAR RIDES HIS NUCLEAR BEAM IN PURSUIT AND...
GETTING STILL LARGER... FATTENING UP ON THE METAL LIKE SOME MONSTROUS HOG! H-HOW CAN I STOP IT?
THE MAGNETIC CREATURE MOVES ACROSS THE COUNTRY-SIDE, LIKE SOME TERRIBLE PLAGUE...
IF IT REACHES THE CITY THERE'LL BE A CATASTROPHE! E-EVERY METAL FIXTURE WILL BE RIPPED LOOSE... BUILDINGS WILL TOPPLE...
THE STEEL PLANT! THAT'S MY ONLY CHANCE!
TH-THE MAN OF THE ATOM!
CLEAR THE AREA! HURRY! MOVE AT ONCE... YOUR LIVES DEPEND UPON IT!

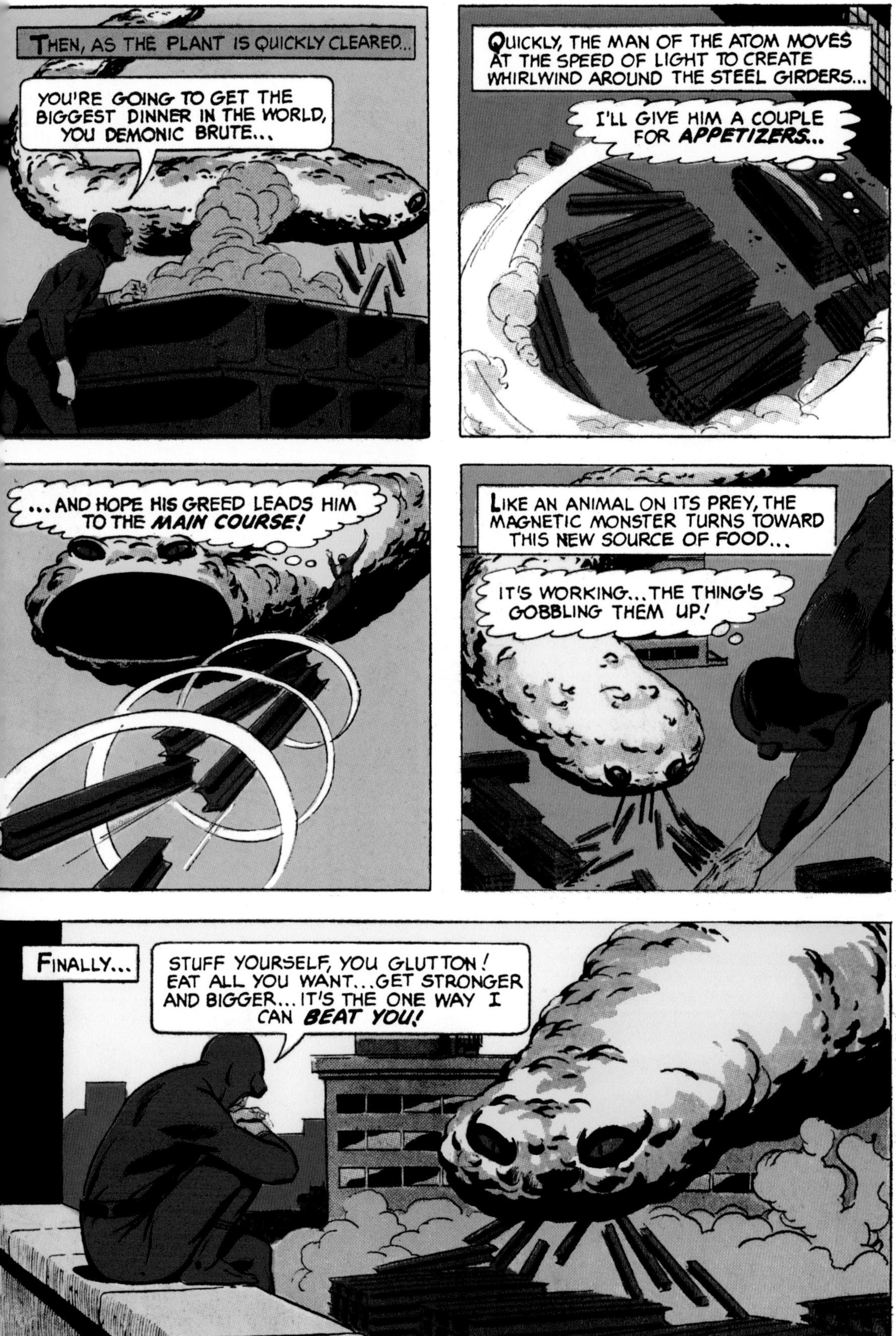
THEN, AS THE PLANT IS QUICKLY CLEARED...
YOU'RE GOING TO GET THE BIGGEST DINNER IN THE WORLD, YOU DEMONIC BRUTE...
QUICKLY, THE MAN OF THE ATOM MOVES AT THE SPEED OF LIGHT TO CREATE WHIRLWIND AROUND THE STEEL GIRDERS...
I'LL GIVE HIM A COUPLE FOR APPETIZERS...
...AND HOPE HIS GREED LEADS HIM TO THE MAIN COURSE!
LIKE AN ANIMAL ON ITS PREY, THE MAGNETIC MONSTER TURNS TOWARD THIS NEW SOURCE OF FOOD...
IT'S WORKING...THE THING'S GOBBLING THEM UP!
FINALLY...
STUFF YOURSELF, YOU GLUTTON! EAT ALL YOU WANT...GET STRONGER AND BIGGER...IT'S THE ONE WAY I CAN BEAT YOU!

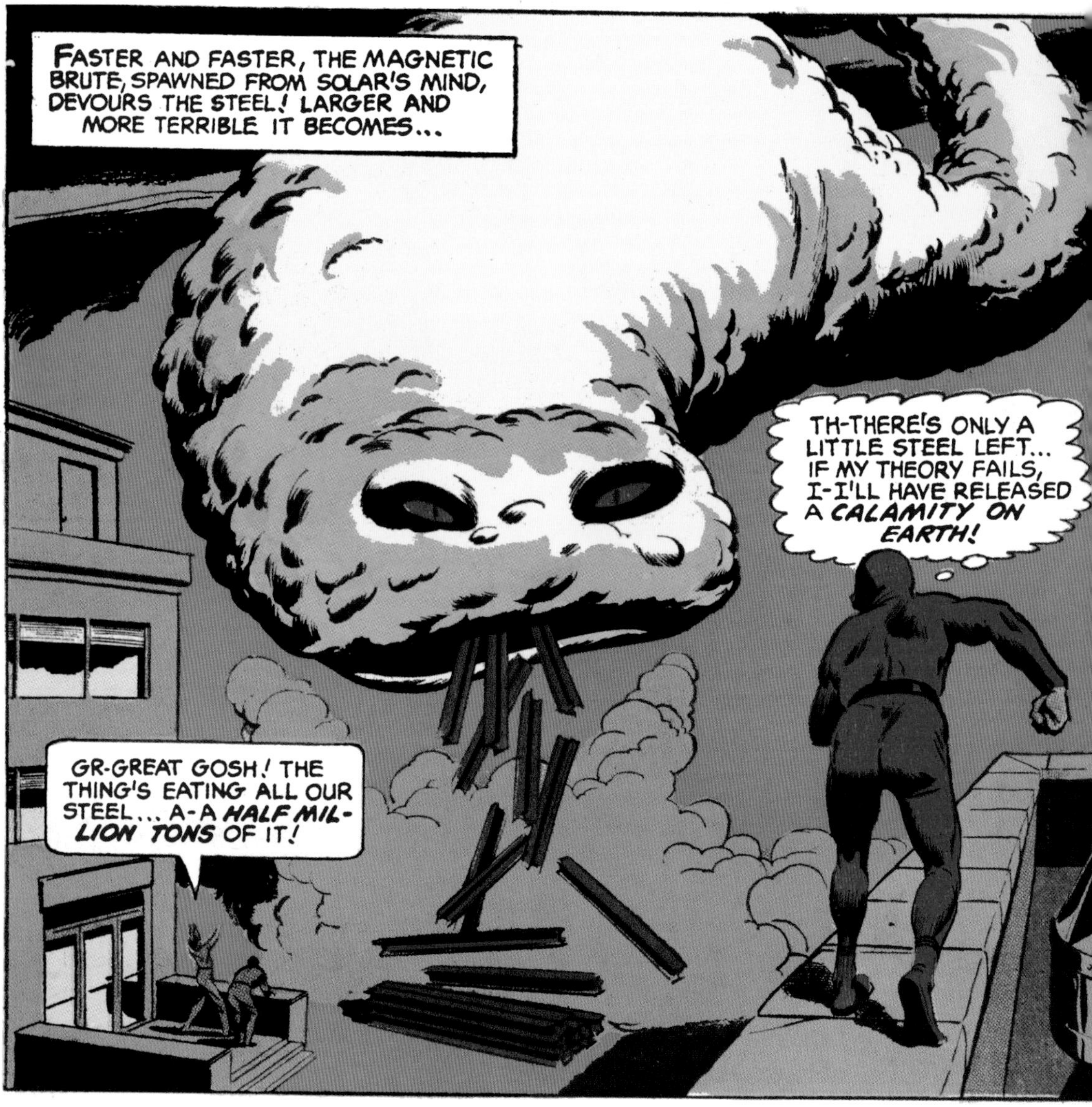
FASTER AND FASTER, THE MAGNETIC BRUTE, SPAWNED FROM SOLAR'S MIND, DEVOURS THE STEEL! LARGER AND MORE TERRIBLE IT BECOMES...
TH-THERE'S ONLY A LITTLE STEEL LEFT... IF MY THEORY FAILS, I-I'LL HAVE RELEASED A CALAMITY ON EARTH!
GR-GREAT GOSH! THE THING'S EATING ALL OUR STEEL... A-A HALF MIL-LION TONS OF IT!

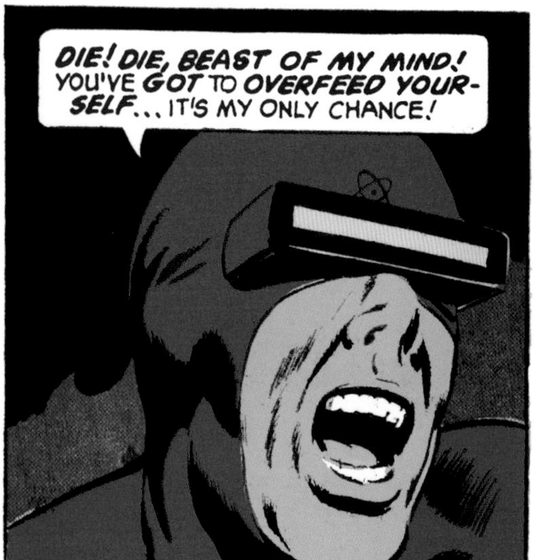
DIE! DIE, BEAST OF MY MIND! YOU'VE GOT TO OVERFEED YOUR-SELF... IT'S MY ONLY CHANCE!

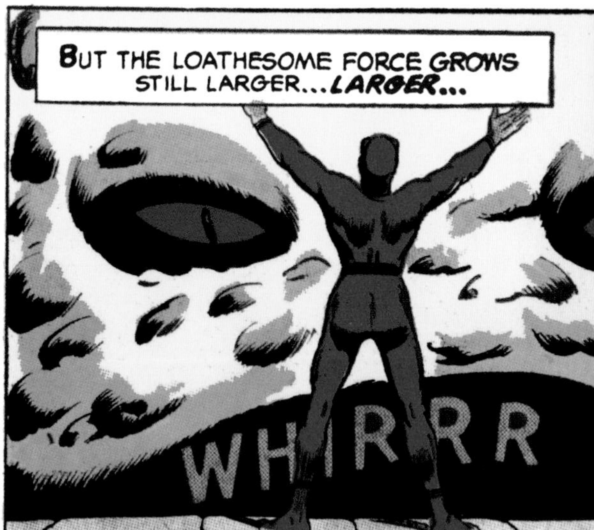
BUT THE LOATHESOME FORCE GROWS STILL LARGER...LARGER...
WHIRRR

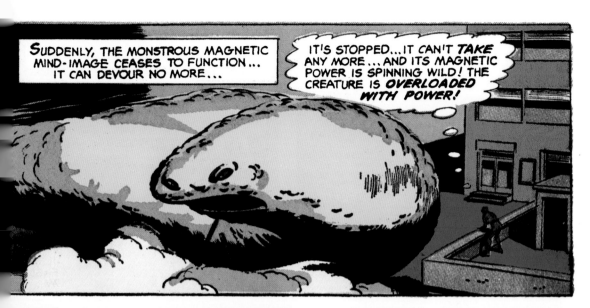

SUDDENLY, THE MONSTROUS MAGNETIC MIND-IMAGE CEASES TO FUNCTION... IT CAN DEVOUR NO MORE...

IT'S STOPPED...IT CAN'T *TAKE* ANY MORE...AND ITS MAGNETIC POWER IS SPINNING WILD! THE CREATURE IS *OVERLOADED WITH POWER!*

THEN...

I'VE...WON... IT'S...*BEATEN!*

HURRY, GAIL... WE'VE GOT TO REACH HIM BEFORE THE OTHERS DO!

POOR SOLAR... HIS OWN MIND IS...*DESTROYING HIM!*

AND LATER...

I-IT LOOKS LIKE THE END, DR. CLARKSON... THE *MAN OF THE ATOM* CAN'T CONTINUE JEOPARDIZING THE WORLD! MY *NEXT* MIND IMAGE MAY REALLY GET LOOSE UPON THE WORLD!

DON'T GIVE UP!...NOT *YET,* SOLAR...THERE'S *ONE* WAY WE MIGHT CURE YOU!

H-HE'S FALLEN DEAD *ASLEEP!* DO...YOU *REALLY* KNOW HOW TO CURE HIM, DR. CLARKSON?

*PERHAPS,* GAIL! HELP ME WHEEL HIM INTO THE REACTOR CHAMBER!

SHORTLY, AS SOLAR ABSORBS THE ATOMIC REACTOR'S SEETHING ENERGY...

I'M GOING TO TRY AND *SHOCK* HIS SYSTEM WITH ROENTGENS WHEN THE NEXT DREAM MONSTER BEGINS TO TAKE FORM...TRY TO BLOT THE IMAGE OUT OF HIS MIND.

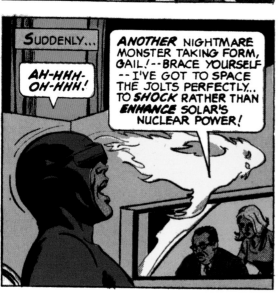

SUDDENLY...

AH-HHH-OH-HHH!

*ANOTHER* NIGHTMARE MONSTER TAKING FORM, GAIL!--BRACE YOURSELF -- I'VE GOT TO SPACE THE JOLTS PERFECTLY... TO *SHOCK* RATHER THAN *ENHANCE* SOLAR'S NUCLEAR POWER!

N-NO... I'M MAKING THE SPURTS OF RADIATION TOO *LONG*... MUST *SHORTEN* THE DOSAGES...MAKE THEM ACT AS A DISTRACTION... NOT A POWER FORCE!

SOLAR'S CONJURED UP A...A *SUN MONSTER!*

FEVERISHLY, THE DOCTOR WORKS THE REACTOR CONTROL DIAL AS...

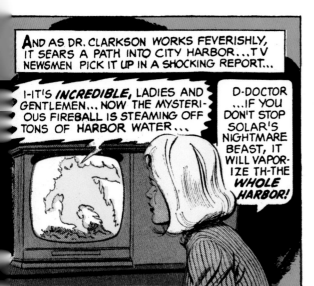

AND AS DR. CLARKSON WORKS FEVERISHLY, IT SEARS A PATH INTO CITY HARBOR...TV NEWSMEN PICK IT UP IN A SHOCKING REPORT...

I-IT'S *INCREDIBLE*, LADIES AND GENTLEMEN... NOW THE MYSTERIOUS FIREBALL IS STEAMING OFF TONS OF HARBOR WATER...

D-DOCTOR ...IF YOU DON'T STOP SOLAR'S NIGHTMARE BEAST, IT WILL VAPORIZE TH-THE *WHOLE HARBOR!*

THEN...

I-I THINK I HAVE THE JOLTS SPACED *PROPERLY* NOW, GAIL... SOLAR'S SYSTEM IS BEING *RHYTHMICALLY* SHOCKED BY THE RADIATION!

AT THIS MOMENT, A YOUNG VISITOR OBSERVES FROM A SIGHT-SEEING OBSERVATION TOWER IN THE CITY AS...

G-GOOD GRIEF! I-IT'S TERRIBLE! B-BUT IT'S GETTING *SMALLER!*

MOST UNUSUAL ...A SUNBALL COMING DOWN THE RIVER FROM THE AREA OF *ATOM VALLEY* ...WHERE *THE MAN OF THE ATOM* FREQUENTLY *APPEARS!*

I-IT PUFFED *OUT!* S-SOMETHING DESTROYED IT, *THANK GOODNESS!*

THE MAN OF THE ATOM POSSESSES THE SOLAR ENERGY OF THE SUN... AND SO DOES THAT FREAK THING...HMMM... *MOST UNUSUAL INDEED!*

WHILE AT ATOM VALLEY...

IT'S ALL RIGHT, SOLAR... WE'VE KILLED YOUR ATOMIC NIGHTMARE FOREVER! YOUR ATOMIC CHEMISTRY IS BACK IN ORDER AGAIN!

(WH-WHEW...) I'M SURE GLAD OF *THAT!*

MY BRAIN FEELS LIKE IT'S BEEN *ZINGED* UP AND DOWN ON A *YO YO!* BUT FOR THE FIRST TIME SINCE BEING CHAINED TO NURO'S REACTOR I FEEL *RELAXED* AGAIN!

MISS SANDERS! YOU HAVE A VISITOR AT SECURITY GATE NO.2!

OH! IN THE EXCITEMENT I FORGOT THAT MY NEPHEW WAS ARRIVING FROM BOSTON TODAY! AND HE'S *QUITE* A LAD...HE WON A COLLEGE SCHOLARSHIP AT *FIFTEEN* YEARS OF AGE! *IMAGINE!* SEE YOU...

SHORTLY...

*HAMILTON MANSFIELD LAMONT...* MASS. INSTITUTE OF TECHNOLOGY...

YES, ANDY ...HE HAS CLEARANCE AS AN ATOMIC RESEARCH STUDENT FOR A FEW WEEKS!

GATE 2

WELCOME TO ATOM VALLEY, HAMILTON!

THANK *YOU, GAIL!* I AM MOST ANXIOUS TO STUDY SOME MOST... ER...*UNUSUAL* HAPPENINGS IN THESE PARTS!

DR. SOLAR CANNOT KNOW THAT IN SHORT ORDER, A BOY PRODIGY IS TO BECOME MORE DANGEROUS THAN ANY OTHER OPPONENT IN HIS CAREER! DON'T FAIL TO *"CHARGE UP"* WITH EXTRA ENERGY FOR THE NEXT ISSUE OF *DR. SOLAR!*

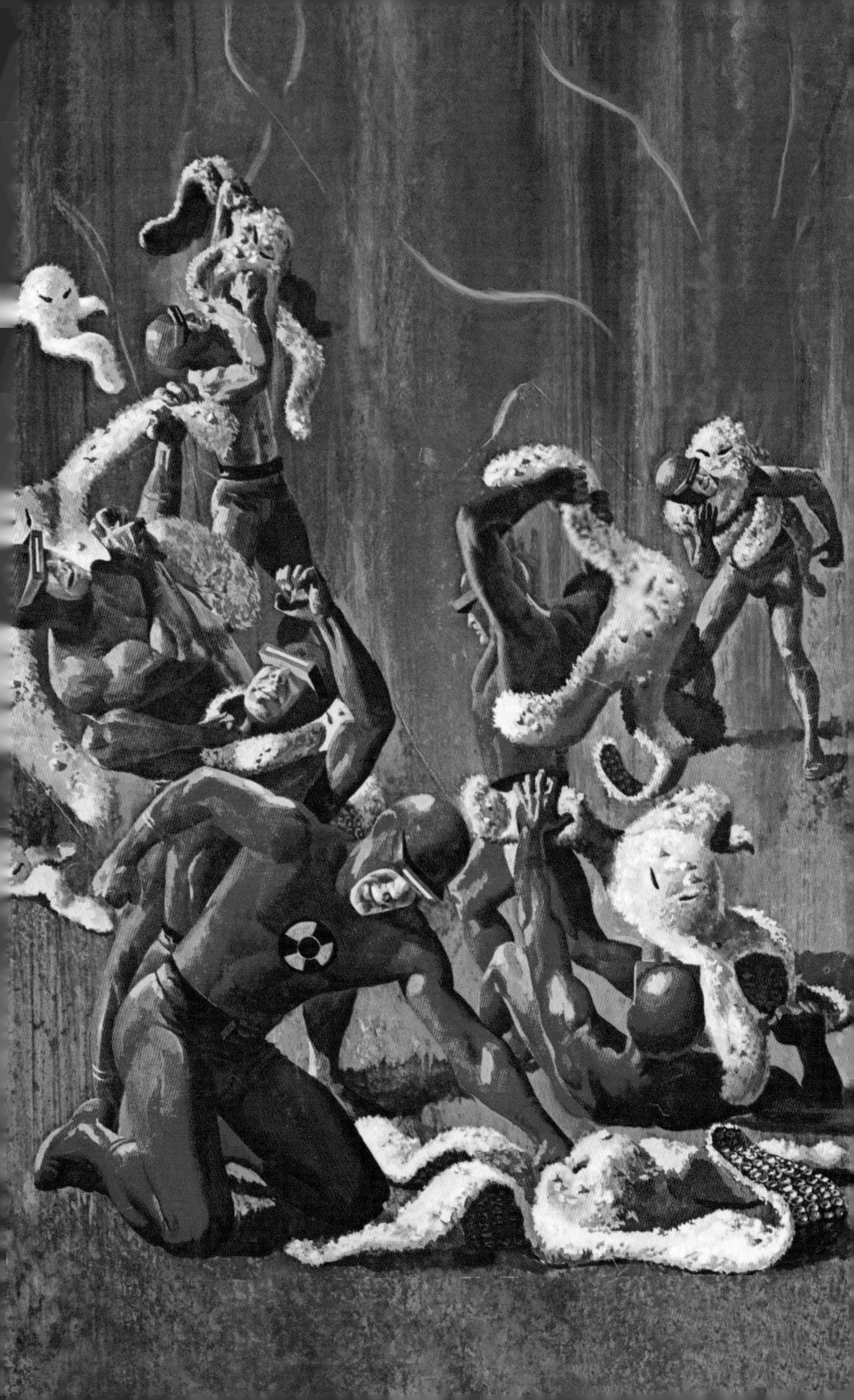

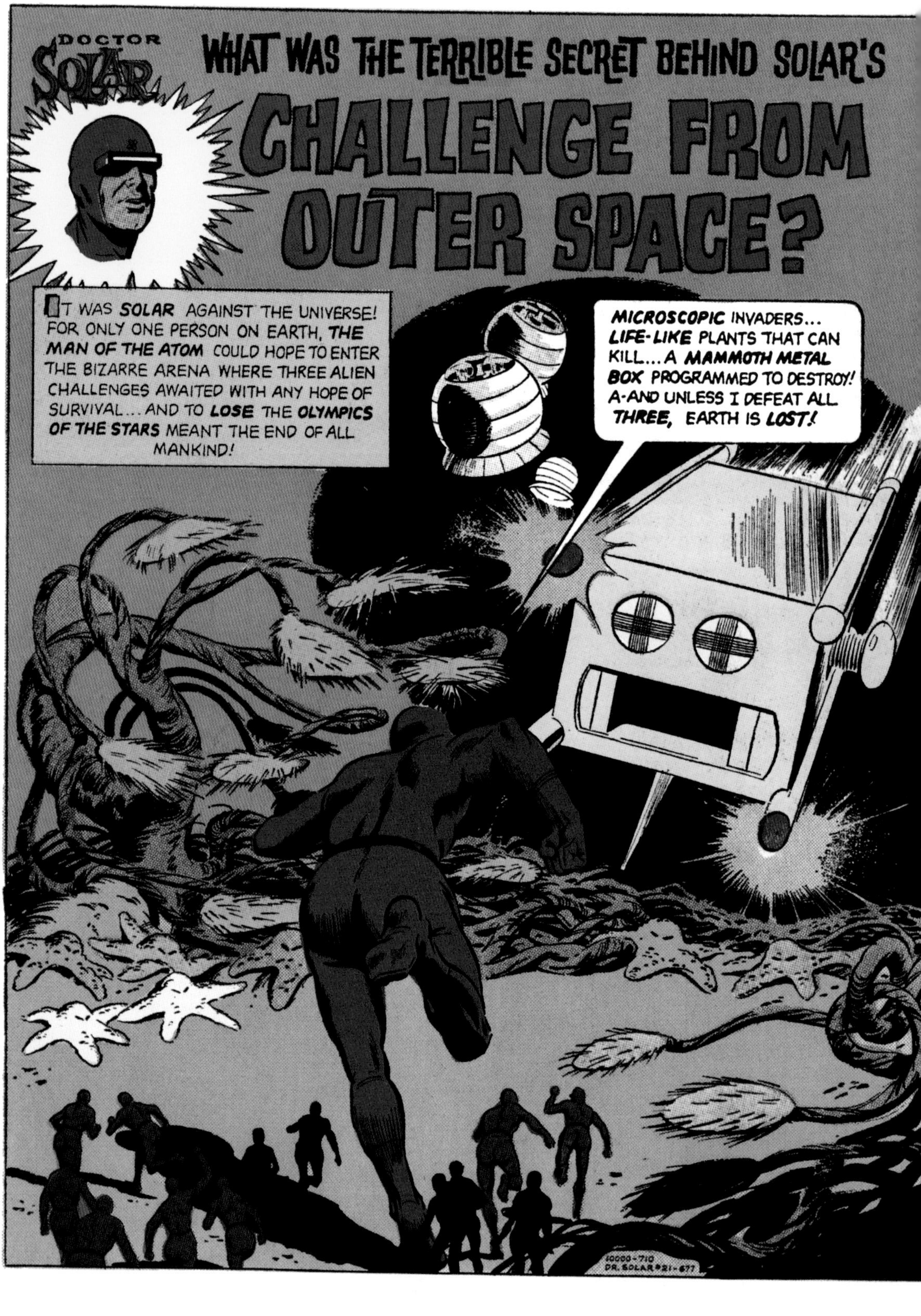
DOCTOR SOLAR
WHAT WAS THE TERRIBLE SECRET BEHIND SOLAR'S
CHALLENGE FROM OUTER SPACE?
IT WAS SOLAR AGAINST THE UNIVERSE! FOR ONLY ONE PERSON ON EARTH, THE MAN OF THE ATOM COULD HOPE TO ENTER THE BIZARRE ARENA WHERE THREE ALIEN CHALLENGES AWAITED WITH ANY HOPE OF SURVIVAL... AND TO LOSE THE OLYMPICS OF THE STARS MEANT THE END OF ALL MANKIND!
MICROSCOPIC INVADERS... LIFE-LIKE PLANTS THAT CAN KILL... A MAMMOTH METAL BOX PROGRAMMED TO DESTROY! A-AND UNLESS I DEFEAT ALL THREE, EARTH IS LOST!
10000-710
DR. SOLAR #21-677

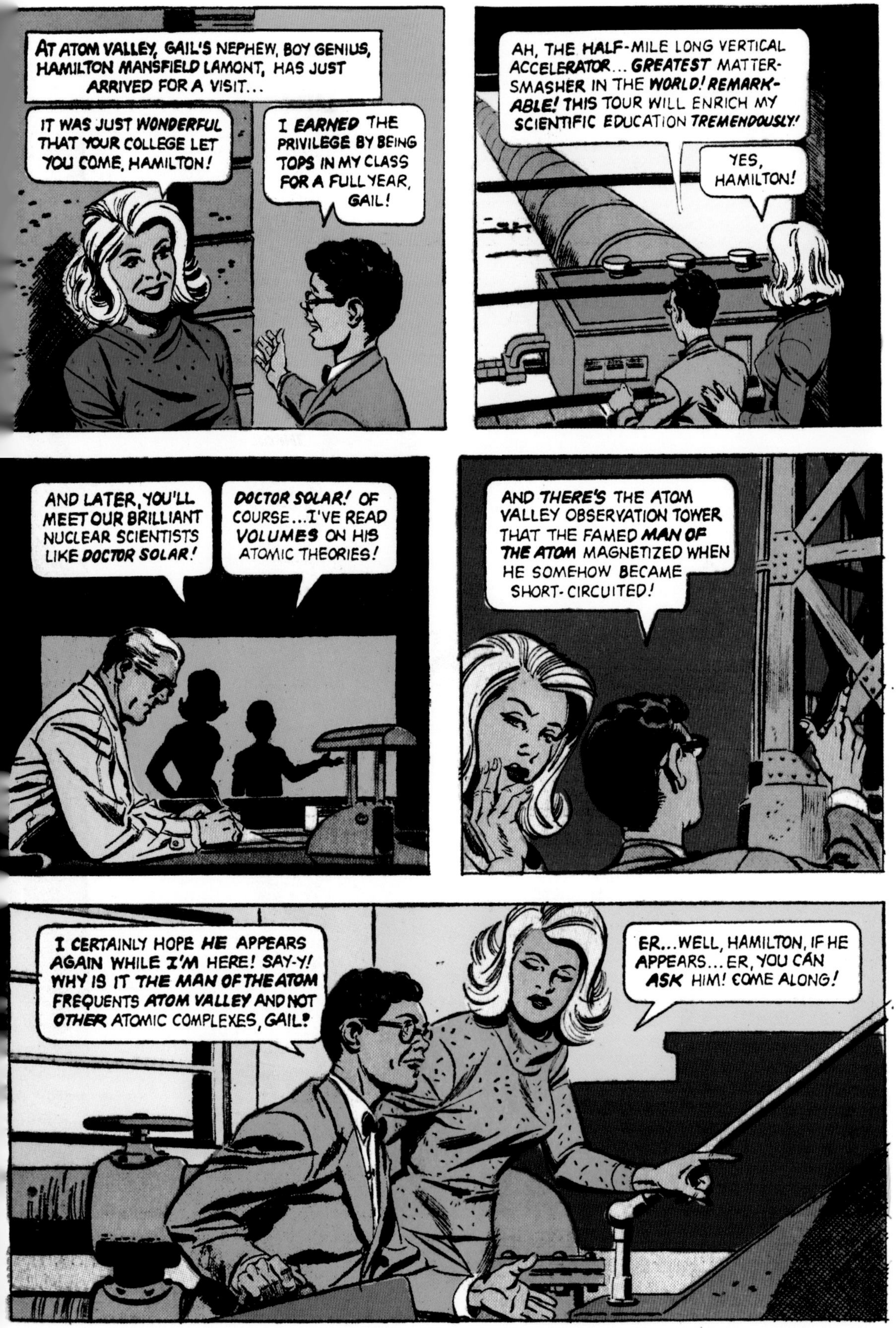
AT ATOM VALLEY, GAIL'S NEPHEW, BOY GENIUS, HAMILTON MANSFIELD LAMONT, HAS JUST ARRIVED FOR A VISIT...
IT WAS JUST WONDERFUL THAT YOUR COLLEGE LET YOU COME, HAMILTON!
I EARNED THE PRIVILEGE BY BEING TOPS IN MY CLASS FOR A FULL YEAR, GAIL!
AH, THE HALF-MILE LONG VERTICAL ACCELERATOR... GREATEST MATTER-SMASHER IN THE WORLD! REMARKABLE! THIS TOUR WILL ENRICH MY SCIENTIFIC EDUCATION TREMENDOUSLY!
YES, HAMILTON!
AND LATER, YOU'LL MEET OUR BRILLIANT NUCLEAR SCIENTISTS LIKE DOCTOR SOLAR!
DOCTOR SOLAR! OF COURSE...I'VE READ VOLUMES ON HIS ATOMIC THEORIES!
AND THERE'S THE ATOM VALLEY OBSERVATION TOWER THAT THE FAMED MAN OF THE ATOM MAGNETIZED WHEN HE SOMEHOW BECAME SHORT-CIRCUITED!
I CERTAINLY HOPE HE APPEARS AGAIN WHILE I'M HERE! SAY-Y! WHY IS IT THE MAN OF THE ATOM FREQUENTS ATOM VALLEY AND NOT OTHER ATOMIC COMPLEXES, GAIL?
ER...WELL, HAMILTON, IF HE APPEARS...ER, YOU CAN ASK HIM! COME ALONG!

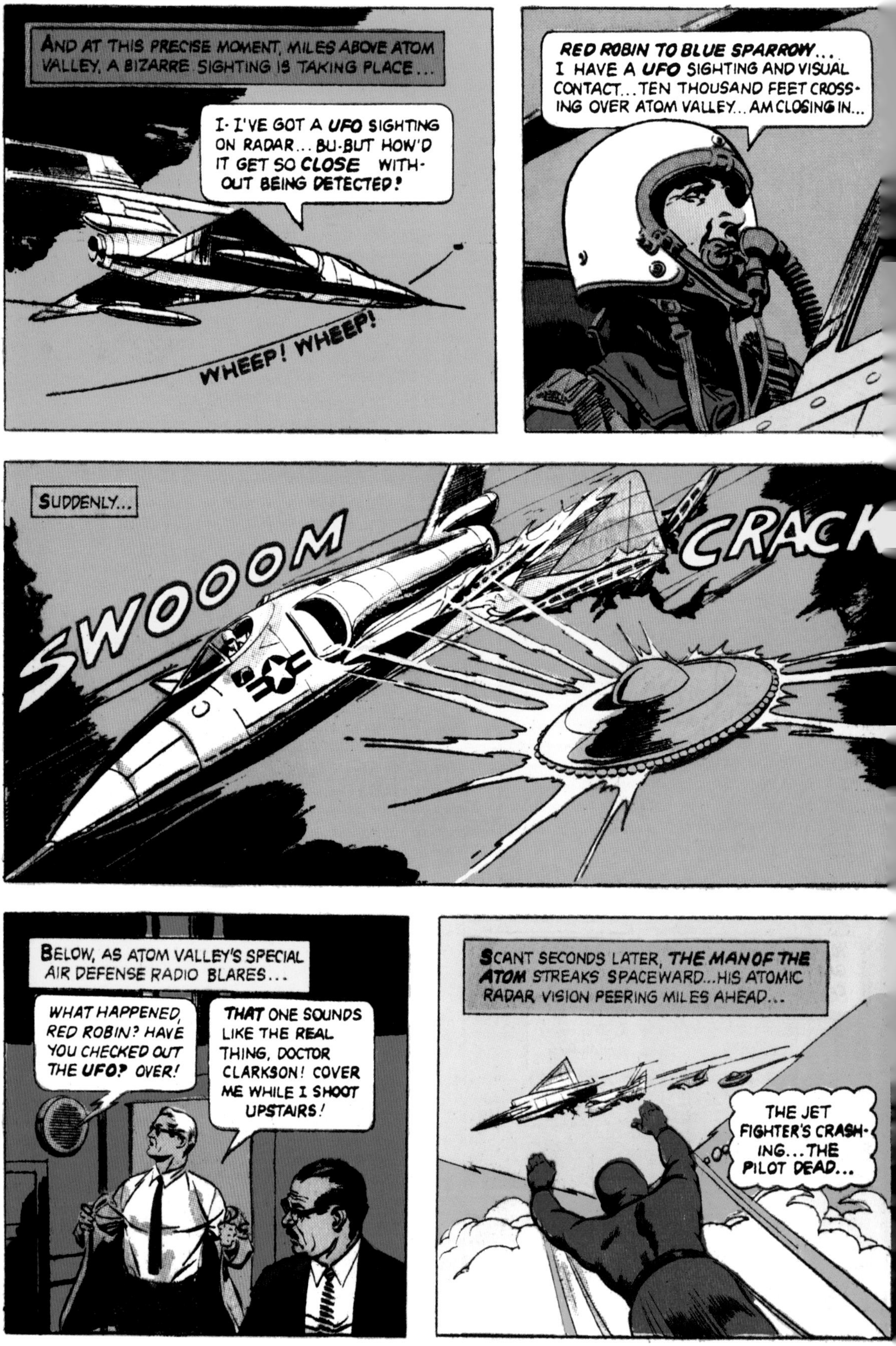
AND AT THIS PRECISE MOMENT, MILES ABOVE ATOM VALLEY, A BIZARRE SIGHTING IS TAKING PLACE...
I- I'VE GOT A UFO SIGHTING ON RADAR... BU-BUT HOW'D IT GET SO CLOSE WITH-OUT BEING DETECTED!
WHEEP! WHEEP!
RED ROBIN TO BLUE SPARROW... I HAVE A UFO SIGHTING AND VISUAL CONTACT... TEN THOUSAND FEET CROSS-ING OVER ATOM VALLEY... AM CLOSING IN...
SUDDENLY...
SWOOOM
CRACK
BELOW, AS ATOM VALLEY'S SPECIAL AIR DEFENSE RADIO BLARES...
WHAT HAPPENED, RED ROBIN? HAVE YOU CHECKED OUT THE UFO? OVER!
THAT ONE SOUNDS LIKE THE REAL THING, DOCTOR CLARKSON! COVER ME WHILE I SHOOT UPSTAIRS!
SCANT SECONDS LATER, THE MAN OF THE ATOM STREAKS SPACEWARD...HIS ATOMIC RADAR VISION PEERING MILES AHEAD...
THE JET FIGHTER'S CRASH-ING...THE PILOT DEAD...

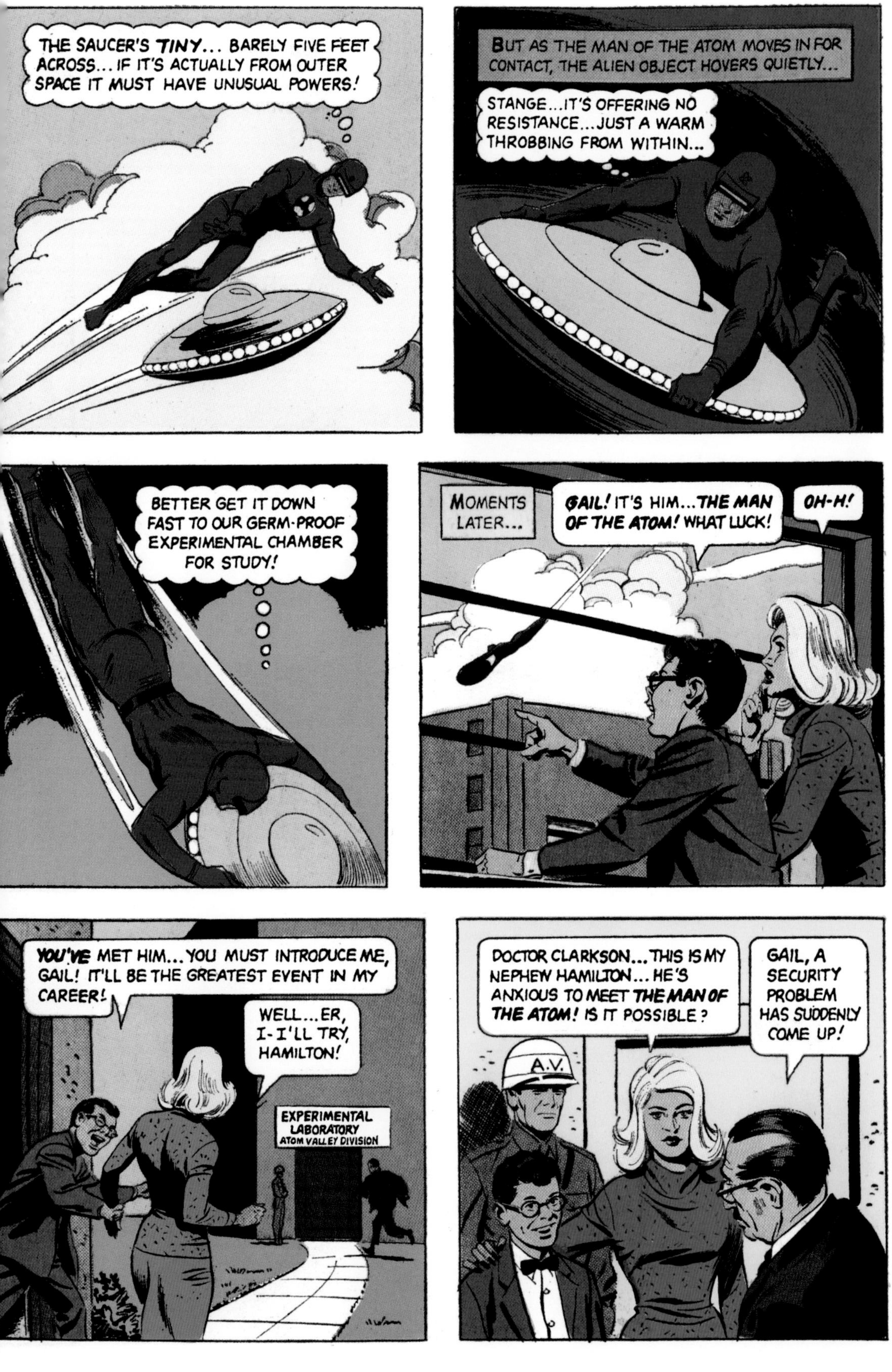
THE SAUCER'S TINY... BARELY FIVE FEET ACROSS... IF IT'S ACTUALLY FROM OUTER SPACE IT MUST HAVE UNUSUAL POWERS!
BUT AS THE MAN OF THE ATOM MOVES IN FOR CONTACT, THE ALIEN OBJECT HOVERS QUIETLY...
STANGE... IT'S OFFERING NO RESISTANCE... JUST A WARM THROBBING FROM WITHIN...
BETTER GET IT DOWN FAST TO OUR GERM-PROOF EXPERIMENTAL CHAMBER FOR STUDY!
MOMENTS LATER...
GAIL! IT'S HIM... THE MAN OF THE ATOM! WHAT LUCK!
OH-H!
YOU'VE MET HIM... YOU MUST INTRODUCE ME, GAIL! IT'LL BE THE GREATEST EVENT IN MY CAREER!
WELL... ER, I-I'LL TRY, HAMILTON!
EXPERIMENTAL LABORATORY ATOM VALLEY DIVISION
DOCTOR CLARKSON... THIS IS MY NEPHEW HAMILTON... HE'S ANXIOUS TO MEET THE MAN OF THE ATOM! IS IT POSSIBLE?
GAIL, A SECURITY PROBLEM HAS SUDDENLY COME UP!
A.V.

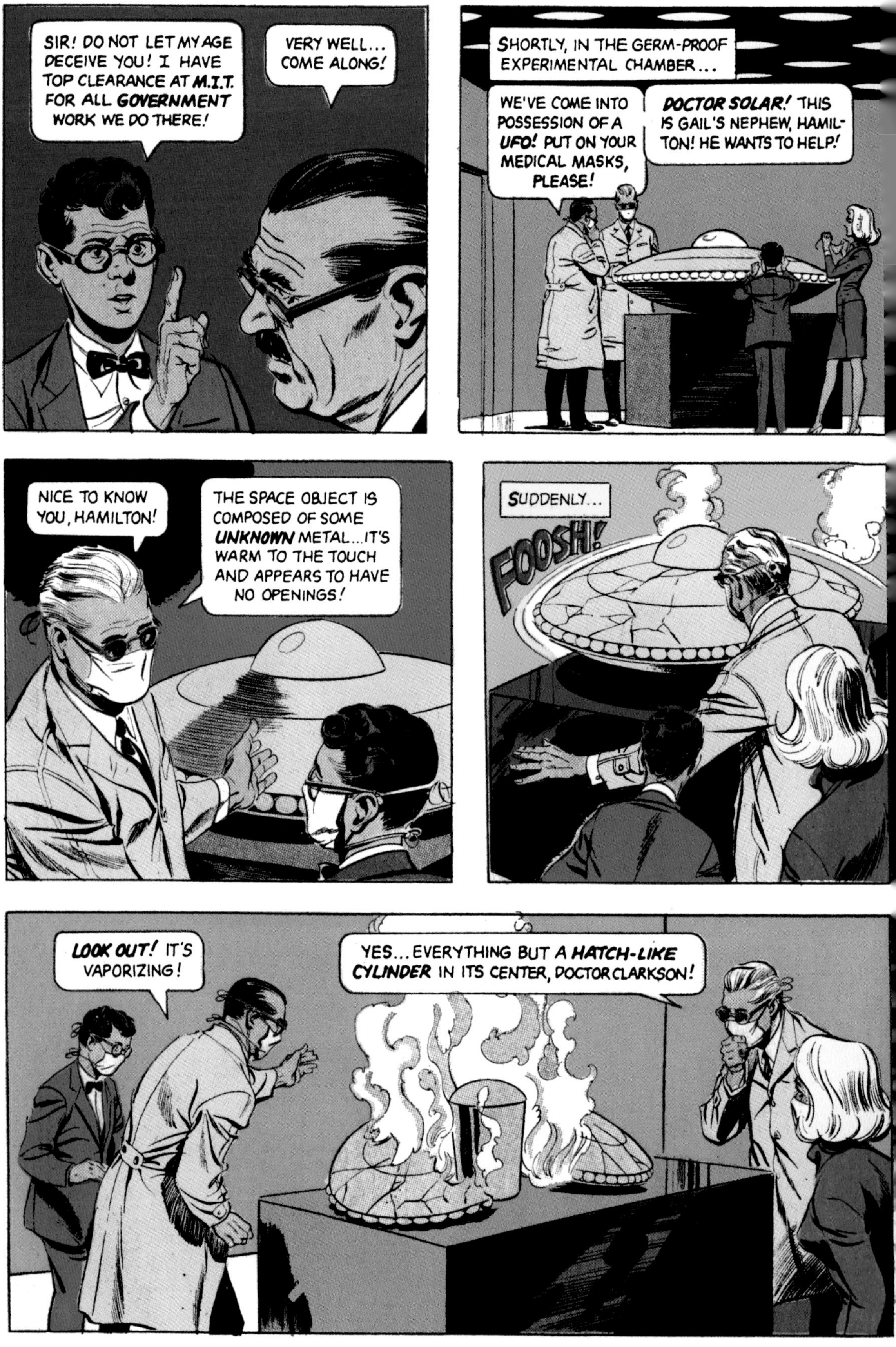
SIR! DO NOT LET MY AGE DECEIVE YOU! I HAVE TOP CLEARANCE AT M.I.T. FOR ALL GOVERNMENT WORK WE DO THERE!
VERY WELL... COME ALONG!
SHORTLY, IN THE GERM-PROOF EXPERIMENTAL CHAMBER...
WE'VE COME INTO POSSESSION OF A UFO! PUT ON YOUR MEDICAL MASKS, PLEASE!
DOCTOR SOLAR! THIS IS GAIL'S NEPHEW, HAMILTON! HE WANTS TO HELP!
NICE TO KNOW YOU, HAMILTON!
THE SPACE OBJECT IS COMPOSED OF SOME UNKNOWN METAL...IT'S WARM TO THE TOUCH AND APPEARS TO HAVE NO OPENINGS!
SUDDENLY...
FOOSH!
LOOK OUT! IT'S VAPORIZING!
YES... EVERYTHING BUT A HATCH-LIKE CYLINDER IN ITS CENTER, DOCTOR CLARKSON!

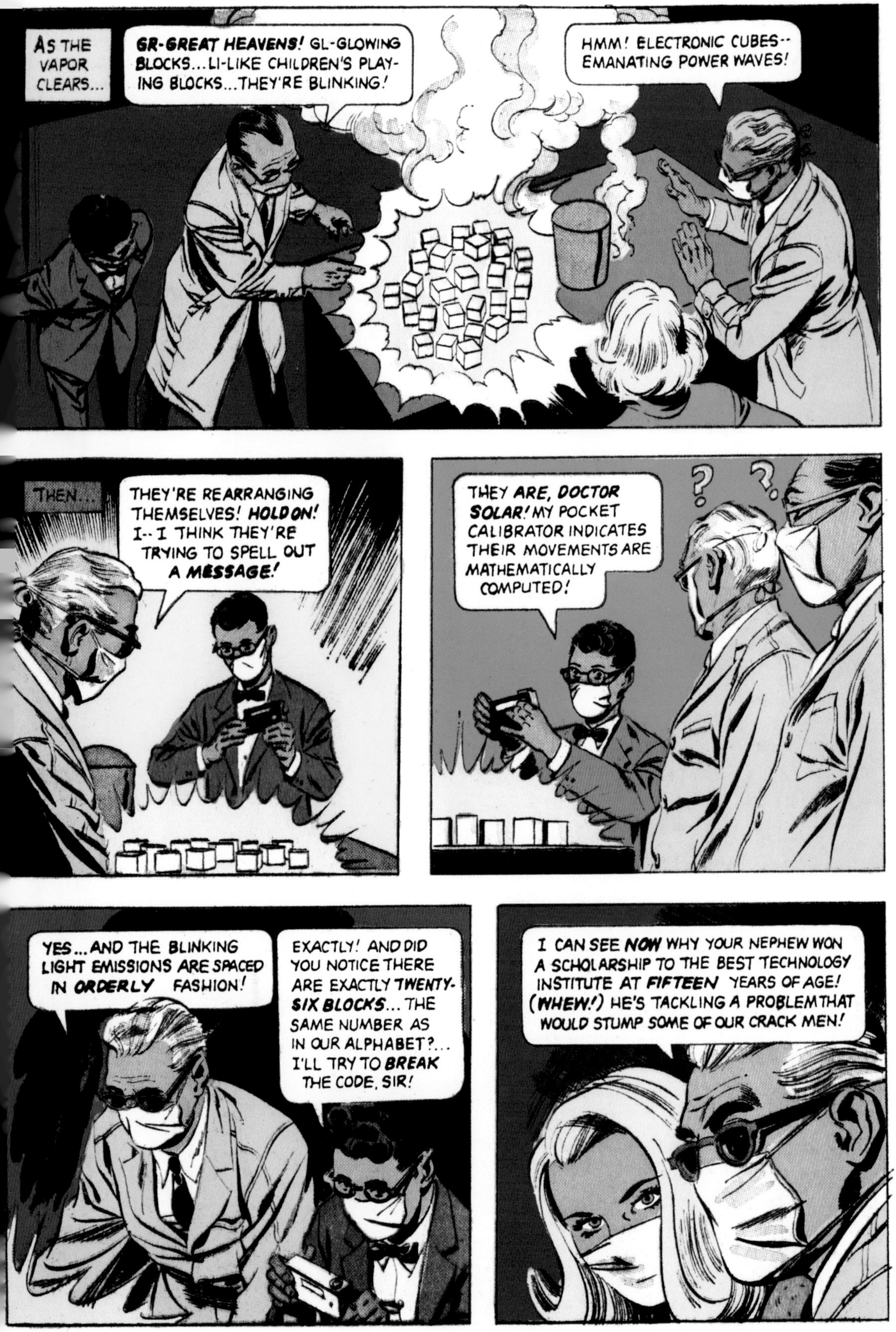
AS THE VAPOR CLEARS...
GR-GREAT HEAVENS! GL-GLOWING BLOCKS...LI-LIKE CHILDREN'S PLAYING BLOCKS...THEY'RE BLINKING!
HMM! ELECTRONIC CUBES--EMANATING POWER WAVES!
THEN...
THEY'RE REARRANGING THEMSELVES! HOLD ON! I-- I THINK THEY'RE TRYING TO SPELL OUT A MESSAGE!
THEY ARE, DOCTOR SOLAR! MY POCKET CALIBRATOR INDICATES THEIR MOVEMENTS ARE MATHEMATICALLY COMPUTED!
?
?
YES...AND THE BLINKING LIGHT EMISSIONS ARE SPACED IN ORDERLY FASHION!
EXACTLY! AND DID YOU NOTICE THERE ARE EXACTLY TWENTY-SIX BLOCKS... THE SAME NUMBER AS IN OUR ALPHABET?... I'LL TRY TO BREAK THE CODE, SIR!
I CAN SEE NOW WHY YOUR NEPHEW WON A SCHOLARSHIP TO THE BEST TECHNOLOGY INSTITUTE AT FIFTEEN YEARS OF AGE! (WHEW!) HE'S TACKLING A PROBLEM THAT WOULD STUMP SOME OF OUR CRACK MEN!

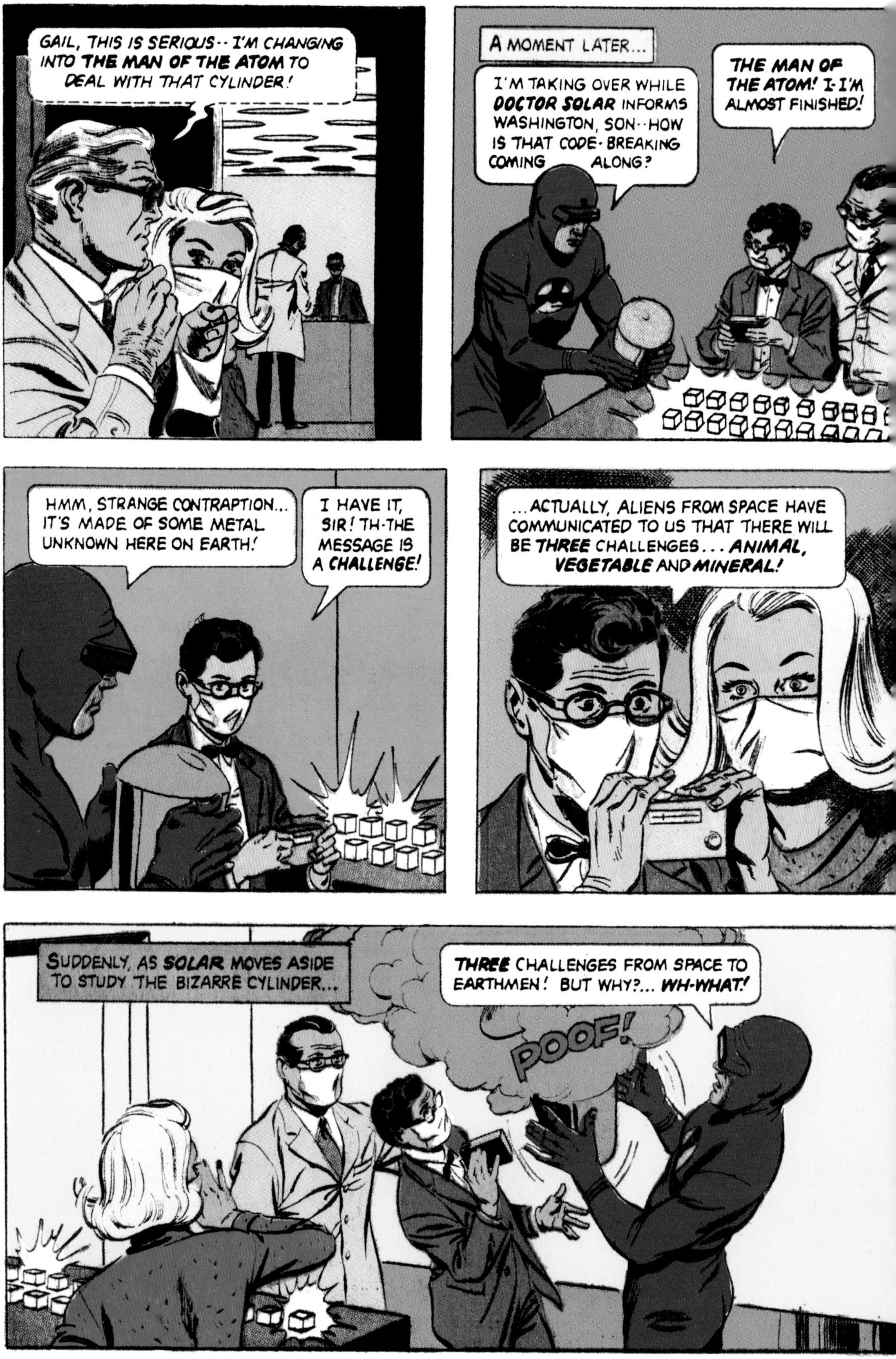
GAIL, THIS IS SERIOUS-- I'M CHANGING INTO THE MAN OF THE ATOM TO DEAL WITH THAT CYLINDER!
A MOMENT LATER...
I'M TAKING OVER WHILE DOCTOR SOLAR INFORMS WASHINGTON, SON--HOW IS THAT CODE-BREAKING COMING ALONG?
THE MAN OF THE ATOM! I-I'M ALMOST FINISHED!
HMM, STRANGE CONTRAPTION... IT'S MADE OF SOME METAL UNKNOWN HERE ON EARTH!
I HAVE IT, SIR! TH-THE MESSAGE IS A CHALLENGE!
...ACTUALLY, ALIENS FROM SPACE HAVE COMMUNICATED TO US THAT THERE WILL BE THREE CHALLENGES... ANIMAL, VEGETABLE AND MINERAL!
SUDDENLY, AS SOLAR MOVES ASIDE TO STUDY THE BIZARRE CYLINDER...
THREE CHALLENGES FROM SPACE TO EARTHMEN! BUT WHY?... WH-WHAT!
POOF!

WHAT IS IT, MAN OF THE ATOM? WHAT'S HAPPENED?
GERMS! VIRUSES FROM SPACE SWARMING OVER ME... I-I'M CONTAMINATED!
OF COURSE! THE FIRST CHALLENGE... MICROBES-- GERMS ARE ANIMAL! QUICKLY! OUT OF THE CHAMBER... I'VE GOT TO REDUCE MYSELF TO MICROSCOPIC SIZE AND FIGHT THEM BEFORE THE WORLD IS CONTAMINATED!
AND AS SOLAR BEGINS TO DIVIDE HIS ATOMIC MOLECULES...
UTILIZE THE WALL OBSERVATION MICROSCOPES TO STUDY THE ACTION... I MAY NEED YOUR HELP!
RIGHT!
THE TINY SOLARS BECOME SMALLER AND SMALLER... THEN, BY FISSION, BURST INTO A MILLION MICROSCOPIC PARTS TO MEET THE INVADERS...
ALIEN GERMS... WAITING TO TEST EARTHMAN'S POWER! I-I MUST DEFEAT THEM!
BUT AS THE MULTIPLE SOLARS BEGIN THE BIZARRE BATTLE...
THEY'RE MULTIPLYING TWO TO MY ONE... OVERPOWERING ME...

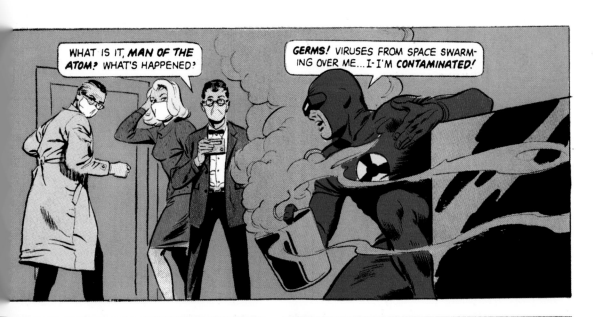

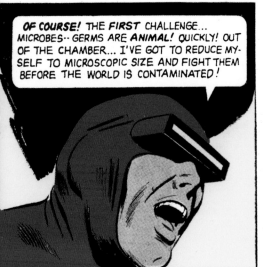

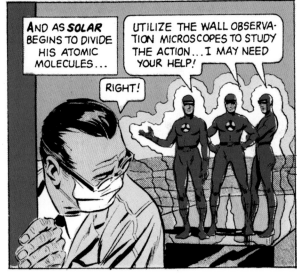

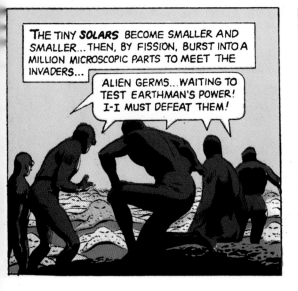

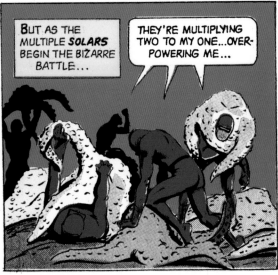

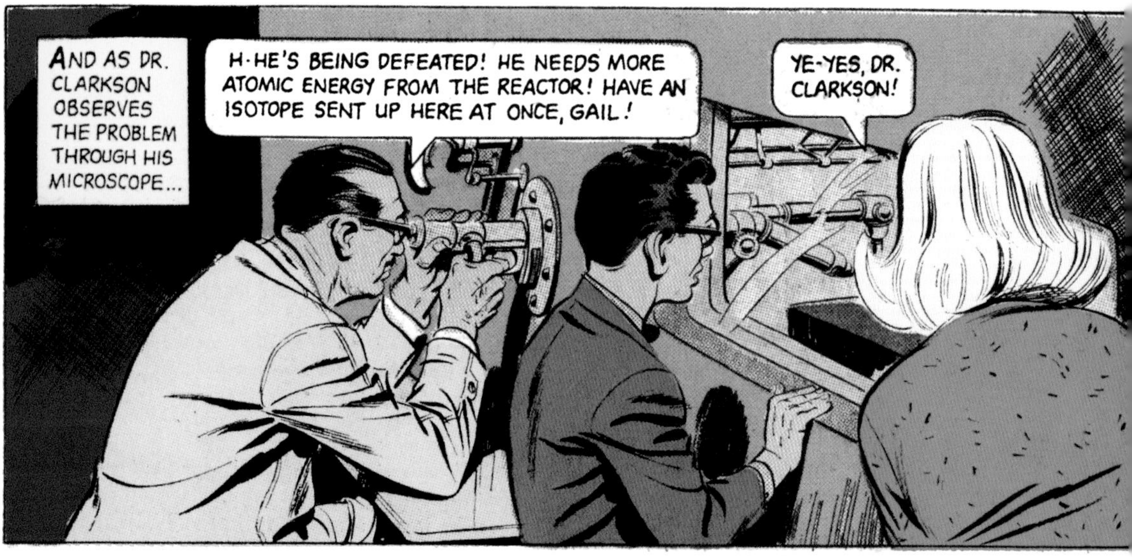
AND AS DR. CLARKSON OBSERVES THE PROBLEM THROUGH HIS MICROSCOPE...
H-HE'S BEING DEFEATED! HE NEEDS MORE ATOMIC ENERGY FROM THE REACTOR! HAVE AN ISOTOPE SENT UP HERE AT ONCE, GAIL!
YE-YES, DR. CLARKSON!

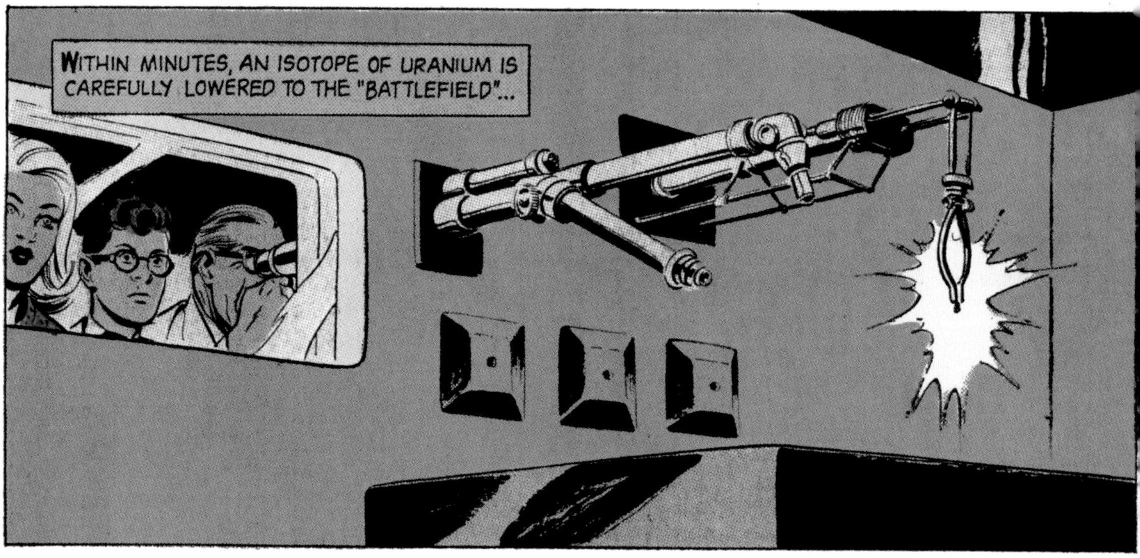
WITHIN MINUTES, AN ISOTOPE OF URANIUM IS CAREFULLY LOWERED TO THE "BATTLEFIELD"...

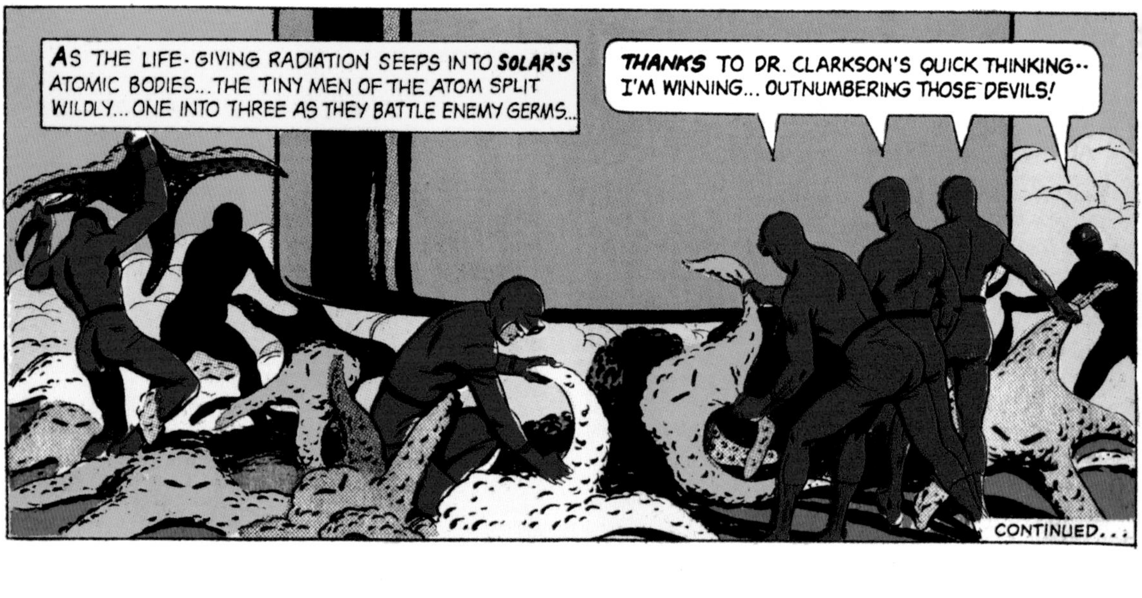
AS THE LIFE-GIVING RADIATION SEEPS INTO SOLAR'S ATOMIC BODIES...THE TINY MEN OF THE ATOM SPLIT WILDLY...ONE INTO THREE AS THEY BATTLE ENEMY GERMS...
THANKS TO DR. CLARKSON'S QUICK THINKING-- I'M WINNING... OUTNUMBERING THOSE DEVILS!
CONTINUED...

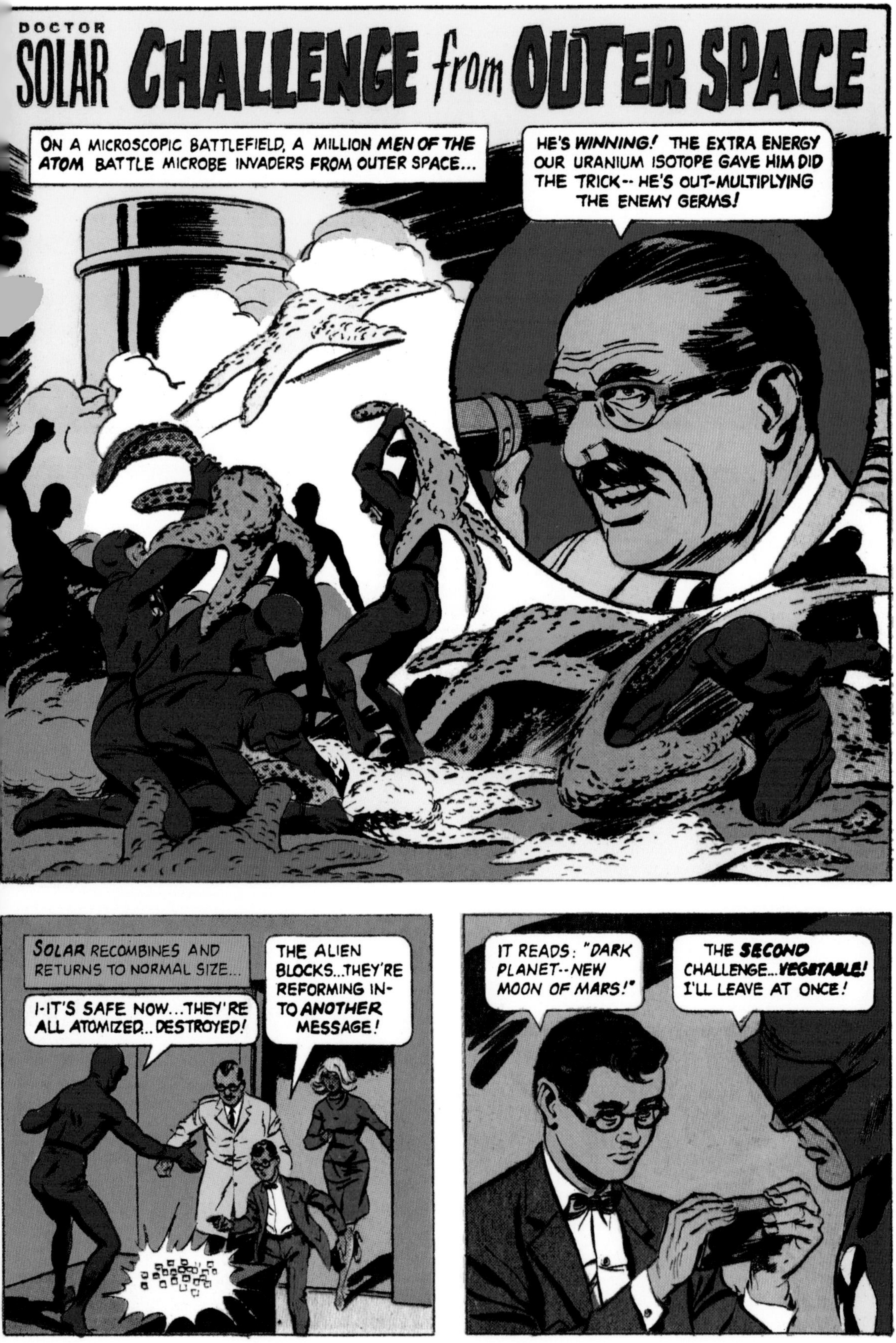
DOCTOR SOLAR
CHALLENGE from OUTER SPACE
ON A MICROSCOPIC BATTLEFIELD, A MILLION MEN OF THE ATOM BATTLE MICROBE INVADERS FROM OUTER SPACE...
HE'S WINNING! THE EXTRA ENERGY OUR URANIUM ISOTOPE GAVE HIM DID THE TRICK-- HE'S OUT-MULTIPLYING THE ENEMY GERMS!
SOLAR RECOMBINES AND RETURNS TO NORMAL SIZE...
I-IT'S SAFE NOW... THEY'RE ALL ATOMIZED... DESTROYED!
THE ALIEN BLOCKS... THEY'RE REFORMING IN-TO ANOTHER MESSAGE!
IT READS: "DARK PLANET--NEW MOON OF MARS!"
THE SECOND CHALLENGE... VEGETABLE! I'LL LEAVE AT ONCE!

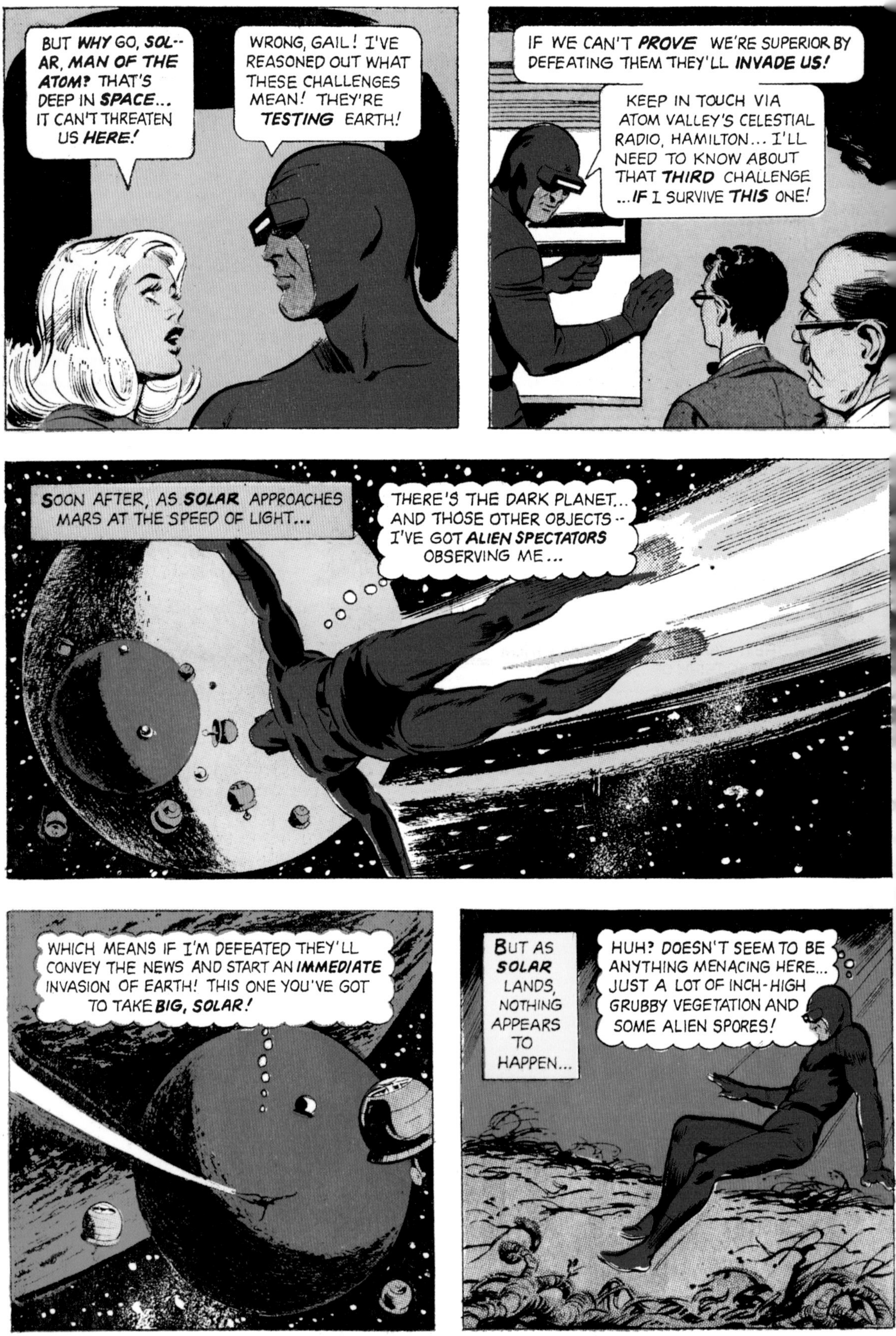
BUT WHY GO, SOL--AR, MAN OF THE ATOM? THAT'S DEEP IN SPACE... IT CAN'T THREATEN US HERE!
WRONG, GAIL! I'VE REASONED OUT WHAT THESE CHALLENGES MEAN! THEY'RE TESTING EARTH!
IF WE CAN'T PROVE WE'RE SUPERIOR BY DEFEATING THEM THEY'LL INVADE US!
KEEP IN TOUCH VIA ATOM VALLEY'S CELESTIAL RADIO, HAMILTON... I'LL NEED TO KNOW ABOUT THAT THIRD CHALLENGE ...IF I SURVIVE THIS ONE!
SOON AFTER, AS SOLAR APPROACHES MARS AT THE SPEED OF LIGHT...
THERE'S THE DARK PLANET... AND THOSE OTHER OBJECTS -- I'VE GOT ALIEN SPECTATORS OBSERVING ME...
WHICH MEANS IF I'M DEFEATED THEY'LL CONVEY THE NEWS AND START AN IMMEDIATE INVASION OF EARTH! THIS ONE YOU'VE GOT TO TAKE BIG, SOLAR!
BUT AS SOLAR LANDS, NOTHING APPEARS TO HAPPEN...
HUH? DOESN'T SEEM TO BE ANYTHING MENACING HERE... JUST A LOT OF INCH-HIGH GRUBBY VEGETATION AND SOME ALIEN SPORES!

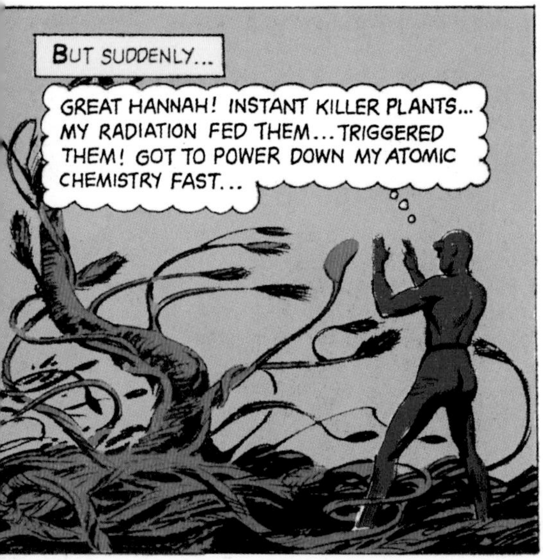
BUT SUDDENLY...
GREAT HANNAH! INSTANT KILLER PLANTS... MY RADIATION FED THEM... TRIGGERED THEM! GOT TO POWER DOWN MY ATOMIC CHEMISTRY FAST...

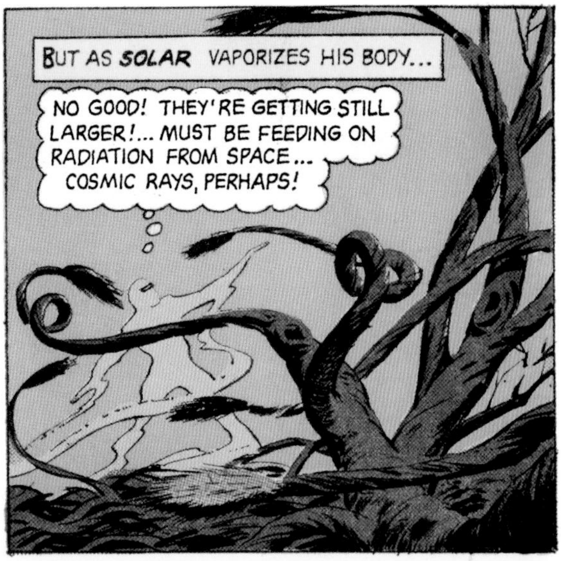
BUT AS SOLAR VAPORIZES HIS BODY...
NO GOOD! THEY'RE GETTING STILL LARGER!... MUST BE FEEDING ON RADIATION FROM SPACE... COSMIC RAYS, PERHAPS!

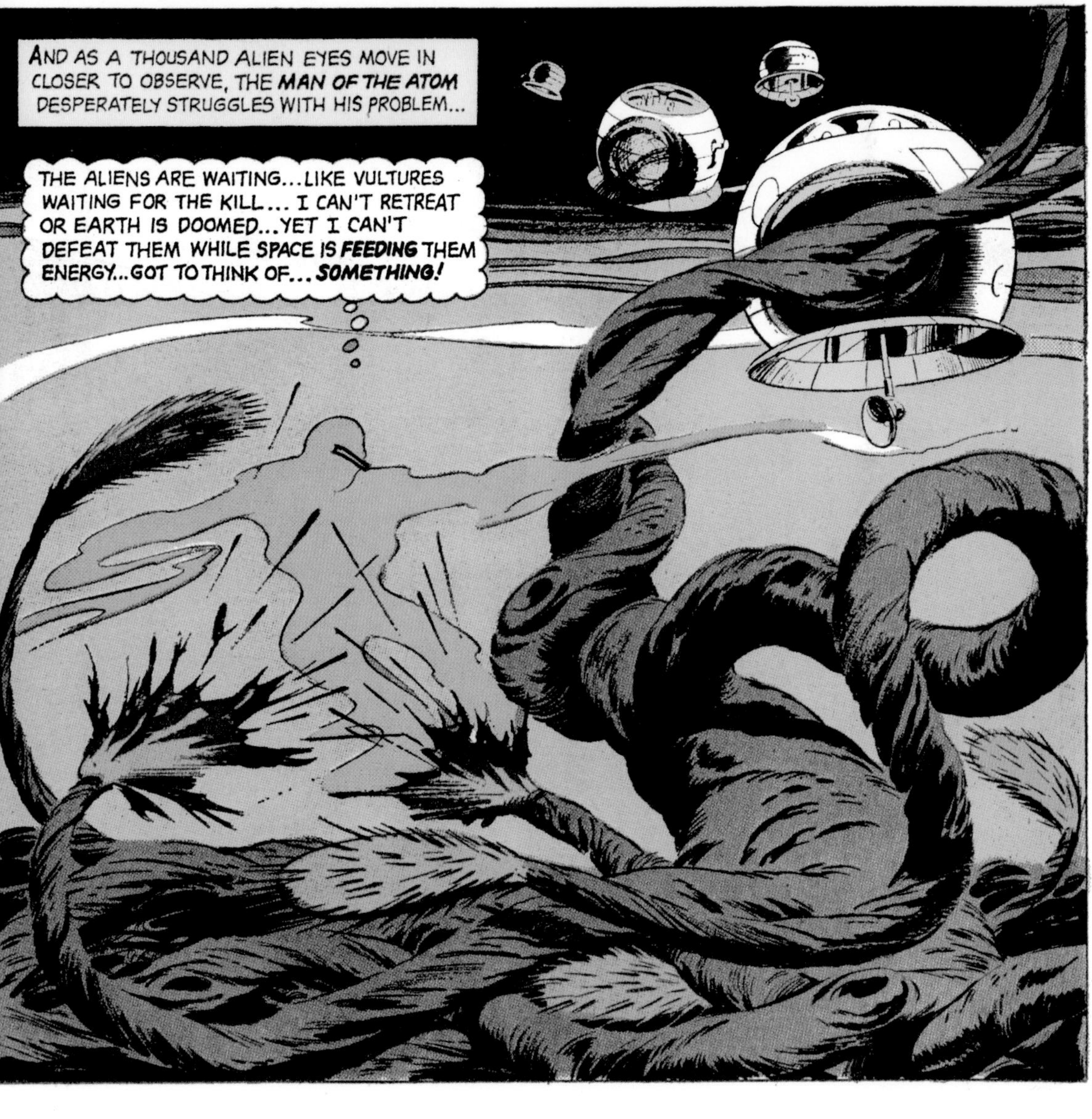
AND AS A THOUSAND ALIEN EYES MOVE IN CLOSER TO OBSERVE, THE MAN OF THE ATOM DESPERATELY STRUGGLES WITH HIS PROBLEM...
THE ALIENS ARE WAITING... LIKE VULTURES WAITING FOR THE KILL... I CAN'T RETREAT OR EARTH IS DOOMED... YET I CAN'T DEFEAT THEM WHILE SPACE IS FEEDING THEM ENERGY... GOT TO THINK OF... SOMETHING!

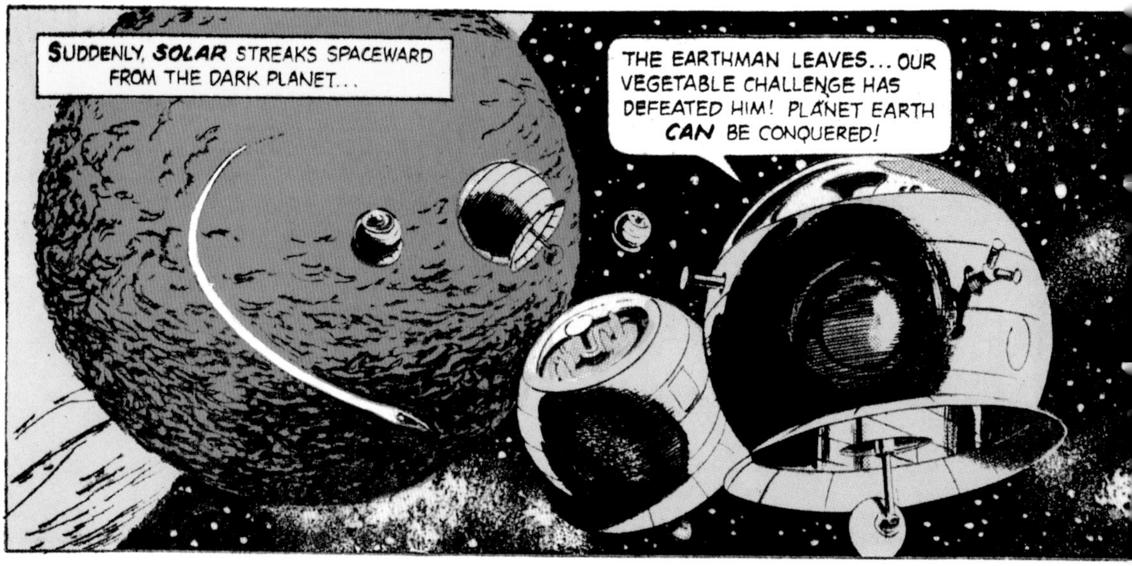
SUDDENLY, SOLAR STREAKS SPACEWARD FROM THE DARK PLANET...
THE EARTHMAN LEAVES... OUR VEGETABLE CHALLENGE HAS DEFEATED HIM! PLANET EARTH CAN BE CONQUERED!

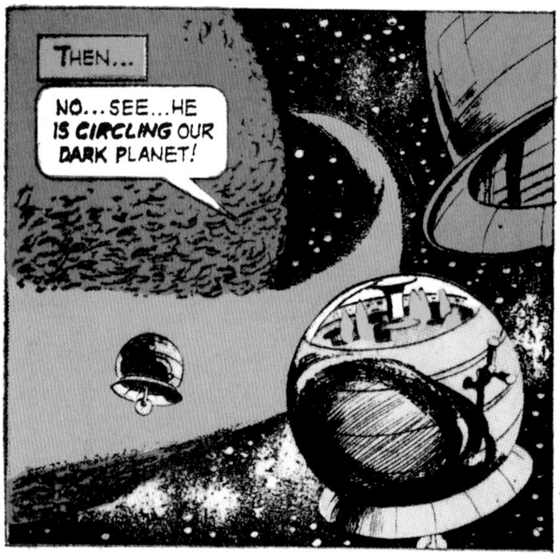
THEN...
NO...SEE...HE IS CIRCLING OUR DARK PLANET!

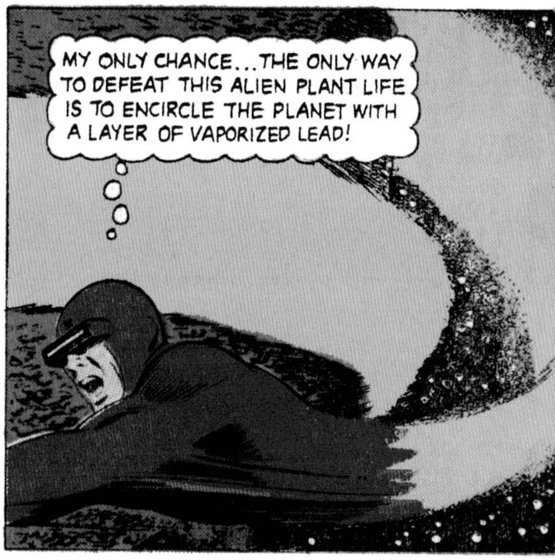
MY ONLY CHANCE...THE ONLY WAY TO DEFEAT THIS ALIEN PLANT LIFE IS TO ENCIRCLE THE PLANET WITH A LAYER OF VAPORIZED LEAD!

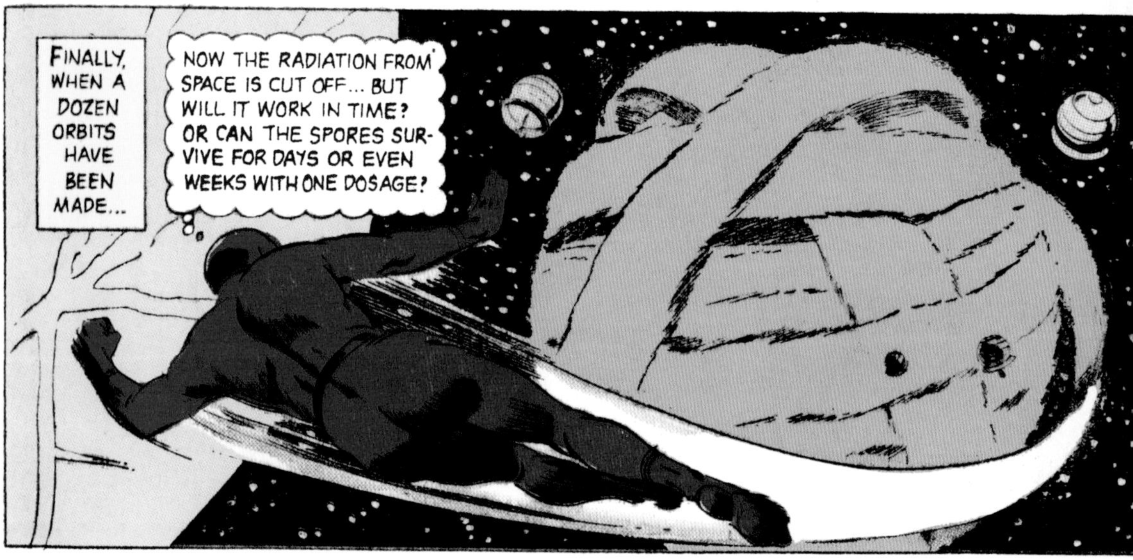
FINALLY, WHEN A DOZEN ORBITS HAVE BEEN MADE...
NOW THE RADIATION FROM SPACE IS CUT OFF... BUT WILL IT WORK IN TIME? OR CAN THE SPORES SURVIVE FOR DAYS OR EVEN WEEKS WITH ONE DOSAGE?

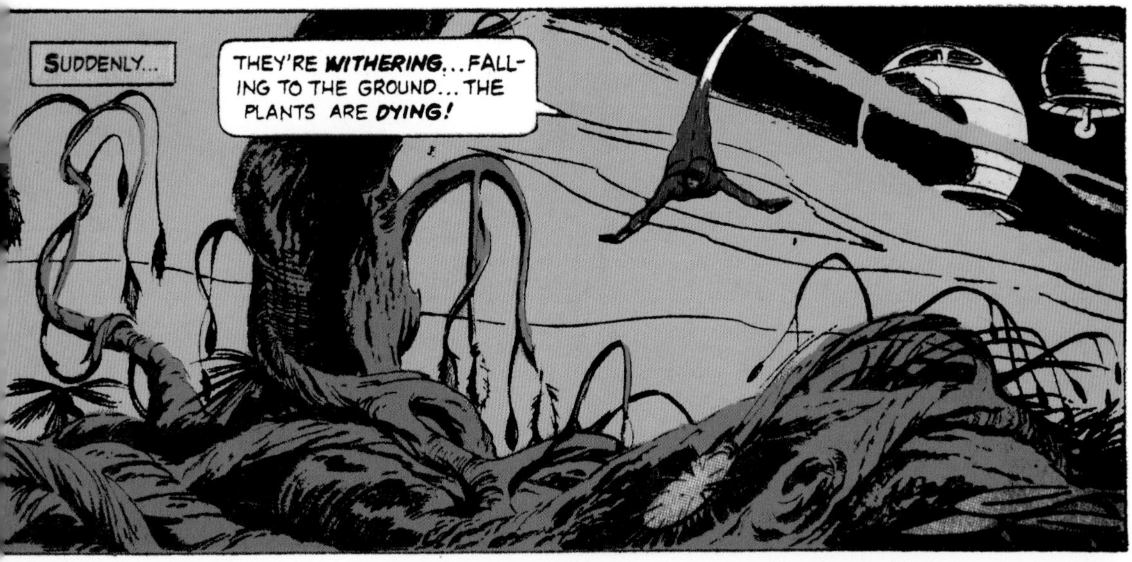
SUDDENLY...
THEY'RE WITHERING...FALLING TO THE GROUND...THE PLANTS ARE DYING!

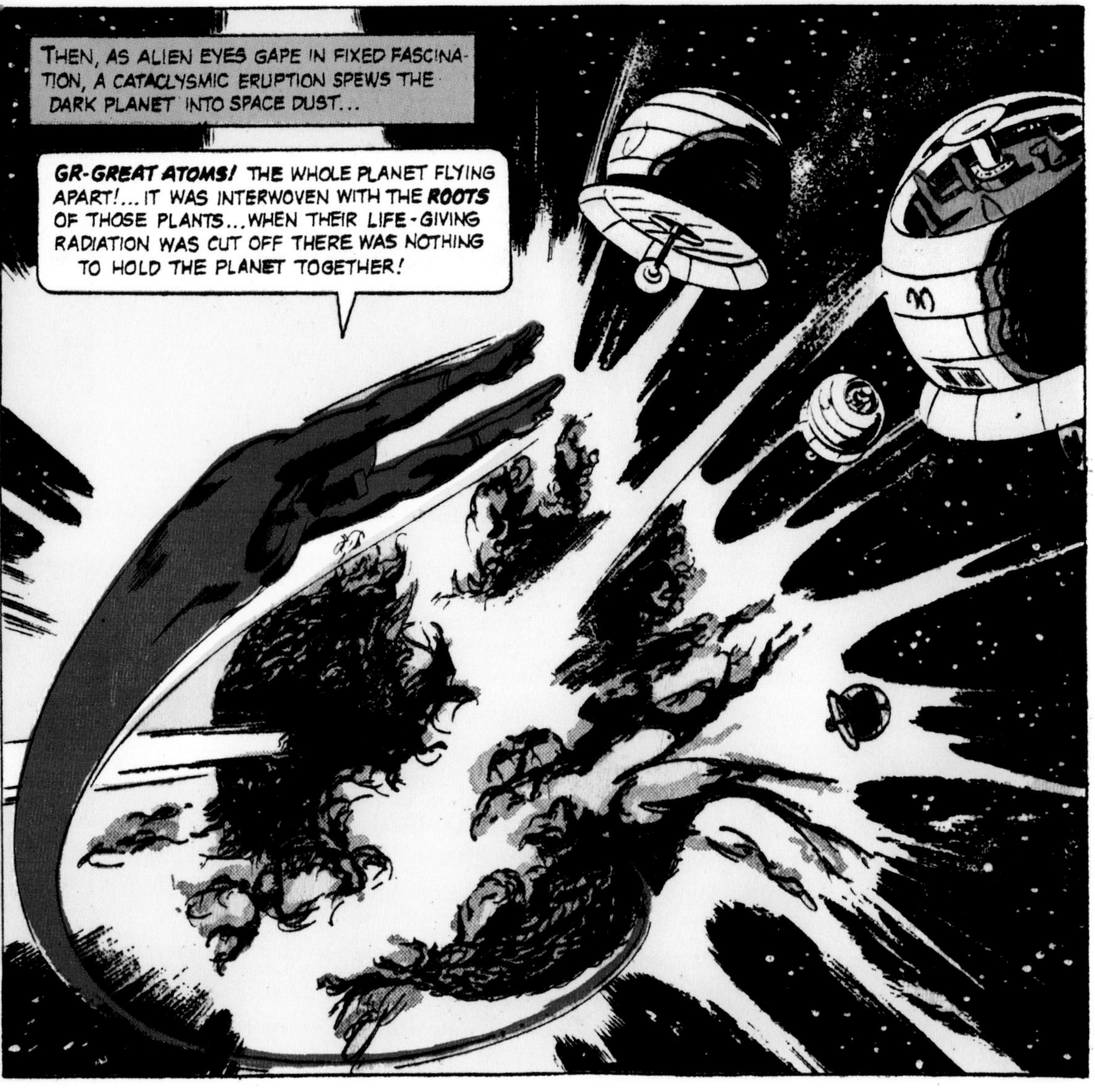
THEN, AS ALIEN EYES GAPE IN FIXED FASCINATION, A CATACLYSMIC ERUPTION SPEWS THE DARK PLANET INTO SPACE DUST...
GR-GREAT ATOMS! THE WHOLE PLANET FLYING APART!...IT WAS INTERWOVEN WITH THE ROOTS OF THOSE PLANTS...WHEN THEIR LIFE-GIVING RADIATION WAS CUT OFF THERE WAS NOTHING TO HOLD THE PLANET TOGETHER!

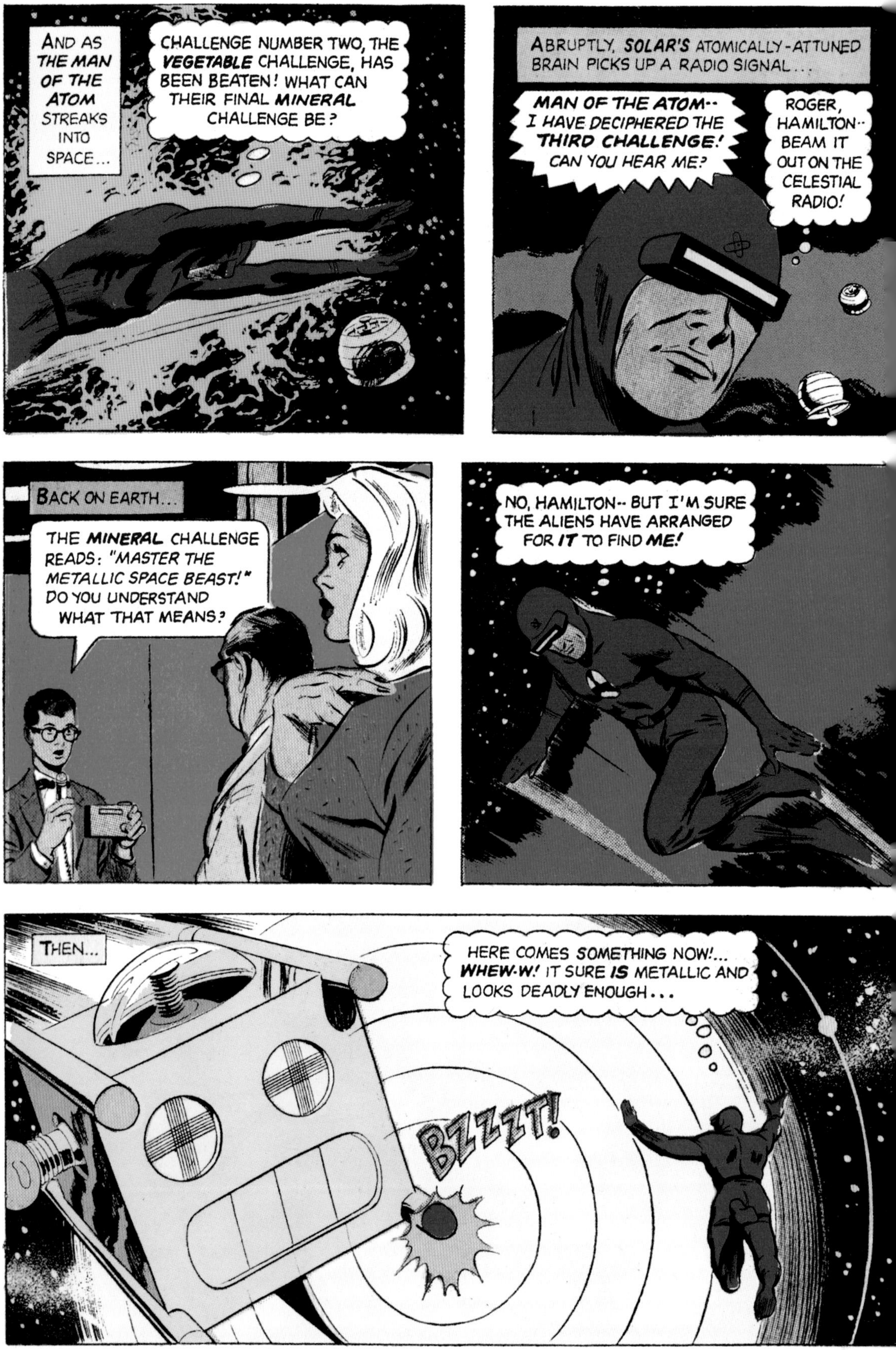
AND AS THE MAN OF THE ATOM STREAKS INTO SPACE...
CHALLENGE NUMBER TWO, THE VEGETABLE CHALLENGE, HAS BEEN BEATEN! WHAT CAN THEIR FINAL MINERAL CHALLENGE BE?
ABRUPTLY, SOLAR'S ATOMICALLY-ATTUNED BRAIN PICKS UP A RADIO SIGNAL...
MAN OF THE ATOM-- I HAVE DECIPHERED THE THIRD CHALLENGE! CAN YOU HEAR ME?
ROGER, HAMILTON-- BEAM IT OUT ON THE CELESTIAL RADIO!
BACK ON EARTH...
THE MINERAL CHALLENGE READS: "MASTER THE METALLIC SPACE BEAST!" DO YOU UNDERSTAND WHAT THAT MEANS?
NO, HAMILTON-- BUT I'M SURE THE ALIENS HAVE ARRANGED FOR IT TO FIND ME!
THEN...
HERE COMES SOMETHING NOW!... WHEW-W! IT SURE IS METALLIC AND LOOKS DEADLY ENOUGH...
BZZZT!

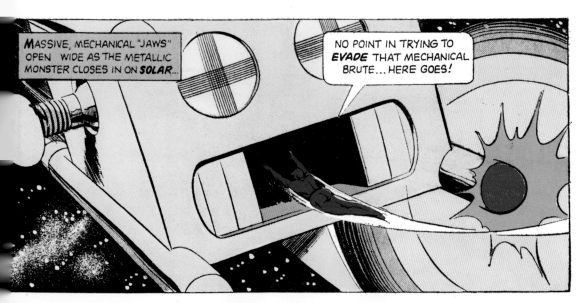

MASSIVE, MECHANICAL "JAWS" OPEN WIDE AS THE METALLIC MONSTER CLOSES IN ON *SOLAR*...

NO POINT IN TRYING TO *EVADE* THAT MECHANICAL BRUTE... HERE GOES!

OBVIOUSLY, THE FINAL CONTEST BEGINS WHEN I GET GOBBLED UP! *LET'S GO, METAL MONSTER!*

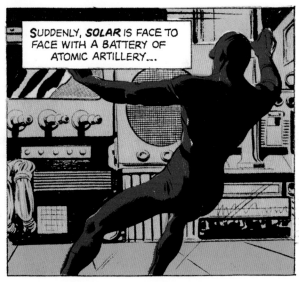

SUDDENLY, *SOLAR* IS FACE TO FACE WITH A BATTERY OF ATOMIC ARTILLERY...

WITHOUT WARNING...

*OOF!!* ENERGY BLASTS ST-STRONGER THAN LASER BEAMS!... ONLY ONE WAY TO SURVIVE...

ZISS! ZISS!

AND AS ALIENS WATCH VIA SPACE-VISION SCOPES...

CONVERT MY BODY FROM ATOMIC MATTER TO *LIGHT ENERGY!*

OBSERVE! THE EARTH-MAN HAS TRANSFORMED TO *LIGHT*-- THE ZICA BEAMS ENERGIZE HIM SO THAT HE GLOWS EVEN BRIGHTER!

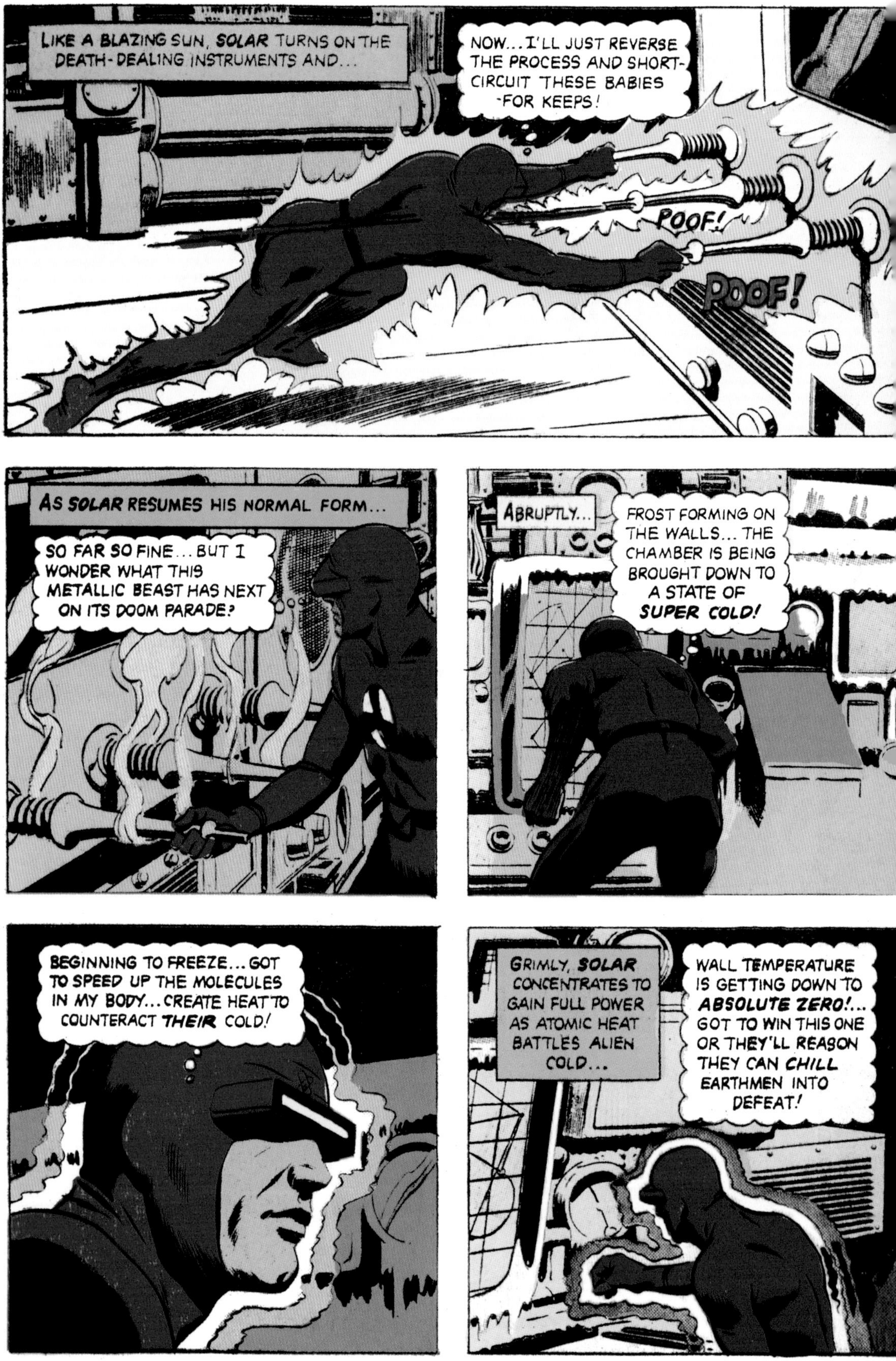
LIKE A BLAZING SUN, SOLAR TURNS ON THE DEATH-DEALING INSTRUMENTS AND...
NOW... I'LL JUST REVERSE THE PROCESS AND SHORT-CIRCUIT THESE BABIES -FOR KEEPS!
POOF!
POOF!
AS SOLAR RESUMES HIS NORMAL FORM...
SO FAR SO FINE... BUT I WONDER WHAT THIS METALLIC BEAST HAS NEXT ON ITS DOOM PARADE?
ABRUPTLY...
FROST FORMING ON THE WALLS... THE CHAMBER IS BEING BROUGHT DOWN TO A STATE OF SUPER COLD!
BEGINNING TO FREEZE... GOT TO SPEED UP THE MOLECULES IN MY BODY... CREATE HEAT TO COUNTERACT THEIR COLD!
GRIMLY, SOLAR CONCENTRATES TO GAIN FULL POWER AS ATOMIC HEAT BATTLES ALIEN COLD...
WALL TEMPERATURE IS GETTING DOWN TO ABSOLUTE ZERO!... GOT TO WIN THIS ONE OR THEY'LL REASON THEY CAN CHILL EARTHMEN INTO DEFEAT!

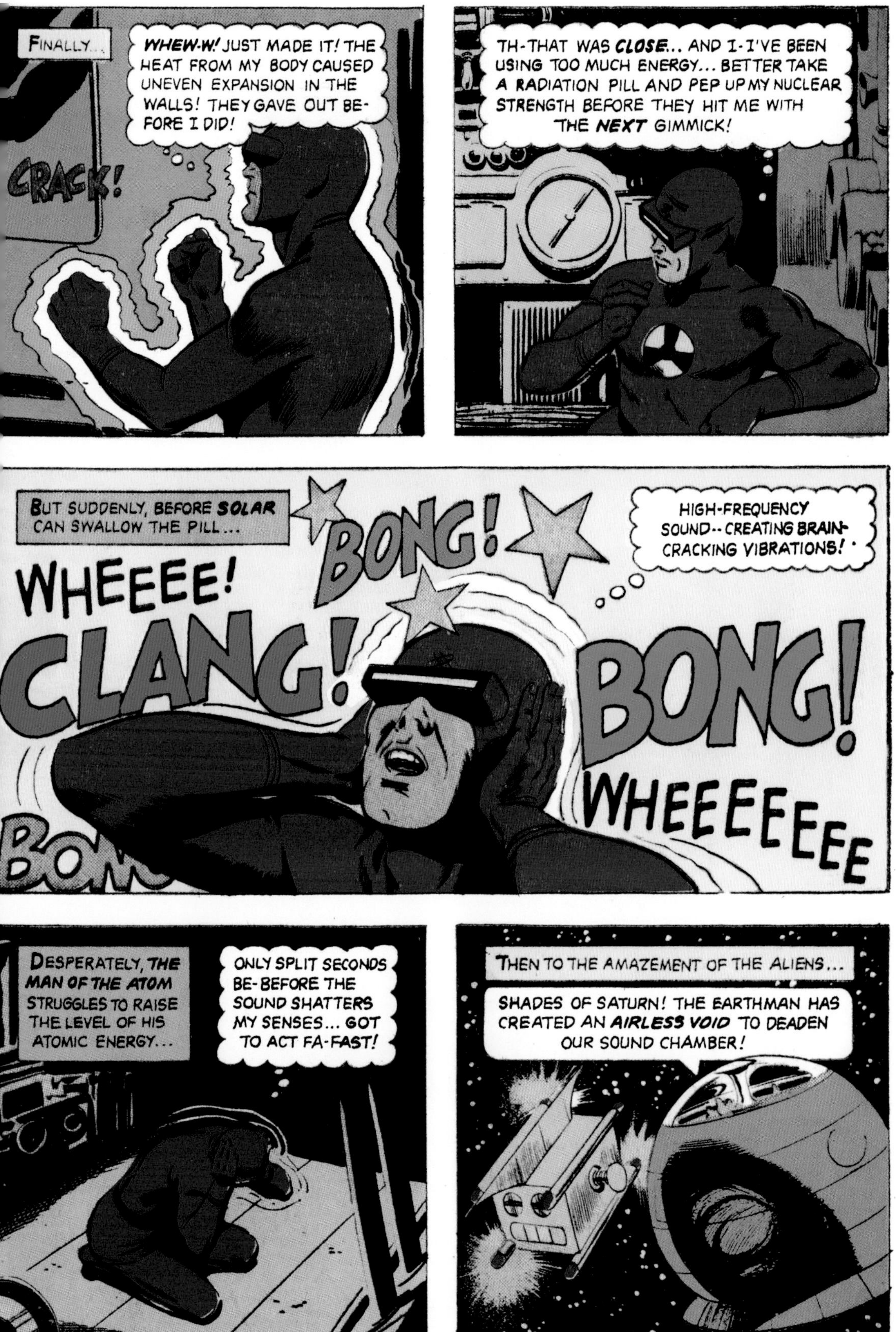
FINALLY...
WHEW-W! JUST MADE IT! THE HEAT FROM MY BODY CAUSED UNEVEN EXPANSION IN THE WALLS! THEY GAVE OUT BE-FORE I DID!
CRACK!
TH-THAT WAS CLOSE... AND I-I'VE BEEN USING TOO MUCH ENERGY... BETTER TAKE A RADIATION PILL AND PEP UP MY NUCLEAR STRENGTH BEFORE THEY HIT ME WITH THE NEXT GIMMICK!
BUT SUDDENLY, BEFORE SOLAR CAN SWALLOW THE PILL...
BONG!
HIGH-FREQUENCY SOUND-- CREATING BRAIN-CRACKING VIBRATIONS!
WHEEEE!
CLANG!
BONG!
WHEEEEEEE
DESPERATELY, THE MAN OF THE ATOM STRUGGLES TO RAISE THE LEVEL OF HIS ATOMIC ENERGY...
ONLY SPLIT SECONDS BE-BEFORE THE SOUND SHATTERS MY SENSES... GOT TO ACT FA-FAST!
THEN TO THE AMAZEMENT OF THE ALIENS...
SHADES OF SATURN! THE EARTHMAN HAS CREATED AN AIRLESS VOID TO DEADEN OUR SOUND CHAMBER!

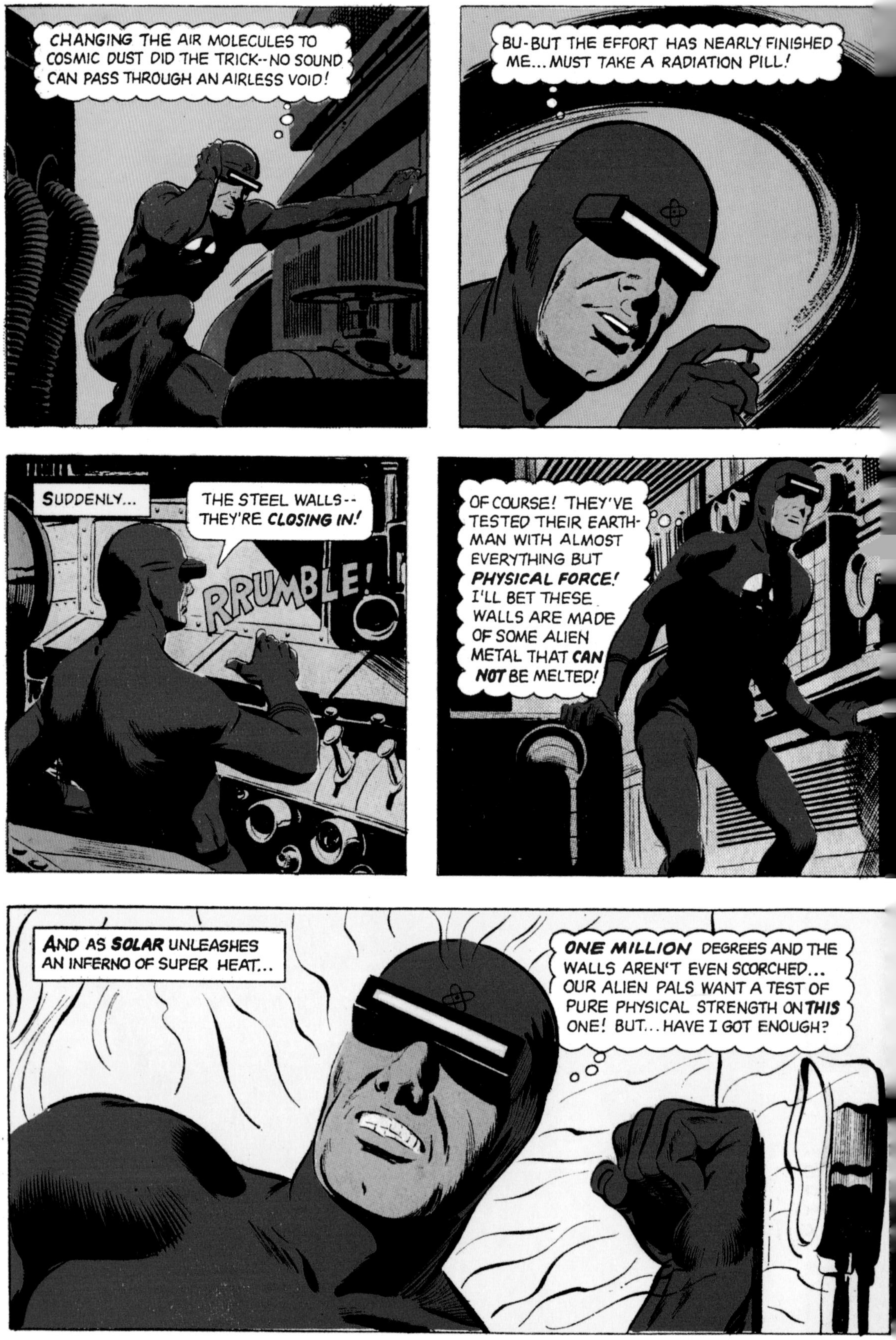
CHANGING THE AIR MOLECULES TO COSMIC DUST DID THE TRICK--NO SOUND CAN PASS THROUGH AN AIRLESS VOID!
BU-BUT THE EFFORT HAS NEARLY FINISHED ME... MUST TAKE A RADIATION PILL!
SUDDENLY...
THE STEEL WALLS-- THEY'RE CLOSING IN!
RRUMBLE!
OF COURSE! THEY'VE TESTED THEIR EARTH-MAN WITH ALMOST EVERYTHING BUT PHYSICAL FORCE! I'LL BET THESE WALLS ARE MADE OF SOME ALIEN METAL THAT CAN NOT BE MELTED!
AND AS SOLAR UNLEASHES AN INFERNO OF SUPER HEAT...
ONE MILLION DEGREES AND THE WALLS AREN'T EVEN SCORCHED... OUR ALIEN PALS WANT A TEST OF PURE PHYSICAL STRENGTH ON THIS ONE! BUT... HAVE I GOT ENOUGH?

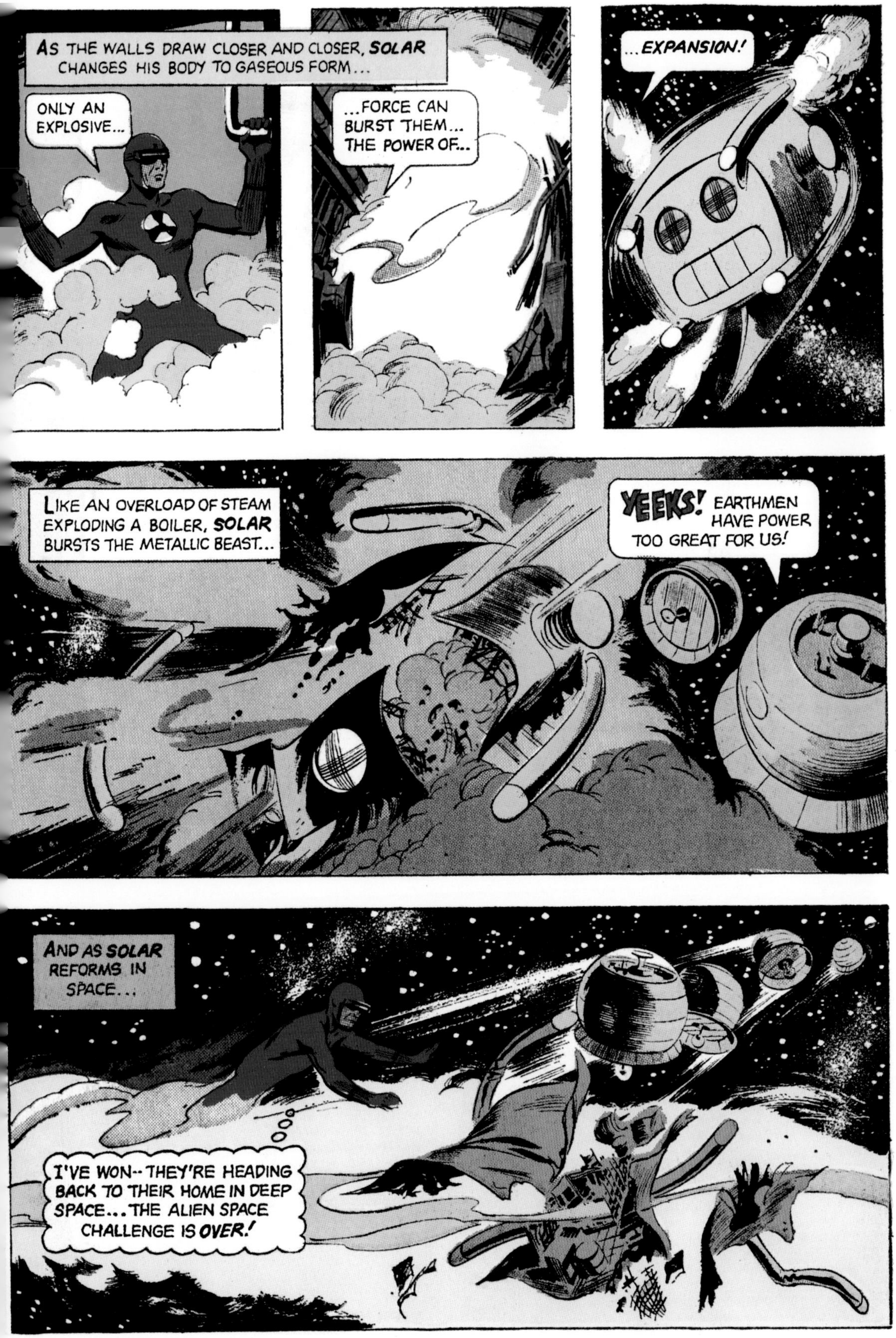
AS THE WALLS DRAW CLOSER AND CLOSER, SOLAR CHANGES HIS BODY TO GASEOUS FORM...
ONLY AN EXPLOSIVE...
...FORCE CAN BURST THEM... THE POWER OF...
...EXPANSION!
LIKE AN OVERLOAD OF STEAM EXPLODING A BOILER, SOLAR BURSTS THE METALLIC BEAST...
YEEKS! EARTHMEN HAVE POWER TOO GREAT FOR US!
AND AS SOLAR REFORMS IN SPACE...
I'VE WON-- THEY'RE HEADING BACK TO THEIR HOME IN DEEP SPACE... THE ALIEN SPACE CHALLENGE IS OVER!

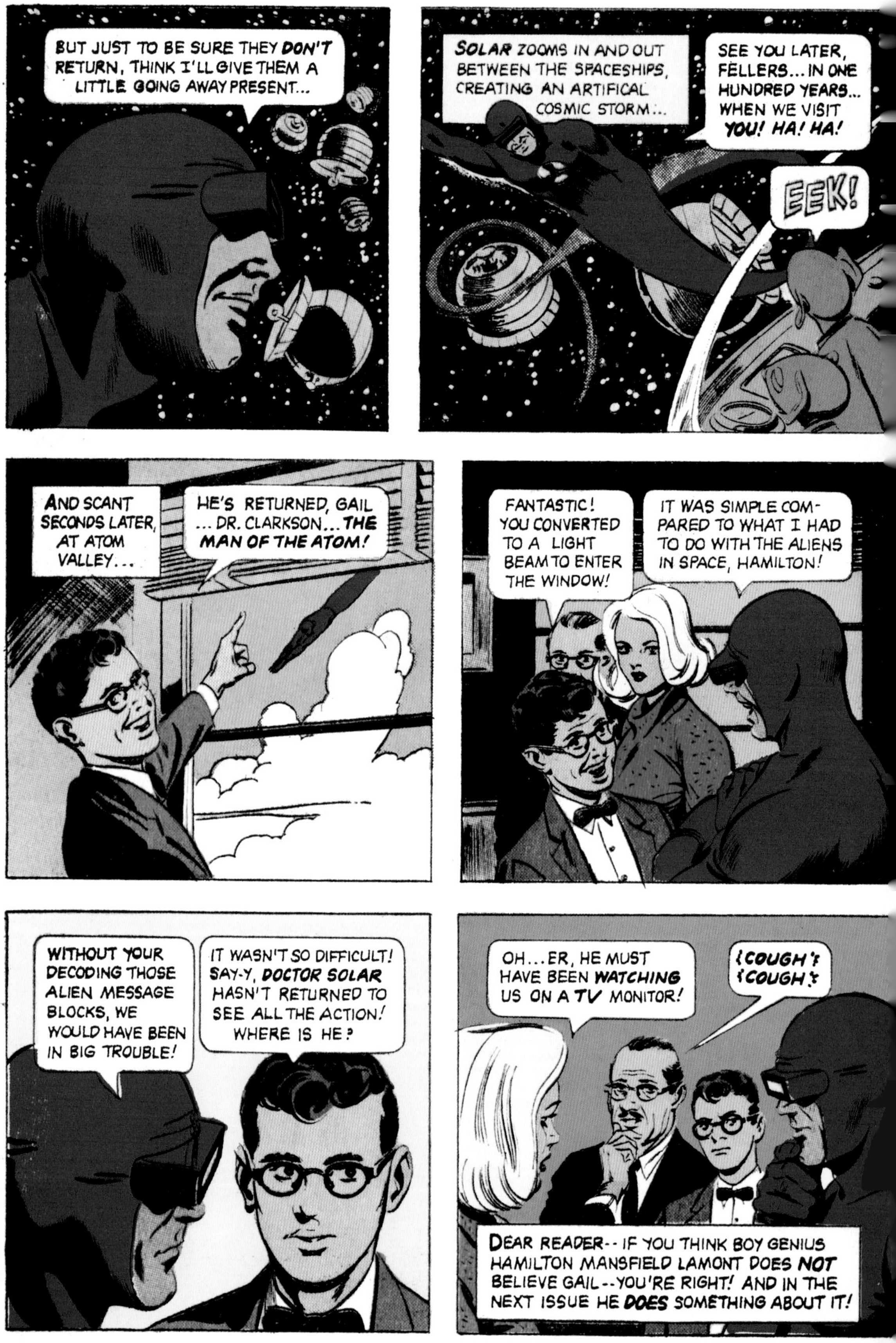

BUT JUST TO BE SURE THEY DON'T RETURN, THINK I'LL GIVE THEM A LITTLE GOING AWAY PRESENT...
SOLAR ZOOMS IN AND OUT BETWEEN THE SPACESHIPS, CREATING AN ARTIFICAL COSMIC STORM...
SEE YOU LATER, FELLERS... IN ONE HUNDRED YEARS... WHEN WE VISIT YOU! HA! HA!
EEK!
AND SCANT SECONDS LATER, AT ATOM VALLEY...
HE'S RETURNED, GAIL ... DR. CLARKSON... THE MAN OF THE ATOM!
FANTASTIC! YOU CONVERTED TO A LIGHT BEAM TO ENTER THE WINDOW!
IT WAS SIMPLE COMPARED TO WHAT I HAD TO DO WITH THE ALIENS IN SPACE, HAMILTON!
WITHOUT YOUR DECODING THOSE ALIEN MESSAGE BLOCKS, WE WOULD HAVE BEEN IN BIG TROUBLE!
IT WASN'T SO DIFFICULT! SAY-Y, DOCTOR SOLAR HASN'T RETURNED TO SEE ALL THE ACTION! WHERE IS HE?
OH...ER, HE MUST HAVE BEEN WATCHING US ON A TV MONITOR!
{COUGH} {COUGH}
DEAR READER-- IF YOU THINK BOY GENIUS HAMILTON MANSFIELD LAMONT DOES NOT BELIEVE GAIL--YOU'RE RIGHT! AND IN THE NEXT ISSUE HE DOES SOMETHING ABOUT IT!

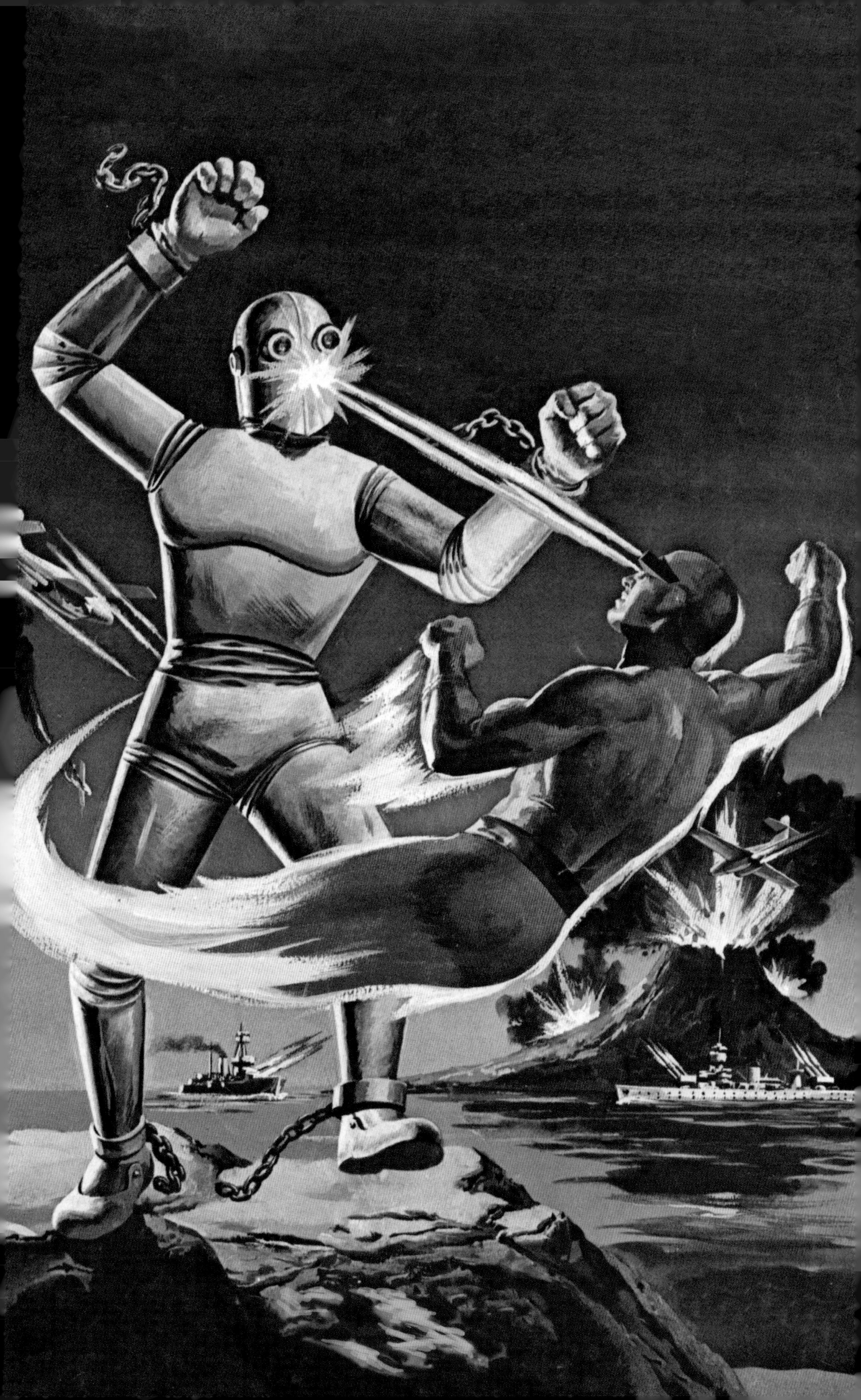

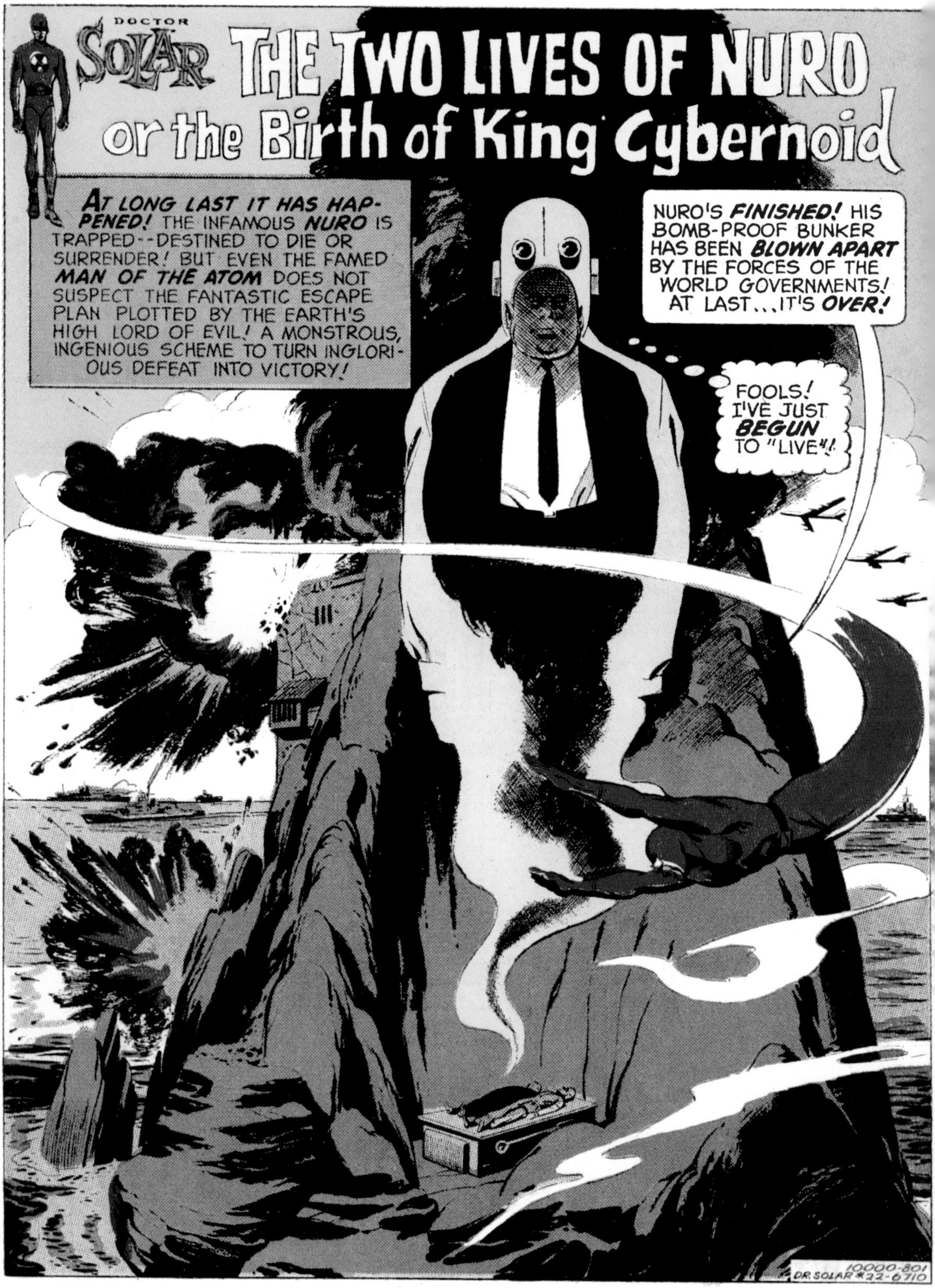
DOCTOR SOLAR
THE TWO LIVES OF NURO or the Birth of King Cybernoid
AT LONG LAST IT HAS HAPPENED! THE INFAMOUS NURO IS TRAPPED--DESTINED TO DIE OR SURRENDER! BUT EVEN THE FAMED MAN OF THE ATOM DOES NOT SUSPECT THE FANTASTIC ESCAPE PLAN PLOTTED BY THE EARTH'S HIGH LORD OF EVIL! A MONSTROUS, INGENIOUS SCHEME TO TURN INGLORIOUS DEFEAT INTO VICTORY!
NURO'S FINISHED! HIS BOMB-PROOF BUNKER HAS BEEN BLOWN APART BY THE FORCES OF THE WORLD GOVERNMENTS! AT LAST...IT'S OVER!
FOOLS! I'VE JUST BEGUN TO "LIVE"!
10000-801
DR. SOLAR #22-6710

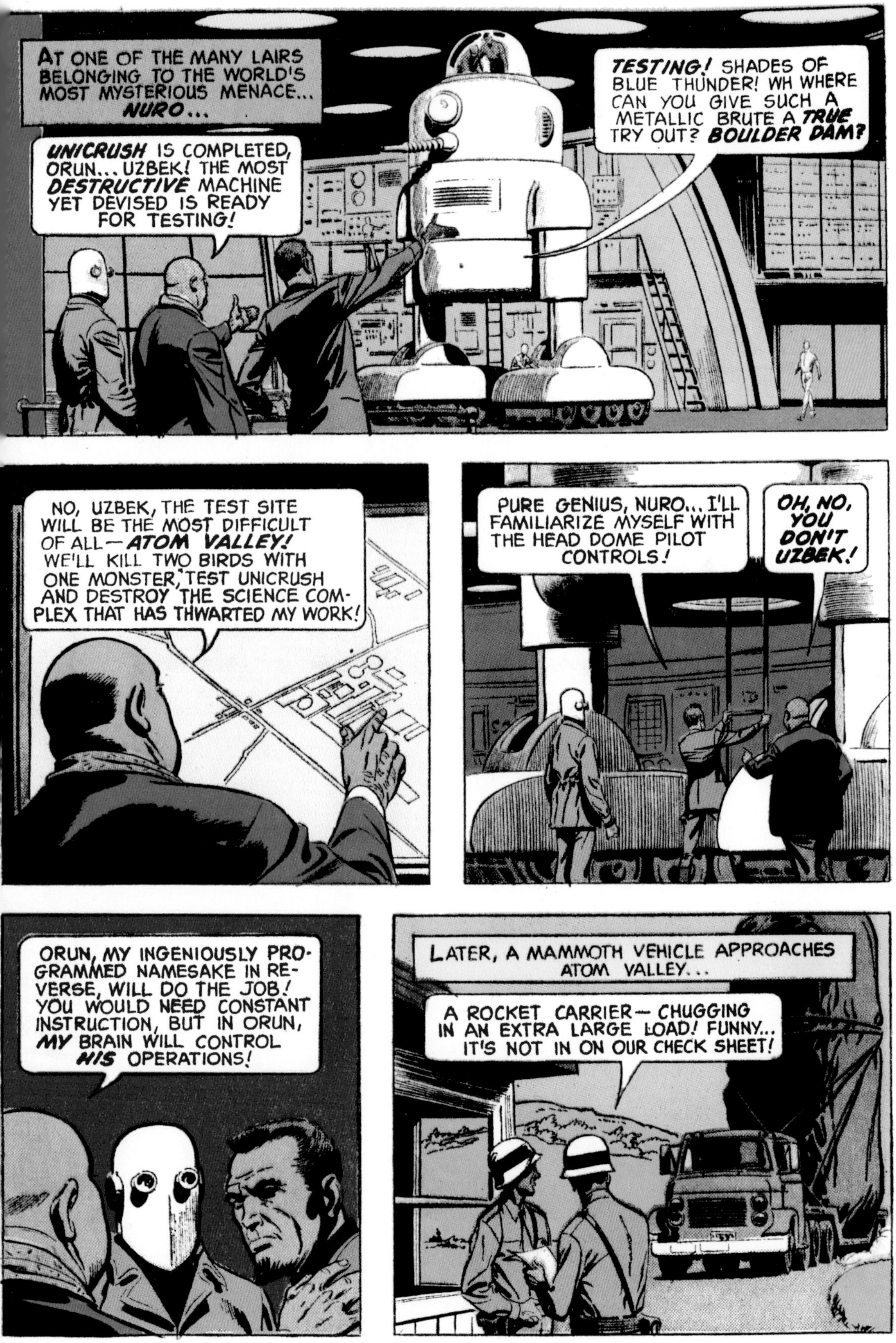
AT ONE OF THE MANY LAIRS BELONGING TO THE WORLD'S MOST MYSTERIOUS MENACE... NURO...
UNICRUSH IS COMPLETED, ORUN... UZBEK! THE MOST DESTRUCTIVE MACHINE YET DEVISED IS READY FOR TESTING!
TESTING! SHADES OF BLUE THUNDER! WH WHERE CAN YOU GIVE SUCH A METALLIC BRUTE A TRUE TRY OUT? BOULDER DAM?
NO, UZBEK, THE TEST SITE WILL BE THE MOST DIFFICULT OF ALL—ATOM VALLEY! WE'LL KILL TWO BIRDS WITH ONE MONSTER, TEST UNICRUSH AND DESTROY THE SCIENCE COMPLEX THAT HAS THWARTED MY WORK!
PURE GENIUS, NURO... I'LL FAMILIARIZE MYSELF WITH THE HEAD DOME PILOT CONTROLS!
OH, NO, YOU DON'T UZBEK!
ORUN, MY INGENIOUSLY PROGRAMMED NAMESAKE IN REVERSE, WILL DO THE JOB! YOU WOULD NEED CONSTANT INSTRUCTION, BUT IN ORUN, MY BRAIN WILL CONTROL HIS OPERATIONS!
LATER, A MAMMOTH VEHICLE APPROACHES ATOM VALLEY...
A ROCKET CARRIER—CHUGGING IN AN EXTRA LARGE LOAD! FUNNY... IT'S NOT IN ON OUR CHECK SHEET!

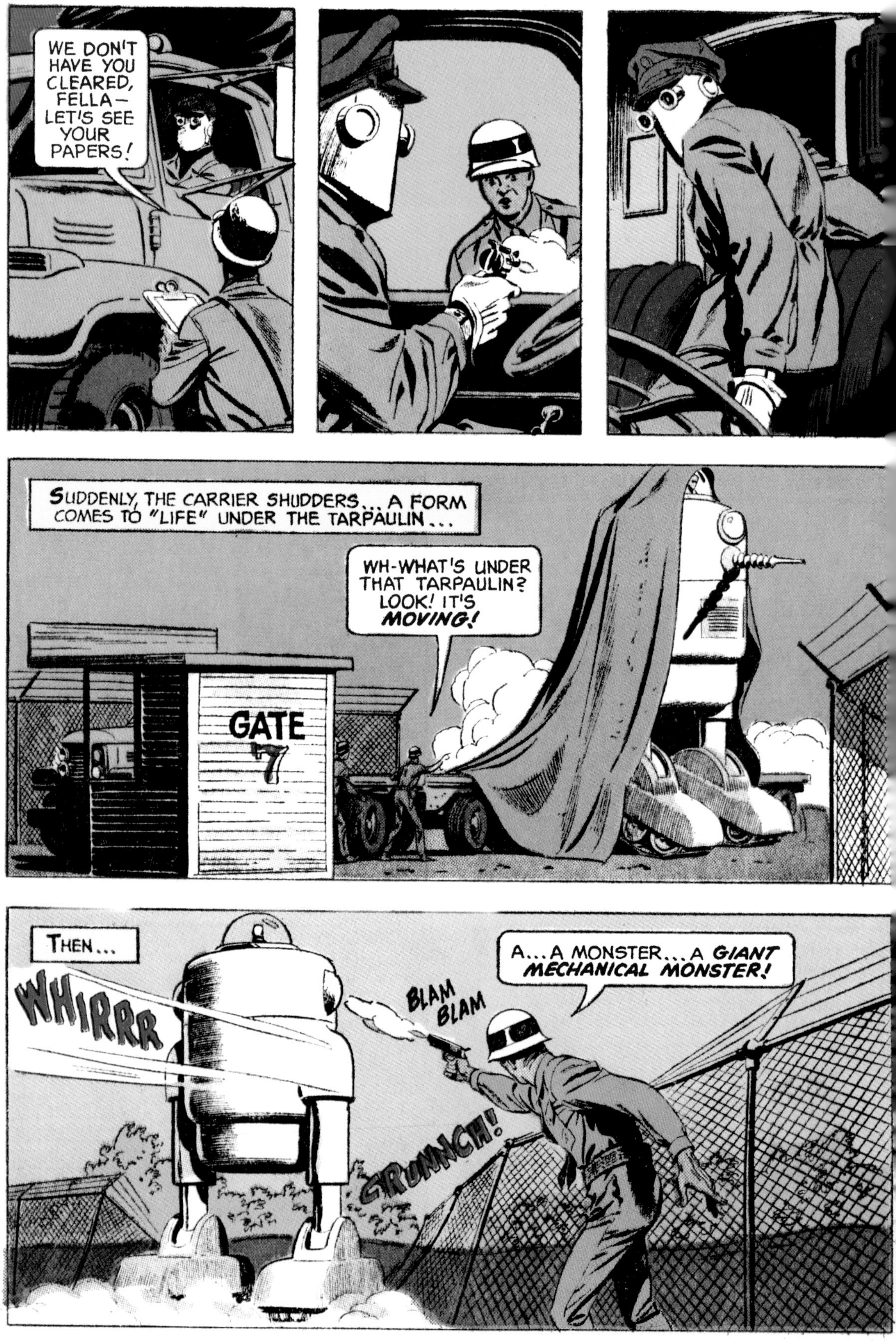
WE DON'T HAVE YOU CLEARED, FELLA— LET'S SEE YOUR PAPERS!
SUDDENLY, THE CARRIER SHUDDERS... A FORM COMES TO "LIFE" UNDER THE TARPAULIN...
WH-WHAT'S UNDER THAT TARPAULIN? LOOK! IT'S MOVING!
GATE 7
THEN...
WHIRRR
BLAM BLAM
A...A MONSTER...A GIANT MECHANICAL MONSTER!
GRUNNCH!

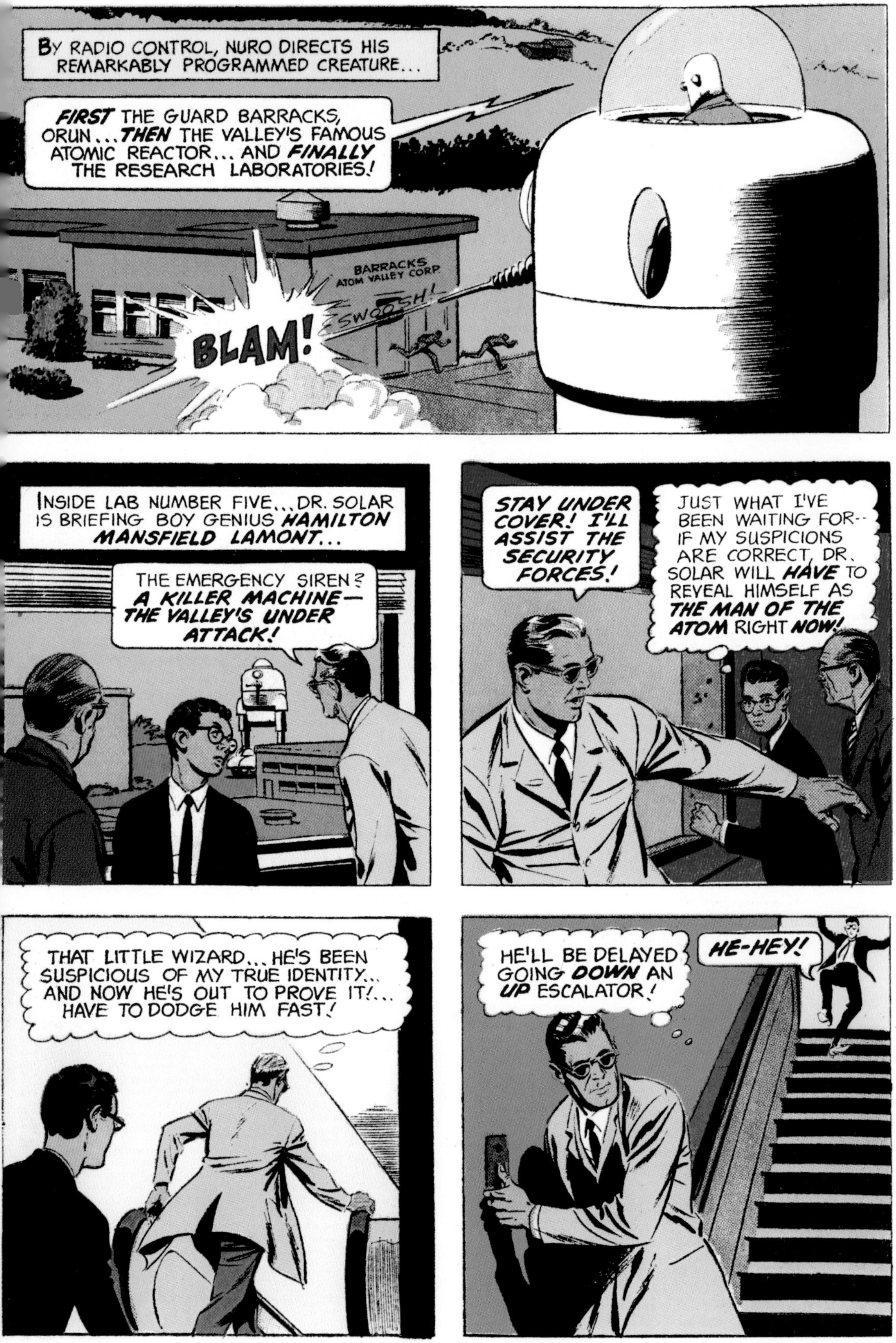
BY RADIO CONTROL, NURO DIRECTS HIS REMARKABLY PROGRAMMED CREATURE...
FIRST THE GUARD BARRACKS, ORUN... THEN THE VALLEY'S FAMOUS ATOMIC REACTOR... AND FINALLY THE RESEARCH LABORATORIES!
BARRACKS ATOM VALLEY CORP.
SWOOSH!
BLAM!
INSIDE LAB NUMBER FIVE... DR. SOLAR IS BRIEFING BOY GENIUS HAMILTON MANSFIELD LAMONT...
THE EMERGENCY SIREN? A KILLER MACHINE— THE VALLEY'S UNDER ATTACK!
STAY UNDER COVER! I'LL ASSIST THE SECURITY FORCES!
JUST WHAT I'VE BEEN WAITING FOR-- IF MY SUSPICIONS ARE CORRECT, DR. SOLAR WILL HAVE TO REVEAL HIMSELF AS THE MAN OF THE ATOM RIGHT NOW!
THAT LITTLE WIZARD... HE'S BEEN SUSPICIOUS OF MY TRUE IDENTITY... AND NOW HE'S OUT TO PROVE IT!... HAVE TO DODGE HIM FAST!
HE'LL BE DELAYED GOING DOWN AN UP ESCALATOR!
HE-HEY!

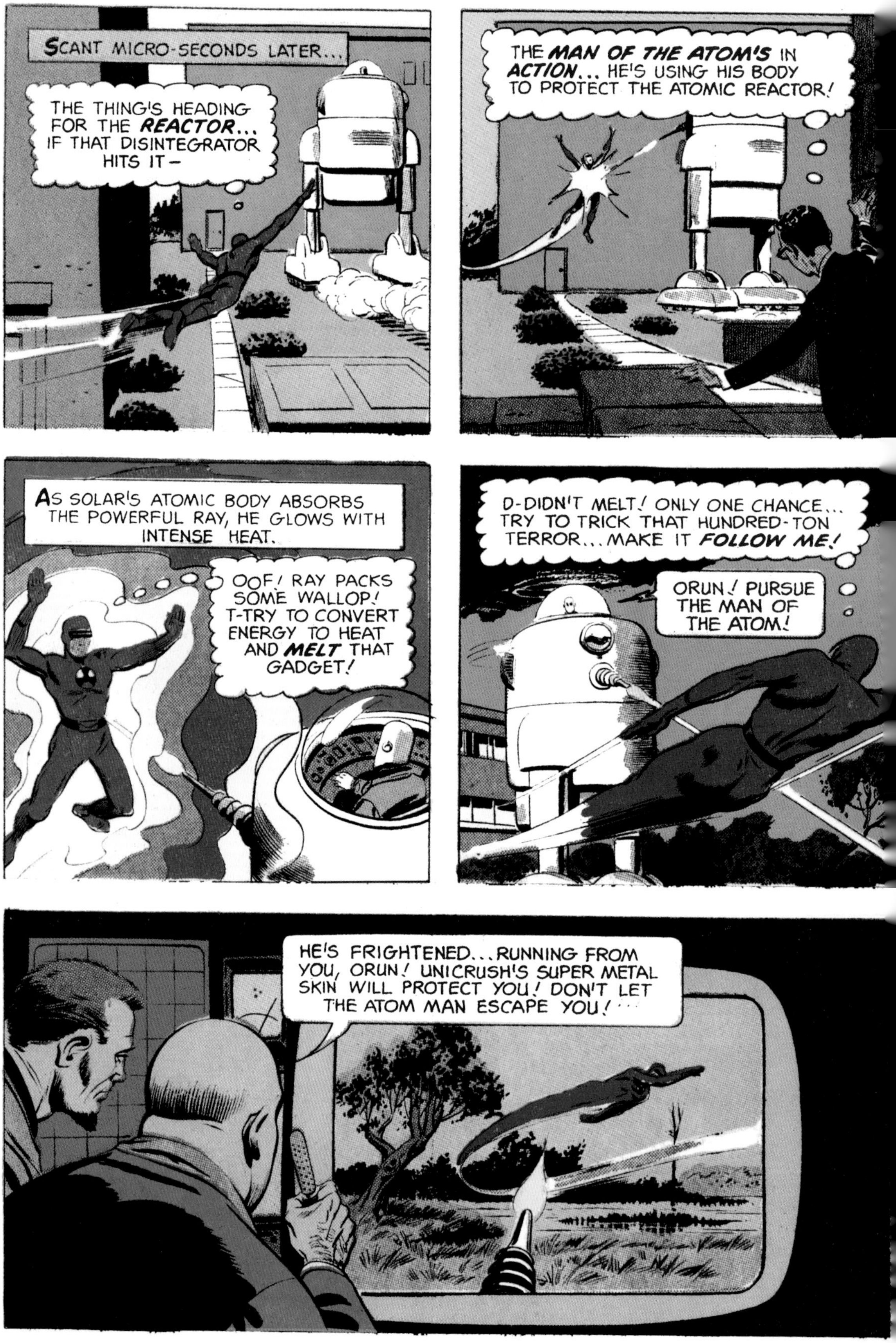
SCANT MICRO-SECONDS LATER...
THE THING'S HEADING FOR THE REACTOR... IF THAT DISINTEGRATOR HITS IT—
THE MAN OF THE ATOM'S IN ACTION... HE'S USING HIS BODY TO PROTECT THE ATOMIC REACTOR!
AS SOLAR'S ATOMIC BODY ABSORBS THE POWERFUL RAY, HE GLOWS WITH INTENSE HEAT.
OOF! RAY PACKS SOME WALLOP! T-TRY TO CONVERT ENERGY TO HEAT AND MELT THAT GADGET!
D-DIDN'T MELT! ONLY ONE CHANCE... TRY TO TRICK THAT HUNDRED-TON TERROR... MAKE IT FOLLOW ME!
ORUN! PURSUE THE MAN OF THE ATOM!
HE'S FRIGHTENED...RUNNING FROM YOU, ORUN! UNICRUSH'S SUPER METAL SKIN WILL PROTECT YOU! DON'T LET THE ATOM MAN ESCAPE YOU!

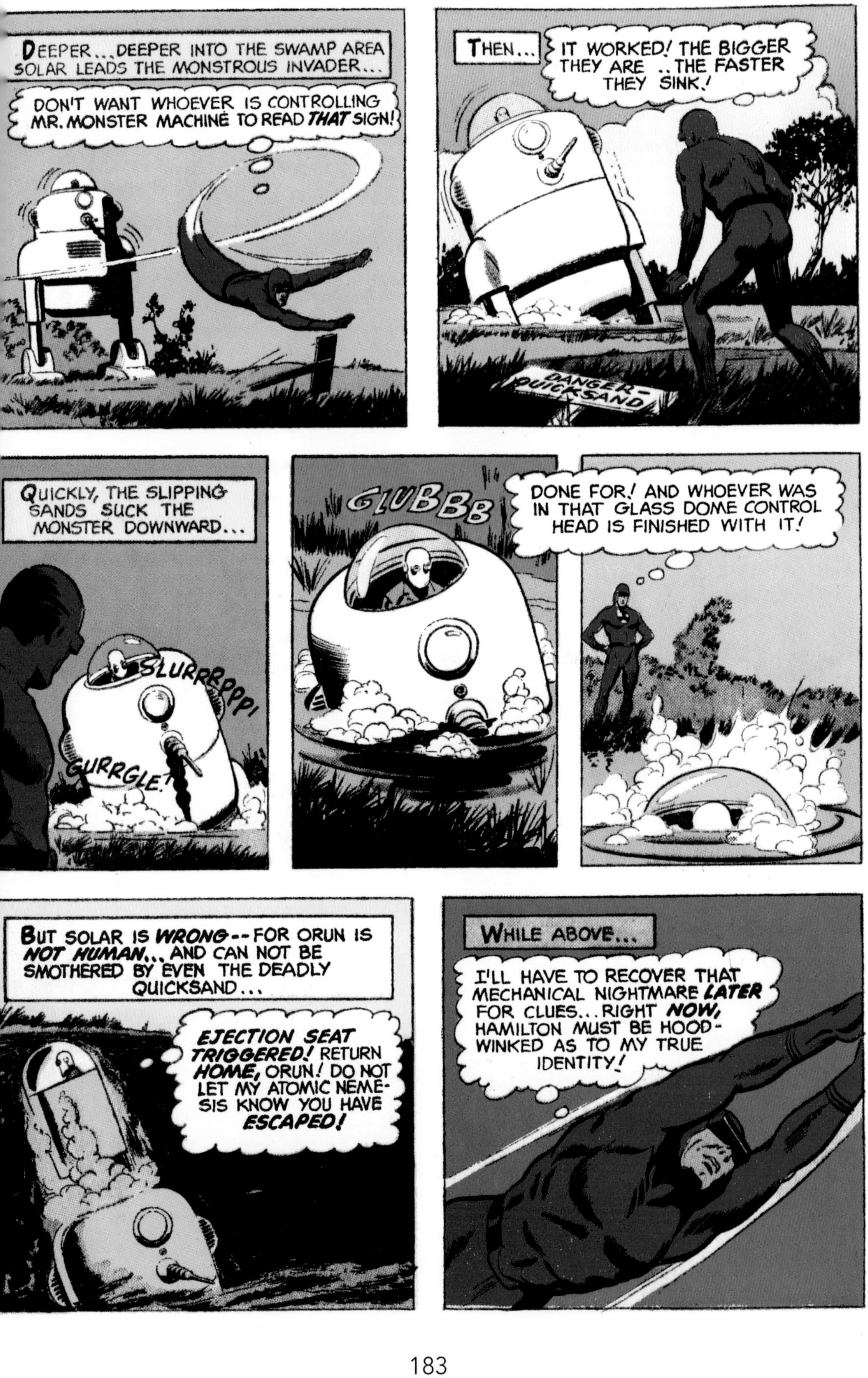
DEEPER...DEEPER INTO THE SWAMP AREA SOLAR LEADS THE MONSTROUS INVADER...
DON'T WANT WHOEVER IS CONTROLLING MR. MONSTER MACHINE TO READ THAT SIGN!
THEN...
IT WORKED! THE BIGGER THEY ARE ..THE FASTER THEY SINK!
DANGER-QUICKSAND
QUICKLY, THE SLIPPING SANDS SUCK THE MONSTER DOWNWARD...
SLURRRPPP!
GURRGLE!
GLUBBB
DONE FOR! AND WHOEVER WAS IN THAT GLASS DOME CONTROL HEAD IS FINISHED WITH IT!
BUT SOLAR IS WRONG--FOR ORUN IS NOT HUMAN...AND CAN NOT BE SMOTHERED BY EVEN THE DEADLY QUICKSAND...
EJECTION SEAT TRIGGERED! RETURN HOME, ORUN! DO NOT LET MY ATOMIC NEMESIS KNOW YOU HAVE ESCAPED!
WHILE ABOVE...
I'LL HAVE TO RECOVER THAT MECHANICAL NIGHTMARE LATER FOR CLUES...RIGHT NOW, HAMILTON MUST BE HOODWINKED AS TO MY TRUE IDENTITY!

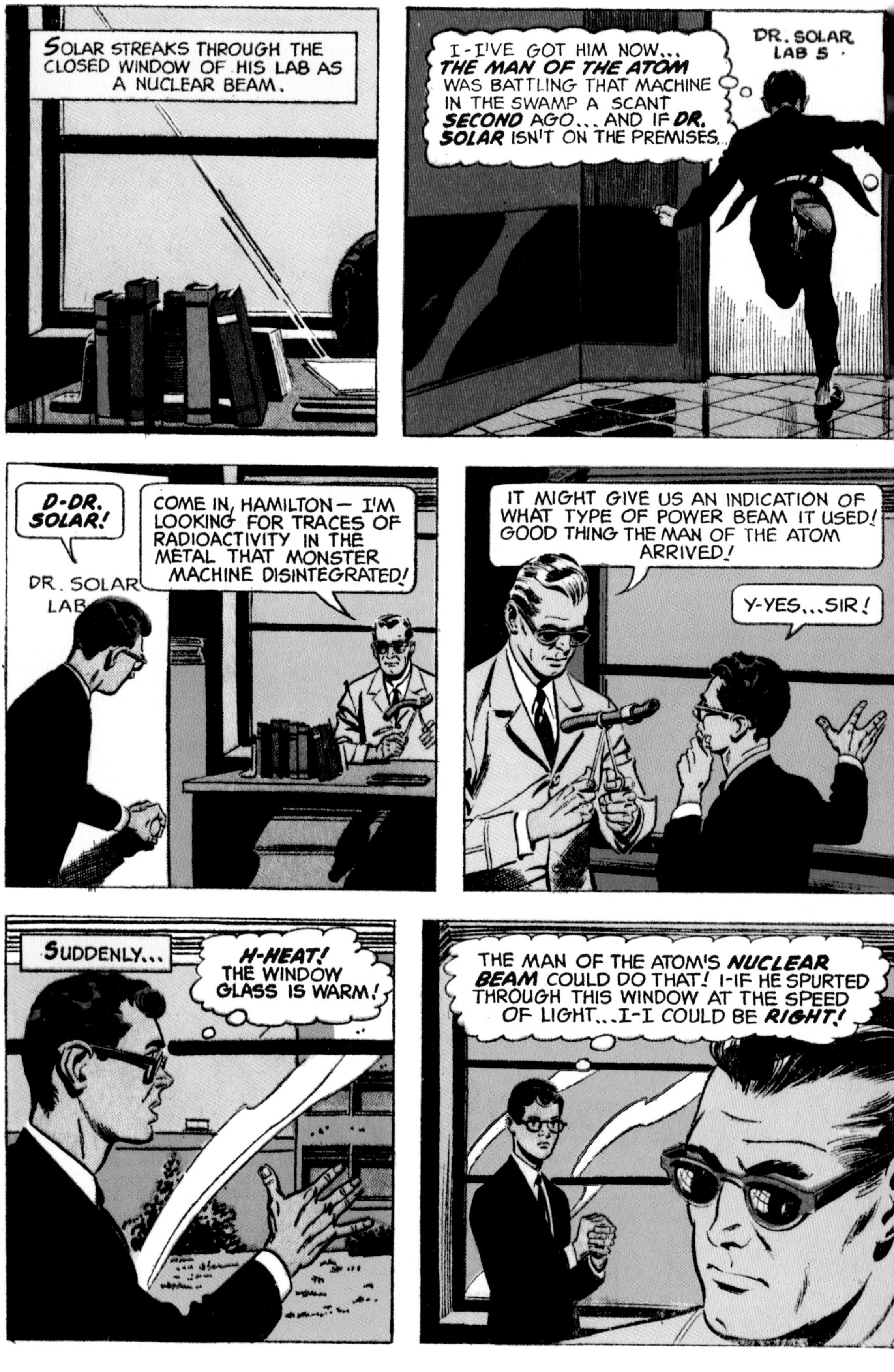
SOLAR STREAKS THROUGH THE CLOSED WINDOW OF HIS LAB AS A NUCLEAR BEAM.
DR. SOLAR LAB 5
I-I'VE GOT HIM NOW... THE MAN OF THE ATOM WAS BATTLING THAT MACHINE IN THE SWAMP A SCANT SECOND AGO... AND IF DR. SOLAR ISN'T ON THE PREMISES...
D-DR. SOLAR!
COME IN, HAMILTON— I'M LOOKING FOR TRACES OF RADIOACTIVITY IN THE METAL THAT MONSTER MACHINE DISINTEGRATED!
DR. SOLAR LAB
IT MIGHT GIVE US AN INDICATION OF WHAT TYPE OF POWER BEAM IT USED! GOOD THING THE MAN OF THE ATOM ARRIVED!
Y-YES...SIR!
SUDDENLY...
H-HEAT! THE WINDOW GLASS IS WARM!
THE MAN OF THE ATOM'S NUCLEAR BEAM COULD DO THAT! I-IF HE SPURTED THROUGH THIS WINDOW AT THE SPEED OF LIGHT...I-I COULD BE RIGHT!

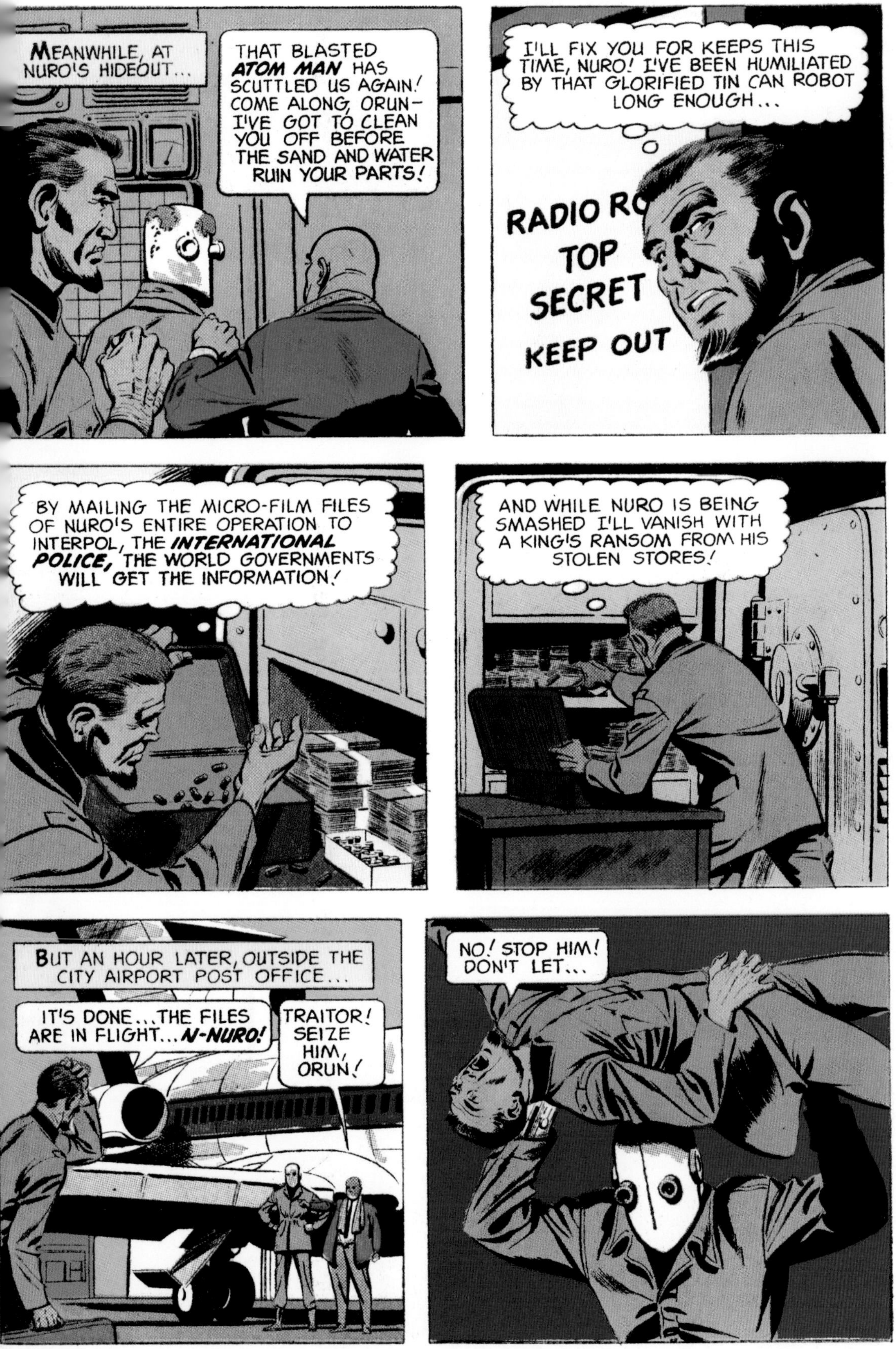
MEANWHILE, AT NURO'S HIDEOUT...
THAT BLASTED ATOM MAN HAS SCUTTLED US AGAIN! COME ALONG, ORUN-- I'VE GOT TO CLEAN YOU OFF BEFORE THE SAND AND WATER RUIN YOUR PARTS!
I'LL FIX YOU FOR KEEPS THIS TIME, NURO! I'VE BEEN HUMILIATED BY THAT GLORIFIED TIN CAN ROBOT LONG ENOUGH...
RADIO RO
TOP SECRET
KEEP OUT
BY MAILING THE MICRO-FILM FILES OF NURO'S ENTIRE OPERATION TO INTERPOL, THE INTERNATIONAL POLICE, THE WORLD GOVERNMENTS WILL GET THE INFORMATION!
AND WHILE NURO IS BEING SMASHED I'LL VANISH WITH A KING'S RANSOM FROM HIS STOLEN STORES!
BUT AN HOUR LATER, OUTSIDE THE CITY AIRPORT POST OFFICE...
IT'S DONE...THE FILES ARE IN FLIGHT...N-NURO!
TRAITOR! SEIZE HIM, ORUN!
NO! STOP HIM! DON'T LET...

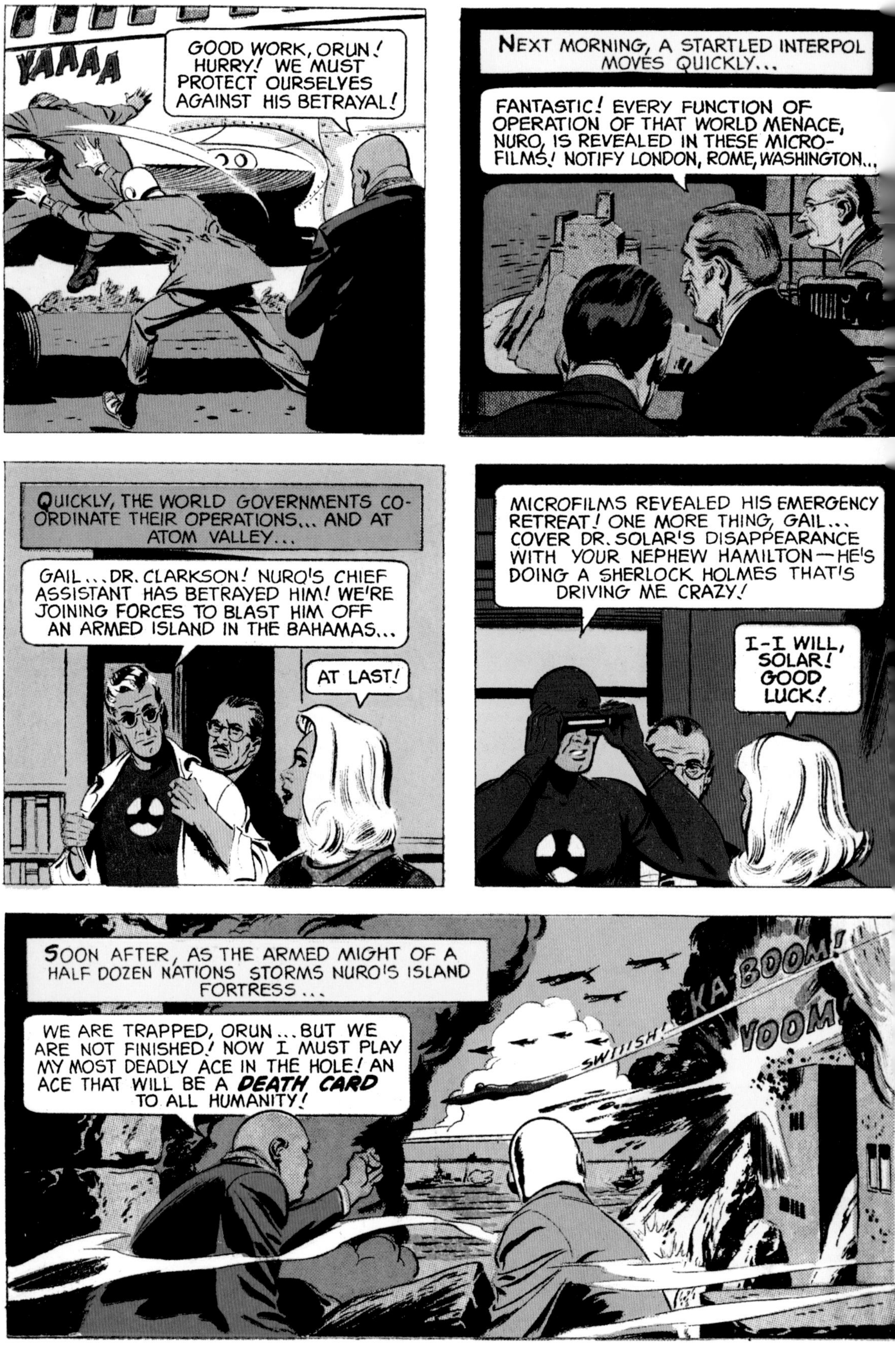
YAAAA
GOOD WORK, ORUN! HURRY! WE MUST PROTECT OURSELVES AGAINST HIS BETRAYAL!
NEXT MORNING, A STARTLED INTERPOL MOVES QUICKLY...
FANTASTIC! EVERY FUNCTION OF OPERATION OF THAT WORLD MENACE, NURO, IS REVEALED IN THESE MICRO-FILMS! NOTIFY LONDON, ROME, WASHINGTON...
QUICKLY, THE WORLD GOVERNMENTS CO-ORDINATE THEIR OPERATIONS... AND AT ATOM VALLEY...
GAIL...DR. CLARKSON! NURO'S CHIEF ASSISTANT HAS BETRAYED HIM! WE'RE JOINING FORCES TO BLAST HIM OFF AN ARMED ISLAND IN THE BAHAMAS...
AT LAST!
MICROFILMS REVEALED HIS EMERGENCY RETREAT! ONE MORE THING, GAIL... COVER DR. SOLAR'S DISAPPEARANCE WITH YOUR NEPHEW HAMILTON—HE'S DOING A SHERLOCK HOLMES THAT'S DRIVING ME CRAZY!
I-I WILL, SOLAR! GOOD LUCK!
SOON AFTER, AS THE ARMED MIGHT OF A HALF DOZEN NATIONS STORMS NURO'S ISLAND FORTRESS...
WE ARE TRAPPED, ORUN...BUT WE ARE NOT FINISHED! NOW I MUST PLAY MY MOST DEADLY ACE IN THE HOLE! AN ACE THAT WILL BE A DEATH CARD TO ALL HUMANITY!
SWIIISH!
KA-BOOM!
VOOM!

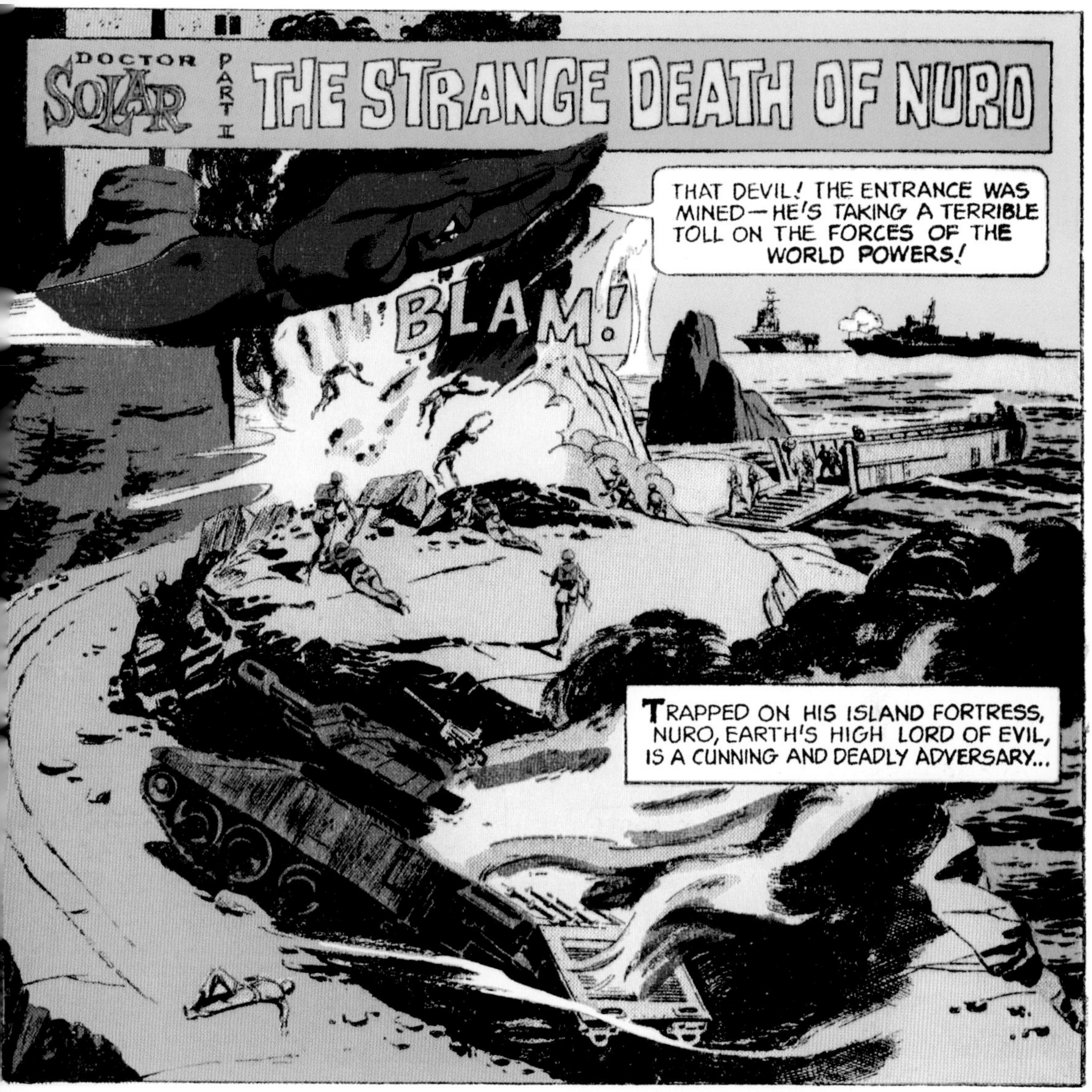
DOCTOR SOLAR PART II
THE STRANGE DEATH OF NURO
THAT DEVIL! THE ENTRANCE WAS MINED—HE'S TAKING A TERRIBLE TOLL ON THE FORCES OF THE WORLD POWERS!
BLAM!
TRAPPED ON HIS ISLAND FORTRESS, NURO, EARTH'S HIGH LORD OF EVIL, IS A CUNNING AND DEADLY ADVERSARY...

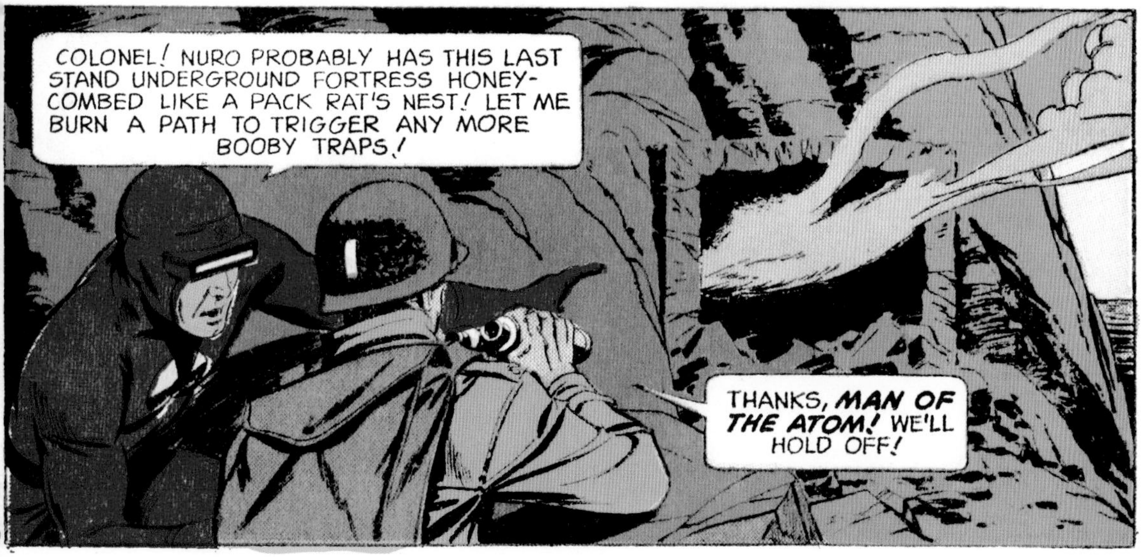
COLONEL! NURO PROBABLY HAS THIS LAST STAND UNDERGROUND FORTRESS HONEY-COMBED LIKE A PACK RAT'S NEST! LET ME BURN A PATH TO TRIGGER ANY MORE BOOBY TRAPS!
THANKS, MAN OF THE ATOM! WE'LL HOLD OFF!

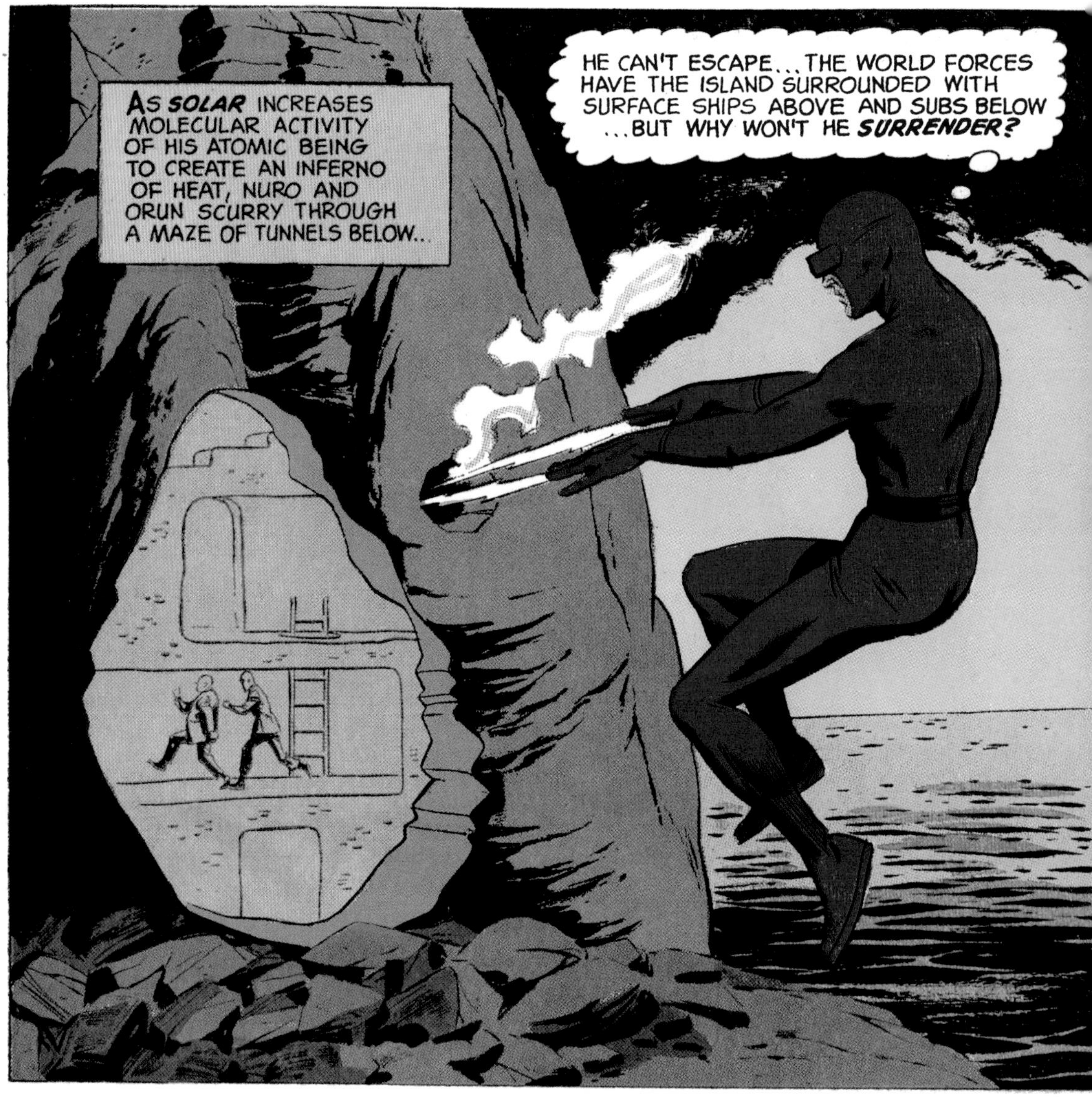
AS SOLAR INCREASES MOLECULAR ACTIVITY OF HIS ATOMIC BEING TO CREATE AN INFERNO OF HEAT, NURO AND ORUN SCURRY THROUGH A MAZE OF TUNNELS BELOW..
HE CAN'T ESCAPE... THE WORLD FORCES HAVE THE ISLAND SURROUNDED WITH SURFACE SHIPS ABOVE AND SUBS BELOW ...BUT WHY WON'T HE SURRENDER?

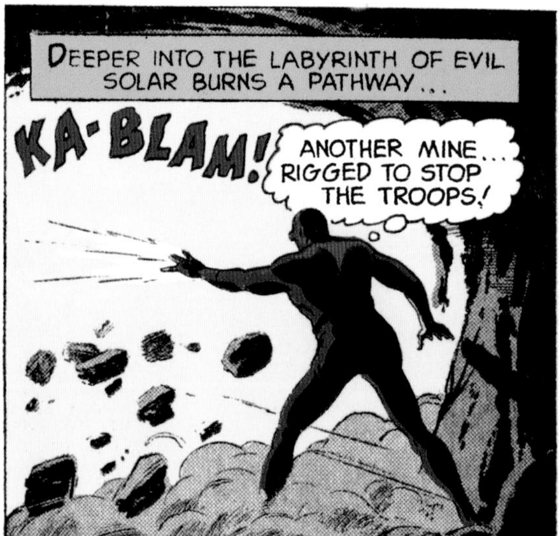
DEEPER INTO THE LABYRINTH OF EVIL SOLAR BURNS A PATHWAY...
KA-BLAM!
ANOTHER MINE... RIGGED TO STOP THE TROOPS!

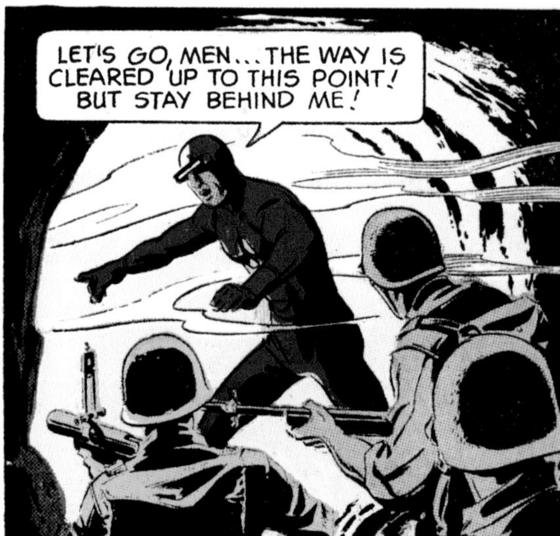
LET'S GO, MEN... THE WAY IS CLEARED UP TO THIS POINT! BUT STAY BEHIND ME!

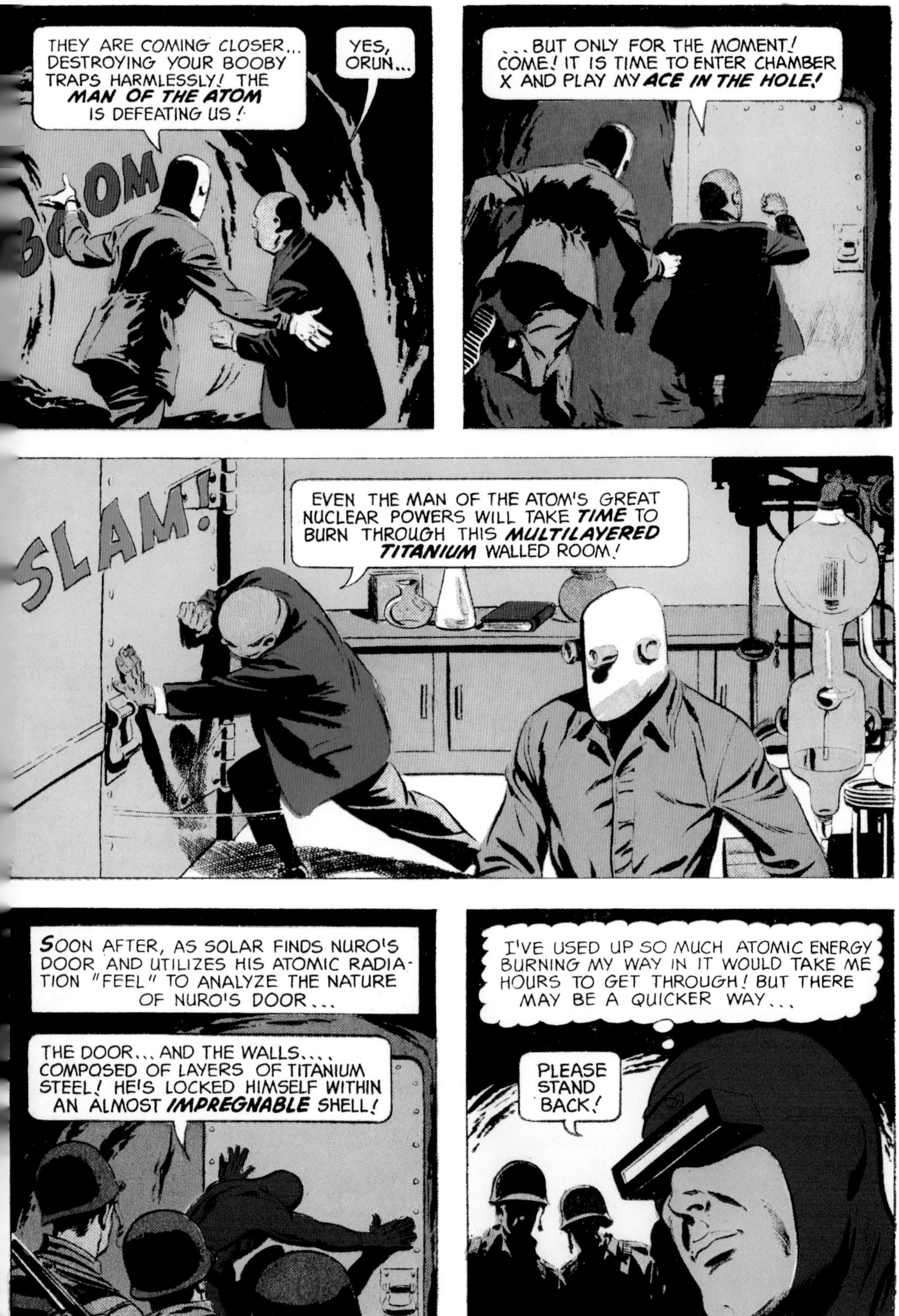
THEY ARE COMING CLOSER... DESTROYING YOUR BOOBY TRAPS HARMLESSLY! THE MAN OF THE ATOM IS DEFEATING US!
YES, ORUN...
BOOM
...BUT ONLY FOR THE MOMENT! COME! IT IS TIME TO ENTER CHAMBER X AND PLAY MY ACE IN THE HOLE!
SLAM!
EVEN THE MAN OF THE ATOM'S GREAT NUCLEAR POWERS WILL TAKE TIME TO BURN THROUGH THIS MULTILAYERED TITANIUM WALLED ROOM!
SOON AFTER, AS SOLAR FINDS NURO'S DOOR AND UTILIZES HIS ATOMIC RADIATION "FEEL" TO ANALYZE THE NATURE OF NURO'S DOOR...
THE DOOR... AND THE WALLS.... COMPOSED OF LAYERS OF TITANIUM STEEL! HE'S LOCKED HIMSELF WITHIN AN ALMOST IMPREGNABLE SHELL!
I'VE USED UP SO MUCH ATOMIC ENERGY BURNING MY WAY IN IT WOULD TAKE ME HOURS TO GET THROUGH! BUT THERE MAY BE A QUICKER WAY...
PLEASE STAND BACK!

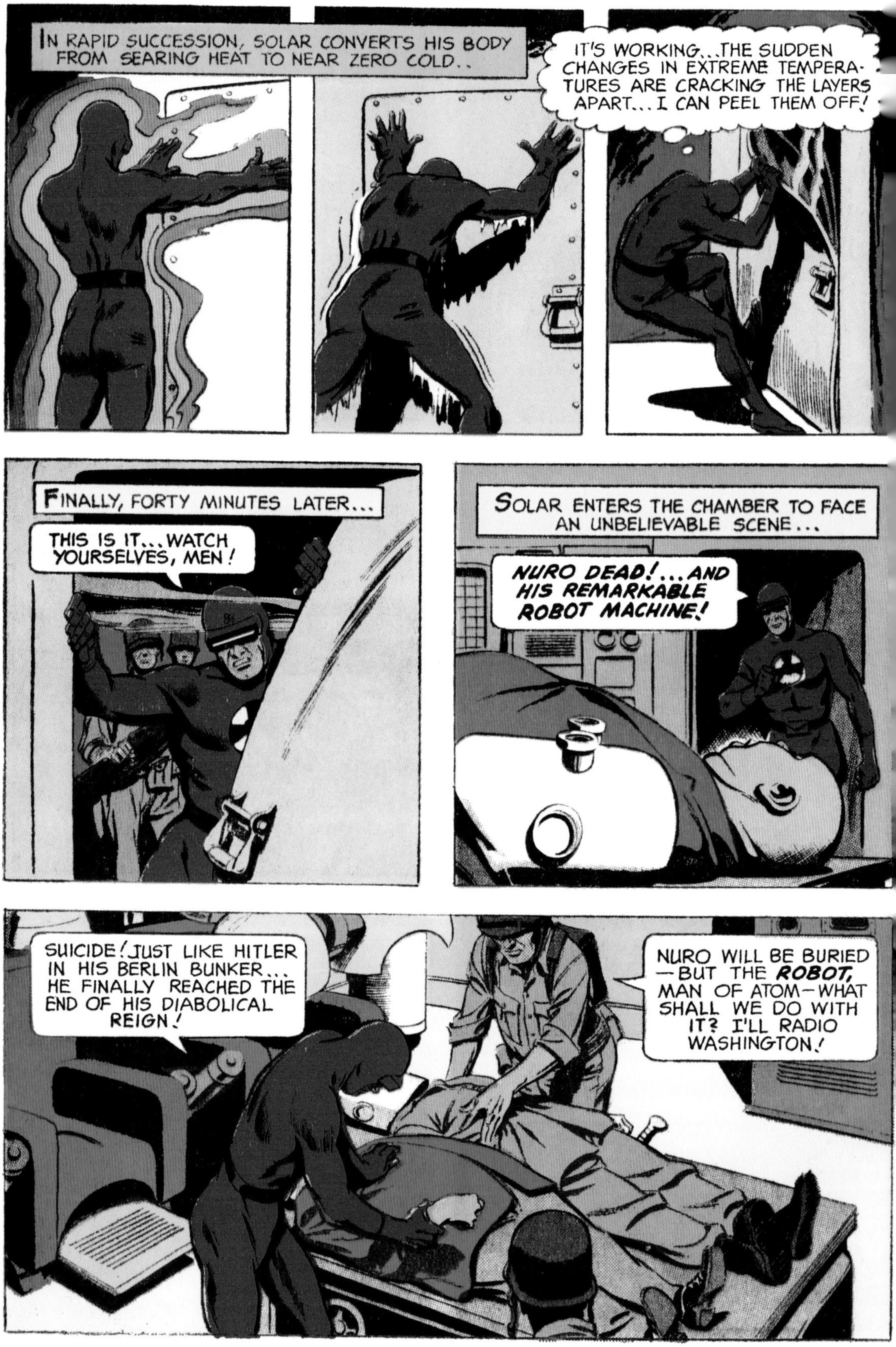
IN RAPID SUCCESSION, SOLAR CONVERTS HIS BODY FROM SEARING HEAT TO NEAR ZERO COLD..
IT'S WORKING...THE SUDDEN CHANGES IN EXTREME TEMPERATURES ARE CRACKING THE LAYERS APART... I CAN PEEL THEM OFF!
FINALLY, FORTY MINUTES LATER...
THIS IS IT...WATCH YOURSELVES, MEN!
SOLAR ENTERS THE CHAMBER TO FACE AN UNBELIEVABLE SCENE...
NURO DEAD!...AND HIS REMARKABLE ROBOT MACHINE!
SUICIDE! JUST LIKE HITLER IN HIS BERLIN BUNKER... HE FINALLY REACHED THE END OF HIS DIABOLICAL REIGN!
NURO WILL BE BURIED—BUT THE ROBOT, MAN OF ATOM—WHAT SHALL WE DO WITH IT? I'LL RADIO WASHINGTON!

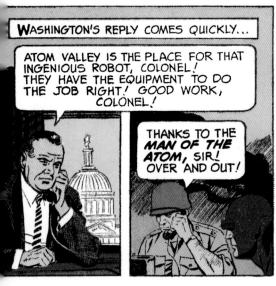

WASHINGTON'S REPLY COMES QUICKLY...

ATOM VALLEY IS THE PLACE FOR THAT INGENIOUS ROBOT, COLONEL! THEY HAVE THE EQUIPMENT TO DO THE JOB RIGHT! GOOD WORK, COLONEL!

THANKS TO THE *MAN OF THE ATOM*, SIR! OVER AND OUT!

LATER AT ATOM VALLEY...

I CAN'T BELIEVE IT! WE'VE PUT AN END TO THE GREATEST MENACE ON EARTH... AND *WE* HAVE HIS MOST TREASURED INVENTION!

YES, DR. CLARKSON! GOSH! WHERE'S DR. SOLAR? HE SHOULD BE SEEING *THIS*!

DR. SOLAR'S FLYING A REPORT ON THE ROBOT TO WASHINGTON, SON! HE EXAMINED IT AT NURO'S FORTRESS!

OH, ER, THANKS, MAN OF THE ATOM!

WHEN DR. SOLAR RETURNS YOU CAN BEGIN A COMPLETE STUDY OF THE ROBOT, SIR!

ER... YES! IT WILL TAKE US SEVERAL DAYS JUST TO X-RAY EVERY INCH OF ITS BODY!

THE MAN OF THE ATOM IS ALSO DR. SOLAR... I'M ALMOST *SURE* OF IT — BUT HOW CAN I *PROVE* IT?

AND THAT NIGHT...

DR. SOLAR... SUPPOSEDLY RETURNING FROM WASHINGTON! OR IS IT THE *MAN OF THE ATOM* COMING BACK IN HIS *REAL-LIFE* IDENTITY?

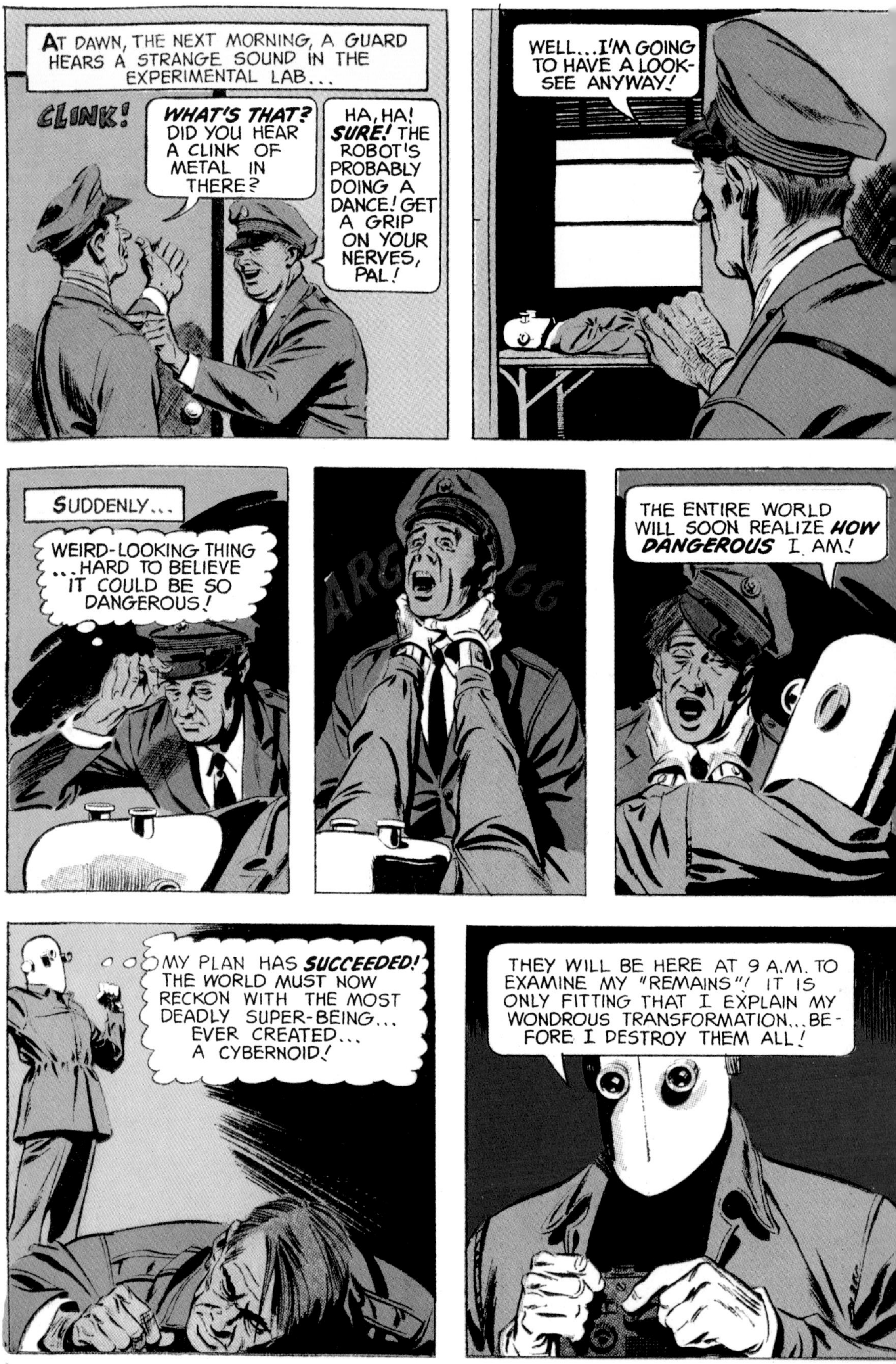
AT DAWN, THE NEXT MORNING, A GUARD HEARS A STRANGE SOUND IN THE EXPERIMENTAL LAB...
CLINK!
WHAT'S THAT? DID YOU HEAR A CLINK OF METAL IN THERE?
HA, HA! SURE! THE ROBOT'S PROBABLY DOING A DANCE! GET A GRIP ON YOUR NERVES, PAL!
WELL...I'M GOING TO HAVE A LOOK-SEE ANYWAY!
SUDDENLY...
WEIRD-LOOKING THING ...HARD TO BELIEVE IT COULD BE SO DANGEROUS!
ARG GG
THE ENTIRE WORLD WILL SOON REALIZE HOW DANGEROUS I AM!
MY PLAN HAS SUCCEEDED! THE WORLD MUST NOW RECKON WITH THE MOST DEADLY SUPER-BEING... EVER CREATED... A CYBERNOID!
THEY WILL BE HERE AT 9 A.M. TO EXAMINE MY "REMAINS"! IT IS ONLY FITTING THAT I EXPLAIN MY WONDROUS TRANSFORMATION...BEFORE I DESTROY THEM ALL!

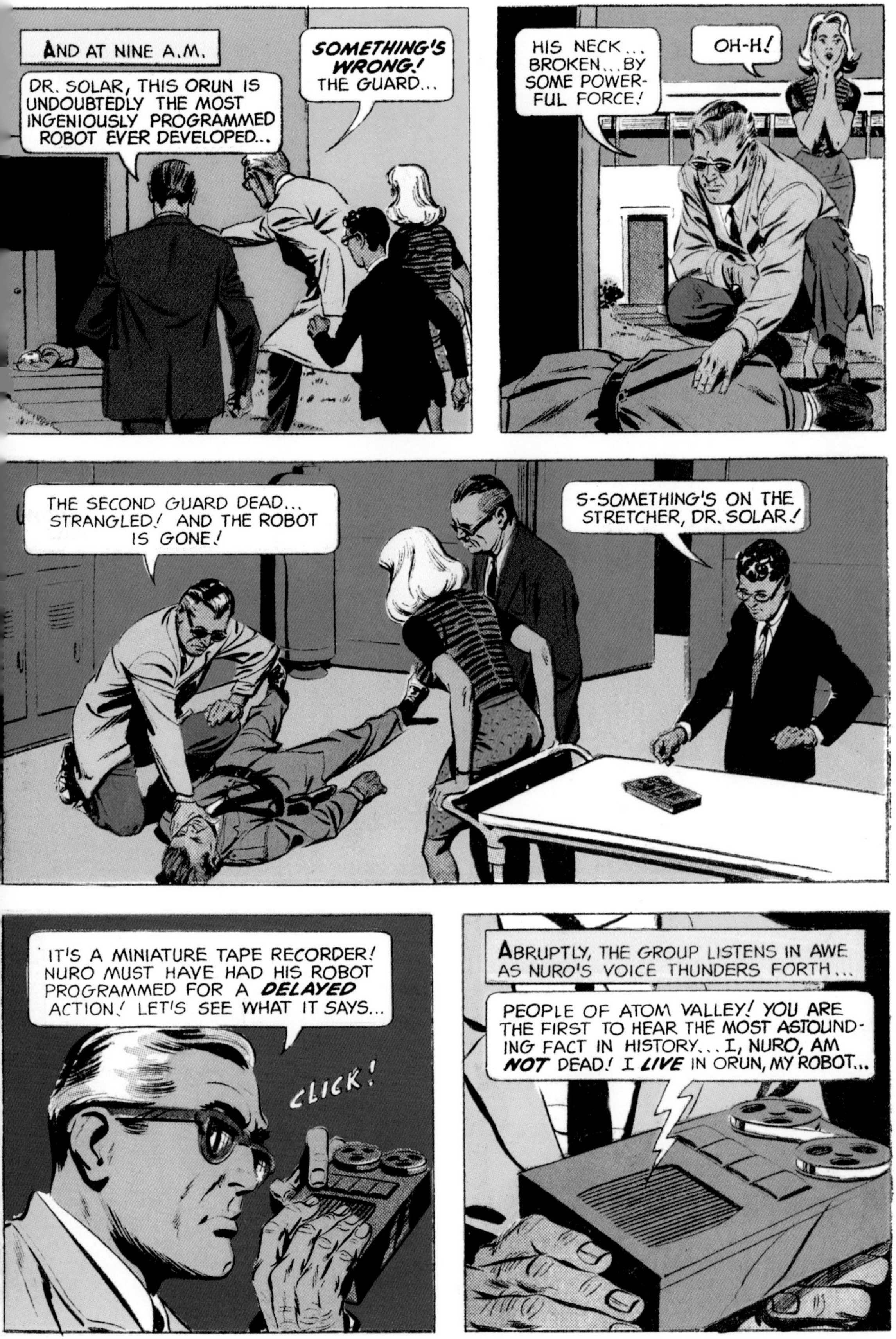
AND AT NINE A.M.
DR. SOLAR, THIS ORUN IS UNDOUBTEDLY THE MOST INGENIOUSLY PROGRAMMED ROBOT EVER DEVELOPED...
SOMETHING'S WRONG! THE GUARD...
HIS NECK... BROKEN... BY SOME POWERFUL FORCE!
OH-H!
THE SECOND GUARD DEAD... STRANGLED! AND THE ROBOT IS GONE!
S-SOMETHING'S ON THE STRETCHER, DR. SOLAR!
IT'S A MINIATURE TAPE RECORDER! NURO MUST HAVE HAD HIS ROBOT PROGRAMMED FOR A DELAYED ACTION! LET'S SEE WHAT IT SAYS...
CLICK!
ABRUPTLY, THE GROUP LISTENS IN AWE AS NURO'S VOICE THUNDERS FORTH...
PEOPLE OF ATOM VALLEY! YOU ARE THE FIRST TO HEAR THE MOST ASTOUNDING FACT IN HISTORY... I, NURO, AM NOT DEAD! I LIVE IN ORUN, MY ROBOT...

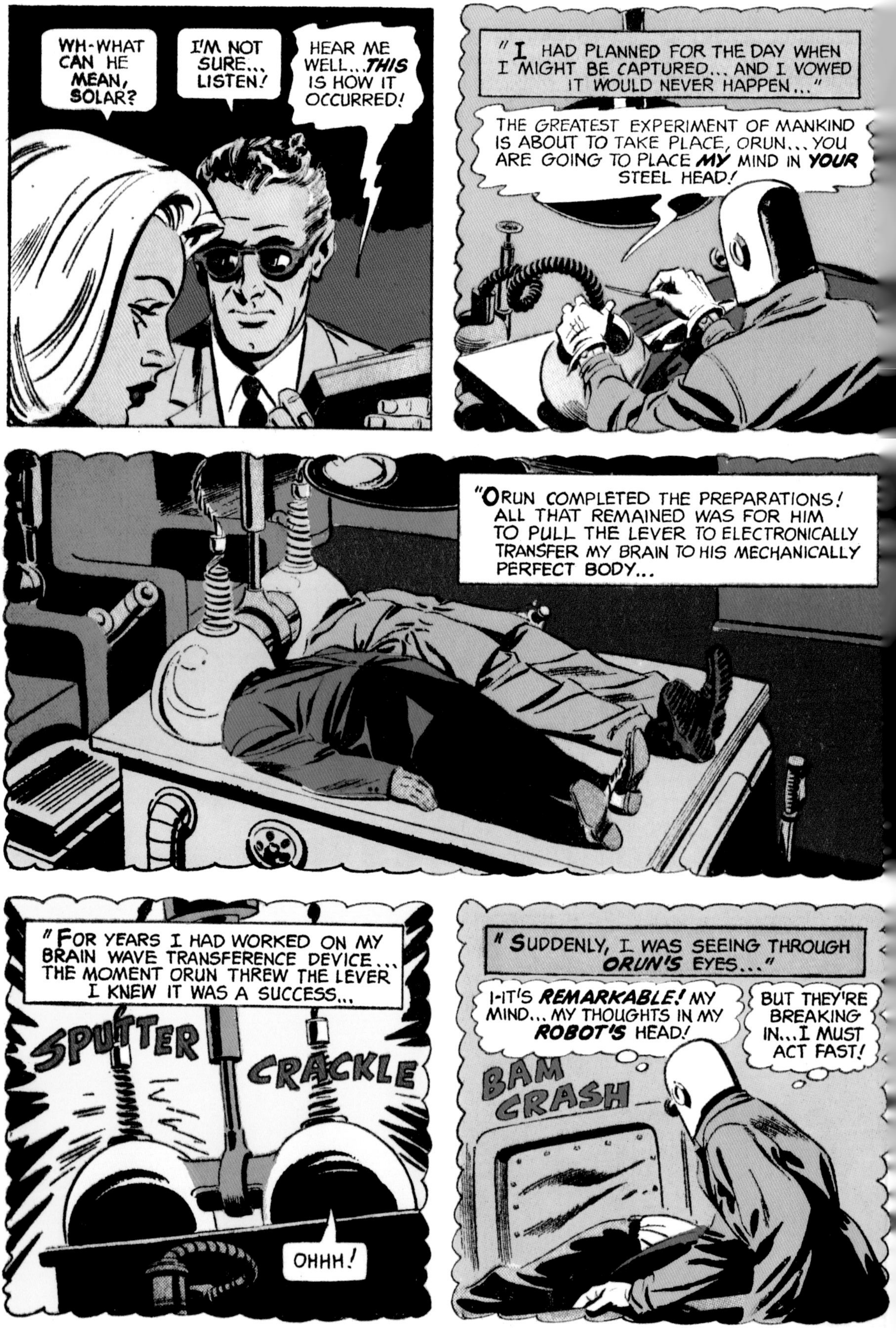
WH-WHAT CAN HE MEAN, SOLAR?
I'M NOT SURE... LISTEN!
HEAR ME WELL... THIS IS HOW IT OCCURRED!
"I HAD PLANNED FOR THE DAY WHEN I MIGHT BE CAPTURED... AND I VOWED IT WOULD NEVER HAPPEN..."
THE GREATEST EXPERIMENT OF MANKIND IS ABOUT TO TAKE PLACE, ORUN... YOU ARE GOING TO PLACE MY MIND IN YOUR STEEL HEAD!
"ORUN COMPLETED THE PREPARATIONS! ALL THAT REMAINED WAS FOR HIM TO PULL THE LEVER TO ELECTRONICALLY TRANSFER MY BRAIN TO HIS MECHANICALLY PERFECT BODY...
"FOR YEARS I HAD WORKED ON MY BRAIN WAVE TRANSFERENCE DEVICE... THE MOMENT ORUN THREW THE LEVER I KNEW IT WAS A SUCCESS...
SPUTTER
CRACKLE
OHHH!
"SUDDENLY, I WAS SEEING THROUGH ORUN'S EYES..."
I-IT'S REMARKABLE! MY MIND... MY THOUGHTS IN MY ROBOT'S HEAD!
BUT THEY'RE BREAKING IN... I MUST ACT FAST!
BAM
CRASH

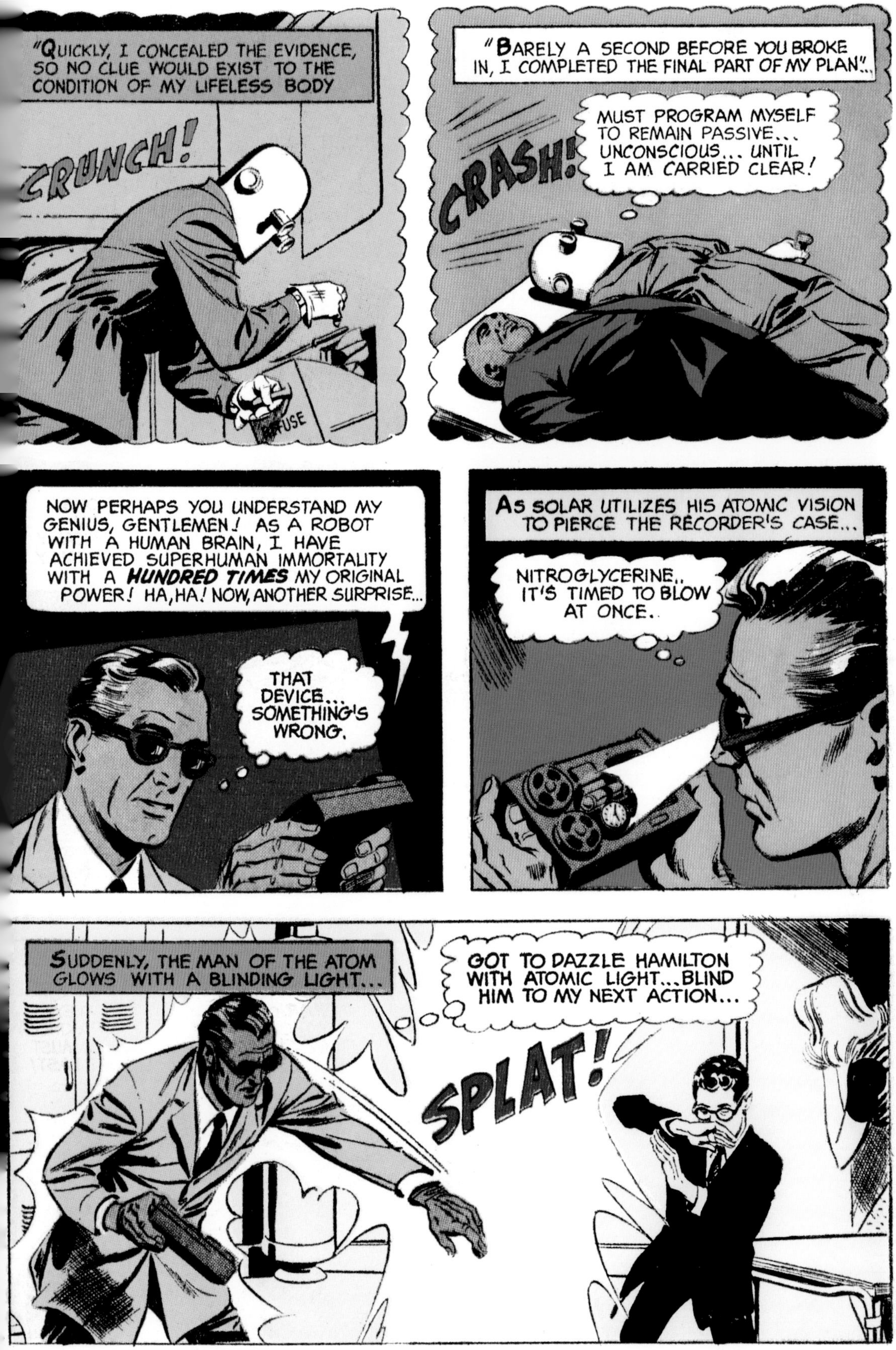

"QUICKLY, I CONCEALED THE EVIDENCE, SO NO CLUE WOULD EXIST TO THE CONDITION OF MY LIFELESS BODY
CRUNCH!
"BARELY A SECOND BEFORE YOU BROKE IN, I COMPLETED THE FINAL PART OF MY PLAN"...
MUST PROGRAM MYSELF TO REMAIN PASSIVE... UNCONSCIOUS... UNTIL I AM CARRIED CLEAR!
CRASH!
NOW PERHAPS YOU UNDERSTAND MY GENIUS, GENTLEMEN! AS A ROBOT WITH A HUMAN BRAIN, I HAVE ACHIEVED SUPERHUMAN IMMORTALITY WITH A HUNDRED TIMES MY ORIGINAL POWER! HA, HA! NOW, ANOTHER SURPRISE...
THAT DEVICE... SOMETHING'S WRONG.
AS SOLAR UTILIZES HIS ATOMIC VISION TO PIERCE THE RECORDER'S CASE...
NITROGLYCERINE.. IT'S TIMED TO BLOW AT ONCE.
SUDDENLY, THE MAN OF THE ATOM GLOWS WITH A BLINDING LIGHT...
GOT TO DAZZLE HAMILTON WITH ATOMIC LIGHT...BLIND HIM TO MY NEXT ACTION...
SPLAT!

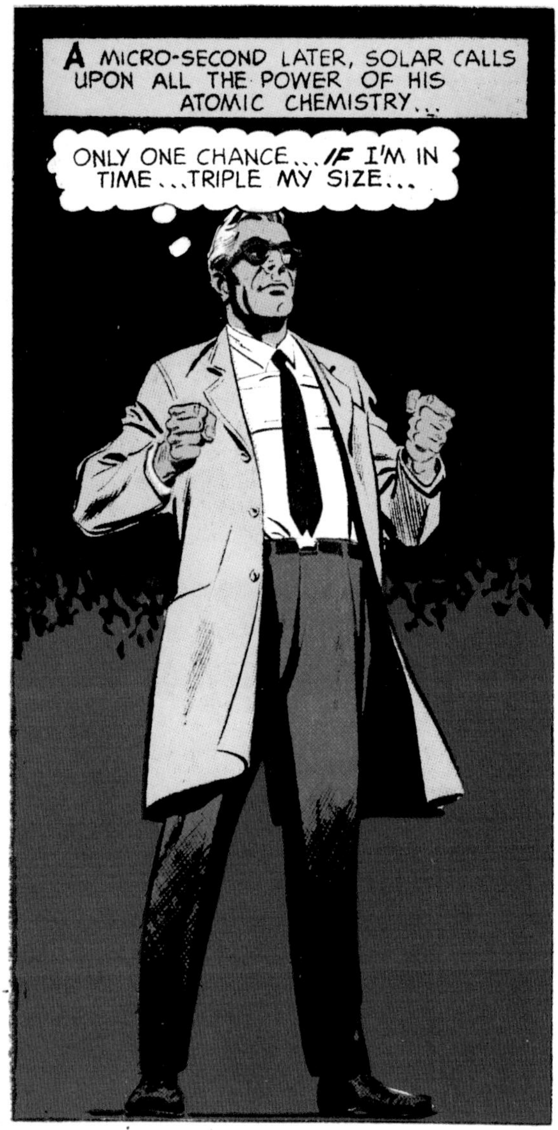
A MICRO-SECOND LATER, SOLAR CALLS UPON ALL THE POWER OF HIS ATOMIC CHEMISTRY...
ONLY ONE CHANCE... IF I'M IN TIME...TRIPLE MY SIZE...

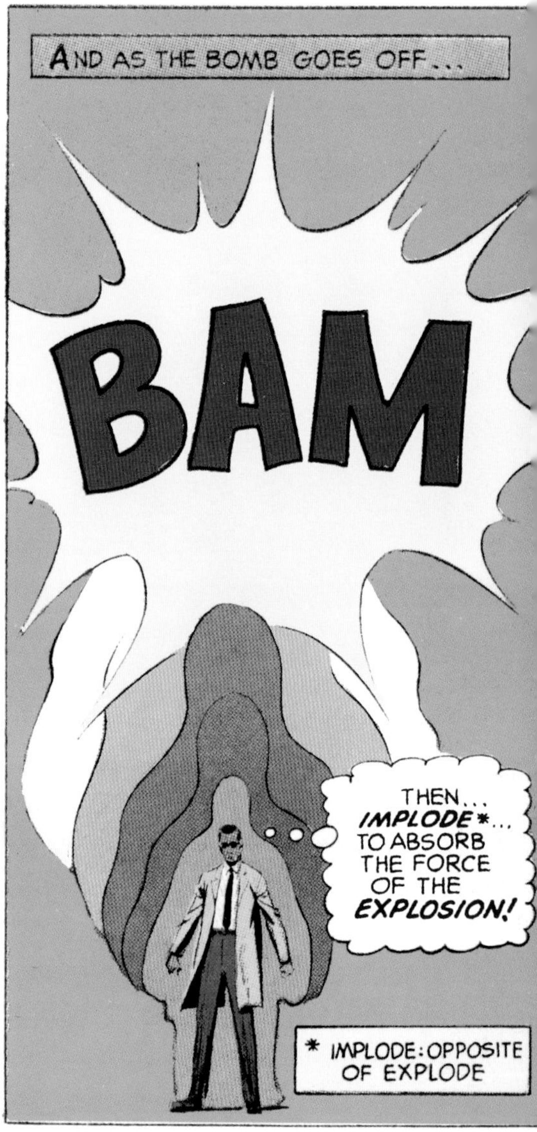
AND AS THE BOMB GOES OFF...
BAM
THEN... IMPLODE*... TO ABSORB THE FORCE OF THE EXPLOSION!
* IMPLODE: OPPOSITE OF EXPLODE

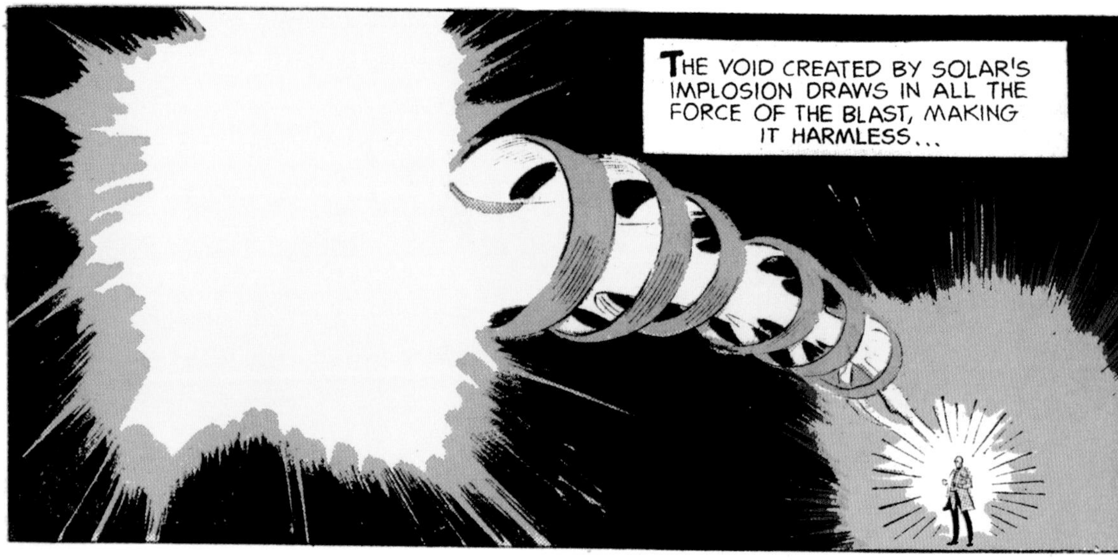
THE VOID CREATED BY SOLAR'S IMPLOSION DRAWS IN ALL THE FORCE OF THE BLAST, MAKING IT HARMLESS...

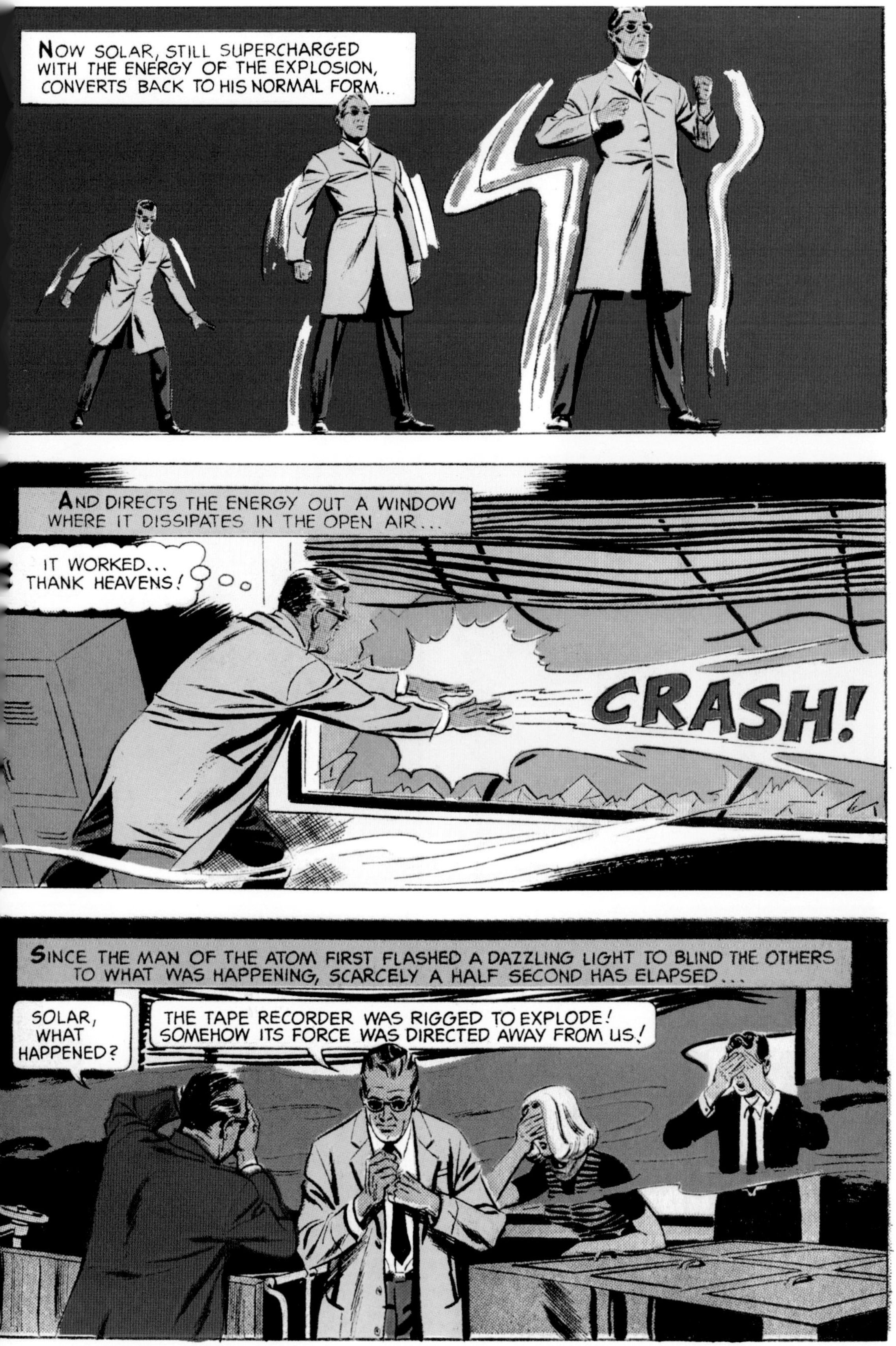
NOW SOLAR, STILL SUPERCHARGED WITH THE ENERGY OF THE EXPLOSION, CONVERTS BACK TO HIS NORMAL FORM...
AND DIRECTS THE ENERGY OUT A WINDOW WHERE IT DISSIPATES IN THE OPEN AIR...
IT WORKED... THANK HEAVENS!
CRASH!
SINCE THE MAN OF THE ATOM FIRST FLASHED A DAZZLING LIGHT TO BLIND THE OTHERS TO WHAT WAS HAPPENING, SCARCELY A HALF SECOND HAS ELAPSED...
SOLAR, WHAT HAPPENED?
THE TAPE RECORDER WAS RIGGED TO EXPLODE! SOMEHOW ITS FORCE WAS DIRECTED AWAY FROM US!

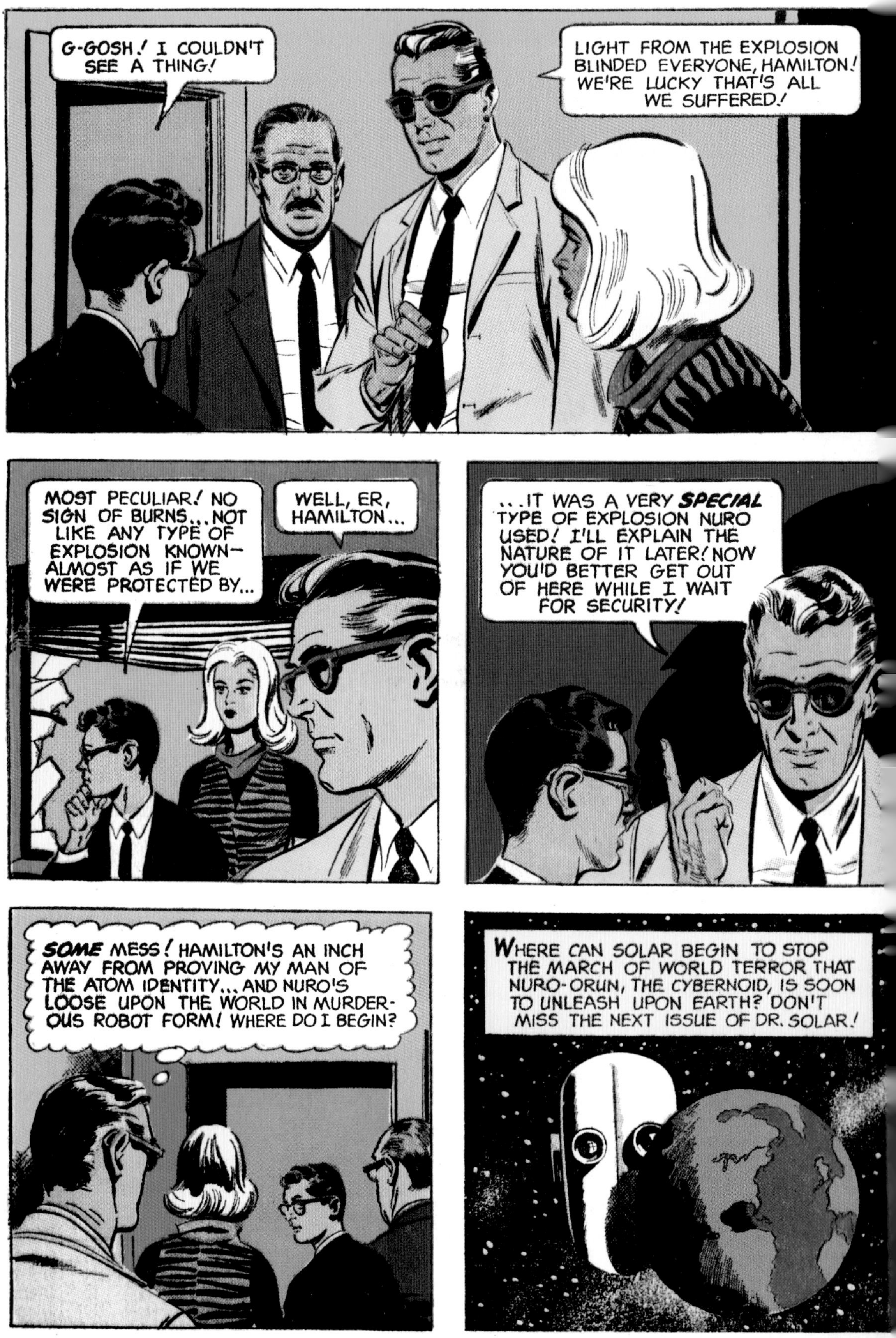
G-GOSH! I COULDN'T SEE A THING!
LIGHT FROM THE EXPLOSION BLINDED EVERYONE, HAMILTON! WE'RE LUCKY THAT'S ALL WE SUFFERED!
MOST PECULIAR! NO SIGN OF BURNS... NOT LIKE ANY TYPE OF EXPLOSION KNOWN— ALMOST AS IF WE WERE PROTECTED BY...
WELL, ER, HAMILTON...
...IT WAS A VERY SPECIAL TYPE OF EXPLOSION NURO USED! I'LL EXPLAIN THE NATURE OF IT LATER! NOW YOU'D BETTER GET OUT OF HERE WHILE I WAIT FOR SECURITY!
SOME MESS! HAMILTON'S AN INCH AWAY FROM PROVING MY MAN OF THE ATOM IDENTITY... AND NURO'S LOOSE UPON THE WORLD IN MURDEROUS ROBOT FORM! WHERE DO I BEGIN?
WHERE CAN SOLAR BEGIN TO STOP THE MARCH OF WORLD TERROR THAT NURO-ORUN, THE CYBERNOID, IS SOON TO UNLEASH UPON EARTH? DON'T MISS THE NEXT ISSUE OF DR. SOLAR!

## FRANK BOLLE
### (BORN 1924)

After serving in the Army Air Force during World
War II, Frank Bolle started illustrating for Magazine
Enterprises in 1948, pencilling comic-book
westerns such as *Best of the West*, *Redmask*, and
*The Black Phantom*. Later, Frank was hired by
Western Publishing to illustrate Golden Books
based on a variety of characters including The Lone
Ranger and Sherlock Holmes.

Bolle also pencilled a variety of comics for Gold
Key, including *Boris Karloff's Tales of Mystery*,
*Buck Rogers*, *Doctor Solar*, *Flash Gordon*,
*Grimm's Ghost Stories*, and *Rod Serling's
Twilight Zone*. At this time, he started *Children's
Tales*, a syndicated Sunday newspaper strip
adapting classic children's stories.

In 1982, King Features Syndicate hired Frank
to draw *The Heart of Juliet Jones*, which he
illustrated until 1999. Bolle now illustrates Alex
Kotzky's syndicated soap-opera strip *Apartment
3-G*.

## PAUL S. NEWMAN
### (1924–1999)

In 1998, the Guinness World Book of Records
named Paul S. Newman the "Most Prolific Comic
Book Writer." Paul was so prolific, in fact, that it is
nearly impossible to list all of his credits. From the
time he started his career in 1947, until his death
in 1999, Paul produced an astonishing body of
work that included over 4,100 published stories
(totaling about 36,000 pages) and thousands of
unpublished plots, pitches, and scripts.

Paul's first assignment was with DC Comics, who
hired him to write a comic based on the television
show *A Date with Judy*. He then found work with
a number of other publishers like Fawcett, Avon,
and Timely/Atlas—where he worked with Stan Lee
on *Marvel Tales*, *Journey into Mystery*, and other
titles.

Dell hired Paul to write *The Lone Ranger* comic
book, which Paul scripted for twenty-four years
along with the daily newspaper strip. Paul wrote
scripts for almost every Gold Key title, including
all thirty-five issues of the *I Love Lucy* comic and
writing nearly every issue of *Turok, Son of Stone*
for twenty-six years.

In addition to comics and syndicated newspaper
strips, Paul wrote a number of children's books,
television sketches, plays, screenplays, magazine
articles, and corporate speeches.